Communicating in Organizations
A Cultural Approach

Communicating in Organizations

A Cultural Approach

Gerald L. Pepper
University of Minnesota, Duluth

McGraw-Hill, Inc.

New York   St. Louis   San Francisco   Auckland   Bogotá   Caracas   Lisbon
London   Madrid   Mexico City   Milan   Montreal   New Delhi
San Juan   Singapore   Sydney   Tokyo   Toronto

This book was set in Palatino by The Clarinda Company.
The editors were Hilary Jackson and James R. Belser;
the production supervisor was Louise Karam.
The cover was designed by Carol A. Couch.
R. R. Donnelley & Sons Company was printer and binder.

COMMUNICATING IN ORGANIZATIONS

A Cultural Approach

This book is printed on recycled, acid-free paper containing 10% postconsumer waste.

1 2 3 4 5 6 7 8 9 0   DOC   DOC   9 0 9 8 7 6 5 4

ISBN 0-07-049286-7

Library of Congress Cataloging-in-Publication Data

Pepper, Gerald L. (Gerald Lee)
    Communicating in organizations: a cultural approach / Gerald L.
Pepper.
    p.   cm.
    Includes bibliographical references and index.
    ISBN 0-07-049286-7
    1. Communication in organizations.   2. Corporate culture.
3. Organizational behavior.   I. Title.
HD30.3.P45   1995
302.3'5—dc20   94-6694

About the Author

I am a lucky person. I live in a beautiful part of the country, Northern Minnesota; I work in an office that gives me a scenic view of Lake Superior; I work with people whose company I enjoy and whose insights and abilities I respect; and I share my home with a wife I love, two daughters I cherish, two dogs, a bird, a newt named fig, and a somewhat aggressive, but nice, rabbit.

I'm also lucky because I have a job that allows me to be paid to do work that I enjoy. Here at UMD I teach classes in organizational and small-group communication, conflict management, interviewing, and leadership. I research (not surprisingly) organizations from a cultural perspective. I also work with a community group implementing a violence-free school project in our school district.

I have been fortunate enough to receive a teaching award and an advising award here at UMD, to see some of my work published, and to consult with a number of public and private organizations. I have taught at both the high school and college levels, have served as the editor of the *Communication and Theater Association of Minnesota Journal*, and received my Master's Degree from Purdue University, and my Ph.D. from The University of Minnesota.

For Kay, Kari, and Jenny

Contents

vii

Part Two
CULTURAL CONCERNS

Preface

When teachers decide to use a textbook, we generally go through a number of motions. We look at the needs of our audience, the students; we look at our own styles and philosophies; we look at the field and the progress that has been made in both theory and application; and we look at the class and what we hope to accomplish in the limited amount of time available. After all of that, we look at the choices. What is available that will facilitate the accomplishment of the goal of the class, complement our own styles and beliefs, and meet our students' needs?

Within the subject area of organizational communication we are blessed with many really good choices for textbooks. I've used a number of them in my classes with varying degrees of satisfaction. In each case, though, I've found myself ultimately unsatisfied with one consistent lack: the way that organization culture was being presented. Despite the quality of the texts and the efforts of the authors, culture is consistently relegated to chapter-length treatments, which makes the subject appear as though it is "just another organizational issue," important enough to merit a chapter, but no more important than any other organizational issue.

I found this light coverage interesting, given that much, if not most, of what has been written about culture argues that it is a pervasive organizational influence. If this was the case, I reasoned, then why wasn't it receiving more treatment in the textbooks?

This book is my response to that question. I don't believe that culture is a secondary subject in the study of organizations. I believe that organizations are cultures, and that any discussion of organizations must also be a discussion of culture, for the two cannot be separated. As such, culture cannot be treated adequately in a single or a couple of chapters; it must permeate the entire book, just as culture permeates all organizational issues. Since no text existed with such a pervasive and thorough treatment of culture, I decided to write this book.

Is culture an adequately substantial paradigm from which to view the diversity of issues encountered in this text? The answer is definitely "yes!" A cultural approach forces an emphasis on the communicative development of belief and value systems as they are demonstrated in the behaviors of organization members. I would ask a critic of a cultural emphasis, "What is there beyond beliefs, values, and behaviors?" The answer is, "nothing." Everything from the buildings, desks, room design, inventory, and hiring policies, through the decision-making norms, levels of participation, socialization strategies, morale surveys, and codes of conduct are cultural reflections. This book is an effort to explain systematically, coherently, and cohesively some of the diversity of the organization from this perspective.

ORGANIZATIONAL PLAN

The book is divided into two parts. Part One, Chapters 1 through 5, presents the theoretical grounding for a communication-cultural explanation of organizations. Part Two, Chapters 6 through 11, presents six of the most informative and important communicative concerns over which culture exerts significant influence. As a whole, Chapters 1 through 11 offer the reader a composite review of communication theory and organizations, the history of organizational design and theory, culture and a cultural approach, socialization, ethics, communication networks, politics, diversity in the workplace, discrimination, and decision making. However, despite what subject is in the title of the chapter, this book's premise is that organizations are cultures, and culture permeates all other organizational issues. So—culture is the lens through which we learn about these issues.

The book ends with Chapter 12: Epilogue. In this epilogue I attempt to lay out the sort of thinking or debate that goes on when researchers and authors wrestle with what should or should not be included in a book. I chose the topic of leadership and the potential impact of leaders on organization culture. The epilogue is meant to demonstrate that not all issues are clear cut, and that there is as much value in the discussion as there is in the conclusion.

Part One: Theoretical Grounding, Chapters 1 to 5

Chapter 1: "Organizations as Communication Events" is about communication theory and organizations. In it, we compare the flawed view of organizations as containers in which communication happens with a more appropriate and complex view of organizations as the communication activities of organization members. This is a communication-theory explanation of organizations which suggests that organizations are continually evolving, changing and unstable, consisting of the communicative relationships between organization members. The chapter includes discussions of transactionalism, negotiated structure, five levels of communication (individual, dyadic, small group, intergroup, technological), and symbolic convergence theory. The joint focuses of communication and culture are not a coincidence. Approaching organizations as communicative events will invariably lead the examiner to shared meanings and beliefs—the essence of culture.

Chapter 2: "Understanding Organizations as Cultures" and Chapter 3: "Discovering Organization Cultures" should be read as a package. In them I pick up where Chapter 1 leaves off. Chapter 1 concludes that organizations are communication activity. Chapter 2, the "formal" culture chapter, says that the result of all that communication is the emergence of shared belief and value systems: organization cultures and subcultures. The chapter explores many of the most complicated questions inherent in a cultural approach, such as, What is culture? Is culture beliefs or behaviors? Is there one general culture or many subcultures in an organization? Why is a cultural approach reasonable? Can culture be managed? and, Can culture be changed? Chapter 3 is intended primarily for those who will be undertaking a bit of culture research themselves, or those who want more details on how culture research results are obtained. The chapter discusses ethnography, interpretive research methods, participant observation, and Bantz's (1993) Organizational Communication Culture Method.

Like Chapters 2 and 3, Chapters 4 and 5 are intended to be a package of information. The intent of the chapters is to give an historical overview of the development of organizational design and theory. However, given that this text takes a cultural approach, the history is linked to the development of a cultural interpretation. I ask, "Didn't organization 'culture' exist before the 1980s?" The answer is that of course it did; it simply hasn't been widely recognized. Chapter 4 traces the early development of the cultural perspective from the industrial revolution up to the 1930s. Included are discussions of organization prehistory, bureaucracy, Frederick Taylor and the principles of scientific management, time-motion studies, and the development of the machine culture. Chapter 5 picks up there, pointing out the cultural implications of "modern" organizational theory. The chapter includes extensive coverage of the Hawthorne Studies, the human-relations movement (satisfaction culture), the human-resources movement (teamwork culture), the sociotechnical systems movement (organismic culture), and the organization as culture movement. The two chapters rely on descriptive metaphors and focus on key individuals in history who shaped the modern organization.

Part Two: Cultural Concerns

Part Two of the book focuses on six key areas in which culture exerts significant influence. Culture is pervasive, affecting and affected by all components of the organization. These six chapters are intended to demonstrate the impact of that influence on some of the most critical organizational issues.

Chapter 6: "Organization Cultures and Socialization Practices" focuses on organizational efforts to create good organization citizens. We see quickly that our "common sense" vision of socialization as a one-way effort by the organization to bring the newcomer along is flawed. A more accurate portrayal of so-

cialization is the two-way process of creating the organizational value and belief system. The active newcomer is discussed in the chapter as a coparticipant
in the socialization process and the reproduction of organization culture. The
chapter revolves around the sense-making model provided by M. R. Louis and
includes discussions of the importance of socialization, newcomer as career
transitioner, socialization strategies, the selection interview, mentoring, commitment, and identification.

Chapter 7: "Ethics and Organization Culture" treats some of the most difficult material in organizational communication theory and research: the difficulty and importance of studying ethics, sexual harassment, whistleblowing,
and corporate social responsibility. Each of these issues is treated extensively.
We'll see throughout the chapter that it is almost impossible to separate an organization's cultures from its ethical practices. The two are created through
the stories of organization members and, once developed, become so intertwined as to be indistinguishable.

Chapter 8: "Culture and Communication Networks" looks at the importance of social grouping on the development of culture. Though networks are not the same thing as culture—networks are spatial while culture is cognitive—the network literature provides interesting insights into
the development of subcultures and the critical importance of keeping
track of group interlocking and potentially closed cultural systems. This is
not a "typical" networking chapter. Coverage includes theory, methods,
and research, of course, but also includes cross-boundary networking, interlocking corporate directorates, small-world research, and superior-subordinate communication.

Chapter 9: "Organization Cultures, Politics, and Conflict" looks at how
culture contributes to power relationships and conflict management. We look
at organizations as rule systems that favor some at the expense of others, overt
and covert power, and how these political power networks come to reflect the
competing subcultural interest groups within the organization. We also look at
conflict management, the influence of gender and the role of women as peacekeepers, bargaining as conflict management, and labor-management negotiations.

Chapter 10: "Organization Culture and the Multicultural Workplace"
examines the complexity of the multicultural workplace. We look at the
experiences of Asian-Americans, Native Americans, Hispanics, African-
Americans, and women as they struggle to receive the same treatment
as the white (non-Hispanic) male experience. The chapter presents occupational representation and income data, discrimination theories, antidiscrimination legislation, and the cultural mandate to recognize and embrace diversity.

Finally, Chapter 11: "Organization Culture, Decision Making, and Environmental Uncertainty" looks at organizations as decision environments. We
approach decision making from a cultural perspective, which means understanding that many decisions will be made that are out of the control of the individual decision maker, but rather, are guided by the organization's culture.

The chapter addresses Weick's work on decision environments, tight and loose coupling, Simon's work on bounded rationality, bounded emotionality, decision making in crisis situations, and executive moral responsibility.

Chapter 12: "Epilogue, or the Culture-Leadership Conundrum" examines the controversy surrounding the question of influence: Do leaders create cultures? and Is the impact of leaders on culture formation greater than the impact of nonleaders? I chose to frame this issue as an epilogue for two reasons. First, the jury is clearly still out on the issue. For every piece that says "yes," another exists that says "no." Second, although I do have a definite opinion that is in accordance with the philosophy of the text, I have decided that greater value would be derived from inviting the student into the debate than just giving my opinion as though the debate has been concluded. Finally, as an epilogue chapter I intended the treatment to represent an experiment with something of an interactive textbook. It is my effort to invite the student to think with me and with you, the teacher of the course. The material offers fuel for thought, but few conclusions. You and your students will find plenty of room for agreement, discussion, and disagreement. I look forward to hearing how it goes.

IMPORTANT FEATURES

I am pleased to point out the following features of this text. In total, I feel that they offer a wide-ranging, user-friendly package that is interesting and accessible for both the student and teacher:

- *Every chapter revolves around cultural questions.* This is a book that puts culture at the center of the explanation, not as a peripheral concern. This unifying theme makes the text material more cohesive than is often the case in textbooks.
- *Each chapter opens with examples that illustrate the material to be presented within the chapter.* The examples are sometimes mini-case studies, sometimes quizzes, sometimes extended examples demonstrating key chapter material. The opening examples are always discussed and referenced in the chapters themselves.
- *Every chapter opens with a preview* of how the chapter content will be presented, followed by a list of key terms used in the chapter.
- *Extensive use has been made of examples, figures, tables, research spotlights, and case studies* in an effort to make the material more interesting, applicable, and accessible. Importantly, every case study is based on real or true events. No cases have been created to artificially illustrate chapter content. Cases were found that genuinely show the applicability of the book's "theoretical" content to real life. Examples include summaries of the Tenerife air disaster, the Exxon Valdez oil spill, the creation of a violence-free school, living with sexual harassment, the search for IBM's new CEO, and Nestle's problems with infant formula marketing.

- *I have inserted review questions into the text itself,* as an immediate retention-and-understanding aid for the readers. Thus, as the student is exposed to new and sometimes complex information, he or she will have the benefit of being questioned immediately. This questioning strategy will help reinforce material, as well as serve as an in-text study guide.
- *This text discusses many issues often missing in other books.* The following is a brief sampling: symbolic convergence theory, in-depth coverage of Taylorism and the Hawthorne Studies, time-motion studies, culture change, the cultural implications of various organizational designs, culture research methods, participant observation, M. R. Louis' model of socialization, the newcomer as an active creator of organizational reality, small-world research, interlocking corporate directorates, mentoring, whistleblowing, labor negotiations, women as informal peacekeepers, the various differences found among Asian, African, Native, and European Americans, and Hispanic women, discrimination theories, antidiscrimination legislation, decision making, social responsibility, and sexual harassment.
- *The book includes an extensive research-base and reference section,* which should help students as they conduct their own research. In addition, some chapters include "Spotlight on Research" sections which highlight both the difficulty and the utility of conducting culture research.
- *A teacher's manual accompanies the book* with test questions and answers, answers to all questions posed in the text, exercise ideas, and teaching tips.

Finally, a word about language and writing. I close this preface by noting three issues concerning writing choices. First, I wrote this book in the first person. I use the terms "I," "me," "mine" without apology. You know who wrote this, so I see little value in referring to myself as "your author," such as: "your author conducted research. . . ." Second, when referring to sexual demarcations, I use the terms he or she and him or her rather than relying on the more formal and less wordy male pronoun only. However, no quotations were altered to change their gender references. Such tampering is not, I believe, legitimate on an author's part. And finally, I tried to write simply and in a way I felt students would find easy to digest. I certainly welcome your reactions/feedback to learn of your and your students' experiences with the book.

ACKNOWLEDGMENTS

I owe an enormous debt of gratitude to a number of individuals who have contributed in direct and indirect ways to the completion of this book. First, I must acknowledge those who influenced my scholarly development. For this I am particularly grateful to Professors Ralph Webb, Barry Brummett, Charles Stewart, Robert Scott, Charles Bantz, George Shapiro, Scott Poole, and Sandra Petronio. These were teachers who forced me, sometimes against my will, to challenge myself. To this list I thank the following who, at various points, challenged me to grow beyond the journals and textbooks: Mike Bokeno, Larry

Williamson, Kirk Milhone, David Bastien, Todd Hostager, Danny Robinson, Roxanne Knutson, Verna Corgan, and Deb Peterson. And I offer a special thank you to John Stone, a good friend, a great reader, and a fine scholar and critic.

I also owe a practical debt of gratitude to my colleagues in the Department of Communication at UMD. I am especially grateful to Virginia Katz who, as department chair, freed up my time to write this book, and to Jackson Huntley, Linda Krug, and Mike Sunnafrank who encouraged and questioned the project all along the way. I also thank our department's executive secretary, Sue Brockopp, who worked long and hard with many of the typing and text processing details of the manuscript.

And then there are the anonymous contributions. I am sure that I could not have had better reviewers. I was constantly amazed at the generosity of their suggestions. They were always blunt, but never cruel; always straightforward, and always willing to offer suggestions and help. The following are those individuals who read part or all of the manuscript: Angela Laird Brenton, University of Arkansas; Connie Bullis, University of Utah; Patrice Buzzanell, Michigan State University; Stan Deetz, Rutgers University; Patricia Geist, San Diego State University; Sandra Ketrow, University of Rhode Island; Karen Krupar, Metropolitan State College; Dean Scheibel, Loyola-Marymount University; John Stone, University of Wisconsin, Whitewater; and Shirley Willihnganz, University of Louisville.

Finally, I thank Jim Belser of McGraw-Hill for his patience with rounds one and two of this production process. And I thank Hilary Jackson, my editor at McGraw-Hill. My wish to all of the writers out there is that they get an opportunity to work with Hilary. She left me alone when I needed to be left alone; she prodded me when I needed to be prodded. But, most importantly, she understood the difference between the two forms of encouragement.

This seems like a long list. It is. But, that's OK, because I am genuinely fortunate to have had so much help along the way. Despite their best intentions, however, this book might still have a weakness or two. I take responsibility for them all. And if you find something about which you take issue, I ask that you write me a note or give me a call. I like to talk about this stuff. I can be reached at: Department of Communication, 469 A.B. Anderson Hall, University of Minnesota, Duluth, Duluth, MN 55812; (218) 726-7274.

Gerald L. Pepper

PART ONE

Perspective

CHAPTER 1

Organizations As Communication Events

Chapter Preview

Why would I open a book that takes a "cultural approach" to organizations with a chapter about communication? The simple answer is that culture is communication, or, to be more precise, a cultural approach to organizations is a focus on the everyday ordinary and extraordinary communication of organization members. To begin the book with "culture," then, would be to presuppose an understanding of communication that may not exist in the reader.

We're not often challenged to view organizations as communication events, as I will ask in this chapter. We are more commonly asked to believe that organizations are containers in which communication happens. According to this container image, communication is the tool used by organization members to do their work. They talk, write memos, engage in conflicts, have romantic interludes, and perform dozens of other behaviors alone and with others that depend on communication.

I believe that this is a seriously flawed picture. Communication isn't something that happens inside the organization. Communication is the organization, or, to put it more in the terms of this chapter, to communicate is to organize. From a communication theory point of view, the communication behaviors of organization members are what constitute the actual organization. The organization, then, is composed of much more than walls, signs, desks, pencils, and computers. The organization is the continuing communicative construction of its members. It is continually evolving as the participants engage in the normal drama of their lives.

This may sound very abstract and confusing—and it is both abstract and confusing. But so are organizations. This chapter (indeed, this whole book) is about moving us out of our more common, stable, safe ways of understanding organizations. Only by shedding these blinders can we begin to gain an adequate understanding of the complex, fascinating, ever-changing event that is the organization.

To create this vision of organizations as communication, this chapter will progress as follows. I'll first present a number of communication scenarios. Read each one carefully and answer the questions that follow it. The chapter will then offer a discussion of the communication-organization overlap in the examples. With these examples as background, the chapter then turns to definitions. I'll take what is called a "transactional" approach to communication. A transactional approach is simply a perspective that emphasizes the notion of process in understanding communication.

The chapter then addresses the issue of communication as structure. After all, if organizations are to be discussed as communication, rather than buildings, we're going to have to come to terms with what communicative structure means. In that section, we'll also look at five forms of communicating—individual, dyadic, small group, intergroup, and technological—that can be viewed as the essence of communicative structure.

With the above as background, I'll offer a definition of organizations that is consistent with a communication approach. The chapter concludes with a compact summary of Ernest Bormann's symbolic convergence theory as a vehicle for demonstrating the organizing processes discussed throughout the chapter.

In short, then, this first chapter is more about communication than about culture. The linear nature of writing and reading demands that something come first. I believe that our understanding of culture will be heightened if we begin by acknowledging the communicative form that we call the organization.

Key Terms

interaction

transaction

structure

negotiated aspect of culture

individual level

dyadic level

small-group level

intergroup level

technological level

organization

symbolic convergence theory

equivocality

fantasy

fantasy chain

fantasy theme

fantasy type

rhetorical vision

rhetorical community

organizational saga

Before venturing any further into this chapter, please look over the following examples and questions. They will be referred to later and will give you a frame of reference for reading the chapter.

Situation 1. Imagine walking down a sidewalk in your town. About a tenth of a mile away you notice another person walking toward you on the same sidewalk. That person also notices you. You continue to walk toward each other, each aware of the other's location, until you are virtually upon the same spot. For some reason, all of a sudden, instead of totally missing one another you find yourself in the terribly awkward position of almost crashing into each other. It takes an embarrassing second or two of jostling one direction, then the other, before the two of you coordinate your positions and walk around each other.

Question. How is it possible that the two of you saw each other from so far away, yet still almost ran into each other?

Question. How is it possible that the two of you avoided each other?

Question. How common is it to run into another person on a sidewalk, on a street, or in a hallway, regardless of how crowded it is?

Question. Are two people coordinating their walking on a deserted sidewalk (or a thousand people coordinating their walking on a crowded sidewalk) an example of an organization?

Situation 2. I live across the street from an elementary school. At various times during the day, as occurs in most elementary schools across the country, the bell rings and out pour hundreds of kids onto the playground. Some of them go to the paved areas to jump rope; some go to the grassy areas to play chase; some go to the open areas to play catch or other ball games; but the majority of the kids go to the equipment area to play— swing on the swings, slide on the slides, walk on the swinging bridge, balance on the balancing boards, and shimmy through the tunnels. As I watch them, I am amazed that though there are hundreds of kids located in a small area, with virtually no supervision, almost no accidents happen. They don't step on each other, they don't walk into the swinging kids, they don't run into each other.

Question. How is it possible that so few accidents occur amid the chaos of a playground?

Question. How chaotic is a playground?

Question. Is a playground full of kids playing an example of an organization?

Situation 3. As I write this, my town, Duluth, Minnesota, is once again experiencing an unusual event—the thirty-fourth annual meeting of the Wally Byam Caravan Club. The event is expected to attract some 2400 of the club's membership to town. But this isn't just "any old convention." The caravaners come to town in Airstream trailers—those shiny silver camping trailers and recreational vehicles that some of you might have seen or own. The members will be in town for about two weeks, attending meetings, conducting club business (they will vote this year whether to admit members who drive the less prestigious, more conventional minivan type of Airstreamer), doing "conventioning," and catching up on old acquaintances.

Their needs will be met by some of the many committees formed to help organize these large gatherings. These committees include a parking committee (to help with the parking needs of around 1200 20- to 30-feet-long trailers and an almost equal number of vans or large cars that tow them, in three different locations around town), a mail committee ("scooter patrol") to deliver the hundreds of messages that arrive each day, a sanitation committee, a communications (telephone) trailer, a medical trailer, and so forth. The club is supported by member dues, has an administrative structure, and exists almost exclusively for the purpose of gathering in these temporary trailer cities as a social event.

> *Question.* Is the Wally Byam Caravan Club an organization?

> *Question.* Are there any significant differences between this club, which exists for the social fulfillment of members, and the kids on the playground, who are also fulfilling social needs?

Situation 4. In 1989, I took part in a unique building experience. I volunteered to help with the construction of a large playground down on the waterfront in town (Duluth is a port city). This playground, referred to as Playfront, is one of many constructed this way by a firm based in New York. The firm travels to communities, talks with kids about what they would like to have on their playground, then designs the playground to meet the kids' standards. The firm coordinates with a local committee of community volunteers who supply all the labor. The firm sends out a core team of four or five individuals who know how to build playgrounds following specific blueprinted designs. Over a week-long period these individuals coordinate the work of hundreds of volunteers who show up, unannounced, to participate in the experience.

The event includes a food tent, where the volunteers are fed, a medical tent, portable bathrooms, and an electric power tent specifically for the power tools used to cut the lumber. The volunteers are split into three groups: those who can run a power tool, those with a skill (can hammer? can saw? can drive a bulldozer?), and those who self-identify as "no skill." The core group polls the individuals for their "skill level," assigns them to jobs ("you go to the electric tent," "you hammer these nails," "you shovel that pile from there to here"), and supervises the whole operation. Somehow, by the end of the week, the playground is built.

> *Question.* Is such an assemblage a reasonable example of an organization?

> *Question.* Clearly, organizing the behavior of the volunteers was happening. But, for the most part, none of the volunteers had the foggiest notion of what the final product would look like, or of what their role was in its completion. Is this an example of being organized?

To communicate is to organize. That is the perspective of this chapter as well as this book. The four examples at the head of this chapter were intended to start you thinking along those lines. Let's look briefly at what those examples showed us about communicating and organizing.

In the sidewalk example, as the two participants walked toward each other they tried to not communicate. The result was chaos—they almost ran into each other. But, when they made the conscious effort to communicate, coordination of activities happened—they went around each other. The process of communication organized the event.

"Coordinated" chaos is the result of playground behavior by the kids in the second example. Interestingly, of course, the overall flow of playground activity appears chaotic only to the outsider. The kids are all getting along just fine. Life in that organizational form is active, flowing, normal to the participants, and chaotic only by the nonparticipative standards of the onlooker.

In the third example, communication is both the goal and the process of the Wally Byam organizational form. Those folks have an elaborate formalized communicative structure that allows for the emergence of the informal organizational form of the temporary Airstreamer trailer court. And, finally, the construction of Playfront Park could not have been accomplished without the successful merging of communicative efforts toward organizing the random assemblage of workers to achieve a goal, the form of which almost none of them knew.

In each of the examples, then, communication proved to be synonymous with effective coordination of activities. Random behavior became organized during communication—not as a result of communication. This is important to note, because it reminds us that we're not talking about a chicken-egg dilemma here. *Neither communication nor organization comes first; they are the same event.*

Communicating and organizing are two sides of the same coin. The process of communicating is the act of organizing, and efforts to organize are communication-bound. Does this mean that all organizing is contrived, based upon some predetermined communicative intent? The answer is an unequivocal "yes" and "no." Yes because clearly any large-scale organizational effort, such as the creation of a newspaper recycling plant, or the design of a playground, or the institution of a degree program, will be governed by an overarching, formalized communicative effort. On the other hand, we can easily see that the relationship between communicating and organizing is much less predetermined and emergent in such situations as workers developing relationships at a newspaper recycling plant, children playing on a playground, and students choosing classes to fit around their sleeping habits rather than choosing what they might most benefit from taking.

- *Do you understand how communicating and organizing are being portrayed as the same effort?*

An additional issue that may be unclear in this discussion of communicating and organizing is the difference between the process of organizing and the result—usually referred to as an organization. Process versus result, verb versus noun. To clarify this issue we'll turn our attention to what "communication" is, then to what "structure" is. We'll find that the two are remarkably similar.

DEFINING COMMUNICATION

Communication is commonly discussed as an *interaction* in which a source transmits a message to a receiver, who, upon receiving and decoding the message, gives feedback to the original source. This is called an interactional view of communication, and is illustrated in Figure 1-1.

This image of communication as an interactive "loop," historically, has served as the reasonable view of "organized" social interaction. This vision of communication, however, poses many problems. First, with it we reduce the complex process of communication to a series of discrete events and parts with minimal relationship to each other. We call these parts source, message, channel, receiver, and feedback. This oversimplification of the communicative process misleads us into thinking that "effective" communication lies in enhancing the source or the receiver or the channel.

In an organization, for example, a manager who is having trouble with his or her workers may be advised to send clearer messages. Clarity, after all, is what is needed in order for the workers to understand what it is that they are to do. Or the advice may be to use less face-to-face interaction, for commands given in that channel are too easily forgotten. Rely more on memos. Or the advice may be that the workers are at fault, and need some development of their listening skills. Or the advice may be to improve how certain messages are worded so that their "tone" is improved.

Each of these pieces of advice on source, message, channel, and receiver may be well intentioned, but each is likely to fail if it is offered without an adequate understanding of the overall communicative process. This brings us to the second problem of the interactional view of communication: It portrays communication as a linear event. It is a presentation of communication as something that occurs from person to person in a clear, straightforward, straight-line fashion. Such linear visions of communication are very "clean"—they're easy to discuss and seem to accurately demonstrate communication behavior. However, communication is actually quite "muddy."

- *Can you explain what an interactional model of communication is?*

FIGURE 1-1. An interactional model of communication
[Original Message]
"Did you understand my instructions?"

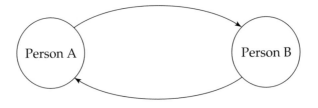

"Yes, I think so."
[Feedback on Original Message]

Communication As Transaction

For a number of years, organizational communication researchers have debated these definitional issues in their efforts to settle upon the most fruitful approaches to understanding organizations (see Daniels & Spiker, 1994; Frank & Brownell, 1989; Goldhaber, 1990; Kreps, 1990; Pace & Faules, 1994). The result of these discussions has been the widespread rejection of interactional models in favor of transactional models.

Transaction differs from an interaction in that with interaction, one still has the notion that meanings are sent from a message source and received by a message receiver, with the receiver then offering feedback. This model of back-and-forth sending and receiving of meaning oversimplifies words as containers of thoughts and feelings. In the *transaction,* however, meaning emerges from the combination of communicative participants within a specific context. Rather than being the content of words, meaning is the result of a complex communicative process that includes words, intentions, contexts, histories, and attitudes.

- *What is the difference between interaction and transaction?*

Participants bring biases and assumptions, feelings and experiences, attitudes and skills into every communicative situation. These individual differences will color message reception, taint message sending, and basically befuddle the best attempts at offering precise, clear statements. Meaning, then, becomes the understanding that emerges from our attempts to communicate with one another. It is the result of the interplay between context and participants.

David Berlo (1960) is generally credited with being the first communication scholar to forcefully make the case that communication is a process rather than a linear series of steps. Berlo contended that process, as a definitional guideline for communication, implied that communication had no beginning or end, and no clear, linear line of movement. This doesn't mean that there aren't messages, sources, receivers, and so forth. It is, rather, a reminder that breaking communication down into these parts is arbitrary and simplistic. Human communication is complex and muddy, and there is only minimal value in making it appear simpler than it is. "Process" is the premise that as humans coordinate their beliefs, behaviors, and so forth with one another, a coordination occurs that we can point to and identify as structure.

- *What was Berlo's contribution to our understanding of communication?*

Communication As Structure

We assume the existence of *structure* when we think about organizations. We say, "Of course the organization is structured. It has walls and a building. It has job titles, positions, levels, bureaucracy, and an organizational chart." These structural assumptions help us visualize organizations as stable, uniform, and lasting. Understanding structure as a communication event, however, offers a different appreciation of organizational stability. A number of scholars have offered insights into the relationship between communication and structure.

McPhee (1985, 1989), for example, built a case for the interaction between formal structure—the predetermined distribution of offices, rank, responsibilities, and so forth—and communication, suggesting that the nature of the communication activities of organization members has a most significant impact on what is understood as the formal structure. McPhee noted that structure is usually discussed as something distinct from the work or communication of the organization. It is within the structure that these things are said to occur. Structure, then, is usually understood to be a container for communication.

Structure is created to fit someone's conception of "organized" and to facilitate the work within its boundaries. But what is usually overlooked is the *negotiated aspect of structure*—the notion that organizational structure is that which is experienced by organizational members much more than anything built of bricks and mortar. As a negotiated dimension of the organization, structure includes working relationships, experiences and interpretations, and power relationships. In short, structure is a form of document, forged, communicated, and responded to over time. It is not something independent of the organizing activities of the organization members.

- *What does it mean to say that structure is negotiated?*

For example, consider the chaos of the playground described at the beginning of the chapter. The playground was designed to meet a number of formalized goals, including enjoyment, safety, and variety. The equipment and play areas were designed and situated so as to fulfill these formalized assignments.

However, the kids (organization members) don't use the playground in quite those ways. Kids launch themselves from swings rather than hanging on while swaying gently and safely back and forth; the ball players play virtually on top of the rope jumpers, who are jumping so close to the school doorway that entrance and exit are difficult; and some kids aren't playing at all. They're just sitting, watching, or standing near the playground monitor waiting for recess to be over. The point here is that structure has less to do with preconceived notions of jungle gyms, balls, slides, and swings than with member notions of use, value, and interest.

At this point, please refer to Case 1-1: The Violence-Free School, which describes a program intended to create a haven for kids aged five through twelve (roughly). What the case shows is the importance of understanding the negotiated character of structure. This school has now changed to include conflict programs, playground conflict managers, open discussions of racial prejudice, family violence, sexism, ethnocentrism, and virtually any other "ism" you might imagine.

Case 1-1 illustrates that structure can be understood as a communicative process. The school is an organizational form. It has an apparent physical structure: walls, desks, closets, library, bathrooms, and so forth. Yet these artifacts seem hollow when used as the primary criteria of what this organization is. The elementary school described in Case 1-1 changed. But no new walls were added, no new desks were brought in, no new teachers were hired, no new parking lots were paved.

The changes were communicative. A new dialogue emerged, one that focused on violence, safety, rights, maturity, development, prevention, racism, abuse, and a host of other issues too often not part of the elementary school dialogue. Organizations as communication events, like the violence-free school, are beyond bricks and mortar. They are relationships that constitute the structure understood as the organization.

- *How was "structure" negotiated in the violence-free school of Case 1-1?*

A number of organizational researchers (Bastien & Hostager, 1988, 1992; Eisenberg, 1990; Weick, 1989) offer us a further provocative explanation for the complex and abstract arguments of emergent structure put forth in this chapter. These researchers built the case that jazz improvisation is a reasonable model or analogy for the organizing behavior that has come to be called "organization." The jazz band is offered as a prototypical example of the organization because, as with the improvisational jazz band, "Organizing is a continuous flow of movement that people try to coordinate with a continuous flow of input" (Weick, 1989, p. 243). This "flow of input" exists as the form that is forced upon the movement. There are many such forms (the family, the group, or the team) but whatever the specific form, it serves as an attempt to make sense of organizational flow. The problem is, of course, that those led by the form may fall into the trap of believing that their map (their structure) is an accurate portrayal of reality. Organizational structure exists as the imposition of form on something in order to make it more accessible, orderly, and understandable than it actually is. Understanding organizations as communication events is difficult, but that should not be a reason for oversimplifying the organization into nothing more complex than a building which houses a number of formalized role-based relationships.

But, is an improvisational jazz group really an example of an organization, or is the example just too far-fetched? Is the school discussed in Case 1-1 an organizational form that much different from any other school? Are the kids on the playground, a family, two individuals who pass each other on the sidewalk? You are faced constantly throughout this chapter with what might be considered nontraditional organizational forms. This was intentional. I doubt that anyone reading this book has trouble conceptualizing 3M, or General Mills, or American Express, or General Motors as organizations. The jazz group, the school, the playground full of kids are all organizations. *Their structures differ but the basic ingredient necessary to constitute organization is there: communicative actions resulting in coordinated activities.* We must stop being lured by the simplicity of physical structure as our definitional requirement for an organization.

- *Can you talk about the improvisational nature of organizational form in your own words?*

Case 1-1:   The Violence-Free School

In 1992 five women who work with the Duluth Domestic Abuse Intervention Program (DAIP) were discussing their frustration with their work. The program was great. Duluth's Domestic Abuse Program is a model of its kind, capturing national and international recognition. This was the first city in the country to require that abusers go to jail and then attend twenty-six weeks of group treatment designed to help the abuser understand and deal with why he or she (mostly he) abuses.

The frustration felt by these women was with where in the cycle of abuse they were having an impact. At the point of spouse abuse, these women were performing interventionist actions; necessary, certainly, but by no means curative. They wondered what they might do to have a greater impact earlier in the abuse cycle; how they might prevent rather than intervene.

Their solution: get into the elementary school system with a program to help kids deal with conflicts in a healthy, socially productive fashion. Stop violence before these kids grew up

to think of violence as an acceptable means of conflict management. So, with some financial help from the Minnesota Women's Fund and Ben and Jerry's Ice Cream Company; a curriculum developed by The Community Board Program of San Francisco; an elementary school building, teachers, and student body offered as a test site by the building principal; the moral support of their colleagues in DAIP; and the enormous reservoir of energy that they themselves possessed, these women launched the Violence-Free School Project.

The project operates as follows. First, a listening process was used: kids were asked to describe the sorts of conflicts in which they were involved. In other words, the participants in the program were asked to give the basic content of the program (the workers designed the work, more or less). Once the issues that needed to be discussed were clear, the steering committee held informational meetings for the teachers in the school. They then recruited volunteers from the third, fourth, fifth, and sixth grades to train as playground conflict

---

Organizational structure is an "image" imposed on communicative behavior (Boulding, 1956). In the next section we'll look at five forms that this communicative structure may take.

FIVE FORMS OF ORGANIZING

The distinction between organizations and organizing blurs when we look at the structures we have come to call organizations. In other words, we forget that the identifiable structures, the buildings and names that have come to mean "organization," actually exist on the unstable foundation of at least five levels of human transaction.[1]

---

[1]These five levels are adapted from Thayer (1979), who wrote of five levels of analysis in human communication: intrapersonal, interpersonal, enterprise, enterprise-environment, and technological.

Case 1-1: *(Continued)*

monitors. Once trained, these monitors, working in pairs, approach disputants on the playground at recess and ask if they would like help solving their dispute. If the disputants agree, all four go into the building into a private room where the conflict managers lay out the ground rules: no interrupting, no name calling, be honest, and have a sincere desire to resolve the dispute.

At an appropriate point the managers ask if the disputants have any solutions. When ideas are raised, both are asked if the solution is acceptable. If and only if both agree, the conflict is declared resolved, both disputants sign a form attesting to the resolution, and the solution is implemented.

The actual training of the volunteer conflict managers takes five weeks. The kids come to meetings after school where they observe members of the steering committee and current conflict managers role play various conflicts. Suggestions are made about how to mediate, along with additional teaching surrounding the conflict process, mediation, role playing, privacy, listening, strategies, and tactics. Once the kids have developed the neces-

sary competence, they are allowed to perform their duties on a scheduled basis out on the playground.

The project has garnered praise and criticism. Civic groups, women's groups, law enforcement agencies, many teachers, principals, and parents have applauded the program. On the other hand, many teachers and parents have also objected strongly to the program. It interrupts the school day; pulls kids out of their normal classes; puts adult responsibilities onto the kids; asks kids to perform roles that they may not be developmentally prepared to perform; imposes a "feminist" ideology on the kids; and puts some kids in the difficult situation of seeing their parents as racist or sexist.

The program has changed the school that houses it. Kids are regularly called into small assemblies to view programs about violence, prejudice, and other issues. The language that the kids use, and thus the dialogue of the school, is now peppered with such words as discrimination, prejudice, racism, conflict, feelings, trust, and values. The school has been forced to take on an unspoken, informal curriculum.

The first and most fundamental level of transaction is the *individual level.* At this level the individual is in direct contact with the environment and with him- or herself. Thus, the environment shapes individual perceptions while the perceptions of the individual serve to cast the form of the environment. At the individual level communication concerns environmental adaptation coupled with internal dialogues (discussions with oneself about how clearly one is seeing things, one's competence, one's abilities, and so forth). This is the level of human perceptions, where attitudes, weaknesses and strengths, frailties and experiences come into play. As shown in Figure 1-2, the individual level serves as the foundation for the other four levels. The organization is built, then, upon the strengths and frailties, the adaptive capacity of the individual as he or she copes with an uncertain environment.

For example, consider some of the differences between a typical college environment and the environment of a business executive's office. I remember my first substantial exposure to such a distinction. While working toward my

Level 5:   Technological level—the human-machine interface

Level 4:   Intergroup level—the we-versus-them understanding

Level 3:   Small-group level—the difficulties of group dynamics

Level 2:   Dyadic level—making sense of someone else's sense

Level 1:   Individual level—making sense of the surroundings

FIGURE 1-2. Five levels of organizing

doctorate I was fortunate to obtain an internship at what was then called Honeywell's Management Development Center (MDC). I was a student at the University of Minnesota, Minneapolis campus. My "college" space was a comfortable studying environment, including an office shared with eight other teaching assistants, assorted books and computer printouts, a window overlooking a window well, manual typewriters, coffeepots and, well, you probably have the image in mind. It seemed quite nice to me at the time.

My surroundings at MDC were a bit different. I had to go past the receptionist to get into the doors of the complex. Once I was inside, the carpeted surroundings struck me as lush to the point that I had trouble adjusting. There was a cafeteria with free drinks (no coffeepots in people's offices!). Each intern shared space with only one other person, and we had our own desks, our own phones, and access to computers. The area was bright, expansive, hushed, filled with artworks, and no less busy than my school surroundings.

I began to notice that the surroundings themselves could become part of an individual's working reality. It became hard for me not to resent the poverty of my school surroundings and prefer the "glamor" of MDC's. Each time I went back and forth between the two I had to adjust my coping mechanisms so that expectations and behavior appropriate to one were not being imposed on the other.

The second level of transaction is the *dyadic level,* most notable because of the problems of mutual adaptation. At the dyadic level the individual must respond to the environment that he or she is actively shaping (individual level) and at the same time shape and respond to the influence of others. This level includes interactions with coworkers, superiors and subordinates, and customers one-to-one. This is a level of extraordinary significance in the organization because in terms of "organizing," the dyadic level is the most fundamental level. *Organizing cannot occur in the absence of at least two people; thus, while the individual is the lowest common denominator in the organization, the dyad is the basic organizational unit.*

- *Why is the dyad the basic organizational unit?*

For example, consider the case of the hurried shoe salesperson. On a busy afternoon in any shoe department in any store in America, you could observe the following scenario being played out by both men and women salesclerks. The clerk may be helping customer one be fitted. On the way to the back room to get number one's shoes, the clerk is approached by customer two with a question and a request for help. The clerk answers the question and asks number two to have a seat and wait, just as the phone rings. The clerk answers the phone just as customer number three comes up to the register to purchase some shoe polish. The clerk deals with the phone customer and rings up the sale at the same time, nodding to customer number two to acknowledge that he or she has not been forgotten, while avoiding eye contact with number one, who is beginning to show signs of impatience. Finally, the clerk makes it to the back room, grabs two pairs of shoes for customer one, takes them out and, while number one tries them on, approaches number two to offer assistance. But, just as the clerk gets to number two, the phone rings and a customer across the aisle catches the clerk's eye. . . .

The third level of transaction is the *small-group level.* One could convincingly argue that the small group is actually an organization in miniature. The small-group interaction includes such variables as roles, leadership, groupthink, power, hierarchy, and conflict. In short, the dynamics of small-group communication are very similar to those of the organization. This level of transaction includes such things as committee work, ad hoc groups, training sessions, and strategy meetings.

Ross (1989) argued that groups are the most effective way to accomplish good decision making. Current organizational practices suggest the same conclusion. Poole and DeSanctis (1990) reported a study that guessed that in the average large corporation, a meeting took place every minute of every day. These meetings might be kaizen groups (workers meet to suggest ways to improve their own work), quality circles (workers generate ways to improve productivity, quality, and so forth), standing committees, informal groups, or task forces.

The fourth level of transaction is the *intergroup level.* This level has all the potential problems of the group level and adds to them the problems associated with bringing groups together to form some common understanding. This is very common in organizations. Groups such as sales must communicate with marketing, finance must communicate with legal, management must communicate with labor, and so on.

In a very real sense, this intergroup level is similar to intercultural communication (communication between people who hold different beliefs or have different ethnic or cultural backgrounds). For example, it may be hampered by ethnocentrism, lack of understanding of other groups, an apparent lack of a common language (for example, the "language" of research and development is quite different from the "language" of sales and marketing), and quite different perceptions of "reality."

Consider the case of the Corporate Growth Team (CGT) discussed by Pepper (1993). The CGT was to do a total organizational redesign at New Public Utility. Overseeing the CGT was a group of five senior vice-presidents of the company. From the very beginning of the project the two groups did not see eye to eye. The CGT felt that the executive level should take responsibility for managing and owning the change effort. The VPs, however, felt that the responsibility for the project rested with the group charged with doing it. The

CGT felt that because they had no real power to create or change programs, their job was to recommend and facilitate, not take ownership. The VPs felt that the change effort was premature, constantly addressed it in terms of financial returns on investment, and avoided having anything to do with the change team.

It isn't hard to imagine what their joint meetings looked like. They were forced, superficial exchanges primarily between the leaders of the two groups. Eventually, at the prompting of the CGT, and to the great relief of the executives, the regularly scheduled meetings between the two groups were ended. They just weren't speaking the same language. What this meant for the company, of course, was that there was no longer any scheduled communication between the two groups charged with accomplishing a total corporate redesign of a major public power utility.

The fifth level of transaction is the *technological level.* Although this level may not seem to reflect the concerns of "human" transaction, we must remember that humans use technology, and then often become dependent upon their technological "toys." Technology includes any form of mediated communication, from the telephone to the word processor, from the conference call to the teleconference. Each form of mediated communication has an impact on human communication. That impact is seen, for example, in how the use of technology affects face-to-face interaction, how the introduction of technology affects workplace climate, how access to technology democratizes the workplace by making information more available to more people, and how mediated communication affects decision making.

The human-technology interface is all too easy to overlook. We've come to take automated bank machines for granted; we forget that most of the junk mail we receive is generated because our addresses are part of huge data banks routinely sold by one organization to another; the phones hanging on our walls have evolved from amazing devices through which information was shared to the means by which a seemingly endless number of sales representatives enter our homes to sell us everything from light bulbs to sandpaper to time share condominiums. Computer programs have been designed to help groups make decisions (see Poole & DeSanctis, 1990). Beepers, those little devices that doctors wear on their belts to let them know when patients need them, have become devices used by drug dealers to let them know when drug users are in need. And, in one of the most interesting current examples of technology use, organizations have entered the video game zone with the emergence of "virtual corporations."

The virtual corporation "is a temporary network of independent companies—suppliers, customers, even erstwhile rivals—linked by information technology to share skills, costs, and access to one another's markets" (Byrne, 1993, p. 99). Through these temporary structures, large organizations can tap the flexibility of small companies to develop products, for example, or enter markets, while small companies can draw upon the research and development capabilities and assets of large companies to develop projects that they might not have the resources to develop themselves. In other words, technological linking capacities are now stretching the boundaries of organizations to include their customers and even their rivals. In the terms of this chapter, the structure of the organization has been expanded through technological links far beyond the walls, desks, carpeting, and hallways of the physical structures we like to call "the organization."

- *Why are the five levels of communication discussed above called the foundations of organizational structure?*

These levels of transaction, then, are the organization, even though it may not look like the stereotypical organizations that we tend to imagine—the ones that are portrayed on television, or that form the New York skyline. The organizational form that emerges from this line of reasoning is one that is in flux, changing with the stream of organizational members participating in their daily routines. And, finally, we must not suppose that these forms do not affect each other. Though they exist as levels of varying complexity, they are not hierarchical or linear. Each will affect the other in both subtle and obvious ways.

In this chapter, so far, we've looked at what constitutes the organization. I've argued that the organization is the form created by the communicative behaviors of the members. In the following section I'll summarize all that has been said into a definitional statement with implications.

DEFINING THE ORGANIZATION

Although not necessarily a conventional explanation, this "communication approach" to understanding organizations is not new. It is found in the works of Bantz (1989), Homans (1975), and Weick (1979a, 1989), among others. Hawes (1974) clearly articulated the theoretical approach of this chapter when he argued that too much organization theory is built on the assumption that "organizations" exist as entities unto themselves, within which communication happens, and that these organizations have qualities that set them apart from nonorganizations, such as permanence, size, and complexity. Hawes found fault with this argument, suggesting that the differences noted may in actuality be questions of degree rather than kind. The group, the family, and the classroom all engage in organizing behaviors. Each is a kind of organizational form.

The interesting question for Hawes was, "How do organizations come into being?" This is a communication question and it centers our attention on a social collectivity definition of organizations as systems of organizing behavior. The definition of organizations to be used in this book, then, is that an *organization* consists of the organizing activities of its members. Though this definition may seem circular, it really is quite descriptive of a communication explanation of organizations. The definition accounts for traditional, pyramidal organizational form just as easily as it accounts for nontraditional, democratic, "feminist" organizational forms, because the key to the definition is the communicative relationships among the members, rather than arbitrary components assumed to define the organization, such as goal-directed, hierarchical, or rule-governed.

A number of issues are implied by this definition:

1. An organization's membership consists of the members of the social collectivity who identify themselves or who are identified as participants of the organization.
2. The organization's form or structure consists of the communicative relationships established by the membership. Thus, the shape of the organization is continually evolving, continually being reformed during the process of organizing.
3. Since organizing is synonymous with communicating, the organization is truly a communication event, built on the communication behaviors of the membership.
4. Because communication is understood as transaction, (a) the minimal unit necessary for an "organization" to exist is the dyad, and (b) the meaning of any organization will be the product of the transactions between members and the organizing environment.

By this definition, then, all of the situations and illustrations offered in this chapter are examples of organizations. This definition, as well as this chapter, presents an image of organizing as organization.

The image of organizations offered in this book is certainly abstract. But we need to understand the nature of this abstraction. The vision of organizations as organizing doesn't do away with desks and walls and buildings and hierarchy and job titles. What it does do is put those variables into a relationship with human participation. When this mix occurs, the organization becomes the outcome of human experience.

- *Why is such a circular definition acceptable within the context of this chapter?*

THE ORGANIZING ACTIVITY:
SYMBOLIC CONVERGENCE THEORY

The organizing-as-communication approach of this book can be compactly illustrated by drawing upon the work of Ernest Bormann of the University of Minnesota. Bormann's symbolic convergence theory (SCT) offers us a working vocabulary as well as a way of demonstrating the organizing processes discussed throughout the chapter. Before moving to the discussion of the theory, though, take a few minutes now to read Case 1-2: Harassment at City High. The case will be referred to throughout the following section to illustrate the sometimes confusing terminology of SCT.

Symbolic convergence theory is a dramatistic perspective on human communication. This means that it speaks of human communication in terms of such things as scripts, plots, actors, action, metaphors, allegories, fables, analogies, and figures of speech. The theory, based upon work by Robert Bales (1970), was developed by Bormann, and others, who noticed that individuals and groups commonly cope with uncertainty by telling stories in an attempt to make sense of what is confusing. Bormann used the term "fantasy" to refer to this process. According to Bormann, the language or symbols of group interaction may be more important than the actual physical group experience.

- *What is a group fantasy?*

Informative and comprehensive discussions of symbolic convergence theory are found in Bormann (1972, 1980, 1982 [with Howell, Nichols, and Shapiro], 1983, 1990, 1992 [with Bormann]), Cragan and Shields (1981), and Putnam, Van Hoeven, and Bullis (1991). At its most basic, symbolic convergence refers to the rhetorical construction of reality through the accomplishment of shared meaning among group members. In other words, as group members transact with each other, their understanding of the group experience—the reality of the event—is shaped by their language. Common understanding emerges as members struggle to make themselves clear and to understand one another. In the language of the chapter thus far, we would say that symbolic convergence is the process of organizing, resulting in the form of organization commonly called the small group.

- *What is symbolic convergence?*

This struggle to understand is necessary because of the equivocality (Putnam, 1989) of the group experience. *Equivocality* is a level of uncertainty. Group members are uncertain of each other, of issues, and of their capacity to work together. They're also uncertain of the environment outside the group. By sharing their various interpretations, group members may become aware of what were previously unknown or overlooked portions of the environment and thus move toward the shared understanding referred to as symbolic convergence.

Finally, symbolic convergence theory is discussed here because it represents a theoretically grounded, well-researched and documented articulation of the communication explanation of organizations put forth in this chapter. Symbolic convergence theory revolves around seven key elements: fantasy, fantasy chain, fantasy theme, fantasy type, rhetorical vision, rhetorical community, and organizational saga. Taken together they offer a concise vision of how organizations can be understood as the sense-making activities of members. Don't let the terms bog down your understanding of the theory. Symbolic convergence theory simply refers to the coming together of symbolic worlds. The jargon of SCT helps illustrate that process. The relationship of these elements to one another is shown in Figure 1-3. Referring to Figure 1-3, as well as Case 1-2, while studying the concepts below should help you understand SCT.

Fantasy, as used here, does not mean the common notion of daydreaming or imaginary visions of events removed from reality. Indeed, Bormann (1990) wrote, "You should not get the impression that the term fantasy . . . means

---

Case 1-2:   Harassment at City High

Janice Little began her sophomore year at City High School with the same sorts of hopes and anxieties that most 15-year-olds have when entering high school. She wondered if she would be lost in the large building, if she would make friends and be accepted, if her grades would remain as high as they were in middle school, and so forth. The last thing she worried about was if she would be labeled a "slut" on the walls of one of the boy's bathrooms, and if that label would haunt her throughout her entire high school experience. Unfortunately, this is just what happened.

Janice is a junior in college now. But the emotional scars of the high school experience have not diminished with the passing years. The ordeal apparently started as someone's idea of a joke. Some boy wrote "Janice Little is a slut" on the wall of the middle stall in the boys' second-floor bathroom. Janice found out about it and discussed it with her guidance counselor, who assured her that it would be taken care of. A week later the writing remained.

As time passed the crudity grew greater and greater. Users of the stall added daily to the list of acts attributed to Janice, including sex acts with dogs, her brothers, and various farm animals. They began to refer to the stall as the "Janice stall," and would remark to Janice that they had used *her* stall that day. Much of this verbal taunting took place on the bus ride home at the end of each school day.

Eventually, Janice withdrew from school and social activities. She didn't date. She did keep complaining to her counselor and the school principal, who both assured her that the graffiti would be taken care of. In their defense, the school authorities claimed that its custodians were not allowed to paint; the district had to hire painters to do that job. Additionally, they claimed that the custodians did wash some of the remarks off, only to have them reappear a day later.

---

that the communication is bizarre like science fiction, or unrealistic like a cartoon, or make-believe like a fairy tale. A group fantasy may and often does deal with real-life situations and people" (p. 104). Case 1-2 presented a number of fantasies, both real and imagined. The story spread about Janice was a fantasy—in this case, a real-life nightmare for her. It is an all-too-common occurrence in public bathrooms across the country that both men and women are portrayed as objects to be used. It is important to note here that a group fantasy is not just imaginary descriptions, like those of Janice. The fantasy is the whole process of describing women on bathroom walls. It is an effort by some men to explain something that they don't understand and want to control.

When group members respond to a fantasy (dramatic episode), such as a story, a joke, or a pun, they publicly proclaim a position (for example, "that was funny,"). When others participate in that proclamation, "chaining" is said to occur. The *fantasy chain*, then, allows symbolic convergence to come about based on the "common ground" demonstrated in the group members' participation in a public response to a fantasy. At its most basic, symbolic convergence refers to the public coming together of private symbolic worlds through

Case 1-2: (Continued)

Finally, Janice complained to her mother. Her mother immediately complained to the principal, who assured her that the comments would be removed. They remained. By the end of her sophomore year the whole inside of the stall was covered with penned, penciled, and even carved comments about Janice. They remained there over the summer and greeted her upon her arrival for her junior year of school. Again, more promises and no action.

Toward the end of that year Janice contacted the local program to aid victims of sexual assault, who assured her that this was sexual harassment and she did not have to put up with it. Again the principal assured her that the stall would be painted over the summer but, upon returning for her senior year, Janice was again greeted by the carved-in comment: "Janice Little is a slut."

Things had now gone too far. Janice and her family got an attorney and filed suit against the school district. The day after the suit was filed the words were painted over. She sought an apology, which she never got. What she did receive was a settlement for $15,000 and a promise by the school district that it would post a sexual harassment policy. The district also promised to check the bathroom walls daily. Janice also received a lot of support from other victims as well as observers of what happened.

And, sadly, Janice received a lot of resentment from males and females. Some accused her of filing suit for the money; some complained that she tarnished the reputation of her school. Some of her teachers in college have expressed anxiety about having her in class for fear that she is looking for ways to "get them." And, one of Janice's detractors took it upon himself to write upon a wall in one of the college bathrooms: "Janice Little is a slut."

Note: Though this is a true story, I have changed the name of the actual victim and the name of her high school.

---

participation in fantasy chains. The sharing of group fantasies, then, is the cornerstone of the theory; it is what brings about symbolic convergence.

- *What is "chaining"?*

In Case 1-2, many people participated in the fantasy of Janice. Each person who added an item to the ever-growing list was publicly stating that he supported the vision put forth in the fantasy. Indeed, it could even be said that the principal, counsellor, and district personnel who knew of the stories but did nothing to stop them were participants in the fantasy as well.

Fantasy themes are stories involving individuals in the past or the future, true or fictitious, that have an impact on the present. Dramatizing messages leads to fantasizing (fantasy chains) based on fantasy themes (the content and style—puns, anecdotes, analogies—of the story). In Case 1-2, the theme of the fantasy was obviously Janice's alleged sexuality. The theme or content of the story was embodied in the carved statement: "Janice Little is a slut." That theme had an enduring effect on Janice's ability to cope with the lies.

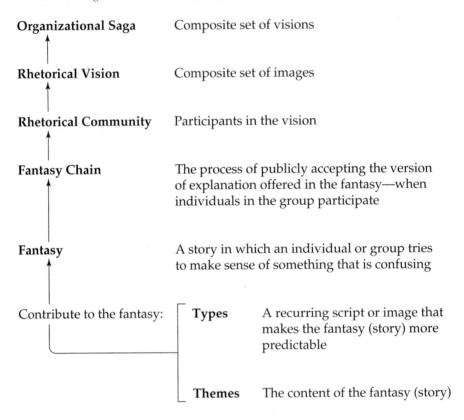

Organizational Saga   Composite set of visions

Rhetorical Vision   Composite set of images

Rhetorical Community   Participants in the vision

Fantasy Chain   The process of publicly accepting the version of explanation offered in the fantasy—when individuals in the group participate

Fantasy   A story in which an individual or group tries to make sense of something that is confusing

Contribute to the fantasy:

Types   A recurring script or image that makes the fantasy (story) more predictable

Themes   The content of the fantasy (story)

FIGURE 1-3. The process of symbolic convergence

- *Do you see the relationship between fantasies, fantasy themes, and chaining?*

When fantasy chains deal with similar themes, characters, and so forth they become a fantasy type. A *fantasy type* is a recurring script in which the players may change, but the general plot remains essentially the same. For example, in the media, certain "types" of shows make programming somewhat predictable. Westerns tend to look like one another, soap operas tend to look like one another, and cop shows tend to look like one another. Additionally, fantasy types may refer to stock characters. As such, heroes of westerns tend to look alike, and absent-minded professor is a term that evokes a generally consistent image.

In Case 1-2 the "type" was obvious. Janice was portrayed as the same "slut" discussed on a thousand doors and walls in a thousand men's and women's bathrooms. The fascinating thing about the development of the fantasy type is that at some point in its development, just the fact that it is typical becomes justification for its existence. Consider, for example, how difficult it would be for a movie maker to present an image of Dracula as a sympathetic, somewhat benevolent character. Breaking the mold established by typecasting is nearly impossible.

The *rhetorical vision* represents the unified or composite set of fantasies. The vision is the overarching understanding created through the integration of scripts, and offers the broad view of the organization. This vision may be very broad, as articulated in slogans like "IBM means service," or "Sears is where America shops for value," or "At Avis, we try harder." More often, however, rhetorical visions are subgroup specific, meaning that the vision of those in marketing represents marketing's understanding of the organization, while the vision of production represents their understanding, and so on.

In Case 1-2 the rhetorical vision forced Janice into the category of promiscuous women. People began to interact with her on the basis of her assumed participation in such a category. However, with the filing of the suit, a new vision unfolded—one that most schools are not accustomed to discussing: sexual harassment. This term then became part of the organizational dialogue. And, unfortunately, Janice was forced into additional new, unfamiliar categories, such as feminist, greedy, and man-hater. The school was forced to take on a new image, with which it will now have to contend, as a context for sexual harassment. Its organizational form evolved into this new structure.

Those who participate in the vision constitute the *rhetorical community*. The rhetorical community is equivalent to a society, a population, a number of people who demonstrate a shared understanding of organizational experience. The vision and the community actually exist in an interdependent relationship. Obviously, the process of sharing experiences may coalesce into a unified vision. Less obvious, but no less important, a vision may draw participation. For example, a charitable organization may ask you to contribute money by presenting a particularly poignant and compelling message on television. You may respond by sending a check and encouraging others to do the same. You're now part of the rhetorical community, prompted by your acceptance of the vision.

In Case 1-2, the local program to aid victims of sexual assault, a local psychiatrist, the courts, and a number of attorneys all became part of the community. Additionally, the story was carried by a number of national magazines, and Janice appeared on at least three talk shows to discuss the case. In the terms of this chapter, with the growth of this rhetorical community, the boundaries of the school, its structure, expanded exponentially.

Finally, the *organizational saga* represents the whole story of the group or community. The story includes the fantasies, rhetorical visions, and future visions of the organization. Sagas can be almost mythic in quality, full of legends and legendary characters. In Case 1-2, sadly, Janice's story will most likely reach legendary status. The posters cautioning against sexual harassment will always prompt questions, which will always bring answers embedded in Janice's story.

Not all fantasies chain out (gain public acceptance), but when they do they act as common ground for future rhetorical events. Dramatizations catch on, become chained out, and come together to form a composite picture of symbolic reality or rhetorical vision. Once the vision is formed, it can serve as a plot line to be alluded to in the future. In the process of fantasizing, the members may personify the group as "our group," making possible the identification of boundaries and of insiders and outsiders. Group fantasizing allows the group to develop a common history, a shared understanding, a tradition, memory, and a basis for reasoning and action. Fantasies that chain out become the group's symbolic common ground, its basis for cohesiveness. The fantasies serve as the socially constructed group reality.

Symbolic convergence theory is complex. But so is the vision of organizations offered in this text. The vision, and the explanation of the vision, are based on the realization that organizations are more complicated than we usually assume. They are not just boxes within which rules and people and positions and roles are each allotted a compartment.

The process of reaching symbolic convergence is how organizing comes about. The language of symbolic convergence helps us see how the organization can be easily understood as communicative process. People come together and share interpretations, and as other interpretations are brought in, the original "organization" expands—changes to accommodate the modified vision.

SUMMARY

This chapter has presented a communication theory approach to organizations. I argued that communicating is the process of organizing, making the organization the process of member communication. Organizations have not been described as containers in which communication happens, but rather as the communication process itself.

Communication was explained as a transactional process in which meaning evolves through the interplay of participants and context. Viewing organization as communication and communication as transaction allows us to question the validity of considering formalized or identifiable structure as something independent of organization members. I suggested, instead, that structure is a communication event, predicated on five levels of human transaction.

Finally, symbolic convergence theory was offered as an overarching theoretical approach to demonstrate the communication-based picture of organizations presented in the chapter. Symbolic convergence theory, as a dramatistic approach to explanation, focuses explicitly on language and the rhetorical construction of reality through the sharing of group fantasies, or the coming together of symbolic interpretations of the world. Thus, a group vision of reality is accomplished through language and symbols that are shared, resulting in the rhetorical community and symbolic convergence.

CHAPTER 2

Understanding Organizations As Cultures

Chapter Preview

All science, all understanding is guided by the inquirer's perspective. Point of view serves to frame the world in a way that makes it understandable and predictable. Point of view also narrows the vision of the viewer by blocking out competing visions. The approach to organizations presented in this chapter—organizations as cultures—is a point of view. It is the argument that organizations are composed of communities of individuals who, through their language use, come to understand organizational reality in ways that align them with some, while making them distinctly different from others in the same organization.

In Chapter 1 we looked at organizations as communication events, structured through the communicative transactions of the members. This emphasis on communication is with us in this chapter, also. The main difference is that in this chapter I'll go into detail about the results of all this communication: the emergence of shared understanding, referred to as organization culture and subculture.

A focus on culture forces the researcher to examine such vague notions as assumptions, values, beliefs, expectations, and shared meanings. The payoff of examining such things is a different understanding of the organization than can be achieved by using any alternative perspective. The understanding derived from a focus on culture revolves around the idea of "shared sense making." In other words, the researcher learns a little about the process by which organization members come to understand their lives in organizations.

This chapter will progress as follows. First, I'll pose one of the most troublesome questions in culture research, for you to consider as you read the chapter: Is culture in the minds of organization members, or is it their behaviors and the surroundings of the organizational context? Or is it actually both? After those questions are posed, we'll turn directly to the first main section: Why culture? I've chosen to begin with that question instead of defining culture at the outset because in answering the question we'll accomplish two goals. First, we'll begin the definitional process. Second, we'll gain some insight into why I've chosen to build this entire book around this concept. Only when we've come to terms with the perspective's importance do we look at specific definitional issues.

The chapter then turns to definitions, noting both the difficulty and the complexity of defining culture. Our discussion centers on "cognitive" orientations, placing culture primarily in the heads and language of organization members. In a natural progression from the definitional issues, the chapter then probes the sticky question of whether organizations are composed of a single, unified culture that can be controlled and managed or of a variety of subcultures, each different and sometimes competing. Finally, the controversial issue of culture change is examined. You will see through the examples that we are really revisiting the issues at the top of the chapter regarding where culture resides.

Throughout the chapter I have inserted a number of very brief summaries of some of the many, many culture studies that have been reported in the last decade. These are labeled "Spotlight on Research" and have been inserted with minimal comment, primarily in the early parts of the chapter, to give you a feel for the sorts of results available to a culture researcher, and to give you a feeling for what it's like to conduct culture research. To do a culture study you would first have to have faith in the importance of the perspective, as you would enter an unfamiliar setting that confused you somewhat as you came to understand it more and more. The chapter, then, reads somewhat like doing a culture study.

Chapter 2 serves as the informational and theoretical background for Chapter 3. In Chapter 3 I'll present a specific tool for cultural analysis—Bantz's (1993) Organizational Communication Culture method—along with a detailed presentation of results found during a culture study of an organizational development team. The two chapters together, then, offer a unified statement of what culture is, why it is important, and how to get at it.

Key Terms

paradigm	ideational definitions
culture	adaptationist definitions
culture as external variable	subculture
culture as internal variable	organization culture
culture as psychodynamic process	organizational culture

Before venturing any further into this chapter, stop to review your thoughts on Chapter 1's portrayal of organizational structure. Remember that structure was referred to as the process of communicative relationships. Structure, then, becomes a mixture of predetermined physical artifacts, such as desks, walls, buildings, and chairs; rules and regulations, such as hierarchical reporting relationships, seniority systems, and decision-making authority, combined with emergent or nonpredetermined actual behaviors and beliefs. These may include the symbolic status inherent in an office with a door, rather than a cubicle, the bypassing of formal authority in order to get projects completed, and the informal "ropes" taught to newcomers as the ways that work "actually gets done here."

The point was made throughout Chapter 1 that neither formal structure nor informal beliefs come first: Organizational "structure" is a combination of the two. In this chapter as well as Chapter 3, we're going to look much more closely at both the theoretical and applied importance of this structure-belief system merger. To set the stage and to get you thinking at the outset, let's consider structure to be all of the formalized dimensions of the organization, including buildings, offices, hierarchy, job titles, and benefit packages. And let's consider culture to be all of the informal dimensions of the organization, including beliefs, values, assumptions, true leadership (rather than designated leadership), and conflict.

Now, put yourself into the supremely powerful position of organizational change agent. You must design and oversee a large-scale change effort toward the goal of accomplishing the CEO's vision of "less competitive, more participatory culture." Where would you begin? Structure is observable, but the link between structural tinkering and attitude adjustment is tenuous at best. You want to change attitudes, beliefs, and values, but you're not sure how to access them. And you wonder what good it would do if no fundamental changes are made in how the work (and workplace) is designed.

You wonder where to begin your culture change effort. At the top, because ultimately top management must support the change? At the middle, because ultimately middle management must implement the change? At the bottom, because ultimately those at the bottom must endure the change? You wonder if a change in the organizational value system is even possible, if it's ethical, and how long it will take. You wonder if structure is, ultimately, the culture of the organization.

The above are culture questions. They are the sorts of questions and issues with which organizational culture theorists must grapple and on which organizational development (OD) practitioners and consultants must take stands. We need to remember that OD efforts do not just affect corporate profitability, they also affect people's lives.

All inquiry, whether "scientific" or "humanistic," is guided by a perspective or a paradigm (Brown, 1977; Kuhn, 1962; Morgan, 1993; Morgan & Smircich, 1980). A *paradigm* is a particular way of thinking about things, and these ways of thinking govern what sorts of questions the researcher can legitimately ask, as well as what sorts of answers are acceptable, given the governing assumptions of the paradigm. Indeed, Morgan and Smircich (1980), in a classic article regarding the importance of paradigm, demonstrated how relatively small, subtle shifts in our basic assumptions about human nature can have dramatic significance in our overall understanding of the relationship between humans and the world around us.

One of the gravest consequences of perspective, of course, is that questions and answers that fall beyond the boundaries of our points of view will be less likely to be considered. A paradigm, then, can actually serve as a blind-er to the researcher, making him or her either unaware of or overly critical of alternatives that fall outside the boundaries acceptable to the researcher (Daft & Wiginton, 1979; Schon, 1979).

The perspective that governs this text is a language focus: Organizations are cultures constructed through the communication (verbal and nonverbal language use) of organization members. And, as any perspective will do, a cultural approach presupposes certain assumptions, suggests certain questions, and steers the researcher toward some aspects of organizations at the expense of others. But this is not necessarily bad, if we recognize the approach as just that—an approach, a way of seeing rather than an answer. If we recognize the strengths and weaknesses of our perspectives, we are in a better position to garner the greatest amount from them. In short, this is not a "neutral" chapter or textbook. It presents a point of view. A cultural bias is here in every chapter for you to ponder, to agree or disagree with, and to guide your thinking and reasoning in a given direction.

- *Why is a paradigm, or a research perspective, both a strength and a weakness for researchers and consumers of research?*

SPOTLIGHT ON RESEARCH

Barley (1983) used a semiotic analysis to study the themes and codes within the culture of a funeral home. He argued that semiotics ("defined as the study of signs or systems of signs, semiotics concerns the principles by which signification occurs," p. 394) offers a technique for examining both meaning construction and the rules for interpretation.

Barley collected data over a three-month period. Preliminary data included observations and interviews designed to discover signs relevant to funeral directors. The early period of data gathering used observation to generate broad, loosely structured interviews. The interviews were transcribed and studied, resulting in fifty-six "domains" or categories to follow up on. This resulted in the later stages of data collection aimed at further identification and verification of categories. Thus, the patterns had to be both generated and corroborated by the subjects.

What Barley discovered was that the key problem faced in the culture of the funeral director was the juxtaposition of living and dead persons and how to most approximate the continuity of life when presenting death. This problem calls for certain regularized behaviors, or codes. Barley found three primary codes: a code of posed features, designed to resemble sleep; a code of furnishings, to make the funeral home most "homelike"; and a code of home removal, necessary to make the death scene most closely resemble the way it would look before the death occurred.

Question: What "meanings" do funeral home personnel attempt to construct in their work with the deceased and the deceased's families?
Question: Do you see why a "cultural approach," as a focus on attitudes and values, would be an appropriate paradigm for such a study?

Let's address the first question on your mind, a question even more fundamental than what "culture" is: Why is a cultural approach useful?

WHY CULTURE?

Why explain organizations as cultures? I might have chosen a systems metaphor, explaining organizations as interrelated, interdependent sets of components, using the human body as an analogy; or I might have used a beehive metaphor, explaining organizations as buzzing hives of seeming randomness, when in actuality there is rhyme and reason; or I might have chosen a prison metaphor, explaining organizations as places that force individuals into roles, requiring blind obedience and conformity, locking the workers' minds behind bars (see Morgan, 1986, for a fascinating discussion of a variety of competing metaphorical images of organizations, including systems, flux and transformation, psychic prisons, cultures, machines, and organisms).

The answer to the question "Why culture?" is that a culture focus facilitates an understanding of organizations that, if identifiable at all within competing metaphors, is certainly less clear. A cultural approach also often highlights the nuances of alternative perspectives. Culture thus helps generate insights into the organizing activity that would be overlooked or presented differently in other approaches.

As discussed when it first burst on the academic scene, a cultural approach challenges traditional assumptions, raises questions, and questions the taken-for-granted. Its most common and interesting challenges are in the areas of norms, assumptions, taken-for-granted communication practices, the informal organization, power and control, and other communication issues within the organization. Reilly and DiAngelo (1990) went so far as to argue that ignoring the culture of an organization is the same as not understanding the assumptions that allow decision making.

The many authors who recommend the examination of organization cultures are remarkably consistent in their reasons and reasoning. The advice for taking a cultural approach tends to center on the importance of accessing the communication and everyday sense-making activities of organization members. Table 2-1 summarizes a number of culture researchers' thoughts on the importance of tapping the everyday life of the organization.

- *What sort of information will a cultural approach to organizational analysis get you?*

The cultural approach to organizations is still in its early stages; no unified model has yet been developed. Pettigrew (1979), one of the earliest organizational culture theorists, offered a three-stage model of concept development. The first stage—introduction and elaboration—is the stage of concept invention or discovery or innovation from another field, as well as the attempts at legitimation. The second stage—evaluation and augmentation—is critique of the concept and its methodology. The third stage—consolidation

TABLE 2-1. The Importance of a Cultural Approach

Conrad (1994): "Cultures are communicative creations. They emerge and are sustained by the communicative acts of all employees, not just the conscious persuasive strategies of upper management. Cultures do not exist separately from people communicating with one another" (p. 27).

Pace and Faules (1994): "Everyday talk reveals organizational sense making and networks of shared meanings that may exist. Taken-for-granted behaviors that allow routine and organizing to exist are embedded in communication" (p. 71).

Smircich (1983a): "A cultural analysis moves us in the direction of questioning taken-for-granted assumptions, raising issues of context and meaning, and bringing to the surface underlying values. The rational model of organization analysis is largely silent on these matters" (p. 355).

Morgan (1986): The construction of culture is the process of creating shared reality. The critical reasons for studying culture are that such examination directs our attention to the symbolic and focuses on the language processes that facilitate shared meaning.

Deal and Kennedy (1982): Cultural analysis is critical because the organization of the future—the atomized organization—will barely resemble its present-day counterpart. Environmental complexity, the accelerating rate of change, more intense competition, a richer, better educated, white-collar workforce, and changes in technology will all demand a break from the rational tradition toward a deeper understanding of the organizing behaviors of the workforce.

Sathe (1985): The effects of culture are seen clearly in many critical organizational practices, including decision making, control, communication, commitment, perceptions, and the justification of behavior.

---

and accommodation—is marked by less controversy and more report and review of what is. This is the stage of "state-of-the-art reviews" commenting on what has been discovered and what remains within the conceptual research agenda.

Reichers and Schneider (1990), drawing upon Pettigrew's model, noted that culture is currently heavily stage one, less so stage two, and clearly not yet a stage-three concept. The implication, of course, is that within a very short period, the study of culture has developed both definitionally and methodologically.

Morey and Luthans (1985) argued that even with the various disagreements concerning definitional and applied aspects, there does seem to be general agreement on the following aspects of culture: It is learned, shared, transgenerational and cumulative, symbolic, patterned, and adaptive.

- *Of what value is understanding concept development as progressing through stages? What will it take for culture research to progress to more advanced stages in the above model?*

Why culture? The study of organization culture is advocated for at least the following six reasons.

SPOTLIGHT ON RESEARCH

Feldman (1988) suggested that culture can serve as a hindrance to innovation. The points are made through a case study illustration of Smith Electronics, an electronics production company that was thirty-five years old and employed three hundred people. Feldman found that the company's founder had instilled a culture of dependency among the workers, and that they had become unable to exercise enough self-direction to accomplish innovation. The company carried an internal focus on engineering at the expense of an external focus on marketing. This lack of understanding of customers' needs resulted in an overly cautious company culture that was handicapped by its own style of operating.

Question: What is the importance of "founders" in establishing workplace culture?
Question: At what point would you guess that a founder's or strong leader's influence over workplace values would begin to wane?

---

1. Culture mandates the explicit focus on communication at all levels of the corporate hierarchy. As individuals articulate who they are in relation to one another in the organization, shared understandings join people into identifiable subgroups.
2. A focus on culture is a focus on the routine, on the everyday sense making that is the process of building a shared reality among organization members. And it is also a focus on the official, on the everyday contrived attempts to build identity and manage the relationships among organizational members.
3. A cultural approach forces a focus largely ignored by the rational model of organizing, one that questions assumptions and brings underlying values and motives to the surface.
4. An understanding of culture offers insights to leaders and managers. This is not to say that the managers can then shape the culture (a controversial contention addressed in Chapter 12). However, they can better understand and participate in the sense-making activities that constitute the organization. Cultures are real and have an impact on the organization. Without an understanding of the culture, one does not have a handle on the feelings, attitudes, expectations, values, and assumptions of the workers.
5. A cultural approach is more in line with the organization of the future. Organized complexity will mandate novel approaches and understandings of organizations.
6. Culture is pervasive. It is not simply a variable that affects the organization, it is indistinguishable from the organization.

DEFINING CULTURE

Culture is one of most difficult approaches to understanding organizing to portray concisely. The primary problem is that culture can be explained and

SPOTLIGHT ON RESEARCH

Smith and Eisenberg (1987) applied a "root metaphor" analysis (extended from the work of Koch & Deetz, 1981) to Disneyland in an attempt to account for employee-management conflict. They argued that metaphor plays an important role in structuring world view, so an understanding of the dominant metaphors of a given group should offer insight into differences between groups of people, such as managers and workers.

In this case, analysis of root metaphors offered insight into changes in world view over time. Open-ended interviews were conducted, documents were analyzed, and structured interviews were conducted with central participants in a twenty-two-day strike in 1984. Results showed the presence of two key root metaphors that governed the understandings of both management and labor: drama and family. The authors suggested that historically, the drama metaphor guided life at Disneyland. This metaphor gave way to a family metaphor in the 1960s. The violation of "family" principles because of "business" decisions by management was seen as the cause of the 1984 strike against Disneyland.

Question: Based on the brief summary given, why would this be called a "culture" study?

---

defined in so many different, sometimes competing ways (see Morgan, 1989, for excellent examples). However, as noted by Barnett (1988), despite some definitional variation, culture research is tied together by the assumption that the language of the organization members is the key to understanding the organization culture. *A "cultural approach" to organizations, then, is a language approach.* By examining the language of organization members as presented in the various message forms available (Bantz, 1993), the culture researcher is able to infer to the level of member beliefs and assumption.

Definitional Foundations

How culture is defined depends, generally, upon from where the investigator believes culture comes. Smircich (1983a) compactly characterized the differences between three alternative explanations for the formation of culture. The first conceptualization views *culture as an external variable*, imported into the organization from outside. In this view (popularized in the many Japanese-form-of-management books), the organization would tend to reflect the beliefs, values, attitudes, and so forth of the host culture. The second conceptualization views the *culture as an internal variable* of the organization. In this view (popularized in many current writings, as well as the "excellence" culture books), the unique transactions of the participants within the organization result in a social reality that may or may not reflect the culture outside the organization. The final conceptualization that may emerge views culture as root metaphor. From this vantage, culture is no longer a variable, but rather is an extension of psychodynamic processes of organization members. *Culture as a psychodynamic process* is an "expression of unconscious psychological processes" (Smircich,

SPOTLIGHT ON RESEARCH

According to Deal and Kennedy (1982), culture governs how people are expected to behave, and culture must be understood because it affects how people feel about what they do. For Deal and Kennedy, culture is composed of the business environment, corporate values, heroes, rites and rituals, and the cultural network (means of communication). Values are the cornerstone of culture, help define the corporate character, and affect performance.

   Deal and Kennedy identified four types of cultures: (1) the tough-guy, macho culture of individualists (for example, police departments, construction, advertising, entertainment); (2) hard-work, hard-play culture of sales (for example, Mary Kay cosmetics, McDonald's, Xerox); (3) bet-your-company culture of high-stake, long-term investments (for example, oil and aircraft companies, NASA); and (4) process culture of the bureaucracy (for example, banks, insurance companies, government agencies). These four culture types will be distinguished in many ways, including dress, housing, sports, language, greeting rituals, and coworker rituals.

Question: What value can be found in generalizing cultural types?
Question: What problems might arise from generalizing cultural types?

1983a, p. 351). Culture, then, would be a reflection of underlying individual psychological states, such as anxiety, self-esteem, or dogmatism. The myths and stories and ceremonies of interest above are still of interest, but the psychodynamic researcher sees these as generative forces that result in the organization, rather than seeing culture as a result of members' social interactions.

- *Why are these three explanations of the sources of culture considered "competing visions"?*

   An example would be useful here. In the area where I live there are three four-year colleges within fifteen miles of each other: the University of Minnesota, Duluth (UMD); the College of St. Scholastica (CSS); and the University of Wisconsin, Superior (UWS). Let's consider the student cultures at each institution from each of the above points of view.

   According to the "culture as external variable" explanation, the cultures of the three institutions should be roughly the same, reflecting the values and belief systems of the Twin Ports area, the Northeastern Minnesota–Northwestern Wisconsin areas, states of Minnesota and Wisconsin, and obviously, of the United States as a whole. It is not clear in this explanation where the primary influence comes from—local community? state? country?

   According to the "culture as internal variable" explanation, the beliefs and values brought into the schools will be less important than the interactions that occur among students once they become organizational members. These interactions will influence the acceptance, rejection, and revision of external organizational values, resulting in the emergence of unique internal cultures or subcultures. Thus, culturally, students from CSS, UWS, and UMD differ in ways attributable to the unique discussions and activities in which they engage as students.

Finally, according to the "psychodynamic process" explanation, the anxieties that go along with the college experience will be the primary shapers of culture. Relevant examples might include the effects of failure on self-esteem, competition, fear, and separation from families.

The important point is that each of the above interpretations is based upon one of the three dominant paradigmatic biases in culture research. In other words, culture researchers put on blinders, just like any other researcher. Their perspectives, as noted at the beginning of the chapter, will allow certain questions and favor certain answers because they are consistent with the researcher's approach and expectations. The three research orientations discussed above must be understood in order to read and conduct culture research.

- *Summarize the differences in the research orientations presented above.*

Both the importance and complexity of the cultural approach can be shown in a quick review of some representative definitional statements. Table 2-2 offers a number of such definitions. Look over the table and note the similarities among the statements. Such definitions emphasize the abstract charac-

---

SPOTLIGHT ON RESEARCH

Nicholson and Johns (1985) portrayed absence as a culturally mediated event and held that different cultures contribute to different levels of absence. Absence was seen not as an individual event, but as a contextually and culturally embedded event. An absence culture consists of the beliefs of a group of people concerning absence.

The absence culture may exert influence directly, in the form of restrictions and norms; directly though more subtly, as when a worker observes the absence behavior of others and then patterns his or her own behavior on that observation; and indirectly, in the form of limitations and other nonspoken expectations of attendance and absence. A point that the authors make is that both the culture outside the organization and that inside the organization influence the development of the absence culture.

Four types of absence cultures were identified. The first, a dependent culture, is found in highly authoritarian organizations, where workers are bound to the rules and order system of the organization. The second type—moral—is a culture bound more by the unspoken norms of the group than by organizationally mandated rules. The third type—fragmented—exists in piecework or factory-type organizations, where attendance and absence are cost-reward ratios of personal consequence. The final type—conflictual—exists in low managerial-worker relationships, where absence is offered as a form of defiance.

Question: Most students skip a class occasionally. In your own experiences with skipping (being absent from class without a good excuse), what type of absence culture best explains your behavior?

TABLE 2-2. Defining Culture

A focus on culture helps us focus on the assumptions that drive the way things are done in the organization (Smircich, 1985).

"Culture is a set of important assumptions (often unstated) that members of a community share" (Sathe, 1983, p. 6).

Culture "shapes the character of an organization" (Morgan, 1986, p. 117).

Culture is "a basic pattern of assumptions . . . that has worked well enough to be considered valid and, therefore, to be taught to new members as the correct way to perceive, think, and feel in relation to those problems" (Schein, 1985, p. 9).

Culture consists of the publicly and privately accepted meanings of a given group that serve to define their understanding of reality (Pettigrew, 1979).

Culture is the way things get done in the organization (Deal & Kennedy, 1982).

ter of culture. And, within that abstract nature, we can also see the importance of accessing culture, for it is at that level of understanding that the research is able to tap the assumptions, values, beliefs, and informal guidelines that organizational members draw upon to guide their daily organizational lives.

- *Without worrying about what any single definition is saying, as a whole what is suggested by the definitions of culture offered here?*

Early Definitional Development

Although all of the researchers discussed in Table 2-2 have influenced the development of cultural studies in the discipline of communication, we can look much more specifically at the work of Clifford Geertz, Michael Pacanowsky, and Nick O'Donnell-Trujillo as potentially the most influential in this field. In *The Interpretation of Cultures,* Geertz (1973) presented culture as a controlling mechanism (plans, rules, programs) for the governance of behavior. For Geertz, cultural patterns—"organized systems of significant symbols" (p. 46)—are what keep human behavior from being simply chaotic acts, devoid of shape or meaning. Culture is the condition of human existence. Thus, cultural patterns guide the development of the human. (Geertz was not writing about organizations. Organizational theorists, however, were quick to see the utility and educational value of applying Geertz's thoughts to organizational patterns of human existence.)

Perhaps Geertz's most influential statement of culture was the following: "Believing with Max Weber, that man is an animal suspended in webs of significance he himself has spun, I take culture to be those webs, and the analysis of it to be therefore not an experimental science in search of law but an interpretive one in search of meaning" (p. 5). This "culture as web" metaphor runs through much of the literature addressing organization cultures. For example,

Tuchman (1978) referred to notions of a news net and webs of facticity when accounting for the coverage and creation of news.

Geertz's work has had a profound impact on the research strategies of organizational culture scholars in this field and was seminal in the thinking of Pacanowsky and Trujillo, who are two of the most active advocates of a cultural approach to organizations. In a number of articles (including O'Donnell-Trujillo & Pacanowsky, 1983; Pacanowsky, 1983, 1988; Pacanowsky & O'Donnell-Trujillo, 1982, 1983; Strine & Pacanowsky, 1985; Trujillo, 1983, 1985, 1992; and Trujillo & Dionisopoulos, 1987) they have discussed the theoretical underpinnings, justification, and methods of organization culture research.

They have argued that the organization-as-culture perspective grew out of a basic disagreement with traditional, dominant methods of organizational research. Traditional research relied on quantification and statistical manipulation. Further, these methods often took communicative behavior for granted, inferring it on the basis of questionnaires and surveys. What those researchers were doing was measuring, not discovering. And culture, Pacanowsky and Trujillo suggested, is not available for measurement, only for interpretation.

Pacanowsky and Trujillo argued for an interpretive approach based on the following: First, rather than being managerially based (and biased), the research should be communication based. This means that the focus of the research is the actual communicative events that constitute the social-communicative reality of organizational members. Second, the cultural perspective is based on Geertz's conceptualization of culture as a web, with its three implications: The web constrains its members, it not only exists but is somehow constructed (in this case, via communication), and it can be described or interpreted. Third, certain indicators help the researcher gain an understanding of organizational sense making, particularly relevant constructs, facts, practices, vocabulary, metaphors, stories, rites, and rituals. Fourth, the paradigm of research is interpretation, not explanation. The researcher seeks to make sense of a culture, not discover laws, for culture does not exist as a cause of behavior. Rather, behavior acts as one form of cultural articulation.

- *Why does the "web" metaphor seem particularly apt when describing organization cultures?*

In sum, the study of cultures in organizations revolves around the communication of the organization members. Through communication individuals coordinate their perceptions and their behavior with other individuals, resulting in pockets of people with a common understanding of some event. We make sense of what's going on around us. And "sense making" is at the center of the study of culture.

The study of communication leads the culture researcher to question such things as beliefs, values, attitudes, forms of presentation such as metaphors, stories, and ceremonies, and components of messages such as duration and format. All of these components and more go into the study of organization cultures. The importance of this line of inquiry (as presented in Chapter 1) is that communication creates the organization, through the construction of cultures.

Culture As Beliefs Versus Culture As Behavior

The definitional approaches to culture discussed in this chapter thus far would be labeled "ideational" by Sathe (1983, 1985), as opposed to "adaptationist." *Ideational definitions* position culture within the organization participants. Culture becomes a cognitive event that must be inferred, for it is not directly observable. Behavior is observable, and on the basis of observations of behavior, the culture researcher infers to the level of assumptions. *Adaptationist definitions,* on the other hand, put culture outside the individual, as something that is directly observable within the organization. From this perspective, culture resides in the observable behavior of organization members and the actual formal design of the organization. These competing definitions have a profound impact on both culture theory and research.

- *Do you see the theoretical importance of approaching the study of culture from an ideational rather than an adaptationist perspective?*

   It is the contention of this text that culture is primarily cognitive, not behavioral. Others have expressed the same opinion (Barley, 1983; Sathe, 1983, 1985; Siehl & Martin, 1990). This is not a rejection of the importance of behavior in understanding culture—indeed, communication, the reflection of culture, is a behavior. It is simply the realization that our perceptions, values, attitudes, assumptions, and beliefs are what shape our transactions with others and with the environment. To place too much emphasis on behavior alone is to deny the source of that which is observable.

   In this section I have simply tried to highlight some of the debate surrounding culture definitions. A result of the definitional dilemma is the identification of organizations as cultures themselves, or as containers of cultures. That debate is discussed in the next section.

ORGANIZATION CULTURE VERSUS ORGANIZATIONAL CULTURE

The distinction between organization culture and organizational culture may seem trivial, but it is not. The term "organizational culture" may lead the reader to make two errors. First, the term implies that organizations have one culture or, at least, one primary or dominant culture. This is the impression given by a variety of popular management books, such as those by Deal and Kennedy (1982), Kanter (1983), Ouchi (1981), and Peters and Waterman (1982). The primary weakness of this impression is that it implies that culture is something an organization "has" (culture as organizational component), rather than something an organization "is." Such authors as Conrad (1994) and Schall and Shapiro (1984) have made it clear that culture is more accurately viewed as what the organization is. These authors as well as this text argue that organizations are cultures (organization cultures).

   The second error that may result from the perspective of a single organizational culture is overlooking the fact that organizations are actually composed

SPOTLIGHT ON RESEARCH

To uncover the political structures of the organization, Riley (1983) attempted to identify the political "master structures" that guide individuals' behavior within the organizations. She focused specifically on organizational symbols and language directed at political behavior, symbolic signification, legitimation and domination in the exercise of power and conflicts. The firms studied were a subsidiary of a large government organization and a training and development firm. She conducted interviews of organizational members across the two firms at three hierarchical levels, transcribed the interviews, and analyzed them looking for treatments of legitimation, signification, and domination.

Her analysis showed clearly that the language of members of both firms demonstrated significant numbers of political symbols that (1) differed according to hierarchical level, (2) demonstrated a high level of political activity, and (3) demonstrated the existence of political subcultures. Riley found a dominant subculture at the upper managerial level, as well as an isolated, self-proclaimed subculture in one division. In sum, Riley warned against viewing culture as an overall organizational entity that exists in a unified, organization-wide form, favoring instead the focus on subunits for analysis.

Question: What makes the focus of your research, such as absence or political activity, subculturally specific rather than the organizational culture?

of many, often competing, subcultures. This point is stressed by a number of authors, including Louis (1985), Martin and Siehl (1983), Morgan (1986), Riley (1983), Sathe (1985), and Van Maanen and Barley (1985). The emergence of subcultures within an organization is natural in the development of work groups. Any large group of people who regularly interact within a workplace can expect subgroups to form on the basis of shared understandings and interpretations of events among members.

The importance of and potential differences between subcultures can be demonstrated by taking the simple example of a nursing home. Many nursing homes are composed of at least the following subcommunities of patients: those who are there by choice, those who for one reason or another are forced to be there, those who are mobile, those who have limited or no mobility, those who are "sick," and those who are "healthy." From a communication or cultural point of view we could ask a variety of simple questions, such as, "Is it reasonable to assume that those patients forced to reside in the nursing home 'experience' the same reality as those there by choice?" or, "Is it reasonable to assume that those patients who can get up and walk around at will experience the same nursing home reality as those who are bedridden?"

In both instances, the answer is obviously "no," the different groups do not experience the same reality. In the nursing home example, no single organizational culture is apparent. Clearly in the example multiple organization subcultures are evident. And any researcher interested in that specific organizational context will have to be aware of those various subcultures.

- *What is the difference between organization culture and organizational culture?*

Given our understanding of culture as communication-based and variable across the organization, rather than unified and singular, it is not surprising that many efforts are made to change what managers perceive to be inappropriate cultures. The final sections of this chapter take up the issue of culture change.

CULTURE CHANGE

Questions of culture change are as controversial as they are complex. The goal of this section is to highlight, briefly, some of this controversy and complexity. Unfortunately, a lengthy discussion of the ethics of culture change is not possible here. The interested reader might look up some of the articles in Frost et al. (1985). What is offered here is an overview of the central ethical issues.

The ethics of culture change are problematic along three lines: (1) the uncertainty over whether culture is in the behavior or the beliefs of organization members, (2) the possibility that culture change cannot be made, and (3) the ethics of altering the values of organization members. First, regarding the question of behavior versus beliefs, it simply is not universally agreed whether culture is primarily in the heads or the behavior of organization members. Most theorists ascribe cultural significance to both. However, until there is agreement on where culture resides, and on the link between behavior and values or beliefs, the culture change agent always runs the risk of manipulating the wrong half of the equation.

The second controversial area is the possibility that culture change cannot be accomplished by any sort of intervention. If culture is something like the belief and value systems of organizational participants, which have developed over the course of their lives, a good argument can be made that short-term intervention will not reach this deep-seated system, and if it could reach these beliefs, they would be too well formed to be subject to change, except by the most extreme of interventionist tactics. And such extreme intervention in a person's belief system would, of course, be controversial in itself.

Finally, there is the question of whether any attempt at altering the value system of employees is ethical. Some might argue that it is not legitimate for the organization to concern itself with this part of its employees, that if the employees are doing their jobs, it doesn't matter what they think. By this reasoning, any effort at culture change is, by definition, unethical.

The people who run organizations, however, must be concerned with profits, and if a change in culture is perceived as a technique likely to enhance profit, managers are obligated to explore that option. Siehl and Martin (1990), though, are among those who argue that a focus on culture to enhance financial performance is misguided; indeed, such attempts by managers or researchers not only misrepresent the potential of culture, but also perpetuate a managerial bias in organizational research. In short, the claim that the "right culture fit" will enhance performance is unfounded. Additionally, they argued that researchers should not have to justify their interest in culture by aligning it with performance outcomes, for culture is both interesting and a legitimate area of inquiry in its own right.

Culture must not be relegated to any arbitrary list of organizational variables. This severely constricts attempts to fully realize its nature and potential. A managerial bias in culture research, such as searching for a quantitative link between culture and financial performance, does little more than promote another means of control of the worker by the manager. The control of thoughts, emotions, and behavior was not the intent of early culture discussions, nor should it be the domain of management now.

- *Summarize the controversy that surrounds associating culture with financial performance.*

Despite the controversial questions raised by Siehl and Martin, culture change is still the goal or part of the process of many organizational development (OD) efforts around the world. OD practitioners have been quick to realize that formal structure is not the only ingredient of organizational reality. But structure is easier to change than culture, so tampering with structure is a common technique in efforts at cultural change. For example, an OD team might advocate movement from autocratic decision making to more participatory decision making, believing that a "participative culture" will be the result.

Tampering with organizational structure and design is equivalent to arguing that culture is in the behavior of organizational members. Is "behavioral" change, then, the equivalent of "cultural" change? We can turn to three discussions of the complexity of culture change to get the beginnings of an answer to this question.

Sathe (1983) noted that behavior change is not the same thing as culture change. People may change their behavior for any number of reasons, including the assumption that if they appear to accept a given program it will get the manager off their backs. But, if true cultural change is accomplished, the workers will exhibit the behavioral change without thinking about it. It will come naturally. To accomplish culture change, the manager must intervene in the processes that cause culture: the socialization of organization members, the behavior of members, the justification given for behavior, and actual cultural communication.

Fitzgerald (1988) echoed Sathe in arguing that there is a critical difference between behavioral change and cultural change, and that we can't begin to change culture until we understand how to change human values. The idea of "managing culture" may in actuality be no more than the mistaken assumption that managing behavior is managing culture. We could argue, for example, that Lee Iacocca's impact on Chrysler was not cultural but was simply good management. The big problem in any intentional effort at culture change is that there is no generally accepted view of how people change their values.

Change can occur, and clearly certain forces, such as cognitive dissonance, leader behavior, and positive and negative rewards, can prompt change. But one is still faced with the question of whether the change is cultural or behavioral. Finally, change attempts usually begin with work on top management's value system, on the argument that any change must be supported by the top. Though the move to reorient top management's thinking makes sense, it does not take into account that workers at the lower levels have value systems of their own, forged throughout their lives and just as rational as those of upper management.

Finally, Gordon (1991) presented the interesting perspective that certain industry requirements will predispose similar cultural development within organizations in the same industry. Gordon clearly was suggesting a relatively homogeneous companywide culture when he used the term. Although he does note that companies and subunits within companies may have unique cultures, he believed that these will develop within the parameters allowed by the industry.

Cultural assumptions and values are taught to new organization members. And certainly differences in assumptions and values can exist within the company, as long as they do not conflict with the basic industrywide assumptions. What happens is that industry assumptions drive the development of value systems that in turn keep the company from conducting itself in contradiction to industry values. These industry standards, then, must be communicated by upper management because they mediate managerial efforts at control. These standards limit managerial discretion in choosing courses of action. Culture change at the behavioral level can be accomplished by a change in management, but change at the level of assumptions is almost impossible without the infusion of new personnel.

So management is influenced by the organization culture, which is predisposed by the industry-driven values (toward customer requirements, competition, and societal expectations). Management then uses control mechanisms (strategies, structures, and processes), in accordance with the culture, to produce outcomes (performance and survival). Gordon gives the interesting example of a power utility. Within public utilities lies the industry assumption that customers need uninterrupted service. Thus, value is placed on reliable service to customers. Since this is the industry's standard assumption, it will influence the development of cultures within utilities, and will form the parameters of managerial control.

Regarding change, Gordon argued that it almost never occurs at the level of assumptions, because that would involve a major environmental shift and necessitate a radical restructuring of the workforce. So change is more common at the behavioral level and then still in the direction of industry standards.

- *Summarize the problems that culture change agents face when they try to address the question of where culture resides.*

Culture Change Examples

Despite the problems noted above, many culture change efforts have been undertaken. To conclude this chapter I would like to briefly summarize a few of those efforts to give you a feel for the problems change agents face when contemplating and conducting culture changes. Before looking at specific examples, though, we should remind ourselves of why cultural change is even considered in organizations. Bice (1990) suggested that management has two primary motives for most cultural change efforts: greater productivity from workers and reducing the number of management levels. All the following examples conform to these motivational guidelines.

Crabb (1990) described the change effort at GPT's Beeston plant in Nottingham, England. The plant was a profitable, well-run branch of GPT's larger network of telecommunications manufacturing plants, employing 3500 people. It was a highly structured, traditionally managed, unionized plant. Before the restructuring it used a piecework pay system and allowed 3000 job descriptions for fifty different employment grades. Changes in the British telecommunications industry prompted management at the plant to consider changes that would allow the plant to become more team-oriented, pushing decision making down the hierarchy. They wanted a more participative workforce, less centrally managed, more autonomous and capable.

The new system, among other things, eliminated job descriptions, replacing them with twelve grade descriptions, and instituted a skill-based and skill-used pay and incentive system. All employees became eligible for profit sharing, timeclocks were eliminated, holiday and sick leave time were equalized across the hierarchy. These across-the-board (hierarchy) changes were found to be much more effective than a Total Quality Management (TQM) program initiated years earlier that focused on top management alone. The TQM program failed because it didn't reach the lower levels of the organization. Crabb argued that these structural changes were necessary precursors to sending a "strong cultural message to the workforce" (p. 41): that things would change, resulting in a united, coherent workforce ready to tackle the business needs of the 1990s.

Fullerton and Price (1991) described the changes at Grampian Health Board (GHB). GHB was a health care provider for about 500,000 people in the Grampian region of Scotland, employing about 13,500 people. Its approach to culture change was prompted by two visions: first, that within its workforce lay huge, untapped potential, and second, that by tapping that potential Grampian might reap greater productivity and effectiveness. To accomplish the change the company followed a five-step program of strategy, structural changes in the hierarchy, management style, resource allocation, and internal communication. The most significant act was the creation of a new "management approach," summarized as a statement of senior management's vision, commitments, and overall mission.

The company expressly set out to change upper management. Its approach was that culture change should begin at the top and trickle down to the lower levels. Three years into their change effort they found that senior management was, indeed, changing in the hoped-for directions. Middle management and the lower-level workers, however, were not only showing no changes in attitudes but in some cases were showing a decrease in their perceptions of the positive qualities of the change initiative.

Based upon the results of the Salt River Project (SRP), a power utility restructuring effort, Ulm and Hickel (1990) put forth the view that culture change is certainly available as a result of structural changes. In an effort to meet the changing demands of the utility industry, SRP initiated a culture change effort. The result was a total corporate restructuring that resulted in the elimination of eight hundred positions. The company proceeded by creating a change group of twenty-one individuals identified as those without whom the company could not survive. This group (beginning in mid-1988) surveyed employees, developed recommendations, and obtained top management approval for their suggested changes.

The company instituted a top-down approach by first, eliminating every job (except the board's). The board then chose a general manager, who chose his subordinates, who then chose theirs, and so on down the line, until the workforce was filled (less the eight hundred positions identified as expendable). It then created a mission statement and goals for employees. Upon evaluating the program in 1989, the company decided that it had succeeded in creating a new culture capable of meeting the new challenges in the utility industry.

Finally, Hammonds (1991) presented the case of Corning, Inc., a company that did nothing less than "reinvent" itself. Corning is a $3 billion corporation that employed 10 percent of the sixty thousand residents of Corning, New York. The company had fallen on hard times. By 1983 it had endured three years of declining profits and had 70 percent of its investments in slow-growth businesses. By 1990, however, return on investments was at 16.3 percent, earnings had risen 11.8 percent, analysts predicted a 1992 jump in earnings of another 15 percent, and Corning's stock had risen 36 percent from its 1983 price.

How did Corning do it? By redefining itself and how it does business. First, it instituted a customer satisfaction–product quality blitz. Over three years, every employee took a two-day quality training course. Second, it formed alliances—nineteen technology and marketing partnerships. Third, the company centralized its research function so that all technology and innovations were shared. Fourth, it formed a partnership with its union, agreeing to a team-based factory design with a performance-based bonus plan. Fifth, the company promoted diversity efforts including formal mentoring plans. Finally, Corning invested heavily in its community, making it attractive to its employees and other businesses.

The examples above, though brief, do give a feel for the sorts of complexities surrounding change. Who should conduct the change? Where should the effort be focused? When will the change be done? Should the effort be directed at formal structure or informal working relationships? These and many other questions make organization culture change a most complex and interesting subject.

SUMMARY

In this chapter I have reviewed much of the information necessary for a basic understanding of organization culture. We looked at the question "Why culture?" in an effort to understand why culture is a reasonable theoretical approach. That section was followed by one on definitional issues. The two sections taken together pointed to a complex theoretical and philosophical approach to organizational analysis that focused on the communicative behavior of organization members as they made sense of their everyday experiences. The cultural approach was argued to be a focus on beliefs, values, assumptions, expectations, and so forth of organization members that result in the creation of understanding. This is a language-centered approach in that culture is the product of communication.

We looked at the differences between understanding culture as something an organization is and understanding it as something an organization has. It was argued that organizations are cultures, constituted through the communicative activities of organization members. This view is certainly consistent with the theoretical explanation offered in Chapter 1. The chapter concluded with a discussion of culture change. It was pointed out that the same sticky issues of Chapter 1—structure and communication—are problematic factors in any change effort.

Interspersed throughout the chapter were selected examples of culture study results. These examples were intended only to demonstrate some of the potential of the cultural approach. It is my hope that reading the research summaries as breaks from the chapter content gave you a richer, fuller feel for what culture is. In Chapter 3 we will look much more closely at the methods of culture research.

Discovering Organization Cultures

Chapter Preview

This chapter is intended primarily for two types of audiences: those who intend to do some cultural research in an organization who would like some guidance on methods and those who are interested in seeing how cultural results are obtained. This chapter focuses on research methods and was written to address two of the great frustrations felt by many students as they work their way through the cultural approach: the difficulty of visualizing just how culture is studied and the difficulty of visualizing what might be found.

These confusions are understandable. A cultural examination isn't a straightforward study of output or productivity or satisfaction, for example. And guessing what might result from a cultural inquiry is just as hard as imagining how that inquiry might be conducted.

I began clarifying these issues in Chapter 2, with the "spotlight" sketches. In this chapter I'll go into much greater detail regarding methods, opening with an examination of the most common methods of cultural research— ethnographic methods, including the interpretive approach called participant observation. After we have a sense of methods, I briefly overview the results of studies by Trujillo (1992), Scheibel (1992), and Van Maanen and Kunda (1989). In these three studies we get a feel for the richness available from a "cultural approach."

The chapter then presents a much longer discussion of a research project that I conducted using Bantz's (1993) Organizational Communication Culture (OCC) method. OCC has been used widely and, with specific reference to this chapter, was the method used by me in my study of the corporate growth team at New Public Utility (NPU). The NPU study usefully lays out culture research methods and results, and results from the NPU study are interspersed throughout this book (you've already seen some in Chapter 1).

Key Terms

ethnography
qualitative research
quantitative research
interpretive research

participant observation
Organizational Communication Culture
  method

Before venturing any further into this chapter, stop for a minute to consider all that you've been asked to accept about organizations thus far in this text. The picture painted is one of amazing complexity, with organizations portrayed as complicated, chaotic environments of participation between members and formal structure. The organization has been called a communicative construction, created during the convergence of participants' symbolic interpretations of their experiences. The organization has been described as composed of many subcultures, which exist as language communities that are often at odds with each other.

Imagine for a moment that you want to understand a group within such a conceptualization of organization; that is, you want to do a culture study. How would you go about discovering who that group really is? The first question that you would want to answer is, "How do you define culture?" Your answer, if you believe this text, is that culture consists of the beliefs, values, expectations, assumptions, and so forth of a group of individuals. That said, how would you go about tapping these dimensions?

Would you do an experiment? Perhaps you would run a pretest-posttest design, then conduct statistical manipulation of the results. Perhaps you would administer a survey to each of the members and, again, do some sort of statistical manipulation of the results. Most likely, however, if you were going to study culture, you would be advised to "enter the field." What this means is that your methods would be field methods rather than survey or laboratory methods.

In this chapter we'll explore the philosophy behind the most popular culture field methods, as well as the method of participant observation—another piece of advice that you'd most likely receive.

DISCOVERING ORGANIZATION CULTURES

Understanding and accepting the fact that organizations are multicultural (composed of a number of subcultures) communication events is much easier than actually researching those cultures. In this section I'll discuss the most common techniques and foci of cultural investigations. I'll center my discussion on the ethnographic approach referred to as interpretivism.

The Ethnographic Approach

Ethnography is a research method whereby the researcher lives among his or her subjects, recording what he or she sees, hears, is told, infers, and learns. It is a method predicated on four important assumptions (Philipsen, 1989). The first assumption is that humans are social animals who choose to live (and work) in proximity to one another. The second assumption is that human behavior is coordinated in such a way that it appears coherent, rather than random. So, humans do not perceive themselves as behaving in a haphazard, chaotic fashion. The third assumption is that different groups will display differences in their communicative actions. This means, of course, that each group is distinct and unique, and that the researcher must not carry biases from one group to the next. Finally, each distinctive group will have a system of rules and foundations that allow for the generation and interpretation of its distinctiveness. This assumption is crucial, for it implies that any group's behavior can be accounted for if the researcher has sufficient access to insider information and opportunities to observe the group in action. Given these assumptions, it is little wonder that many have suggested that ethnographers are particularly well-suited to examine life in organizations (Schwartzman, 1993), which are, after all, social communities.

According to Geertz (1973), ethnographic description "is interpretive; what it is interpretive of is the flow of social discourse; and the interpreting involved consists in trying to rescue the 'said' of such discourse from its perishing occasions and fix it in perusable terms" (p. 20). In his poetic fashion, Geertz was suggesting that ethnographic description is intended to illuminate the meaning of the mundane, the importance of what is generally taken for granted. *Ethnography is the method of anthropology, the tool used by outsiders in their effort to describe what insiders know but may overlook.*

The process of doing ethnography is cyclic, as opposed to linear, because the ethnographer continually asks questions, confirms or disconfirms, checks the questions, records observations, checks them against the questions, revises again and again throughout the course of the study. In the ethnographic process the most important period is the early entry period, including the time of gaining entry. The access issues that are raised can be telling comments on the sort of culture the researcher will be entering.

Ethnography is not neutral. Atkinson (1992) made this important point when he noted that even the writing of ethnographers is carried out within the conventions of writing style and the context of other ethnographic writings. Not even the recording of field notes is neutral, for the researcher relies on conventions of grammatical markers and narrative style that are not evident in actual speech.

The field of the ethnographic researcher, like the form of description chosen to tell the ethnographic tale, is a construction of the researcher him- or herself. Boundaries are produced and imposed by the researcher as he or she observes and records. The researcher is part of that field, influences it, and must note that influence in his or her observations.

- *What is ethnography? Why is it a useful approach for explaining organization culture? What are the implications of noting that ethnography is not neutral? Does this lack of neutrality invalidate ethnographic research?*

Interpreting the Field

As with any line of research, the analysis of organization cultures proceeds in many directions. However, the directions that cultural analyses take tend to be guided by what are referred to as interpretive research methods. Although a growing number of authors are calling for a "mixed-method" approach to the study of culture (see Denison, 1990; Morey & Luthans, 1985; Rousseau, 1990), combining *qualitative research* (very generally, nonstatistical, nonlaboratory) and *quantitative research* (very generally, hard-data-based, numerical representations of data with statistical manipulations), interpretive methods are both favored and discussed here because, as Smircich (1985) noted, the organization should be seen as a symbolic form to be interpreted or read, with the focus on symbols. And interpretive research methods are most able to tap the symbolic nature of communication.

Interpretive research in organizations is an attempt to explain the central importance of communication in the act of organizing. Interpretive researchers do not deny the existence of "formal" organization or its importance. They do try to account for the existence and importance of the formal organization as a product of communication. Thus, the organization is approached as the accomplishment of communication. Investigating the organization, then, becomes a study of communication.

An interpretive researcher approaches the organization as something to be read, to be interpreted (Conrad, 1983; Putnam, 1983). What is to be interpreted centers on the messages that are created by the organization members.

- *What is an interpretive research approach to understanding organization culture?*

In order to interpret these organization messages, researchers need to gather organizational messages for analysis. In an early, seminal article on the subject, Pacanowsky and O'Donnell-Trujillo (1982) argued that:

> In order to build a plausible interpretation of how organizational members communicatively make sense of their interlocked actions, it is necessary to have recourse to instances of members communicatively making sense, and recourse to the body of knowledge that members draw upon in order to make sense. What is required then are details—detailed observations of organizational members "in action" and detailed interviews (formal or informal) of organizational members accounting for their actions. (p. 127)

In other words, Pacanowsky and O'Donnell-Trujillo were calling for the researcher to become part of the workforce that he or she was attempting to describe—not necessarily as a paid employee, but at least as a presence at the worksite, observing the workers working and noting how they go about making sense of their daily experiences.

Once a part of the activities, the interpretive researcher sets about gathering both formal and informal messages for analysis. A variety of methods have been used to decipher the details of organizational life. These include "account analysis" (Tompkins & Cheney, 1983), "metaphor analysis" (Koch & Deetz, 1981; Pepper, 1989; Smith & Eisenberg, 1987), "story analysis" (Boje, 1991; Brown, 1985), performance analysis (Trujillo, 1985), fantasy theme analysis (Bormann, 1972), and even fictional narrative as a method of presentation (Pacanowsky, 1983). The techniques of culture analysis—ethnographic methods—are directed at interpreting the symbolic construction of social reality, as if that reality were a text.

To accomplish this description in the organization, the interpretive or naturalistic researcher (Bantz, 1983, p. 64) might use techniques such as participant observation and interviews to interpret things like organizational documents, memoirs, training and instructional manuals, message design, and the use of space. Schein (1983, 1984, 1985) wrote extensively concerning the techniques and focuses of culture studies, and that work is instructive here.

Schein suggested that three levels of culture exist: artifacts (the physical, visible level), values, and basic, underlying assumptions (the most important level). To uncover these levels, the researcher must go beyond surface features to get the insider view of organizational reality. This allows the insider to realize, through the process of trying to explain it, what the culture is.

To accomplish this understanding, Schein advised the interpretive researcher to use the following techniques: (1) gain access and note what surprises you, (2) observe and check, (3) find an insider willing to explain and capable of explaining to you, (4) reveal what you find puzzling, (5) with the insider try to account for your perceptions, (6) form hypotheses, (7) check and consolidate, (8) seek to the level of assumptions, (9) revise earlier findings to suit later ones, and (10) formally report. Other sources of cultural information include formal structure, information and control systems, and myths, legends, and stories. Schein stressed that only through interpretive methods can the researcher reveal culture, for more formal (quantitative) methods will not reveal the richness of organizational detail.

- *Given all that you've learned about culture so far, why would interpretive methods be best suited to revealing culture?*

Participant Observation

One of the most common forms of culture research is *participant observation.* Because of its extensive use, it merits some elaboration here. Many good sources describe the method. This discussion is based primarily on Jorgensen (1989).

Jorgensen made the point that only by participating in the experiences of the subjects can the researcher understand the everyday world of the "natives." This everyday world is inaccessible to the outsider: It can only be inferred, at best. *By experiencing this everyday world, the participant observer allows the categories of understanding to emerge from the actual forms of participation, rather than taking preconceived categories into the study and seeking corroboration in the observations.*

This point is crucial to our understanding of culture research, interpretive methods, and participant observation: the research must be allowed to form its own issues of significance. The researcher is not supposed to predetermine what information will be of value before entering the observed group. The researcher certainly can tap sources of expected information. But it would be inappropriate, for example, for the researcher to decide before the research that the relationship between the men and women of the group will be significant, or that the group is overly dependent on technology, or that individuals derive satisfaction from setting their own goals, or that conflict is a competitive game among a group. The researcher may, in the course of the observations, actually discover each of these things. But the researcher must let the categories of the results come from the group itself and must not impose a predetermined, expected order upon the observed group. To put this slightly differently, the researcher doesn't know what to look for until he or she finds it.

- *What does it mean to not take predetermined research expectations into the field with you?*

Participant observation is a method for gaining access to the subjective worlds of the participants, because any understanding of the world of the subjects must begin with an insider's perspective.

The assembling of the data becomes the process of theory construction, of making wholes from parts, of arranging facts to form explanations, of testing ideas and refining conclusions. And the participant observer understands that every generalization is simply part of a long-term process of interpretation toward the goal of representing the group's reality.

Of critical importance to the researcher is how deep he or she is allowed to get into the site. The goal of participant observation is to gain as many different perspectives as possible, so as to confirm or disconfirm any given piece of information. Through this diversity of perspective, the participant observer is actually in a better position to gain objective findings. In other words, the more subjective the observer is allowed to become, the more objective the findings. The more removed the researcher is from the inside, the more likely that the findings will be inaccurate.

- *Summarize the process of studying culture as a participant observer.*

At this point, we have an adequate understanding regarding the methods of interpretive research. Let's now turn our attention to some results, for the best way to understand interpretive methods is to examine the results of some interpretive studies. When looking at such results the reader must always keep in mind that the goal of interpretive research is to bring to the forefront issues that the reader and even the organizational members may not naturally and normally see. These are issues that are most likely so much a part of the everyday routine that organization members take them for granted. They perform these discussed rituals or behaviors without being aware of their significance. The interpretive researcher notes an event and interprets it according to the context of the research site itself. This interpretation is then fed back to the participants (usually) for verification and, if we're lucky, reported in a paper.

Below are four summaries of interpretive efforts. I'll report the first three with only minimal comment, letting you draw your own conclusions about the value of interpretive methods. The final report will be in greater detail as an aid to those planning to conduct their own interpretive inquiry.

THREE CULTURE STUDIES

Life Beneath the Bleachers

Trujillo (1992) spent two years and five hundred hours of fieldwork observing and analyzing the culture of baseball ballparks. He based his analysis on the following theoretical premises of interpretive research: Interpretive researchers search for the way organization members make sense of or interpret their surroundings; interpretive researchers assume that organizations are composed of layers of meaning, and that uncovering one layer, such as a single subculture, is missing the complexity of the whole; and interpretive researchers approach organizations as in process, continually evolving through member participation.

Through interviews and observation, Trujillo developed three interpretive views of the baseball ballpark: as business, as community, and as drama. As business, baseball has evolved into a form of "industrialized labor." The "behind-the-scenes" workers best typify this interpretation. Included in that category are vendors, cleanup crews, and ticket takers. These workers perform standardized, mechanical tasks much like those performed at any other industrial site. With this industrialization, the ballpark has been transformed into a revenue-generating facility within which employees supply labor for the good and profit of the owners.

As community, the ballpark represents a place where "family" members can come together to enjoy the national pastime. They can observe together, eat together, cheer together, share in the excitement of the contest together. The ballpark becomes, in a very real sense, a symbolic home for the community of fans (tourists) and workers (local residents).

As drama, baseball is a show, it is entertainment. But it isn't a passive form of "couch potato," televised entertainment. The fans are active participants in this production as the production is being staged for their benefit. They cheer, they boo, they yell for no reason, they arrive and depart, they do the "wave," and all the while they contribute to the emergence of the organizational form of baseball as theater.

These three visions of baseball ballparks, as business, community, and drama, are not competing visions, but simultaneous visions, happening concurrently. They add up to a complex cultural event that transcends the simple interpretation of baseball as sport. Perhaps this complexity explains why baseball has endured for so long as the "national pastime."

Trujillo's analysis of the ballpark changes how we, as "spectators," can now enjoy the game. He has made us see that the "game" is much deeper than eighteen overpaid men hitting and catching balls for our amusement. As "business," baseball is an industry of wealth, profit and loss, and, in the case of many of the laborers at the ballpark, minimum-wage, behind-the-scenes hard work. The glamour of the game fades beneath the bleachers. In the stands themselves, the ballpark exists as a structure within which families can play together. The ballpark encloses the community of fans in a safe, known organizational form where each person can feel part of a group with a sense of purpose. Finally, Trujillo has helped us understand how we are part of the organizational form, as contributors to the unfolding drama of the game. As drama the ballclub as organizational form evolves into the entire ballpark as all parts work together to create the momentary form that we call "the game."

Temporary Identities in Clubland

Scheibel (1992) reported a study that he conducted among fraternity and sorority members who were minors and who used (or tried to use) fake identification cards to gain access to bars in order to drink alcohol and listen to music. To conduct the study, Scheibel used participant observation, document analysis, and interviewing. What he found was a fascinating world—dubbed "Clubland"—which included a subculture of individuals willing to risk embarrassment, fines, and perhaps worse punishment, all in an effort to consume alcohol.

"Clubland" is a world of bars, music, and predominantly young people. It is governed by many formal and informal rules, not the least of which is the state mandate (in Arizona) that those under the age of twenty-one cannot drink in the bars. One reaction to the law is the effort of some minors to obtain and use fake IDs. A good fake ID "is often a state-issued document that is of legitimate form but that includes illegitimate content" (Scheibel, 1992, p. 165). The quality of a fake ID is judged by its effectiveness, pure and simple.

The process of faking identity is complex and interesting, and includes the following components. The individual must secure the ID. Once obtained, the ID must be learned—that is, all the information on the ID must be memorized, as well as any tangential information. For example, the user must know the birth date on the ID as well as the zodiacal sign that corresponds with the birth date.

Obtaining and memorizing the ID are only the first (and perhaps the easiest) parts of the process. The users of the IDs must rehearse their performances, knowing that they only get one chance, and a brief one at that, to give a convincing performance to the bouncer, bartender, drink server, or whatever other gatekeeper stands in their way. The users must decide if they will give their performance singly or in groups and, if in groups, in what order they will proceed. If they go in groups they must decide what will happen if one of them is rejected, or if the gatekeeper is suspicious, how the others will act to throw the gatekeeper off guard.

On the other side, Scheibel found that the gatekeepers themselves played their own parts in the fake ID process. These individuals often viewed themselves as controlling the situation. Depending on how they acted, the minor would have to adjust his or her performance appropriately. The gatekeeper might choose to confiscate the card, might sell it back to the minor and keep the money, might pretend to be willing to sell it back to see if the minor is going to implicate him- or herself, or might simply allow attractive men or women to enter while being overly cautious with unattractive men and women. This control by the gatekeepers affects the practices and performances of the minors. Especially important are the users' attitudes (must be "cocky") and their use of flirting to distract the gatekeeper.

Scheibel's analysis of Clubland indicates a complex social environment that is dictated by the interplay between context, gatekeepers, and users of fake IDs. The value of a cultural approach is shown constantly throughout the study in the richness of detail provided in the comments of participants. According to this study, a fake identity is a communication-based persona, enacted within a context of suspicion, fear, distrust, emotion, flirting, distraction, and tension. These components would be very hard to observe, if even possible to observe, in any way other than through participant observation.

Culture and the Management of Emotions

Van Maanen and Kunda (1989) examined the role that culture plays in emotional structuring within organizations. They argued that culture is a significant agent in the conscious and unconscious efforts by management to structure the organizational emotional level: "Any attempt to manage culture is therefore also an attempt to manage emotion" (p. 46). The cultural management of emotion carries several features: First, emotional management often occurs outside normal working hours, or within the normal work routine during "time-out" periods; second, symbols are the primary tools of emotional management; third, emotional management is a collective activity; and fourth, emotional management is planned and orchestrated.

The ritualistic planning and management of emotion is a key way that management can attempt to "teach" the workers of the organization just how they are supposed to understand those organizations. It is a form of control through which managers try to influence what members think and feel. And, since we spend so much time at work, since work is so much a part of our personalities and identities, any mismanagement of our emotional lives may have a profound affect on our overall lives.

What the cultural management of emotion refers to is the explication of the range of acceptable feelings on the part of employees. They exist as the feelings necessary for the performance of one's organizational role. The control of emotion refers specifically to the creation of an organizational emotional social structure. Management of this structure will be most apparent in those face-to-face contacts organizational members have with each other and with the public, suppliers, vendors, and so forth. The greater the amount of contact, the more "rules" necessary to govern correct emotional behavior. It can be suggested that the more an organization values culture and its effect on work, the more rules will exist to govern emotion and feelings within that organization.

Van Maanen and Kunda supplied two brief case studies, one of ride controllers and other "blue-collar" labor at Disneyland and one of engineers at High Technology Incorporated, to demonstrate their points about emotional management. Emotional management at Disneyland included sophisticated, involved hiring and socialization procedures, limited individual autonomy, widely dispersed sources of monitoring adherence to the accepted emotional range, and the recognition that even with all of the work put into emotional education, sometimes the workers fail. Most of the time, however, they don't.

At Tech, emotional management was made explicit in rules, handbooks, and socialized expectations. It was also managed in more subtle ways, including allowing engineers a great deal of autonomy, limited formal bureaucratic structure, and a conscious effort on management's part to teach and cultivate the right culture.

Recognized in both of these case studies is the difficulty of transmitting culture. The real teachers of culture and emotional rules are experience and peers. Length of experience in the organization where one learns to live the culture, where one's peers constantly demonstrate the culture with its expectations, is where emotional maintenance strategies really come into play. The organization may profoundly influence the process, through its rules, socialization strategies, and monitoring of cultural adherence. Members come to know and understand the organization, investing part of their self-image in the organization and its ways, thus making an emotional investment.

Emotional management is a form of control—control of the heart (p. 89), through the manipulation of the symbolic side of organizational life. These attempts at control may be of limited effectiveness; indeed, management has only limited ability to truly structure such aspects as emotion. Such efforts at control become frightening, however, when we consider that the result may be workers who conform to cultural expectations with which they disagree, and over which they have limited control.

Van Maanen and Kunda's explication of emotional management is simultaneously frightening and heartening, for they offer many examples of workers who resisted management's attempts to control their range of emotional expression (especially in the cases of ride operators at Disneyland). Still, for the most part, employee emotions are seen as a legitimate domain for management influence and regulation.

THE ORGANIZATIONAL COMMUNICATION CULTURE METHOD

This final example will be more detailed than the first three, because I want to highlight a well-defined method for approaching the analysis of organization cultures: Bantz's (1993) *Organizational Communication Culture method* (OCC). The method springs from Johnson's (1981) seminal discussion of organizational meanings and expectations. Johnson argued that the organization is constituted through the communication of its members, how they understand the organizational reality (meanings), and how they demonstrate their understanding (expectations). The OCC method (diagrammed in Figure 3-1) is a technique for unraveling meanings and expectations.

The first step in using OCC is to locate communicative events, both temporary *displays*, such as hallway conversations, meetings, and interviews, and permanent *documents*, such as buildings, room layouts, memos, and yearly financial statements. Within the communicative displays and documents lie messages, the analyses of which are the core of the OCC method.

The analysis of messages is the researcher's attempt to locate the daily sense-making activities of organization members. The analysis process centers on four message components: (1) *vocabulary*, the language of organization members; (2) *themes*, those repetitive topics that are noticeable and that carry meaning in and of themselves; (3) *temporality*, the rhythm or frequency of messages; and (4) *architecture*, the structure of messages, including the use of space.

FIGURE 3-1. The Organizational Communication Culture method

Gather Messages:	**Communicative Interactions** (temporary messages, such as conversations)	
	Documents (permanent messages, such as room design, newsletters, memos)	
Analysis:	**Vocabulary**	**Metaphors**
	Themes	**Stories**
	Temporality	**Fantasy themes**
	Architecture	
Inference of Expectations:	**Norms**	
	Roles	
	Motives	
	Agenda	
	Style	
Inference of Meanings:	**Constructs**	
	Relations among constructs	

Note: The analysis and inference processes are more simultaneous than sequential. As the researcher analyzes more and more messages, he or she will be drawing inferences that will affect the subsequent gathering and analysis of messages. Also, norms, roles, motives, agendas, and styles will serve as sources for further message analysis. The analysis and inference of expectations processes are aimed at identifying critical constructs and relations among those constructs.

The analysis process includes both the gathering of examples of messages, to be "decoded" using the four categories listed above, and the unraveling of the messages and identification of three symbolic forms: metaphors, stories, and fantasy themes. Symbolic forms serve to shape the organization members' understanding of their experiences. *Metaphors* serve to articulate one domain of experience in terms of another ("This place is a zoo," "My boss is a real Hitler"), *stories* are scripted constructions of organizational life that carry some sort of moral, and *fantasy themes* (discussed in Chapter 1 under symbolic convergence theory) are encapsulations of whole domains of experience.

From message analysis the researcher should be able to infer organizational *expectations*—evidence of organizationally based meanings or understandings. Five forms of expectations are particularly telling: (1) *norms,* the accepted behavior of members; (2) *roles,* behavior that is expected given the behavior of others; (3) *motives,* the publicly stated reasons for behavior; (4) *agenda,* the structuring of time; and (5) *style,* how members communicate with each other.

From message analysis to the inference of expectations the researcher is then able to accomplish the goal of the method—the inference of organizational *meanings*. Organizational meanings are the shared reality of the members, and the inference of meanings is the researcher's attempt to demonstrate an understanding of the everyday world of the group being studied. The inference of meanings is centered on two areas: constructs and relations among constructs.

Constructs are distinguished from concepts in that a concept is an individual interpretation, say of success or teamwork or competition, whereas a construct is a group or shared interpretation. The goal of OCC, as of any participant observation study, is to understand the construct level, not the concept level. *Relations among constructs,* obviously, refers to how constructs interact with one another to form a shared, common organizational reality.

In sum, the participant observer using Bantz's OCC method should be able to arrive at a verifiable, comprehensive understanding of the everyday experience of organization members. Understanding their reality is the goal of the research. Participant observation serves as the method for uncovering this reality, and OCC is a strategy for helping the participant observer interpret his or her observations.

The following is an account of a culture study that I conducted among the members of a corporate growth team, assembled by a large public power utility to facilitate a wholesale organizational redesign at the company. The reader interested in seeing a more detailed report should consult the appropriate chapter in Bantz (1993). (Please note at the outset here, that though I have chosen to illustrate each of the categories of the OCC method, seldom would any single study report on every focus.)

Life in the CGT

New Public Utility (NPU) is a diversified public utility whose core business is supplying electric service to industrial and residential customers in a 26,000-

square-mile area. At the time of the study it was a highly profitable business with assets over $1.5 billion, operating revenues of approximately $500 million, and twenty years of dividends to shareholders. The company employed about 2300 people.

The Corporate Growth Team (CGT) was formed in 1989 because NPU's CEO felt that deregulation was on the horizon for the utility industry, and if that came about, drastic changes in how work was done at NPU were necessary. He wanted a leaner, flatter organization that had a culture of participation. He wanted workers to feel comfortable making decisions that they "should be making" and managers to feel comfortable relinquishing control over much of the detail that was hampering their ability to do what was most important for them to be doing.

There were fourteen members of the CGT, twelve organizational development (OD) consultants, and two secretarial/support staff (nine men and five— including the team leader—women). All the CGT members came from within the company, representing experiences as diverse as line work, operations analysis, personnel management, supervisory functions, industrial engineering, control room work, accounting, and forestry. The group was told that it would exist for two to five years (although I was told at various times that the promise was a timeline of two to five years, three to five years, and indefinite). The members had to resign from their old positions to join the CGT, but were "promised" that when the group disbanded places in the company would be found for them.

My examination of this group began as all culture studies begin, with my efforts to gain access to their work space. Remember that this is not an insignificant request, for you are asking that these people give you basically unhindered access to their work space and lives. In my case, I asked to be a participant observer for five months. I told them that I would be on site for approximately 15 to 20 hours per week, that I would need open access to all meetings, memos, documents, decisions, retreats, and so forth, that any information I gathered would belong to me (confidentiality issue), and that I would be willing to lend my expertise in communication issues if they desired my assistance.

It took three months of courting before permission was granted. The group gave me much more than I asked for, including a desk in their immediate work area, a phone with voice mail, a mailbox, supplies, and the promise to withhold nothing from me.

During my efforts to gain entry, a number of significant things happened that would later have an effect on my results and my understanding of this group. Two should be recounted here to remind you of the importance of gaining entry as the first phase of ethnographic research. First, the leader of the group, during one of my screening interviews, asked me about the only question that I had forgotten to prepare for: "What will we be getting out of letting you come in?" I'm embarrassed to admit that the question caught me off guard. Its simplicity was a harsh reminder that only in academia do we operate on the assumption that "research" is valuable in its own right. In organizations, research is valuable to the degree that it can be applied. This was a cor-porate change team, empowered to implement change in a multi-billion-dollar corporation. It was composed of savvy, competent, learned professionals who were not fond of answers that included phrases like "heuristic value" and "learning about yourself."

The second important preparatory lesson occurred during another of my screening interviews, when one of the group members upon first meeting me introduced himself as the group's devil's advocate. It struck me as strange at the time, but fortunately when I was with the group I remembered to be on the lookout for instances where such a remark could be validated or discon-firmed or at least explained. As it turned out, that label was not only appropri-ate, but went a long way toward explaining that member's role and level of dissatisfaction with this group and with the company as well.

I did gain entry to the group and began to observe and note in earnest. The two key message forms, documents and communicative interactions, are summarized next.

Key Documents

Documents have two key qualities that make them invaluable sources of infor-mation for the culture researcher. First, they are enduring and thus can be re-ferred to any number of times. Buildings, rooms, memos, and the like are not going to disappear in the blink of an eye. Second, they are scripted. Their ap-pearance has usually been planned to meet some end. Documents, then, can be used for information about the group being examined as well as the crafters of the documents (if different from the group).

The primary documents that I examined included internally produced video magazines, organizational development and effectiveness surveys, the CGT office itself, the many flipcharts, posters, wallboards, calendars, and post-ings around the room, hundreds of pages of internal documents and memos, and articles and books about NPU and the utility business generally.

Key Communicative Interactions

Unlike documents, communicative interactions are temporary and, thus, pose a significant challenge for the researcher. Gathering information about them is likely to be more obtrusive and the information obtained less complete than with documents. Also, the researcher will most likely affect interactions he or she is observing and thus may alter their quality.

The following interactions were important in this research: one-on-one in-terviews, formal one-to-group interviews, over 300 hours of on-site observa-tion, participation with the team in two team-building retreats (they called them "advances," not liking the connotations of the word retreat), formal par-ticipation in a number of the group's activities and informal participation in many more, interviews with the current and former team leaders, senior exec-utives, NPU's chief executive officer, and just about anyone else who came within talking distance of me.

Analysis of Messages

Before offering analyses of the documents and interactions that I gathered, I want to remind the reader that this report is being kept extremely brief. Many of the examples that would make the report more informative and, most likely, more interesting, have been omitted. My intent here is to give a feel for the OCC method and a taste of what the results of a culture study look like. I encourage the reader to seek out expanded results in Pepper (1993).

I also need to remind the reader that this information is being presented in a simple, straightforward, linear fashion, very unlike the way in which material is gathered. I do this for convenience but acknowledge that reading this may be more troublesome because you won't understand the significance of the early data until the results at the end. For example, you most likely won't understand the significance of "the turd on the table" as a key vocabulary item. Please tolerate this ambiguity and stay with the report until the end.

Key Vocabulary

Attending to the vocabulary of the members being observed is extremely important in culture research, for the language used may key important themes. Unfortunately, in culture research the best time to attend to vocabulary is during the first critical observation periods when the location and the group are still new and unknown to the researcher. This is the time when the meanings of language will be most unclear to the researcher. The problem, of course, is that the researcher may miss important terms or critical nuances of usage because he or she is not yet an insider.

Within the CGT the following emerged as some of the most important vocabulary: micromanagement, advance (used instead of retreat, when referring to off-site planning trips), KRA (key result area), feedforward (instead of feedback; again, as with advance instead of retreat, a vision of movement forward, a positive outlook), consensus, the turd on the table, personal agenda, light bulbs and drinking fountains, teamwork, consultant, client, SET (senior executive team), and groupies. This listing gives you just a glimpse of the language that had to be learned to converse with the CGT.

Each of the above has a whole domain of meanings and usages that, once exposed by the researcher, may prove valuable in developing the understanding of the group studied. As just one example, the "turd on the table" reference was not only vocabulary, but also indicated a key theme, metaphor, fantasy theme, norm, and style. All language that is unclear or seems to have a special role to the group must be recorded by the researcher.

Key Themes

Themes represent topics that are repeated with sufficient regularity to imply some importance to the group beyond other topics. Themes are keyed by specific reference, repeated conversations, subtle indications of importance, or any number of other ways. In the CGT the following were some of the impor-

tant themes found: team (keyed by references to teamwork and group); procedure (keyed by references to consensus, buy-in, structure, and restraints);
identity (keyed by references to individuality, autonomy, self-criticism, and accountability); and leadership (keyed by references to management bashing,
objectives, loyalty, and outcome clarity).

Key Temporality Issues

Themes are relatively easy to find: The researcher can't help but notice many
of them. Temporality issues, on the other hand, are often quite hard to notice.
The researcher needs to consciously attend to temporality, for the sequencing
of work can be a critical issue in any work group. In the CGT the following
emerged as some of the major temporality issues: internal meeting dynamics,
external meeting dynamics, time spent in meetings focused on group development versus project reporting, the attitude of response rather than the ini-
tiating model of the previous leader, and the group's designated three-year
timeline.

Key Architectural Issues

In this study, architectural issues were a bonanza finding. From a research
point of view, I was blessed in being allowed into this group because they
were housed in a large, open room. Each of the team members had an open
cubicle along the walls of a huge room, in the middle of which was a large
table at which they held their meetings. For an observer, this situation was
ideal. For any culture researcher, architecture is an important form of document, to be read and interpreted just like a written memo.

Among the important architectural elements, the following were quite
important: the center meeting table (which had seating for more than twenty
people and made any meeting an open event), the room design itself (which
allowed for no privacy unless individuals actively sought it), hierarchy within the group, how time was structured, traffic flow in and out of the office,
the personal use of space and the designation and violations of personal
space, and the tendency of subgroups to make decisions on behalf of the
large group.

Analysis of Symbolic Forms

Once the information is gathered it is further analyzed for its symbolic importance. This analysis stage is very important for the method, and the whole cultural approach to organizations is predicated on the assumption that organizations are communicatively, and thus symbolically, constructed. The primary
symbolic components focused upon in the OCC method are metaphors, stories, and fantasy themes. As much as I would like to give a full detailing of
each of the following, because they are quite interesting, such an account is not
possible in the space allowed. So for each symbolic type I'll just mention the
key forms.

Metaphor Analysis

Metaphors are very important in our lives: They allow us to understand our present experiences in terms of our past. A metaphorical understanding occurs when one domain of experience, say conflict, is understood according to the parameters of another domain of experience. We might suggest that conflict is a war, laden with barrages, attacks, counterattacks, and tactics.

In the CGT the following metaphors had special significance: the team as Lone Rangers; teamwork as a restraint; dancing in unison versus in tension; the turd put on the table; outsider as team member; fifth floor as wilderness; and being drivers versus passengers on the OD train.

Story Analysis

Many culture researchers have written about the importance of stories in the understanding of organization cultures. The researcher equipped with a tape recorder is especially ready to document and analyze stories. I was not so equipped and so had to listen closely and reconstruct stories throughout the research. The following proved to be some of the many important, continuous stories: CGT's relationship with SET (senior executive team or "groupies"), the vision that justified the OD effort in the first place, the ultimate fate of the CGT members once they disbanded, and the passage of leadership from the first leader who "abandoned" the group to the present leader.

Fantasy Theme Analysis

As discussed in Chapter 1, the analysis of fantasy themes can be an invaluable tool in the understanding of the development of group culture. Two fascinating fantasies will be mentioned here. The first I call the Emperor's New Clothes. This fantasy referred to the lack of a clear identity for the CGT and the OD effort generally. Because the effort was pushed by the king (CEO), everybody in the company was expected to see it.

The second fantasy was the turd on the table. This referred to the effort to call something what it actually was; to stop covering up and pretending that things were what we wanted them to be. As the fantasy was displayed on occasion: "It may look like a Baby Ruth, but that ain't no Baby Ruth. Don't call it a Baby Ruth if it's actually a turd." This was a technique for bringing conflict out into the open.

Inference of Expectations

Once the data have been gathered and analyzed, the researcher is in a position to begin inferring expectations. More realistically, though, what the researcher is actually doing is both inferring and corroborating what he or she has already guessed. This is not a linear method or process. The researcher will have already drawn any number of tentative conclusions that fall under the category of inferences of expectations. This category generally involves behavior, so it should not be surprising that the items in the category are pretty much observable.

Norms

Norms refer to accepted behavior. A group that overlooks a member's consistent tardiness, for example, is allowing tardiness to be normative. In the CGT the following norms were evident: speaking for others, long Monday meetings, the tendency to work alone or in dyads, a formal, cautious relationship with the SET, an informal, intimate relationship with each other, and a decision-making style of action instead of reflection.

Roles

Roles refer to behavior that is expected in light of the behavior of others. Many roles are available for comment in any culture study. For this report I'll simply lump some of the major behavior under the headings of: (1) the role of low profile (CGT members consistently acted as advocates for the OD effort without assuming a visible, identifiable lead); (2) lack of role clarity within the group coupled with the acceptance of stereotypical role playing (such as devil's advocate) within the group; and (3) role of truth revealer or wise counsel to other groups, especially the SET.

Motives

In the OCC method, motives refer to explicitly stated (and thus observable) explanations for behavior. Motives are not psychological states inferred by the researcher. They might be inferred, but cannot be reported unless corroborated by the individual to whom the motive is attributed. Almost to the individual, the CGT members included the following among key motives: a rebel self-image, simultaneous group and individual self-promotion and humility, a safety motive behind their relationship with the SET, the "bottom line," the group's time line for project completion, and a basic faith and trust in the CEO to follow through on his promise to the group.

Agenda

Whereas temporality refers to pace, agenda refers to expectations for how time is structured. Among the many agenda issues of importance in the CGT, the following should be noted. The three-to-five-year time line was of critical importance, for it prompted discussions and feelings about going back to divisions that had been left, the members' future work lives, and the possibility that their time together was nearing its half-life. A second agenda issue dealt with getting work done rather than self-reflection. The group was built on the foundation that it needed to get out in the organization, be visible, do rather than plan. Indeed, in a conversation with the first leader of the group, I was told that if he was still the leader he would lock the office door from Tuesday through Friday. This attitude carried on in the group in contradiction to the second leader's inclinations. A third, interesting agenda issue dealt with the group meetings with the SET. These occurred every other week, always on Mondays, always on time, always for one hour exactly (whether the content merited an hour or not), and were always agenda driven (unlike the group's normal meetings).

Style

Style refers to observable communicative behavior. There obviously will be many, many style issues and reflections. I'll lump some of my style observations into four general categories here. First, the members exhibited their own individual, unique styles, often quite distinct and different from each other, yet all styles were readily, and basically unconditionally, accepted by the group. The fishbowl atmosphere of the room was a key factor in the openness that permeated the overall working environment. It was simply impossible to work for very long without being interrupted or joined or challenged or asked to comment by someone else. Dyads and groups were the primary communicative context, and group meetings tended to be characterized by strong beginnings and fizzled endings. Finally, projects tended to be perceived as owned by individuals rather than the team. When someone lost a project, he or she was, essentially, counseled as if he or she had suffered some sort of grief over losing the possession.

Inference of Meanings

Once the data have been gathered and analyzed, the researcher is in the position to draw conclusions. Those conclusions, in the OCC method, take the form of the identification of constructs and relations among constructs. It is important to note the distinction between construct and concept. Whereas concept refers to an individual interpretation and meaning, construct refers to group interpretation and meaning. The OCC method is a tool for examining cultures—group belief systems—not individuals.

Constructs

The most evident constructs found in the CGT were faith; the "bottom line"; the center table and space/design issues; Key Result Areas; meetings and the general format of business; the "turd on the table" philosophy of problem solving; problem identification (if not always problem solving); the three-year time line; identification and accountability issues; personal agendas and issues of self-presentation, self-reliance, the acceptability of others, project ownership, team, teamwork and restraints; the role of the OD consultant; and SET and leadership issues.

These constructs, in isolation, tell us little about the group. Each represents a piece of the overall pie—a domain of experience and understanding, but not the whole. For the fuller, more complete picture of the culture of the CGT we need to look at the relations among the constructs.

Relations among Constructs

In the study I found six key sets of relationships: accountability and identity issues, openness issues, agenda issues, leadership issues, the "bottom line," and individual faith in the company. A full-blown account of this group culture would detail each of these six sets of relationships, but such a full-blown account is not appropriate here. Indeed, even partial accounts, such as the discussion of accountability/identity and openness that is included in Bantz (1993), take a substantial amount of space to develop.

My goal in offering this level of detail concerning the OCC method, along with the brief description of results, was to give you a method to use in your own work and a feeling for what the method might reveal. Studying organization culture is fun and remarkably difficult. It isn't just sitting and watching. It includes the painstaking observation, reflection, checking and double checking of inferences, note taking, detailing of behavior, interviewing, and participating in the group's events. It also includes becoming an insider without actually being an insider. This means building trust and often becoming friends with those being studied.

The ethnographic method of participant observation can be facilitated by any number of research methods. The OCC is one of those methods. It was created specifically to address communication issues, from the point of view that culture is a communication event. It is definitely a method to be considered by anyone hoping to obtain insight regarding group communication.

SUMMARY

This chapter has been a focus on research only. It opened with a discussion of the dominant cultural research paradigm—the ethnographic approach. We saw that this approach is a qualitative philosophy designed to tap the communicative meanings created by the behavior of group members. The chapter focused specifically on interpretive research methods, especially participant observation, and looked at the results of a number of studies that used interpretive methods to explain organization culture.

The chapter then detailed the Organizational Communication Culture method. The method was reviewed and results were given of a study I conducted of a corporate organizational development team—the CGT. The results highlighted the method and showed the sorts of results available when using the method in culture research.

CHAPTER 4

Foundations of the
Cultural Perspective

Chapter Preview

The history of organizational development is an interesting story, full of turbulent times and colorful characters. Chapters 4 and 5 present some of that history, beginning here with an overview of early organizational development, taking us up to about the 1930s. The period from the 1930s to the present will be covered in Chapter 5.

I've chosen to present this history in a way that allows us to recognize that organization culture was alive and well long before any present-day theorist named it and identified it for further comment. Each of the historical periods covered in Chapters 4 and 5 will be discussed and then summarized in terms of cultural significance. In other words, my goal is to demonstrate that cultures have been part of organizations for as long as organizations have been part of society. Too much of our current treatment of culture leads the reader to believe that culture is a new invention. It isn't. It is more accurately seen as a recent recognition of what organizations have always been: communicatively constructed systems of beliefs and values.

The historical periods discussed in Chapters 4 and 5 will be characterized by descriptive metaphors, chosen to encompass the essence of the period. The beginning period of formal organization history will be referred to as the machine culture; the second period as the satisfaction culture; the third period as the teamwork culture; the fourth period as the organismic culture; and the final period as the period of organization *as* culture. These metaphorical frames will allow us to sort our understanding into more manageable, albeit overly discrete, descriptions of this history.

This chapter specifically traces formal organization history back to its roots in medieval craft guilds. This brief discussion reminds us that organizations have been around forever, simply taking different forms throughout the years. The chapter then presents the development of formal organizations through the industrial revolution, ending with the birth of modern organizational form. This chapter, as the first of two historical overviews, will cover only the key creators and foci of early organizational theory, especially the birth of modern organizational theory—the latter half of the twentieth century to about 1930, Frederick Taylor, and the principles of scientific management.

Key Terms and Individuals

machine culture

satisfaction culture

teamwork culture

organismic culture

organization *as* culture

industrial revolution

charismatic authority

traditional authority

rational-legal authority

particularism

universalism

soldiering

scientific management

initiative and incentive

time-motion studies

Fayol's bridge

Henry Towne

Max Weber

Charles Perrow

Frederick Taylor

Frank and Lillian Gilbreth

Henri Fayol

Before venturing any further into this chapter, take a minute to think about some of the organizations that are familiar to you. For example, consider your church, or a club that you belong to, or your university, or the military, or a job that you have had. You might reflect on media-created organizations, such as the hospital of *St. Elsewhere,* the law firm of *L.A. Law,* the police department of *Hill Street Blues,* or the bar of *Cheers.*

When thinking of these organizations ask yourself some questions about them. Some important ones might be: How are the workers treated by management? How do the workers treat each other? How bureaucratic are the organizations? Do they have enough or too much bureaucracy? Have the organizations been designed in a way that promotes or blocks free and open communication? What hierarchical levels can you identify? How responsive are the organizations to events outside themselves? What internal dynamics cause reactions in these organizations?

Now consider the differences between those organizations that are clearly and formally designed, with a set, prescribed hierarchy, and those that are not designed around hierarchy, such as some food cooperatives, some volunteer-based organizations, such as sexual assault hotlines, and many voluntary social groups, such as bowling teams. What differences do you know of, or would you expect, in areas such as communication, decision making, formality levels, conflict, access to information, how people are treated, pay, and motivation?

All historical perspective is arbitrary. How history is framed, what is highlighted and what is overlooked, is as much a reflection of the historian as of the reality of the historical events. Writing a brief overview of the history of organizational design is similar to writing any other history. Certain events and people will be emphasized to the exclusion of others. Chapters 4 and 5 are only an overview of the people and events and ideas that have shaped the modern vision of organizations. I will argue that formal organization theory has been driven by five different, though not mutually exclusive, metaphorical conceptualizations of workers and workplace culture. Those visions are:

1. The *machine culture:* This was the beginning vision of formal organizational design and theory. It was the attempt to construct a working environment around the capabilities of the machines of the industrial revolution. The workers and workplace became extensions of these machines, supervised by managers acting as machine operators.

2. The *satisfaction culture:* In response to a series of studies called the Hawthorne Studies and a basic disillusion with the precepts of the machine metaphor, a new guiding metaphor emerged—the worker as child. Children have needs that caregivers try to meet. Managers in this vision are benevolent parents. They listen to the concerns of their children and try to satisfy these needs.

3. The *teamwork culture:* The vision of children with needs was changed to a vision of workers who could derive satisfaction from workplace factors. These workers could contribute, they were vital, creative forces within the organization team. They were a source that could be tapped and relied upon. It wasn't that they needed less; rather, it was that organizational designers began to focus on what the organization itself could supply. What the organization could offer the worker was a workplace, a specific working environment, rather than the personal relationship of the satisfaction culture.

4. The *organismic culture:* At some point, organization researchers and practitioners came to realize the importance of the environment outside the company walls, as well as the interrelationships of workers and departments within those walls. This was a recognition of complexity and relatedness, of systemic thinking, of contingency theories. The organization became seen as a living organism, growing and dying and subject to diseases, neuroses, growth and decline cycles, and so forth.

5. The *organization* as *culture:* This vision explicitly recognized culture as a definitional quality of organizations. Throughout the history of organization theory, culture was a present but overlooked organizational factor. In the machine period, the "culture" of the organization was understood as efficiency; in the satisfaction period, "culture" was understood as needs-based relationships; in the teamwork period, "culture" was understood as a participation/productivity mix; and in the organismic period, "culture" was systemic complexity. The unifying theme in all of these visions is that culture was imposed from the top down. Culture was what upper management thought it was or wanted it to be.

- *What are the basic differences implied in each of these five ways of explaining organizational design?*

With the organization culture approach (discussed in Chapters 2 and 3), theorists suggested that culture might actually be a bottom-up phenomenon, and that it was a communication event existing in every organization. And, whether theorists and practitioners thought that culture had to emerge or could be mandated, whether it was behavior or beliefs, whether it was organization-wide or group-specific, virtually no commentator could disregard culture and its potential impact.

Before getting more deeply into these metaphorical visions, two additional issues should be mentioned. First, these approaches to organizing, though presented as representative of specific periods, should not be viewed as distinct, nonoverlapping historical eras. Any history is a story of historians' choices: The reader is always left to wonder why some people and events have been chosen to the exclusion of others for mention on the time line of history.

The time line presented in this chapter should be subjected to the same scrutiny as any other time line. I argue that formal organization theory can be divided into the following periods:

Machine culture or classical period: 1900–1930s–present

Satisfaction culture or human relations period: 1930s–1960s–present

Teamwork culture or human resources period: 1960s–present

Organismic culture or systems period: 1960s–present

Organization *as* culture or cultural period: 1980s–present

Dates give the impression of beginnings and endings. Such is not the case here. The fashioning of organization theory has been a cumulative process, whereby successive periods have built upon the perceived inadequacies of past periods. No period can reasonably be said to have eradicated the past, nor does the emergence of a competing vision result in total conversion of all or even most adherents of past visions. The point here is that it would be just as inaccurate to argue that classical design ended with the Hawthorne Studies (about 1932) as it would be to suggest that culture played no role in organization theory until the 1980s. The process of organization design and theory has now come to highlight "culture." One of the goals of Chapters 4 and 5 will be to highlight culture in the periods before the 1980s.

The second issue to be discussed here has to do with "prehistory." Where will a historical chapter begin? Does the beginning point imply that organizations did not exist before this date? This historical chapter begins with a period that has been called the beginning of formal organization theory, which does not mean that organizations did not exist before this period. This is a chapter about *formal* organization theory, but before getting to it we should take a short detour into the land of preformal organizational design.

THE ROOTS OF FORMAL ORGANIZATION

Kieser (1989) traced the roots of formal organization theory back at least as far as medieval Germany. He outlined the emergence of formal organization structure as a "natural" development of the medieval craft guild, a form of organization that is not formal in the current sense. The development of the formal organization followed the path of societal adaptation to the external environment: Specifically, resource scarcity, population growth, and the need for greater efficiency all fueled the speed of societal and organizational change.

The guilds had many rules regulating economic functions, acquisition of materials, how many (and which) journeymen could be employed, wages, working hours, and how customers could be solicited (they couldn't). Profiteering was sinful, and it was dishonorable to improve on products and thereby gain advantage over other guild members. So innovation was frowned upon. Indeed, much more innovation occurred in medieval monasteries, populated by more educated men whose work was "the Lord's," than in the medieval guilds.

The demise of the guilds began in the late 1400s. The guilds were being pressured by competing forces, causing them to tighten their rules and cartels, making them even more exclusive and stifling to innovation, making them more susceptible to outside competition. The guilds fell into disfavor in Germany and by the 1600s had virtually collapsed in the new competitive, profit-making economic environment.

The guild was not a typical organization. It was a way of life, isolated and separate from other ways of life. This separatism and isolation, combined with elitism and monopolistic control efforts, were eventually their undoing.

Medieval German craft guilds were quite unlike the American version of formal organization prehistory. Before 1800 America had an agrarian, home-based economy (Powell, 1988). During this period, men *and* women shared responsibility for the creation of goods produced in the home and consumed by the family, or sold or bartered in central marketplaces.

In other words, before the industrial revolution this country was characterized by a system of home-based production in which the members of the family were intimately involved in manufacture and product development. With the *industrial revolution*, roughly the latter half of the eighteenth century through the nineteenth century, came factories and factory production. With the factories came wages and the emergence of urban economies. Families left the farms for the cities, *and the people who created the factories were faced with a mammoth problem: how to organize masses of people who had virtually no experience as organized labor.*

The early response tended to be best guesses, trial-and-error forms of organizing. The work was hard, management might or might not have been kind, and rules and policies were at the discretion of whoever was in charge. Formalized theory was not available at that time. It was these conditions, then, that resulted in the emergence of early formal organization theory. *Formal theory began as a reaction to the perceived problems of these early attempts to organize.*

- *Summarize the roots of formal organization theory.*

The remainder of this chapter will highlight the progression of formal organization theory from the early 1900s through the development of the machine metaphor. Chapter 5 will begin with the Hawthorne Studies and trace the development of organizational design up to the present. The two chapters together, then, will give us a comprehensive understanding of the thoughts and key thinkers that have shaped our current understanding of the workplace. Finally, in line with this text's overall focus on culture, each section will conclude with a summary statement regarding how culture was understood during that period.

THE CLASSICAL MODEL OF ORGANIZING: CREATING THE CULTURE OF THE MACHINE

We have already seen that management and organizing didn't just begin in the twentieth century. The pyramids represent an enduring example of management and the organization of labor. However, management as a systematic field of study has as its beginning the 1886 meeting of the American Society of Mechanical Engineers, and a paper by *Henry Towne* in which he called for recognition of management as an art similar to engineering (Duncan, 1989). Towne's paper was heard by Frederick Taylor (an early contributor of major significance, discussed later). Study of the beginnings of the systematic study of managing and organizing must focus on the theorists and the society of the late nineteenth and early twentieth centuries.

- *What date and event can be assigned as the beginning of management as a formal field of study?*

The roots of management go back to Great Britain and Scotland, and the beginnings of the worldwide industrial revolution. It would be a hundred years before the revolution hit the United States. The industrial revolution owes its beginning to the invention of steam power, but the emergence of a mass market made the increased production of goods a necessity. In response, greater numbers of unsophisticated laborers were added to the workforce, mandating organizational systems and the emergence of management as a profession. The earliest applications of management were centered on the efficiency of the factory and the demands of organizing these hundreds and thousands of workers, who were unaccustomed to specialization and the division of labor, the first real tasks of management.

With the industrial revolution came the recognition of the value of machines, the value of low-skilled labor that could operate or tend the machines, and the value of interchangeable parts, leading to the invention of the assembly line. And the American factory system was born. The capacity to massproduce, of course, led to the demise of the small shop run by generalists who performed all of the roles of manufacture.

- *What about the industrial revolution made the formal study of management so important?*

Certainly the best example of the movement toward mass production is the creation of the assembly line. The first nonmoving assembly line was introduced by Oldsmobile in 1901. Using this technique and interchangeable parts, the plant increased output from 400 cars in 1901 to 5000 cars in 1903. The car sold for about $650. It was Henry Ford's luck (genius?), however, to create the first mass-market(able) automobile. Ford wanted a car that the average consumer could afford. He got his wish in 1913. That year, armed with the lessons of other auto makers, including Oldsmobile's, Ford introduced the moving assembly line. Before the line, the Model T cost $850, much more than the average consumer could afford. After the line was introduced, the car could sell for $400 and be produced in about 2 hours. One should not assume, however, that there were not problems along the way. According to Morgan (1986), when the assembly line was introduced, turnover rose to 380 percent per year. Turnover was stabilized only through the creation of the five-dollar workday.

The assembly line was specialization, division of labor, and interchangeable parts (key building blocks of bureaucratic design) all in one. Minimal thought was required and still a cost-effective, quality product could be produced. And the savings were spectacular. Duncan (1989) reported that in 1911–1912, about 6800 Ford employees produced more than 78,000 cars. The next year saw a doubling of both number of employees and number of cars produced, and in 1914, the first full year of the moving assembly line, production again doubled while the workforce was reduced by 1500.

- *What role did the assembly line play in the emergence of formal organization theory and design?*

The first attempts at formal organization theory, then, were essentially approaches to management. They were founded on the assumption of bureaucratic form. In the remainder of this section I'll demonstrate the emergence of formal theory—the classical model of organizing—through discussions of many of the major theorists. I'll begin, though, with the question "Why bureaucracy?" What was it about bureaucratic design that impressed the early theorists and practitioners?

Why Bureaucracy?

The two most influential writers cited in most discussions of bureaucracy are Charles Perrow and Max Weber. Beginning with Weber, an overview of these two authors' work will give us substantial insight into the bureaucratic form and the reasons for an early reliance on bureaucratic design.

Max Weber

Max Weber was a German sociologist who lived from 1864 to 1920. He was a prolific scholar whose work with understanding other cultures became known in this country during the 1940s. So it was not Weber's writings that influenced the development of the early American attempts at bureaucratic design. Rather, it was his teachings and applications of those who had studied in Germany that had the impact in the early days.

Bureaucratic design was, for Weber, one form of social control. Weber (1946, 1947; see also Weiss, 1983) was interested in forms of authority, in what would cause people to allow others to have authority over them. In his work he identified three forms of legitimate authority: charismatic, traditional, and rational-legal.

Charismatic authority is based on the follower's belief in extraordinary qualities of a leader. The legitimation of this form of authority rests on the degree to which the follower values characteristics that he or she sees as beyond the normal, everyday level. This form of authority is based on complete trust in the person because of the qualities of that individual.

Traditional authority is vested in the way things have always been done. It is based on tradition and precedent and on the value of maintaining their directives, and it is legitimized by history. Obedience here is a question of loyalty to the individual charged with the traditional position of authority.

Rational-legal authority is legitimized through recourse to legal sanctions. Under this form of authority certain individuals are given the right to dictate binding rules that extend both to themselves and to others who may not write their own rules. This is an impersonal authority system.

Unlike traditional and charismatic authority systems, the rational-legal bureaucratic form is subject to a number of "rules" or criteria, including: participants can be ruled only in official matters, not private; hierarchical organization; division of labor and specialization; freedom of selection in terms of joining or quitting the organization; members are chosen on the basis of qualifications, not elected or appointed; there is a salary scale; the member's position is his or her primary occupation; a system of promotion exists; and all members are subject to disciplinary measures (Weber, 1947, pp. 333–34).

Bureaucratic authority is vested in a system of rationality and legality. Weber (1946) wrote that:

> Bureaucratic rule was not and is not the only variety of legal authority, but it is the purest. . . . In legal authority, submission does not rest upon the belief [in] and devotion to charismatically gifted persons, like prophets and heroes, or upon sacred tradition, or upon piety toward a personal lord and master who is defined by an ordered tradition. . . . Rather, submission under legal authority is based upon an impersonal bond to the generally defined and functional "duty of office." The official duty—like the corresponding right to exercise authority: the "jurisdictional competency"—is fixed by rationally established norms. (p. 299)

- *Summarize the differences between charismatic, traditional, and bureaucratic authority.*

Charles Perrow

The work of *Charles Perrow* (1972) is both an impassioned defense of bureaucratic organizational design and an important criticism of the human relations model of organizational theory (discussed in Chapter 5). According to Perrow, the traditional bureaucracy was one based on rule of thumb, or precedent ("Everyone is doing it"; "I was told it would be OK"). The rational-legal bureaucracy was a refinement on this system, whereby tradition was replaced with (theoretically) rational, legal sanctions. It is a bureaucracy of written rules and explanations, governing codes of conduct that are applied across the board.

Perrow highlighted seven components of the rational-legal bureaucracy:

1. Equal treatment for all employees.
2. A reliance upon expertise, skills, and experience relevant to the position.
3. No extraorganizational prerogatives of the position (such as taking dynamite or wallboard—that is, the position was seen to belong to the organization, not to the person. The employee could not use it for his personal ends.
4. The introduction of specific standards of work and output.
5. The keeping of complete records and files dealing with the work and output.
6. The setting up and enforcing of rules and regulations that served the interests of the organization.
7. A recognition that rules and regulations were binding upon managers as well as upon employees; thus, employees could hold management to the terms of the employment contract. (p. 4)

These are the components of the bureaucracy in its ideal form. This ideal, however, is seldom realized, for three reasons. First, the organization can never block all extraorganizational influences from the workers' lives. So workers will never act totally in the best interests of the company. Second, bureaucratic efficiency breaks down when faced with the need for rapid change because of changes in the environment, and such changes are constantly occurring. Third, the human organization member is a fallible, imperfect designer and enforcer of the bureaucratic ideal.

The primary criticisms of bureaucracy, according to Perrow, are that it is inflexible and unresponsive, that it stifles the creative energy of its employees, and that bureaucracies, because of their design and their pervasiveness, have established enormous power over the thinking and behavior of the many and placed that power into the hands of the few.

Regardless of these criticisms, Perrow's position is clear. He wrote that the bureaucratic form of organizing is "superior to all others we know or can hope to afford in the near and middle future; the chances of doing away with it or changing it are probably nonexistent in the West in this century" (p. 7).

It is not hard to see Weber's and Perrow's points of view. Their arguments are that only bureaucracy can succeed in purging *particularism* (favoritism in all its forms, including rule of thumb and tradition) from the workplace in favor of *universalism* (applying uniform criteria of competence to all employees equally). So, for them, the bureaucratic model offers the greatest hope of overcoming bad administration through its systems of rules, division of labor, hierarchy, and checks and balances. Nonbureaucratic and other organizational structures simply don't have this check-and-balance nature, so their potential for injustice is greater.

- *Summarize the basic components of the rational-legal bureaucratic form, along with the key reasons that recommend it.*

In this section I've outlined the development of the early organizational design attempts. Having discussed the prehistory of formal design efforts and the dominant form that those early efforts took—bureaucracy—we are now in a good position to understand the context in which the early theorists embedded their work. We can also watch the development of organizational design efforts. We turn our attention now to the primary contributors to the development of the classical model.

FREDERICK TAYLOR AND THE PRINCIPLES OF SCIENTIFIC MANAGEMENT

Frederick Taylor is clearly the most important figure in the development of the classical school and one of the most important and controversial figures in the history of management and organizational theory. As "The Father of Scientific Management," Taylor developed a method for achieving efficiency that revolutionized the workplace. In this section we'll spend quite a bit of time on Taylor, his methods, and his critics, beginning with Taylor's own work, *The Principles of Scientific Management* (1967/1911).

Taylor argued that scientific management was developed in response to a need for "the competent man" and the recognition that the company had to train the worker for the level of competence necessary for both the company's and the workers' maximum gain. There existed a need for "systematic management" to create the leadership necessary to overcome what Taylor believed to be an enormous loss of human resources. In the following rather long quotation, Taylor explained his philosophy and approach:

> The principal object of management should be to secure the maximum prosperity for the employer, coupled with the maximum prosperity for the employe[sic]. The words "maximum prosperity" are used, in their broad sense, to mean not only large dividends for the company or owner, but the development of every branch of the business to its highest state of excellence, so that the prosperity may be permanent. In the same way maximum prosperity for each employe means not only higher wages than are usually received by men of his class, but, of more importance still, it also means the development of each man to his state of maximum efficiency, so that he may be able to do, generally speaking, the highest grade of work for which his natural abilities fit him, and it further means giving him, when possible, this class of work to do. . . . The majority of these men believe that the fundamental interests of employes and employers are necessarily antagonistic. Scientific management, on the contrary, has for its very foundation the firm conviction that the true interests of the two are one and the same; that prosperity for the employer cannot exist through a long term of years unless it is accompanied by prosperity for the employe, and vice versa; and that it is possible to give the work-man what he most wants—high wages—and the employer what he wants—a low labor cost—for his manufactures. (pp. 9–10)

Taylor accused the average worker of working to only about 50 to 75 percent capacity, and said that should they attempt to do more, their coworkers would ridicule them for not "soldiering"—"the greatest evil with which the working people of both England and America are now afflicted" (p. 14). Scientific management was Taylor's remedy for these problems, and its application was to eliminate soldiering and its effect on productivity, which affects the prosperity of nations and, ultimately, the prosperity of human kind. *Scientific management, then was proposed as a possible cure for poverty and suffering along with economic decline!*

Taylor argued that *soldiering* came in two forms: natural, or the inborn tendency of humans to be lazy, and systematic, or that based on the worker's relations with his or her coworkers. Taylor allowed, of course, for those few workers who are beyond the rest in energy and vitality, but, over the course of time, even they slowed to the pace of their fellow workers. Natural laziness was a problem, he argued, but it paled in comparison to systematic soldiering. One of the causes for systematic soldiering, the biggest cause, was the worker's fear of establishing a piece-rate system, based on the maximum level of production. Because of this fear, it was in each worker's interest to work at a minimum level, lest the minimum be raised (without a corresponding increase in wages), forcing the worker to continue to work at the higher output level.

- *What are natural and systematic soldiering?*

Scientific Management

In the companies where *scientific management* had been employed, those cases where the best workers and the best implements and the best techniques had been established through careful study, Taylor found uniform prosperity, strike-free environments, and workers making from 30 to 100 percent more in wages than comparable workers in companies not using scientific methods.

In order to implement this new system of management, the manager must apply the four principles of scientific management (see Table 4-1), coupled with acceptance of the revolutionary attitude that accompanies the principles. These four requirements, as simple as they sound today, constituted a revolution in managerial thought. And the revolution was fueled by the success of the various applications of the system.

TABLE 4-1. Frederick Taylor's Principles of Scientific Management

1. Scientifically design each job.

2. Scientifically select and train each worker.

3. Work closely with the workers to ensure that the work is being performed correctly.

4. Divide the work between management and the workers, so that managers are performing those tasks for which they are better suited (planning, training, supervising, and so forth).

• *Summarize the principles of scientific management.*

Taylor cited the example of changes in the handling of pig iron at Bethlehem Steel Company. The job required that the worker bend over, lift a 92-pound piece of iron, walk a few feet, usually up a plank to a railroad car, and drop it on a pile. At the outset of the study the working crew was an efficient group with a good foreman. They loaded about 12.5 tons per day per man. Upon scientifically examining the task, it was discovered that the average man should be able to move 47 to 48 tons per day. The task, then, was to convince the men in the crew that they should be moving that much more tonnage, without causing a strike, and indeed, convincing them that they'd be happier doing this much more work.

The workers were observed for a few days during which time a single man was chosen as the most likely person to be able to meet the task demands. The man earned $1.15 per day loading pig iron. They enticed him with the prospect of a $1.85 day and gave him the rules: When taught, don't disagree. Listen, follow orders, don't think for yourself, just do as you are told. (Taylor's justification here was that this particular worker was not very intelligent, and this "tough talk" was not cruel but, rather, focused him on the project.)

The next day the training occurred and the worker loaded the 47.5 tons. According to Taylor, the man worked at that pace for the next three years. For his work he was paid $1.85 per day, whereas before he had never earned more than $1.15 per day. Only one man out of every eight in the seventy-five-man work group was found to be scientifically suited ("a man so stupid that he was unfitted to do most kinds of laboring work, even" [p. 62]) for accomplishing this much. The rest of the group was fired, but, according to Taylor, immediately rehired for other jobs at Bethlehem.

In another example at Bethlehem, it was discovered that the most efficient shoveling occurred with a load of twenty-one pounds. There were many different kinds of shoveling, so management had to supply about ten different sizes of shovels, each adapted to the product it was shoveling, so that it would hold about twenty-one pounds. This eliminated the old practice of each man bringing his own shovel, which, though it may have been suited for one project, may have been entirely unsuited to another. So, each man was treated as an individual, provided with the proper implements to accomplish his work, properly trained, and paid. In the third year of application, the number of workers at Bethlehem had gone from 400 to 600 down to 140, average tonnage moved went from sixteen to fifty-nine, and the average pay went from $1.15 to $1.88 per day. And, Taylor argued, the workers were happier than ever. They were saving money, happy with their working conditions, and basically proud of their work.

However, we should note that things were not always so rosy at Bethlehem. Taylor left Midvale Iron Works at age 35, famous and successful, to pursue the life of a management consultant. What followed was a period of failures and ups and downs, resulting in two nervous breakdowns. When the opportunity at Bethlehem became available, Taylor jumped at the chance. He surrounded himself with admirers, and his success is well documented. Unfortunately, with each success, Taylor became more and more dogmatic, which isolated him from his peers. When Taylor left on a vacation his colleagues took the opportunity to throw him out. According to Duncan (1989), "He was no longer welcome at Bethlehem Steel, and his loyal colleagues were fired. Even the vice-president who had hired him was forced to resign" (p. 54).

Many more examples of success are available, but the point has been made. Taylor emphasized that scientific management is not a single technique, but a whole program that emphasizes science, harmony, cooperation, maximum output, and the development of human potential. Scientific management was movement away from restricted output, movement toward maximizing the individual capacity to produce, independent of the actions of others, and would move companies and nations toward greater prosperity. Production costs would come down, harmony in the workplace would increase, and individuals would be able to accomplish their greatest levels of efficiency and productivity.

The cultural implications of scientific management are profound. As discussed in Chapter 2, culture is best understood as the product of sense making by organization members. Scientific management is the attempt by managers to impose a version of "sense" on the workplace. The manager's version is seen as the correct interpretation of what the organization is and should be. The nonmanager, then, is expected to follow mindlessly, accepting the interpretations of his or her experience offered by management. So, for example, if management says that things are good, they are; if management says that layoffs are in the best interests of the company, they are; if management says that retrenchments are actually reallocations, they are.

Everybody's a Critic

Taylor and his work fell under intense scrutiny and criticism, both in his lifetime and after (Fry, 1976; Locke, 1982). Scientific management had become very unfashionable shortly after the publication of Taylor's book in 1911, essentially because many followers adopted the principles as means of control, rather than adopting the philosophy of management provided in the work as a whole. These abuses prompted a congressional inquiry and a law passed in 1915 banning the use of timing devices in government facilities.

The criticisms of Taylor have centered on the following issues: his vision of people as motivated by money only, his failure to recognize the worth of the person beyond a unit of measurement, his ignoring of the social and psychological workplace variables, his push for efficiency through coercion, and the assertion that Taylor plagiarized much of his work from his close collaborator Morris Cooke. Some of this criticism is warranted, some is not.

Taylor's work evolved during a period in history that promoted such conceptions of work and the worker. This "progressive era" was marked by calls for greater efficiency, driven by the industrial revolution, the growth of capitalism, and the increase in technological developments. The machine drove organizational design and theory, and Taylor was able to develop a technique for joining the worker and the machine.

Taylor began as an apprentice at Midvale Iron Works and was able in his rise to loftier positions to see ways to innovate on the management principles of the day. We need to remember that Taylor was not the first to advocate efficiency. Taylor was especially critical of the then-popular management philosophy of *initiative and incentive*, which called for the worker to design as well as do the work. Taylor felt that this put too much burden and responsibility on the worker and too little on management. He called upon management to take on the tasks of planning, controlling, and directing through the four principles of scientific management.

Taylor was by no means a humanist. He did see people as lazy, as prone to loafing and "soldiering." Taylor rejected the informal work group as dysfunctional, ignoring its potential advantages in the workplace. He blamed the practice of initiative and incentive for the emergence of systematic soldiering and advocated the application of scientific principles, especially task design and a bonus system, instead. There is no doubt that Taylor desired to disrupt any semblance of group collusion, by rewarding individual excellence and weeding out those who could not live by those rules.

Taylor believed that management should be based on facts rather than tradition, personal opinions, guesswork, and so forth. These were the principles that guided management before Taylor and he argued strenuously against them. Taylor also argued for a change in the relationship between labor and management that would do away with the common violence and strife of the day. Taylor suggested that at the most basic level, the concerns of labor and management were the same: increased production, fair wages, and lower costs. These, he argued, could come about through the application of scientific management.

Many of Taylor's techniques and ideas are still popular today. For example, Taylor argued for breaking tasks down into their simplest components to do away with guesswork, he fought for standardized tools and procedures and for the assignment of a specific amount of work to the worker, roughly comparable to goal setting today. This included feedback, which under Taylor's system was given to every worker every day. Taylor argued that workers were motivated most by money, and suggested a 30 to 100 percent pay raise for most when they succeeded in learning the correct methods for doing their jobs. He also advocated individual work rather than group work, suggesting that groups were actually obstacles to the ability of the individual to succeed at the highest levels, because of systematic soldiering. Taylor held management accountable for the training and selection of workers, and finally, after efficiency evaluations, Taylor argued for shorter working hours and rest pauses as techniques for maximizing productivity.

The reader can make up his or her own mind regarding Frederick Taylor. Critics and supporters are not hard to find. However, before moving totally away from Taylor we should take a brief look at one of Taylor's most enduring legacies—the time-motion study.

- *Why was Taylor such a controversial figure? Summarize Taylor's contributions and put them up against the criticisms. Are you a supporter of Taylor's methods and philosophy?*

Time-Motion Studies

Time-motion studies are a technique for measuring work efficiency by timing and monitoring the movements made during the completion of a given task. Taylor, for example, measured the shoveling of workers at Bethlehem. In a more current example, I recently visited a fast-food restaurant and was confronted with the following: I was greeted as I walked in the door with my wife and two kids. A young woman was at the counter, smiling pleasantly, but clearly anxious about our hesitancy to make a speedy order. It was only upon actually moving to the counter that I noticed the woman standing behind our server with a clipboard and a stopwatch. Once we gave our order it was like watching poetry in motion as our server glided from one station to another filling our order in an obviously choreographed sequence of steps as her movements were being timed and watched by her supervisor.

Although Taylor is the best-known advocate of time-motion studies, he clearly was neither the first nor the only practitioner of these techniques. *Frank and Lillian Gilbreth* are recognized as the key founders of motion research. Frank Gilbreth embraced Taylor's ideas (though the two were never associates) and brought them to bear on the study of motion. Gilbreth turned down an offer to attend M.I.T., choosing instead to study the methods of bricklaying by joining the profession. When he was 36, Gilbreth married Lillian Moller, who became a Ph.D. in psychology, and the two embarked on a lifelong study of the mechanics of motion.

Frank Gilbreth introduced the field of motion study in his examination of bricklayers, in which, after training, he was able to increase the average production from 120 bricks per man per hour to 350. The importance of the science of movement should not be underestimated. Morgan (1986) wrote, for example, that when General Motors increased the speed of its assembly line in the late 1960s, workers were called upon to perform eight different motions in a 36-second span of time. The Gilbreths developed a variety of motion picture devices for photographing and analyzing everything from the most gross to the most minute movements.

Other contemporaries of Taylor who demonstrated the potential of time-motion studies included Harrington Emerson who, in the early 1900s, saved the Santa Fe Railroad $1.5 million annually. In 1913, Emerson published *The Twelve Principles of Efficiency,* and these principles (summarized in Duncan, 1989, pp. 36–40) are worth noting: clear goals, common sense, expert advice, discipline, justice, good record keeping, scheduling, standards, applying efficiency standards to the present as well as planning for the future, planning, written guidelines, and adequate rewards. And Morris Cooke deserves recognition as the person who applied scientific management outside the manufacturing sphere. According to Duncan (1989, p. 40), "Cooke was one of only four men . . . that Taylor acknowledged as true followers who were authorized to teach his system." Among his many accomplishments, Cooke, as director of public works for the city of Philadelphia, managed to find ways to cut over $1 million from the cost of garbage collection.

Results like these do not go unnoticed by contemporary efficiency experts and managers. The following examples (found in Mundel, 1985) are offered to give you a feel for more current applications of time-motion studies. Recently, time-motion studies resulted in a revised process that allowed a publishing company to put out a magazine twice the original size for less money than the original; a method for assembling bearing and oil seals that increased production 2.25 times, while making the work easier; a method for sorting day-old chicks that increased the number inspected by 95 percent, with improved results; a project in a diesel-engine fuel-pump manufacturing plant that increased production from 20,000 to 60,000 units per month without employee reductions or automation; a shipyard project that resulted in a 45 percent reduction in the labor required to build a ship; and a citrus-picking program that resulted in a reduction of employees from 9000 to 7000, while increasing picking by 40 percent and increasing workers' earnings by 20 to 40 percent. These are examples that cannot be taken lightly. The methods and philosophy of time-motion studies are with us today and have continually proven themselves to be of value to managers.

The philosophy of time-motion studies, on the other hand, is more controversial. Mundel (1985) stressed that time-motion studies must not be conducted as if there were no relation to the people being affected. The social needs of the employees must at all times be considered when using these methods. Especially important are perceptions of piece-rate systems, incoming automation or mechanization, layoffs and workforce reductions, and "big-brother" peering over the shoulders of workers.

- *What are time-motion studies? What impact have they had on workplace productivity? Why are they controversial?*

HENRI FAYOL'S GENERAL THEORY OF MANAGEMENT

As a contemporary of Taylor (American) and Weber (German), *Henri Fayol* (French) is considered one of the three most important contributors to the emergence of the field of management. Fayol lived from 1841 to 1925. At nineteen he was hired by the Commentary-Fourchambault Company, where he spent his entire career. He began as an engineer and moved up in the company, eventually becoming managing director, and was credited with saving the company from bankruptcy.

Most argue that Fayol (1949/1916) produced the first general theory of management text. Fayol's is, like Taylor's, a remarkably small book filled with practical advice. According to Fayol (see Table 4-2), six groups of activities compose the industrial undertaking: technical, commercial, financial, security, accounting, and managerial. The managerial activities are of interest here.

Fayol held the manager accountable for four functions: planning, hiring, coordinating, and harmonizing. The individual who would excel at these tasks would need certain physical, mental, moral, and educational qualities, special knowledge, and experience. Fayol felt that managers should be trained just as engineers are, but, at that time, no formal theory of management existed for this purpose. His book was one answer to this lack.

The managerial function, according to Fayol, was composed of fourteen principles: division of work, authority, discipline, unity of command (important that employees receive orders from one superior only), unity of direction (a planning process whereby all managers are moving in the same direction), subordination of individual interests to the general interest, remuneration, centralization, scalar chain (the formal authority network), order, equity (fairness plus justice), stability of tenure of personnel, initiative, and morale.

Regarding the scalar chain of command, Fayol made clear that the chain was important, but should not be used in those instances where its use was actually an encumbrance to the communication process. He wrote: "So long as F and P remain in agreement, and so long as their actions are approved by their

TABLE 4-2. Fayol's General Theory of Management

Activities that Compose the Industrial Undertaking		Fourteen Principles of the Managerial Function
Technical		1. Division of work
Commercial		2. Authority
Financial		3. Discipline
Security		4. Unity of command
Accounting		5. Unity of direction
Managerial—Manager accountable for four functions:	Planning, Hiring, Coordinating, Harmonizing	6. Subordination of individual interests to the general interest
		7. Remuneration
		8. Centralization
		9. Scalar chain
		10. Order
		11. Equity
		12. Stability of tenure of personnel
		13. Initiative
		14. Morale

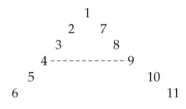

FIGURE 4-1. Fayol's bridge

immediate superiors, direct contact may be maintained, but from the instant that agreement ceases or there is no approval from the superiors direct contact comes to an end, and the scalar chain is straightway resumed" (p. 35). The visual image of this notion is referred to as "Fayol's gangplank," or *"Fayol's bridge"* (see Figure 4-1).

With Fayol, then, we bring this lengthy discussion of the machine metaphor, the classical period of organizational design, to a close. This period in history was marked by profound changes in how work was conceived, conducted, and managed. The classical period laid the foundation for the rest of the story of organizational design.

SUMMARY

From an organization culture point of view, the classical period, with its emphases on division, specialization, efficiency, fine-tuning the workers, hierarchy, structure, control, and its emerging principles and theories of management and organizing, was a time when "culture" was imposed from the top down. Workers were discouraged from sharing ideas with each other, groups were seen as detrimental to the overall good of the company and the workers. Laborers were supposed to hold the thoughts and attitudes forced on them by management.

However, workers of course talked to each other and had beliefs, feelings, assumptions, and visions of work and the workplace. What these visions were, from organization to organization, is a mystery. One point, however, is clear. The vision imposed from the top was not always the vision shared at the bottom of the hierarchy. The workplace rebellions and the growth of labor movements and unions in the first fifty years of this century are testimony to the cultural gaps between labor and management.

For many in these early days, a formal and formalized work environment, governed by rules and wages, was a new experience. For many of these workers this was their first exposure to being told what to do and when to do it. The long hours, the physical and mental demands of the work itself, and the sometimes capricious styles of management all must have set a foundation for cultures of resentment and rebellion.

Management, also, had a vision in these early days. Their emerging field was one of confusion, where formal theory was usurping the rule-of-thumb methods of the past. Those who were accustomed to the old ways must have felt threatened by these new methods. Their power as well as their competence was being questioned by the formalization of management.

The culture of the machine, then, was one of learning. It was the attempt by management to develop a science of control, and the attempt by labor to understand the new forms and structures of work. Such concepts as science, labor, management, structure, divisionalization, control, wages, incentives, cause and effect, mechanical, efficiency, precision, productivity, and mechanization guided the creation of the machine cultures of the classical period.

- *Summarize the "culture of the machine."*

We will turn our attention now to the next model of organizational development: the satisfaction culture. Beginning with the Hawthorne Studies, we'll look at how thoughts about workers and the workplace evolved from the 1930s to the present.

CHAPTER 5

The Emergence of Cultural Understanding

Chapter Preview

This chapter continues the discussion begun in Chapter 4 on the history of the development of organizational theory and the role of culture in that development. Chapter 5 begins with an examination of the Hawthorne Studies, possibly the most important series of organizational studies ever conducted. The years have not been kind to the Hawthorne results; many of them have been discounted by current writers. However, the fact remains that this research led to nothing short of a revolution in the relationship between workers and management, and a resultant shift in dominant design theories.

We'll move from the Hawthorne Studies to an examination of the work of several of the dominant thinkers of the Human Relations model. I will make it clear how the model advocated the satisfaction of worker needs, prompting the use of the satisfaction metaphor when describing this period. From human relations we move to human resources and a subtle, but important, shift in thinking about the workplace. It became clear that a fully operating example of the human relations model was impossible and, many argued, not desirable. So, management thought shifted to taking advantage of the potential of the workforce and to meet their needs to derive satisfaction from their work. Enrich the workplace and you will have satisfied workers.

With the human resources models came a recognition of organizational and environmental complexity. Contingency theories and the rise of system theories and explanations were the result. We'll explore the nature of system inquiries, including STS (sociotechnical systems analysis). System theory and modeling is a recognition that goes beyond anything that came earlier in terms of understanding the complex nature of organizations.

This chapter concludes with a discussion of the development of the organization culture approach. Since culture has been discussed in detail in earlier chapters, the focus in this chapter is on how culture was conceptualized throughout the development of the various historical models.

Key Terms and Names

Hawthorne Studies
Theory X
Theory Y
hierarchy of needs
TORI theory
Managerial Grid
linking pin model
system theories
equifinality
sociotechnical system analysis
open and closed systems
Elton Mayo
Fritz Roethlisberger

Chester Barnard
Mary Parker Follett
Douglas McGregor
Abraham Maslow
Jack Gibb
Raymond Miles
Robert Blake and Jane Mouton
Rensis Likert
Henry Mintzberg
Ludwig von Bertalanffy
Kenneth Boulding
Fred Emery
Eric Trist

Before venturing any further into this chapter, recall from Chapter 4 the early models of organizational development, focused on bureaucratic design and theory. After looking at Chapter 4, with its discussion of bureaucracy's strengths and weaknesses, and the development of scientific management, you were most likely left wondering if anything better came along. After all, it is quite common for us to lament daily our "oppression" by the bureaucracies that surround us.

Well, other models did come along, some of them discussed in this chapter. But before getting to them, stop for a moment and ask what you would do if you were designing an organization. Would you create a structure that overcame the limitations of bureaucracy? Would such a structure also remove the advantages of bureaucratic design? In short, how would you design an organization? Would your design be an improvement on the bureaucratic form?

THE HUMAN RELATIONS MODEL: FACILITATING THE SATISFACTION CULTURE

Unlike the classical period, the next significant era in organizational history is not so well-defined or clearly articulated. Its proponents, however, were every bit as committed to their vision of organization and the workers. This vision, which I have labeled the satisfaction culture, was brought on by a most important research project—the Hawthorne Studies—that serves as a transition between these two historical periods. So we will turn our attention now to the *Hawthorne Studies* and their impact on organizational thinking, followed by a discussion of the thoughts of some of the key contributors to the satisfaction metaphor, or what many have called the human relations period of organizational history.

The Hawthorne Studies

The General Electric Company (not surprisingly) wanted to sell more light bulbs, which meant an increase in the use of electricity, which interested Commonwealth Edison. GE and CE had influence on the National Research Council, which then became interested in electricity and light bulbs. Its honorary chair, Thomas Edison, and one of its members who worked for ATT, persuaded the council to formally develop a project on industrial lighting at the Hawthorne Works, a Western Electric Company located outside Chicago in Hawthorne, Illinois, that assembled telephones for ATT.

Working in conjunction with the NRC, then, the Hawthorne Works set out to conduct a series of illumination studies to determine an optimal level of lighting within the workplace. This was an application of Frederick Taylor's ideas to the lighting industry. The company felt that if it could prove that productivity was affected by lighting, it might use the information to increase the sale of light bulbs.

The studies were carried out at the Hawthorne plant from 1927 to 1932, by the company and various departments of Harvard University. The most comprehensive account of the studies is Roethlisberger and Dickson's *Management and the Worker* (1939). (The interested reader should also see Duncan, 1989; Homans, 1950; Landsberger, 1958; Mayo, 1946/1933.) The principal researchers were *Elton Mayo* and *Fritz Roethlisberger* of Harvard and William Dickson of Western Electric. The following is the sequence of the experiments.

Phase One

Phase one of the studies (the illumination experiments) was not conducted in affiliation with Harvard. These illumination experiments were actually conducted before the noted researchers were brought in, between 1924 and 1927, in collaboration with the National Research Council. These studies, however, supplied the stimulus for the Harvard-affiliated research. The illumination experiments were a three-part sequence of studies.

In the first, the level of lighting was increased in three departments. The productivity of one department varied erratically, and productivity in the other two increased, but, again, erratically, so that the researchers were not sure of the true cause of the change. For the second part of the study, more control was exercised. The lighting intensity experiment was performed on two groups doing similar work and composed of similar workers (age, experience). One group served as a control group. No changes were made in its lighting environment. The other group, the experimental group, worked under various lighting conditions. *The results proved confusing, for productivity increased in both groups, to the same degree.* The third part of the illumination experiments was devised to test the idea that the results in part two had been due to the combination of artificial and natural lighting in the workplace. For part three, the experiment of part two was replicated using only artificial lighting. The lighting in this case was decreased and, for the third time, the results were perplexing. Productivity increased again in both the control and experimental groups, decreasing only when workers were working in an environment described as "bright moonlight" (Perrow, 1972, p. 98).

The results showed, then, that workers produced more under conditions of increased lighting intensity (the hoped-for result), as well as decreased intensity, as well as no changes. Obviously, the changes in productivity had to be attributed to something other than the lighting. This recognition prompted the second significant phase of the research, best explained as another three-part series.

- *Briefly summarize the lighting experiments. Why was this an application of the philosophy of scientific management, discussed in Chapter 4?*

Phase Two

Part 1: Rest Pause Experiments. This is where the Harvard group came in. An attempt was made to gain more control over possible intervening factors that could have confounded the illumination series. This experiment was referred to as the relay assembly test room series. The researchers chose six women telephone relay assemblers. The type of work performed was controlled by the workers themselves, not paced by a machine; the assembly production was so standardized that even small changes in production were easy to measure; before the women joined the experimental group, their performance was charted (for two weeks) to serve as a baseline measure; and the emphasis of the study was, again, on physical determinants of productivity, rather than psychological.

Period one of the experiment consisted of separating the women from the rest of their work group. Before this was done, the women were informed of the nature of the experiment and told not to perform any differently than they would normally. The point of the rest pause experiments was to measure the fatigue level of the workers and monitor how fatigue affected productivity.

Period two of the experiment was simply the establishing of a baseline measure. No changes were introduced for the first five weeks of the study, in order to determine the impact of removing the women from their normal work group. During period three of the experiment, which lasted eight weeks, the women's payment plans were changed to more directly reward individual performance. Periods four through thirteen were the actual periods of manipulation. These periods lasted for over twenty-six months, with only one period being less than four weeks in duration. During these periods the experimenters manipulated many variables, including giving longer or shorter breaks, offering snacks and not offering snacks, shortening the work day and lengthening it. *The end result, overall, was a continuous increase in productivity, even though some experimental conditions were the same as previous conditions.* Especially important to note here is that period twelve was a reinstatement of the original working conditions (forty-eight-hour week, no rest pauses), and period thirteen was a reinstatement of the morning rest periods. In both instances productivity increased, and the overall finding was that no matter what variable was manipulated, productivity just kept increasing.

- *At this point, can you guess why productivity kept increasing?*

Second Relay Assembly Group Experiments. To further assess the impact of the wage incentive program on the first group, a second group was created and, instead of being totally segregated from the large group, remained in their regular department placed next to one another. The only variable manipulated here was wages. This group was given the same incentive system as the first, with the same results.

Mica Splitting Test Room. In this experiment, run concurrently with the second relay assembly group, a group of women were run through five experiments concerning working conditions (rest pauses and length of workday). The results were not necessarily consistent with those of the rest of the study. Productivity did increase, but only to a point. During the fourth period productivity leveled out. Large gaps in productivity among the women were noted, which had not happened in previous conditions. Finally, the researchers noted that the group never formed the close personal ties of the relay groups.

In short, by this time in the experiments the researchers were unable to make any definitive claims. None of the changes in supervisory methods, wage systems, or working conditions alone could be suggested to reliably account for the findings. To help clarify, the researchers looked to worker attitudes.

Part 2: Employee Interview Program. A wide-scale interview program was conducted. Ten thousand interviews were done, resulting in over 86,000 comments on eighty interview topics. In the early portions of the series, the interviews took about 30 minutes each. Later, after techniques were refined and members became more comfortable with the process, they lasted one to one-and-a-half hours each.

Part 3: The Effect and Formation of the Group. With this portion of the studies, the researchers were convinced that they had to look beyond physical factors to account for the changes they had noted. Their conclusion was that attitudinal factors, in terms of the individual's place within the group, played a central role in that person's level of productivity and satisfaction with work. The researchers turned to observational techniques to gather these data. This led to the best-known of the Hawthorne Studies, the bank wiring room observations.

The researchers had already determined from the interview portion of the studies that wages could not account for all of the findings, or even a majority of the findings, because groups had their own standards to which the individual members had to adhere. The group supervisors could not control this phenomenon, nor could the group leaders. The wiring room observation study was set up to observe more formally the process of group formation and informal interaction norms.

Fourteen bank wirers were observed from November 1931 to May 1932. The researchers introduced no changes, they simply observed the workers. Productivity was pretty much "straight line" throughout the course of the observations, mostly because daily results were often overreported. The group as a whole participated consistently in this subterfuge. Also, when supervisors found defects or replaced workers the group found ways to undermine that supervisor's authority.

Thus, there existed a strong sense of group unity that defied corporate standards. Though the group conformed to a common set of production norms, it was found that they actually constituted a unique subgroup that was quite different from other subgroups. It was level of conformity to group norms that determined how included or excluded each individual was in relation to the group.

The results of the Hawthorne Studies were amazing for their times. The studies found that workers had needs beyond money, especially a need to be recognized by their superiors; that within the larger group there were informal work groups, which exerted pressure on members to conform to group standards in defiance of company standards; and that paying attention to workers' needs was a way to increase productivity. This was the finding that came through again and again—the explanation for why productivity increased even in the control groups.

- *Summarize the Hawthorne Studies and their key results.*

A NEW VISION EMERGES

On the strength of the Hawthorne Studies, a new vision of work and worker emerged: the human relations school. No longer was the worker a faceless, replaceable cog in the machine. Instead, the worker was a feeling, needs-driven individual within the workplace, willing and capable to work, if understood, and if his or her needs were being satisfied. This sympathetic image, however, did not protect the advocates of this approach from criticism.

The human relations school of organizational analysis and understanding has come under continuous and sometimes harsh attack, based in good part on the Hawthorne Studies. Of these criticisms, one of the most scathing is the accusation that the worker is portrayed as little more than a pawn to be manipulated by management toward its own ends. The human relations school focuses explicitly on the needs of the worker, but the potential managerial bias must be recognized. Will the worker be an end unto him- or herself, or a means to a managerial end?

In one critical report, Franke and Kaul (1978) presented their quantitative analysis of the Hawthorne data. The authors found that, rather than being the result of social solidarity, more pleasant relationships with management and coworkers, and pleasant working conditions, the increase in productivity was the result of managerial pressure to produce, the fear of being terminated during the depression, and rest pauses to reduce fatigue. So, rather than refuting the philosophy of scientific management, the Hawthorne Studies actually demonstrated scientific principles.

In short, just as occurred with Taylor and scientific management, devotees and detractors of a human relations approach to the workplace are vocal and dogmatic. Whether one agrees or disagrees with the Hawthorne results, it is undeniable that the series of studies opened the door to a new vision of organizing, based on the satisfaction of human needs and a recognition of the informal group and group norms. It is also clear that the Hawthorne Studies gave the first clear evidence of subcultural variation in the workplace.

In the remainder of this section we'll look at a number of the most influential advocates of the human relations philosophy. Reviewing their work will give us a much better feel for the wide differences between the scientific and human relations schools. Two of the most noted writers in these areas were Chester Barnard and Mary Parker Follett.

Chester Barnard

Both George (1968) and Perrow (1972) cited *Chester Barnard* as one of the most influential theorists in organizational history. As president of New Jersey Bell, Barnard had the opportunity to both observe and practice management and organization design. In his most influential work, *The Functions of the Executive*, Barnard (1938) set out to comment on two processes: cooperation in the process of organization and the role of authority or the executive process.

He argued that the organization is based on cooperation and that cooperation is based on individual motivation ("psychological forces"). Individual behavior is modified through collective expectations to become the rational, formal organization system. The organization should be understood as a social system, more than the sum of its parts as those parts interact cooperatively with one another, toward maintenance of the system rather than toward ends of the individual. He identified three primary components of the organization: communication, cooperation, and common purpose. Communication allows the other two components to be achieved and so plays a central role in organizing.

Barnard noted the existence of the informal organization and gave some discussion of its importance. He argued that: (1) the informal organization may occur within the formal; (2) it does not carry a joint purpose and so lacks structure and form; (3) it does affect beliefs, values, customs, habits, and so forth; (4) it creates the conditions for the emergence of formal organization, for it is around the personal, vaguely formed beliefs and ideas that formality wraps itself, giving the personal agenda the structure and status of collective goal; and (5) whereas the formal organization is quite logical, the informal organization, based on an individual, noncollective goal-directed mentality, is quite illogical. Cooperative action is both the catalyst and the outlet of rationality. The role of the informal organization within the formal organization is to enhance cohesiveness by protecting the individuality of the individual.

(With these thoughts, Barnard was clearly recognizing the presence of what came to be called organization culture.)

Regarding authority, Barnard wrote of four conditions that must be met in order for the worker to accept authoritative communication: (1) The communication must be understandable, (2) it must not be seen as inconsistent with the purpose of the organization, (3) it must not be seen as incompatible with what the worker believes, and (4) the worker must be able to do what the communication asks. Authority resides within communication. It is not a component of a person.

For communication to be authoritative, the following conditions should be met: The channels of communication should be known; formal communication channels should be available to all members; lines of communication should be short and direct; formal lines of communication should not be bypassed; the individuals in the communication chain should be adequate to the tasks; and communications should be double-checked to verify the legitimacy of the source. Executives in formal organizations, then, serve two critical functions: the development and maintenance of a communication system, and promoting cooperative relationships among the organization members so that the work of the organization can be accomplished. (For an interesting criticism of Barnard, see Perrow, 1972, pp. 89–95).

- *Summarize Barnard's position on the importance of communication in the work of the organization executive.*

Mary Parker Follett

Mary Parker Follett (1868–1933) was ahead of her time, a business philosopher of immense proportion. Born in Boston, Follett was educated at Radcliffe College and lived the life of social activist, lecturer, business consultant, and philosopher. She was trained in law, history, and political science, and her work was influential in both the United States and England. As an example of her range, while also demonstrating the unity of her thought, consider a sample of the topics Follett wrote about: systems theory, conflict management, superior-subordinate relationships, the profession of management, power and control, leadership, and participatory management.

In this brief section we can address only some of this range. Follett argued that there are three methods for dealing with conflict: domination, compromise, and integration. She strongly advocated integration—an early theme that she came back to repeatedly throughout her career. In an oft-cited piece, Follett (1940/1925) discussed the process of order giving as an issue of integration. She noted that the commonsense explanation of order giving—"The boss gives the orders and the worker obeys them"—neither makes sense, nor adequately explains what actually goes on in organizations. Moreover, it's bad policy.

Follett maintained that orders should flow naturally out of the situation in which the order giver and receiver find themselves. The order should not be seen as the whim of the boss; rather, it should be seen as a by-product, a natural conclusion of a flow of events. If the order is seen as reasonable, there will be less basis for resentment by the receiver and a better chance for a good, productive working relationship between worker and management in the future. Management is training the worker in the habits of ordering, and their paths are being integrated.

This is not meant to give the impression that management should lose its base of authority. On the contrary, Follett does not suggest eliminating the hierarchy, just reexamining it. She wrote, "Moreover, perhaps I have not said explicitly that the participation of employees . . . should take place before the order is given, not afterwards. After the order has been given the subordinate must obey. I certainly believe in authority—of the right kind" (p. 69).

Finally, Follett (1940/1932) spoke of four principles of organizing: coordination through having the concerned parties come together, coordination at the early stages of the organizing process, the understanding that coordination is both reciprocal (it is not just the adjustment of one person to another, but rather, mutual adjustment) and continuing (the need for coordination never ends). Problems cannot be solved in the sense of being gone, but they can be managed through the continuous process of integration and coordination. Managers and workers must break out of the managerial molds that constrain them and keep them from understanding the emergent nature of working relationships and the relationships between the organization and the political/national communities.

- *Do you understand the importance of coordination, integration, and unity in Follett's philosophy? What do Follett and Barnard have in common?*

In sum, Barnard and Follett can be seen as the philosophers of the human relations movement. Together they advocated a reassessment of management toward the greater recognition of the informal work group, the responsibilities of management, coordination of workers, integration of roles, and understanding of the organization as system. The Hawthorne Studies, Barnard, and Follett help explain the transition from the classical model, but do not make clear what the human relations model actually was. For that understanding we now turn to a number of other key contributors to the model itself.

Fritz Roethlisberger and William Dickson

Roethlisberger (1965) wrote: "It is my simple thesis that a human problem requires a human solution. First, we have to learn to recognize a human problem when we see one; and, second, upon recognizing it, we have to learn to deal with it as such and not as if it were something else" (p. 9). His point was that the Hawthorne experiments clearly demonstrated the inadequacy of trying to apply nonhuman bandages to human ailments. Lighting, rest pauses, and snacks all failed where simple human contact and understanding succeeded. That was the lesson of the Hawthorne Studies.

TABLE 5-1. Hawthorne Plant Worker and Employer Expectations

Worker Expectations	Employer Expectations
• Job security	• Employees will work hard and efficiently, without sacrificing quality
• Satisfactory relationships with coworkers and supervisors	• Coworker interaction only when absolutely necessary
• Feelings of belongingness	
• Recognition without being taken advantage of	• Workers will try to understand the logic behind employer's point of view
• The option to develop skills, and recognition for skill development	• Limit complaints
	• Act responsibly and maturely
• Financial and fulfillment needs met	• Cooperation and loyalty.

Note: Adapted from Dickson and Roethlisberger (1966), pp. 245–48.

In an enormous example of putting principles into action, Dickson and Roethlisberger (1966) reported the counseling program run at the Hawthorne works. Their report and the program itself went a long way toward answering the question, "What is it that employees want?" After the Hawthorne Studies were concluded, Western Electric, in conjunction with Roethlisberger and others at Harvard, initiated a massive employee counseling and interviewing program to determine what needs the employees had and offer what remedies they could, primarily in the form of a friendly, listening ear.

The program was massive. Between 1936 and 1956, when the program was discontinued, 574 counselors conducted more than 237,000 employee interviews. Employees at all hierarchical levels were included. The authors summarized the results as falling into three categories: employee concerns, company standards, and group norms and rewards.

Employee concerns included safety, belongingness, treatment, autonomy, and achievement. Company rewards and standards included output, quality, attendance, pay increases, merit increases, downgrading, transfers, and discipline. Group norms and rewards included helping each other, friendliness, protection, access to secrets, isolation, and ostracism.

In summary form, the authors outlined what they found that employees wanted from their employers (see Table 5-1), and vice versa. The job and, according to the authors, the success, of the counseling program was to close the gap between these two sets of expectations.

Douglas McGregor

Douglas McGregor (1960) made a critical point that the process of training managers will probably have less impact on how those managers act than the assumptions that drive management theory. The assumptions of the nature of the managerial task become the key determining factor in what type of manager the person is and what type of management the person demonstrates. McGregor contrasted what he argued were the dominant assumptions about workers, *Theory X*, with the necessarily emerging set of assumptions, *Theory Y*. McGregor (1966/1957) also highlighted the manager's task given both X and Y assumptions (see Table 5-2).

In commenting on Theories X and Y, McGregor noted that Theory X is centered on the scalar chain of command, with communication going downward. Theory Y, on the other hand, focuses on integration. The problem, of course, is that the hierarchy and "chain of command" are so ingrained in our way of thinking about management that it is hard to see the strength of any other system.

TABLE 5-2. Theories X and Y

Theory X	Theory Y
1. Work is distasteful, and people will avoid it if they can.	1. Work is natural and may serve as a source of satisfaction.
2. Because of their dislike for work, in order to get people to perform adequately, they must somehow be controlled, through force, threat, direction, or other control measures.	2. Workers will be committed to goals they help set, with the greatest amount of commitment directed at objectives that, if met, will fulfill ego and self-actualization needs.
3. People lack ambition and prefer to be directed, because they do not want responsibility.	3. If trained to seek and allowed to accept responsibility, workers will.
	4. Greater intellectual and creative potential exists than is currently being tapped.

MANAGERIAL ASSUMPTIONS

1. Management carries the responsibility of organizing all aspects of work, including equipment, money, and people, toward the goal of profitability.	1. Management carries the responsibility of organizing all aspects of work, including materials, money, and people, toward the goal of profitability.
2. The behavior of people is to be directed and controlled toward the ends of the company.	2. Because their input has not been sought, people have been trained to be passive at work.
3. Since people naturally will avoid working, they must be persuaded or otherwise controlled so that the necessary work is accomplished.	3. Management does not motivate the worker. The worker is already motivated, for the motivation lies within him or her. The manager's job is help the worker develop his or her own potential.
	4. Management should provide the environment that allows the worker to accomplish his or her goals while working toward the organizational goals.

Integration is the requirement that both the needs of the individual and those of the organization be met. If not, both the organization and the person will suffer, whereas with Theory X, only the requirements of the organization are considered. Theories X and Y, of course, are blinders, highlighting certain ways of directing the activities of others while obscuring others. But it is important to understand that both Theory X and Theory Y are assumptions and strategies. Tactics come about in the course of attempting the strategy.

- *What are the differences between Theory X and Theory Y?*

Abraham Maslow

Abraham Maslow created an entire approach to psychology, much too complex to be covered in depth here. However, certain elements of Maslow's work, especially his *hierarchy of needs,* have played a prominent role in most of the discussions of the human relations approach. Good discussions of the hierarchy can be found in Maslow (1943, 1954, 1968).

Maslow argued that each person has an "inner nature," which, in part, consists of basic needs (see Figure 5-1), hierarchically stacked from physiological to psychological. The lower-level needs are, essentially, means toward the ultimate end of self-actualization. These needs are discussed briefly below.

Life: This is the most basic or lowest level of needs. These are elementary, life-sustaining needs of food, water, salt, sugar, oxygen, and so forth—the physiological needs of the human organism. *Security:* At the next level are needs for shelter and safety. This level of needs encompasses those beyond simple shelter needs. The search for stability, protection, even "meaning of life" philosophies may be a search for security.

The third level of the hierarchy, *belongingness,* is the need for affection, to be included and to include others. This is the search for love and warmth, for acceptance. The fourth level, *respect,* is the need for self-esteem, to feel good about oneself, have pride in one's work and life. This is the search for self-respect, self-confidence, some sense of prestige among one's peers, and the rejection of feelings of inferiority.

FIGURE 5-1. Maslow's hierarchy of needs

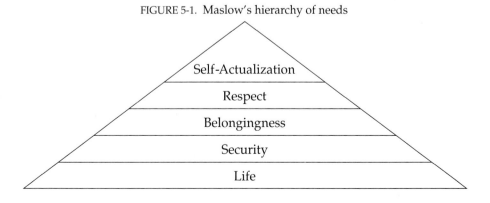

Finally, the highest level of the hierarchy is *self-actualization.* Self-actualization refers to the inner experience of full functioning. It occurs when an individual reaches his or her potential. Self-actualization is what a person *can* be.

- *Summarize Maslow's hierarchy of needs. Do you see how such a theory would play a significant role in the satisfaction culture?*

Jack Gibb

Jack Gibb's contributions to human relations theory and its application to organizations are centered in two bodies of work: his characterization of supportive versus defensive communication climates (Gibb, 1961), and his TORI theory (Gibb, 1978). Gibb argued that the communication of group or organizational members will have an effect on climate and group cohesiveness. Thus, he advises the development of a communication climate characterized by supportiveness rather than defensiveness (see Table 5-3).

A supportive climate is one that would be characterized by communication that is descriptive rather than evaluative, problem-oriented rather than controlling, spontaneous rather than strategic, empathetic rather than neutral, equal rather than superior, and provisional rather than certain. The essential problem in a defensive climate is that it makes trust, which is essential for effective communication, more difficult to achieve and maintain.

Trust is the focus of Gibb's (1978) *TORI theory.* He built his comprehensive approach to trust around the dialectic tension between trust and fear, arguing that the two are the primary catalytic processes in life. Trust is integrating and "wholizing," while fear is constraining and blocking. In a trusting environment people are nourished and systems function well.

The process of discovering trust consists of four elements, encompassed in the acronym TORI. The *T* refers to the individual trusting him- or herself. It is the discovery of one's uniqueness. The *O* refers to opening, self-disclosing to others and being open to them. The *R* refers to realizing, or the process of becoming, of actualizing one's potential. And the *I* refers to interdependence, or the creation of community and being together.

TABLE 5-3. Gibb's Supportive and Defensive Communication Climates

Supportive Climate	Defensive Climate
Descriptive	Evaluative
Problem-oriented	Controlling
Spontaneous	Strategic
Empathetic	Neutral
Equal	Superior
Provisional	Certain

Gibb (1978) offered TORI as the means for diagnosing organizational effectiveness. He contrasted high-productivity and low-productivity focuses. A high-productivity focus is one of increased trust, that allows for personal development and the free flow of communication, that focuses on the "big picture" without losing track of the individual with his or her own unique needs and potential. A low-productivity focus, on the other hand, is a work climate that is overly scripted, depersonalized, overcontrolled, with an inordinate amount of focus on efficiency and products, power, status, and rules.

- *Summarize the differences between supportive and defensive communication climates, and the importance of climate in building a trusting organization.*

From an organization culture point of view, the human relations period was critically important, for it marked the beginnings of "formal" acceptance and recognition of a cultural understanding of organizational dynamics. The Hawthorne Studies and the human relations theorists highlighted the informal organization, composed of attitudes and feelings of workers. The period's recognition of and attention to the "psychological workforce" was a giant leap away from the mechanical vision that preceded it.

During this period the workforce came to be seen as children in need of attention and nurturing, specifically the thoughtful attention of the parent/managers. The needs varied from worker to worker, of course, but it was always recognized that the needs were there in some form or another. Likewise, the workplace came to be seen as composed of work groups with varying needs, sometimes competing, but always there.

In contrast to the terms that distinguished the classical period, such concepts as needs, belonging, attention, satisfaction, dissatisfaction, counseling, motivation, self-actualization, informality, relationships, subgroups, integration, and environment became the identifiers of the movement. And, as with the classical period before it, "culture" in this vision was an attempt to impose an interpretation of order from the top down.

However, unlike the classical period, in the human relations period the attempts to impose culture were understood as flawed. Researchers began to see culture as a two-way street, whereby managers and workers alike created a vision that constituted the workplace reality.

This should not be misunderstood to mean that management placed undue value on the workers' interpretation. Workers still were expected to perform according to management's vision. The difference here was one of attitude. Management became benevolent rather than dictatorial. This benevolence took the form of concern regarding the needs of workers, the children in the workplace system. Like good parents, management struggled with the problem of how to let the children find their own "best" while still being directive.

- *Summarize the cultural implications of a human relations perspective on organizing.*

THE HUMAN RESOURCES MODEL:
BUILDING THE TEAMWORK CULTURE

Whether the human resources model is distinct from the human relations model before it, or simply a definitional refinement, is a matter for each reader to decide for him- or herself. The model was coined by *Raymond Miles* (1965) in an article in which he introduced the idea of a human resources vision of participation as an alternative to the human relations perspective.

The human relations model was aimed at making employees feel needed by giving them some participation in matters of limited importance. Participation was advocated to increase cohesiveness and thereby morale, leading to greater productivity and compliance with formal authority. In the human resources model, on the other hand, participation was advocated because better ideas might surface through the tapping of employee potential. The manager shares information and the employees contribute sometimes creative, useful suggestions.

Miles listed a number of differences in attitudes, type of participation, and expectations that distinguish the human relations from the human resources models (see Table 5-4). Giving the human resources model a name should not be understood as recognizing it as a distinctly different understanding of organizing. The primary value of separating human resources from human relations is that the resources perspective more clearly brought in the concept of contingency theories and social systemic thinking. At the same time that Miles was defining the model, the model was being developed in a number of different ways. In this section I'll overview the work of four theorists: Blake and Mouton, Likert, and Mintzberg.

Robert Blake and Jane Mouton

Robert Blake and *Jane Mouton* (1964) are best known for their development of the *Managerial Grid* as a tool for plotting preferred managerial style and selecting managerial candidates based on their preferences. The grid plots individuals according to two preferences: relative concern for production and relative concern for people. The individual is charted on two nine-point axes, resulting in five styles of management (see Figure 5-2).

The 1,9 manager (country club) would be characterized by a great deal more concern for the feelings of subordinates than for actually getting the work done. This is a "feel-good" managerial style, appropriate in groups such as volunteer organizations, clubs, and many youth groups. This is a style for those situations in which the feelings of the customer or client or worker are more important than the task or product. The 1,1 manager (impoverished) would be characterized by minimal concern for both people and task. This is laissez-faire management, in which neither the participants nor the work benefit from the manager's contributions.

The 9,1 manager (task) would be characterized by concern for task over the feelings of the workers. Getting the job done is the goal of the 9,1 manager,

TABLE 5-4. Summary of the Human Relations and Human Resources Models

Human Relations	Human Resources
1. People have basic needs, especially the needs to be liked and respected.	1. People need to be liked and respected, and they additionally need to make creative contributions toward objectives.
2. People want to feel as though they are part of a group.	2. The majority of workers are an enormous untapped source of creativity and initiative.
3. If people's goals are met, they will cooperate.	3. The manager's job is to create an environment that will tap this potential.
4. The manager needs to fill the role of team builder.	4. The manager should encourage participation in all departmental matters, especially the most important ones.
5. The manager should be willing to explain him- or herself, listen to subordinates, and allow for some autonomy in routine decisions.	5. The workers' areas of responsibility should be continually expanded.
6. Sharing information with subordinates makes them feel important, satisfying needs for recognition.	6. As participation improves, so will the quality of decision making and performance.
7. Feeling needed will reduce employees' resistance to authority.	7. If they help set the objectives, subordinates will work hard to achieve them.
8. Reduced resistance to authority and increased morale should lead to increased performance.	8. Increased performance and the opportunity to contribute will increase subordinate satisfaction.

FIGURE 5-2. Managerial Grid

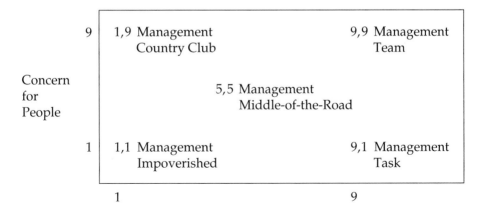

Concern for Production

sometimes at any expense. When faced with the choice of preserving the feelings of subordinates or maintaining relationships, the 9,1 manager's response would be "There is a job to do." This style would be appropriate in settings such as surgeries, airplane cockpits, and the military.

The 9,9 manager (team) would be characterized by a maximum concern for both task and people. This manager encourages participation because he or she believes that it will result in a higher-quality product. This is consensus decision making, appropriate, but seldom applied, to most organizations.

Finally, the 5,5 manager (middle-of-the-road) would be characterized by the tendency to compromise. This is the style of politics, where feelings are considered on a par with task, but the governing assumption is that you probably can't get all of one without sacrificing some of the other.

- *List and define the five styles from the managerial grid.*

Rensis Likert

In two key works, *Rensis Likert* (1961, 1967) presented his *linking pin model* of organizing. According to Likert, organizations are composed of "families" of subgroups, each responsible for its portion of the organization and each supervised by a lead person who acts as the head of that family, a member of a group of peers, and a subordinate. Groups thus overlap, with the supervisor serving to link the groups.

The most effective supervisors, Likert argued, were employee-centered, viewing their jobs as managing people rather than work. They allowed for maximum participation from their subordinates in helping them accomplish their goals. Likert identified four types of management systems:

1. *System 1: Exploitative-authoritative.* Fears, threats, downward communication, centralized decision making.
2. *System 2: Benevolent-authoritative.* Use of rewards to build subservient employee attitudes, patriarchal with some low-level decision making allowed at the subordinate level.
3. *System 3: Consultative.* Rewards and punishments, some increased involvement in decision making, downward and limited upward communication.
4. *System 4: Participative.* Group management using full capacity of the group, all-way communication, group setting its own goals and methods. Maximum involvement.

System 4 management is accomplished through the linking pin organizational structure (see Figure 5-3). In Figure 5-3 the participants in this work group or organization are represented as four hierarchical levels. The *A*s, at the lowest level, are supervised by *B*s, who also represent the lowest level of subgroups supervised by *C*s, who also represent the lowest level of subgroups supervised by *D*, and so forth.

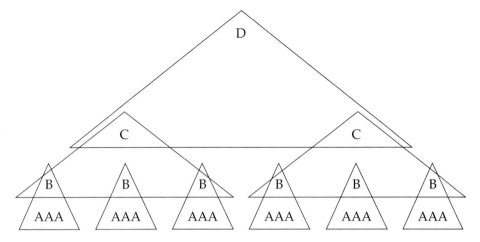

FIGURE 5-3. Linking pin organizational structure

Henry Mintzberg

The influence of *Henry Mintzberg* has been widespread. His most significant work for our purposes deals with contingent configurations of organizational design. Mintzberg (1980) argued that effective structuring required coordination between design factors—how the organization accomplished its goals of differentiation and unification (job specialization, behavior formalization, training and indoctrination, unit grouping, unit size, planning, and control systems)—and contingency factors, such as age and size, technical system (level of bureaucracy), environment, and power.

Mintzberg proposed five structural configurations:

1. Simple structure: Occurs when the strategic apex (top managers) dominates decision making through centralization.
2. Machine bureaucracy: When standardization of processes is the strongest pull; that is, when the technostructure (such as planners, work schedulers, and accountants) exerts the greatest influence.
3. Professional bureaucracy: This occurs when members of the operating core (the majority of employees and staff who produce the product) exert their power, resulting in an appreciation of skills and competence, and relatively autonomous working conditions.
4. Divisionalized form: When middle managers accomplish enough autonomy to control their own domains, making their own decisions, mandated only by standardization of output.
5. Adhocracy: When decision making and power are decentralized, and support staff gain in influence because of their expertise; when a collaborative environment is in effect, characterized by mutual adaptation and adjustment. This is the bringing together of competent people.

From an organization culture point of view, the human resources vision of organizing is significantly more mature than the human relations model was. The resources approach proceeds from the assumption of contingency and subgroup variation. Rather than assuming a homogeneous workforce, the resources model expects each workplace to be characterized by differentiation and unique components that demand different treatments.

"Culture" in this model is not something that can be seen as fully imposed from the top down. The defining quality of the model is participation, and participation breeds subgroup identifiability. With this model workers are no longer children, they are mature contributors. They are no longer seen as parts of a machine, but as the builders of the machine. Each organization, then, could be viewed as a unique construction of its members.

The principle of "participation" has proven to be the approach's defining strength as well as its most significant weakness. Organizations that suddenly adopt participative philosophies often find employees unable or unwilling to accept the new responsibilities (Eisenberg & Goodall, 1993). In order for participation to work as part of the organizational environment, it must be culturally embedded through the communicative practices of both management and labor.

According to Marshall and Stohl (1993), this embeddedness will revolve around the degree to which organization members are empowered and involved. Participation must include employee-initiated efforts to control their own environments and affairs, and it must allow for the employee to become integrated into the communicative network. In short, employee participation must include the opportunity to develop relationships with one's managers and supervisors, as well as others throughout the organization.

The key definitional identifiers of the approach are such concepts as participation, job satisfaction, contingency, creative potential, resources, environment, adaptation, social system, style, preferences, team, and subgroups. The teamwork model, then, is clearly a natural extension of both the machine and satisfaction models. It shows growth in theory and maturity in thinking on the part of theorists. It explicitly focuses on manager and worker as team, rather than relying too much on hierarchy.

The model developed at a time when organizational members and researchers were coming to understand the complexity of the internal and external environments of the organization. The model, with its emphasis on contingency designs, is a reflection of this increased understanding.

- *What are some cultural differences between the satisfaction and teamwork models?*

THE SOCIAL SYSTEMS MODEL: UNDERSTANDING THE ORGANISMIC CULTURE

While the human resources models were being developed and contingency theories were taking form, *social system theories* (also called sociotechnical or general systems theories) were also being developed. The hallmark of the human resources period was the increased understanding of organizational complexity. Systems theorists deserve most of the credit for bringing that complexity to light. Thus, we really can't separate systemic thinking from a human resources approach to the organization. A human resources approach is an actual model—a philosophy of design that argues for organizational configurations that are contingent on the workforce and the circumstances in which the organization finds itself. *System theory is the recognition of complexity, which finds its form in the various contingency models advocated by human resource theorists.*

Definitionally, "A 'system' is a complex of interrelated parts which function as a whole" (Johnson, 1981, pp. 39–40). The notion of the sociotechnical system arose out of the logistical problems encountered in World War II, of coordinating the efforts of machines and soldiers. In industrial organizations, the same problems were found—those of coordinating the specialized workforce with the technology of the organization. *Sociotechnical system analysis,* then, refers to this process of accomplishing a human-machine integration.

A system analysis allows the researcher to understand the intimate relationship between a system and its environment. System research has reminded us that you cannot dabble with one component of a system without affecting the other components (see Frank & Brownell, 1989; Katz & Kahn, 1978).

System theory has a terminology and perspective of its own. It is easier to understand the approach if the language is made clear up front. Toward that end I've included a list of key terms in Table 5-5. The remainder of this section will be devoted to presenting the development of the general system approach to understanding organizations. As with the previous sections, this one will focus on the work of key contributors.

- *After reviewing Table 5-5, do you understand the remarkable increases in organizational complexity posed by system theorists?*

Ludwig von Bertalanffy and Kenneth Boulding

The development of the system approach is usually traced to the influential writings of *Ludwig von Bertalanffy* and *Kenneth Boulding.* According to von Bertalanffy (1968) the notion of seeing objects such as biological organisms as systems occurred to him in the 1920s. At that point in history, however, the sciences were dominated by mechanistic thinking, which viewed the scientific domain as sets of cause-effect, mechanical chains. System thinking was greeted with great doubt as trivial—applying math to biology was no great advance in understanding—or as misleading in its use of analogies, such as viewing society as an organism.

Von Bertalanffy's ideas were first presented in 1937 at a University of Chicago philosophy seminar, but the first publications did not occur until after the war. By this time, the intellectual climate had changed. Model building

TABLE 5-5. Key Systems Terms

1. *Object* (component): A part of a system, such as the desks, teachers, and students within a college. It is important to note that objects and their attributes are secondary in importance to their functions and relationships in the system.

2. *Attributes:* These are properties of objects, such as female teachers and wooden desks.

3. *Relationships:* The tie between objects. System analysis focuses on relationships.

4. *Subsystems:* A subsystem is a component or a set of components within a system. For example, a specific department of a university may be considered a system unto itself or a subsystem of the university system. The subsystem is a level of analysis.

5. *Suprasystem:* A higher-level system than the system itself. Any system is a subsystem of a suprasystem.

6. *Boundary:* The edge of a system. Boundaries are either theoretically permeable, resulting in an open system, or nonpermeable, resulting in a closed system. Boundaries separate systems from their external environments.

7. *Open system:* A system that inputs energy from outside its boundaries and gives some sort of waste back to the environment.

8. *Closed system:* A theoretically self-sustaining, self-perpetuating system that does not need to import its energy sources. The only true example of a closed system is the universe, which, theoretically, has nothing beyond its boundaries.

9. *Environment:* The time and space conditions in which a system is embedded. A distinction is sometimes made between relevant and irrelevant or turbulent and stable environments.

10. *Input:* Importation of energy from the external environment. This includes materials, people, and information.

11. *Throughput:* The transformation of the energy into a form that the system can use. Sometimes referred to as the transformation process, this is the change or conversion of energy. For example, throughput would include the process of photosynthesis and digestion and the conversion of peanuts to peanut butter, time cards into paychecks, and sick patients into healthy ones.

12. *Output:* Exporting a product into the environment.

13. *Systems as cycles:* Input and output continually reinforce each other in a cyclic fashion. For example, the organization takes in raw materials and transforms them into a product, which is sold in the marketplace, bringing money into the organization allowing it to purchase more raw materials.

and generalizations were more accepted by the academic community, and developments in other fields made the time right for a more fully articulated system theory. Such developments occurred in the areas of cybernetics (mechanized feedback loops), information theory (attempts to quantify information and measure its impact in physics), game theory (the mathematical analysis of

TABLE 5-5. *(Continued)*

14. *Negative entropy:* Rather than follow the universal law of movement toward randomness, organizations move toward nonrandomness, or greater organization.

15. *Negative feedback and coding:* Open systems must have the capacity to code negative feedback in order to make adaptations to the environment.

16. *Steady state:* Systems do not fluctuate wildly in any direction. Rather, they maintain a relatively steady state of equilibrium or homeostasis.

17. *Differentiation:* Systems are characterized by functionally specialized parts.

18. *Integration and coordination:* The differentiation of parts must be coordinated somehow so that unified functioning occurs.

19. *Equifinality:* According to this principle, despite different starting points or different paths, systems can reach the same goals. Suppose, for example, that a period of economic decline hits the retail industry. The goal of the industry might be defined as financial prosperity. One company might choose to lay off 10,000 employees, another might choose to diversify and capture alternative markets and thereby increase its profits. These are two paths to the same goal—equifinality.

20. *Technical systems:* The tools and methods (system) designed to accomplish the transformations required by the organization.

21. *Social systems:* The interdependent roles being played out by organization members. (See Katz & Kahn, 1978, for a discussion of organizations as open systems of roles.)

22. *Sociotechnical systems:* The combination of social and technical systems and their impact on the environment.

23. *Sociotechnical systems analysis (STS):* Instead of focusing on the human "problems" of the organization ("This problem must be someone's fault"), STS is a method for assessing the human-technical interplay toward the goal of redesigning the system to address the problems differently.

24. *Variance:* Any unplanned disturbance that has a negative effect on the system. A variance is usually understood as a limitation in the sociohuman system design.

25. *Variance matrix:* A chart of all variances, plotted on a matrix, so that key variances can be identified, causal chains plotted, and variance loops found. An example of a loop might be a managerial program intended to increase motivation. After six months of the program it might be discovered that the program had actually decreased motivation. This finding would loop back to the onset of the program, casting doubt on the past six months of effort.

rational decision making), operations research, and human engineering (coordinating the efforts of humans and machines).

The substantial development of system theory occurred when Kenneth Boulding, Annatol Rapoport, Ralph Gerard, and von Bertalanffy spent time together in 1953 and 1954 at the Center for Advanced Study in the Behavioral Sciences in Palo Alto. Here was formed the Society for General Systems Research. And so we really see an interesting historical progression. The ideas were formulated in the 1920s, but more or less withheld because of the scientific climate of the times; presented on a small scale in the 1930s, but again kept from the public at large because of scientific blinders; presented and applied on a relatively wide scale in the 1940s (including computer applications, decision making, information and communication theory); formalized as an accepted part of the academic community in the 1950s; and applied on an enormously wide scale from the 1960s to the present. At this time there is virtually no department in the university that is not affected by system thinking.

The other seminal thinker, Kenneth Boulding, offered an early typology of levels of systemic complexity. Boulding (1968/1956) lamented the tendency of science to compartmentalize itself into a state of such isolation that one branch of science is unable to communicate with another. The goal of general system theory, as he stated it, was to develop "a framework of general theory to enable one specialist to catch relevant communications from others" (p. 4). So the economist might gain insight from the biologist, the biologist from the sociologist, the sociologist from the political scientist, the political scientist from the economist, and so on.

Boulding arranged eight levels of systems to facilitate discussion and research, and to point out that *systems are of greater or lesser degrees of complexity* (see Table 5-6). The value of this sort of typologizing is that it reminds us of the

TABLE 5-6. Boulding's Typology of System Levels

Level 1: Static. Boulding referred to this as the level of *frameworks.* This is the lowest systemic level, consisting of structural characteristics of crystals, atoms, molecules, and so forth. At this level the system theorist is, essentially, a cartographer.

Level 2: Clockworks. This is a level of simple, predictable, mechanical precision. It is the study of mechanics, physics, clocks, and machines.

Level 3: Control mechanisms. This level includes cybernetic systems with feedback structures, such as thermostats. This level differs from the mechanical level (level 2) in that these systems are regulated by feedback and rules of homeostasis at any given level, not simply the level determined by the chain or sequence of events.

Level 4: Open system. This is the "nonlife," simple, open system, demonstrated by such things as flames, cells, and rivers.

Level 5: Lower organisms. This level is characterized by simple differentiation or division of labor, such as is found in a plant. At this level there exist no elaborate sensory receptors or higher-level cognitive functions.

Level 6: Animals. At this level there is some rudimentary consciousness, more sophisticated sensory receptors, mobility, self-awareness, and a much greater increase in the amount of information taken in and processed.

Level 7: Human. Self-consciousness, self-reflexivity, temporal awareness, use of symbols.

Level 8: Symbolic systems. This is the level of language, mathematics, art, morals, roles within society, logic, and so forth.

complexity of the world and cautions us against drawing too many conclusions based on reasoning from lower levels of systemic development.

- *Do you see where organizations fit in Boulding's typology?*

Fred Emery and Eric Trist

Fred Emery and *Eric Trist* (1973) argued that attention must be given to both the technical and social aspects of systems. A system analysis is one of the interplay between the technical and human resources and processes necessary in the accomplishment of the organizational objective. This is the foundation of the open sociotechnical system concept, one which obtains its energy from outside itself, transforms that energy into usable materials, and gives some sort of output to the environment.

Environments, they wrote, are very complex, always changing. They identified four types. The first, *placid randomized,* is an ideal type of environment, a nonexistent end of a continuum, a theoretical limit that would represent the least turbulent, most stable environmental condition. Organizational survival in this sort of environment is not a matter of choice, for all choices are relatively equal. What the organization needs is available and plentiful. Vendors at a flea market and game booths on a fair midway are examples. Their customers will arrive, so their strategy is simply to accomplish the sale before the customer leaves.

The second type of environment, *placid clustered,* is described as a more "textured" environment, yet still placid. It is one in which the organization has a greater chance at predicting and anticipating (surviving), because advantageous and harmful components of the environment are relatively clustered together. These clusters make themselves known to the organization. The organization, then, to survive, must develop a strategy based upon the known characteristics of the environment. Because the environment is not so random, the organization can plan to maximize its opportunities. An example might be a decision to open a specialty sock store in a mall in which no such outlet exists. The customer traffic can be anticipated, but it would be difficult to predict what proportion of the traffic would be motivated to visit this specific store.

The third type of environment is labeled *disturbed reactive.* This is an environment characterized by overlapping but similar systems, hence, "the environment that is relevant to the survival of one is relevant to the survival of the other" (p. 49). This is a competitive environment in which the information known to one system may be known by the others, so strategies and tactics become much more complex. The actions and intentions of competing systems must be taken into account when formulating plans. However, in this type of environment, the environment as a whole is still considered fairly stable. This is the sort of environment that the K-Marts, Targets, Shopkos, and Wal-Marts of the world know well.

Finally, *turbulent* environments represent the most complexity. These are highly textured forms, characterized by changing dynamics of the systems within the environment, as well as changes in the environment itself. The microcomputer and electronics industries are often discussed this way. However, even more complexity is found, for example, in a forest area that has inadvertently been overcut, setting off a complex chain reaction in the ecosystem that was not anticipated. When the turbulence occurs in a human social system, the complexity is compounded. Environments are becoming increasingly complex as populations grow and demand more food, as demographic shifts occur, as military budgets grow out of proportion to their necessity, as the world grows smaller and increasingly relies on technology as its salvation, as industry pollutes the world for generations to come.

- *Do you understand the four types of environments and how they contribute to various degrees of organizational complexity?*

The above work helped establish the theoretical foundation for the more applied form of system theory—sociotechnical system analysis (STS). This is a highly complex form of organizational analysis that attempts to explain the interrelationships between the human and technical organization. According to Trist (1981; Ketchum & Trist, 1992), an STS analysis may look like the following:

1. An initial social and technical scanning is made of the target system.
2. All transformations that occur within the system are identified.
3. Key variances and their interrelations are identified.
4. A variance table is constructed to identify the degree to which the variances are controlled by the social system.
5. Social system members' perceptions are obtained regarding their roles and the forces that contribute to or constrain them in fulfilling these roles.
6. Neighboring systems, such as maintenance and support, are evaluated.
7. All boundary crossing systems (suppliers, customers, and so forth) are evaluated.
8. All assessments are considered in light of the overall managerial system of the organization.
9. The process culminates in design proposals.

An STS approach, then, is an effort to merge the social and technical aspects of the organization into a composite understanding of systemic complexity.

From an organization culture point of view, the sociotechnical system model of organization understanding is a mixed blessing. On the one hand, the explicit identification of subsystems, the acknowledgment of systemic diversity and interdependence, and the identification of systemic levels of complexity are all in sync with a cultural explanation of organizations. On the other hand, system analyses are aimed at finding causality and building sequential explanations for variances. This movement toward measurement and causality is reminiscent of the classical period of organizational design.

System analysis is identified by concepts such as system, wholeness, equi-finality, boundary, environment, levels, sociotechnical, organization as organism, cybernetics, feedback loops, causal chains, environmental turbulence, differentiation, and integration. Understanding the organismic culture, then, involves the portrayal of the organization as a unified though differentiated set of interdependent parts. Cultures come into being, grow and adapt to their environments, specialize, and die.

THE CULTURAL MODEL OF ORGANIZING: THE ORGANIZATION AS CULTURE

The organization culture model was presented in some detail in Chapters 2 and 3. What I'd like to do in this final section of Chapter 5 is highlight the different visions of culture that characterized the development of organization theory outlined in this chapter. Table 5-7 offers a review of the development of the organization culture model throughout the historical periods summarized earlier.

What is most obvious about the development of the cultural approach is that it is: (1) a culmination of a hundred years of thinking about organizations; (2) a reaction against those approaches that overmechanize and overcontrol the workplace; and (3) a large departure from the models that preceded it. This departure is primarily in the areas of organizational design, managerial control, and the role of communication.

Regarding design, a culture approach to organizations strongly suggests that formal design is of secondary importance to the actual communication of organization members. This attitude is in clear violation of the precepts of the machine, satisfaction, and systems metaphors, all of which revolve around the imposition and control of structure.

The culture metaphor suggests that structure is a symbolic act of communicating with another individual. So the formal structure may exist on paper but plays a limited role in actually dictating communication flow. The symbolic structure of the organization, the informal rules, roles, norms, the beliefs and assumptions and values of members, and their behavior play a much more crucial part in the overall organizational composition.

By this reasoning, then, those who design organizations face a difficult, two-part task. On the one hand, organizations must be designed for effectiveness and efficiency, with some degree of formalization. On the other hand, this formalization must not be understood as the only form of structure, nor as the most important. This formal design certainly influences the symbolic structure, but it is not the structure of greatest concern to the culture theorist.

Regarding managerial control, the culture theorist suggests that managers have limited control over most dimensions of the workers' lives. Again, this is in contradiction to the models that preceded the culture perspective. Workers

TABLE 5-7. The Development of the Organization Culture Vision of Organizing

Machine culture	Satisfaction culture	Teamwork culture	Organismic culture	Organization *as* culture
Classical period	Human relations period	Human resources period	Systems period	Culture period
1900– Present	1930s– Present	1960s– Present	1960s– Present	1980s– Present
Mechanical vision of workplace	Parent-child vision of workplace	Participatory vision of workplace	Interdependent subgroups vision of the workplace	Symbolic vision of the workplace
Culture imposed from the top down	Culture imposed from the top down	Top and bottom jointly create culture	Subcultural complexity a variable to be managed	Culture is what the organization is, not some-thing imposed
Identifiers such as division, efficiency, hierarchy, control, structure	Identifiers such as feelings, needs, esteem, benevolence, concern	Identifiers such as contributions, participation, enrichment, contingencies	Identifiers such as complexity, variables, interdependence, environments, feedback	Identifiers such as values, beliefs, symbols, subgroups, communities
Culture should be controlled.	Culture should be taught.	Culture can be developed and managed.	Culture is a variable to be controlled.	Culture can be described, probably not controlled.
Driven by desire for efficiency	Driven by desire for workplace harmony	Driven by the recognition of environmental complexity	Driven by the recognition of environmental complexity	Driven by the recognition of the importance of symbols

bring beliefs, feelings, attitudes, expectations, understandings, and so forth into the workplace with them. When there, they revise these understandings, enhance them, and reshape them, resulting in a composite portrayal of organization reality; a portrayal that makes good, sound, rational sense to the worker him- or herself.

How much of this process of sense making can management control? Probably not much. Management can shape the formal environment, but as already noted, that will probably have a limited impact on the sense-making activities within the workplace. Management can also try to shape the informal environment. It can develop mission statements, hold company picnics, and declare Fridays to be casual dress days, all in an attempt to shape the organization symbol systems. However, just as communication is not the product only of what the source intended, these attempts are destined to be interpreted by the organization members. And, if the members interpret them differently than management intended, then management's efforts at control may not only fail, but actually work against management.

As an example of one company's attempts to control the symbol systems of employees, consider the case of Specialty Publications (pseudonym for a real company in the United States), a major publisher of trade periodicals. Specialty had recently undergone hard economic times. The company was rife with rumors of takeover bids, layoffs, and division closings. Employee morale was low, and profits were declining.

In an effort to "fix things," upper management tried three symbolic things. First, it gave all full-time employees the option of taking Friday afternoons off (if they had worked their 40 hours already), and second, Fridays became casual dress days. These first two manipulations pleased the workers, on the whole, but had no impact on morale because they were perceived by the workers as inconsequential efforts to divert their attention from the real communication failures of the company.

So management turned to a third strategy for offsetting the rumors rampant among workers. It implemented something called the ECE (Employee Communications Expeditor) program. With this program, nineteen individuals were chosen by management to become ECEs. These individuals were to be fed "factual" information from top management and then were expected to spread the information among the workers. When asked why the managers just didn't write up the information in memo form, management responded that the workers distrusted memos, and that the grapevine was more trusted and a more used source of information in the company.

This attempt by management to control the informal employee symbol system failed dismally. Management forgot that it was management itself that was suspect, not the information being given in the memos. This program was seen as just another management initiative, and a devious one indeed, to control and manipulate the workers.

Regarding the role of communication, as highlighted above and throughout Chapters 2 and 3, a cultural approach to organizations makes the argument that organizations are communication events in and of themselves. Throughout the history of organization design, communication has been understood in a number of very similar ways. It has consistently been seen as a management tool for accomplishing its goals. In the machine metaphor, communication was used by upper management to create worker efficiency; in the satisfaction metaphor, communication was upper management's tool to satisfy workers' personal needs and thus increase efficiency; in the teamwork metaphor, communication was the technique of obtaining worker input, leading to enhanced productivity; in the organismic metaphor, communication was the device for accomplishing integration among the system's units, thereby increasing the operating efficiency of the organization as a whole.

However, with the cultural metaphor, communication is not a tool or a technique or a device to be used in these ways. The organization is a communication event in itself, to be described and interpreted and understood in its own right, not toward the goal of decreasing, increasing, or changing anything. Indeed, many suggest that even when understood, the culture as composed of the communication of members cannot be changed, short of replacing the workforce.

SUMMARY

In these last two chapters I have reviewed the development of formal organization theory. Beginning with the classical period—the machine metaphor—I highlighted some of the dominant writers and thinkers along with the overriding emphases of each successive period.

The classical period was developed around the potential of the industrial revolution and the machines that were driving the development of industry. The demands of theorists were to create a workforce out of people unaccustomed to factory life, develop an organizational structure that could facilitate efficiency, and develop a body of theory that was generalizable enough to be taught systematically.

The human relations period was developed around the misgivings of the classical period. It was thought that the scientific principles of the machine metaphor had overlooked the human needs of the workforce. This period of design, then, focused its attention on the worker as a person, on the assumption that a "fulfilled" worker was a productive worker.

The human resources period was developed around the inability to fully articulate and implement a human relations ideal. Managers as parents turned out to be an unworkable vision, and worker needs were retranslated into workplace needs. The new vision was one of job enrichment rather than personal enrichment.

The systems period was developed around the recognition of internal and external complexity. The organization was seen as complex and in need of integration, environments were viewed as ambiguous, demanding adaptation by the organization. What seemed clear in earlier times was now contingent. The organization was now almost too complex to understand.

The cultural period was developed around the recognition of the importance of symbols and the tendency of workers to develop their own interpretations of workplace reality. These interpretations determined how the workers acted and were largely out of the control of management. Organizations became understood as communication events, rather than being understood as containers within which communication happened.

PART TWO

Cultural Concerns

CHAPTER 6

Organization Cultures and Socialization Practices

Chapter Preview

Beginning with Chapter 6, this book now moves away from the theoretical, definitional, and historical focus of the first five chapters to examine a number of the most significant areas in which culture exerts its influence. We've already discussed the pervasive nature of culture, and in the remainder of this text we'll look specifically at culture's effects on socialization (Chapter 6), ethics (Chapter 7), communication networks (Chapter 8), politics and conflict (Chapter 9), gender and minority issues (Chapter 10), decision making (Chapter 11), and leadership (Chapter 12).

In this chapter we'll look at the important process of organizational socialization. Socialization commonly refers to the efforts of the organization to "teach the ropes" to the newcomer. This limited, one-directional perspective of socialization will be challenged here. In its place I will offer Meryl Reis Louis's conceptualization of an active newcomer, one who participates in creating the entry experience.

The importance of socialization will be discussed, noting that socialization efforts are necessary to create stable, consistent workforces that demonstrate the characteristics that the organization wants. Organizations put a lot of effort into socialization strategies and programs. However, too often organizations operate on the misguided assumption that their efforts to socialize are of primary importance in creating organizational citizens. The premise of this chapter is that the efforts of the newcomers to understand and interpret the organization are of equal or greater value in successful socialization.

From an organization culture point of view, socialization efforts by both the organization and the newcomer are crucial. Through its formal socialization efforts, the organization is presenting its value system to the newcomer. Through the organization's informal socialization efforts, subcultural values as well as inconsistencies in the stated overall value system are discovered. And as the newcomer participates in the socialization process, he or she is actually actively commenting on which values he or she will try to internalize.

The chapter opens with a discussion of the importance of socialization, noting that socialization is an active process that includes both the organization and the newcomer. The chapter then moves to the newcomer experience. In that section the popular "stage" representation of socialization will be contrasted with the more instructive model of active socialization advocated by Louis (1980a). We'll look at newcomers both as new hires and as individuals making career transitions, and we'll examine the impact of change.

The chapter then looks at socialization strategies. This is an important section because it highlights the organization's formal efforts to bring newcomers in. We'll also look at the selection interview, a formal strategy that too often goes unrecognized as a socialization tactic. The chapter then turns directly to the individual as active agent in socialization. This section also highlights the importance of mentoring in successful socialization efforts. The chapter ends with a discussion of the goals of socialization—commitment and identification—and how those goals differ. Once the differences are examined, however, it becomes clear that any formal socialization program must meet both goals. The chapter concludes with a discussion of the idea that socialization is a form of cultural reproduction that must be controlled by the organization, but that can only be controlled to a limited degree, given a recognition of the active role played by the newcomer.

Key Terms

socialization
functional dimension
hierarchical dimension
inclusion dimension
content knowledge
strategic knowledge
implicit knowledge
custodianship
content innovation
role innovation
anticipatory socialization
encounter period
metamorphosis
change
contrast

surprise
role
transition
career
career transition
newcomer
mentor
mentee
identification
common ground technique
antithesis technique
transcendent "we" technique
commitment
transorganizational pluralism

Before venturing any further into this chapter, you might want to reflect on some of your past experiences as a new person within a group—when you got a new job, when you came to college, when you joined a fraternity or sorority, or when you received a promotion at work. Try to recount your experiences, both pleasant and painful. What was it like to learn "the ropes"?

In preparation for this chapter I asked a few of my colleagues to recount some of their newcomer experiences. Here are a few of the things (as amazing as some of them sound) they experienced at various points in their careers.

Situation 1. "I had been a waitress and was now trying out a secretarial position. On my first day on the job I was trying to learn to do everything that would be expected of me. I did not know the proper protocol for even the simplest things, including answering the phone. So my supervisor was handling the phone calls. At the end of one she slammed down the receiver, picked up the phone book, and threw it at the three-level letter tray on my desk. She was angry. I was scared . . . I didn't know what to make of it."

Situation 2. "I was a new graduate student, on campus to accomplish my Master's Degree. On the first day of class I showed up five minutes early. Nobody was there, not a person in the entire lecture hall. I was worried that I had gotten the room wrong or did not understand the schedule. I was worried that I was being a 'dumb newcomer.' I went to the department office to inquire as to the whereabouts of my classmates, not to mention the professor. I learned then that the norm for the department was for classes to begin ten minutes late."

Situation 3. "I was working as a receptionist for a local manufacturing firm. On my first day at work the manager called me into his office to go over the budget for the year. He kept asking me questions like 'How much do you think we'll spend on electricity this year?' Obviously I had no idea, I'd only worked there for one morning. He kept me in there for three hours. I determined later that he just wanted someone to be with him, just to sit there and keep him company while he worked on the budget."

Situation 4. "My first day as a teacher there I was extremely nervous. I wanted to do a good job and make a good first impression on my students. I was new to the campus and so, other than as casual acquaintances, knew virtually nothing about my colleagues—what they were like, how they acted, how to befriend them. I went into my first class in the morning and found two of the men seated in the middle of the front row of the class, slouched down in their chairs in the 'pelvic thrust position.' I asked them if they were going to observe the class. Their response was, 'Yeah, teach us something.' I asked again if they intended to stay for the whole time. Their response was, 'Yeah, show us what you got.' I complained to the division head. His response was, 'Don't rock the boat.'"

Situation 5. "I had been hired as a clerk in a book store, responsible for shelving, dusting, handling customers, and so forth. The store was very small and the layout such that the buyer's (boss's) office was not visible from the middle of the floor because of the 'L' shape of the room. At that time our rules were that we got one 20-minute break for every 4 hours that we worked. Other than that time we were not allowed to sit down. On my first day of work I was feeling a little ill. The boss was nowhere to be seen, so I just sort of leaned/sat against a lower bookshelf. I hadn't relaxed for 10 seconds when I heard my name bellowed across the room by my boss: 'Get your butt off that bookcase.' It was only later that I learned that she had a system of three mirrors set up in her office so that she could observe the workers on the sales floor."

Everyone will experience being socialized "into" a group. Some will know the experience better than others, some will adapt better, some will seek it out more than others. The experience will come in many forms. To some it will be going off to college; for others it will be getting a first job. For some it will be going to prison; for others it will be changing careers. For some it will be accepting a promotion; for others it will be moving to a new culture.

The circumstances vary widely, but the socialization experience is the common denominator of each example. *Socialization* involves the formal and informal practices of bringing new members into a group and the efforts of the newcomer to make sense of the experience. The efforts of both the organization and the newcomer are explored throughout this chapter. To begin, we need to look specifically at why socialization is important.

- *What sort of "sense" was made by each of the newcomers in the experiences described at the beginning of the chapter?*

IMPORTANCE OF SOCIALIZATION

Work is more than just a job or a way to spend time. It represents a way of life, complete with rules, norms, values, roles, changes, and relationships. When new members enter organizations or members make significant changes within the organization, they are taught the way that life is to be conducted within that new environment. This presentation of lifestyle can be referred to as organizational socialization. This presentation, of course, can take many forms. But whatever form it takes, the result is intended to be the construction of an organization citizen capable of functioning within the confines and culture of the organization.

Socialization Requirements

Socialization programs are necessary to continue the organization's stability over the long run, by orienting newcomers to their expected roles (Van Maanen & Schein, 1979). These roles, with their corresponding requirements, revolve around three dimensions: the *functional dimension* (the tasks to be performed), the *hierarchical dimension* (the individual's rank within the organization), and the *inclusion dimension* (the social or interpersonal domain of the organization).

These three dimensions make up a model (Figure 6-1) of the organization that suggests that a socialization program must direct the newcomer to these three sets of requirements. They exist, essentially, as boundaries to be crossed by the individual in transition. Additionally, these roles call for content, strategic, and implicit knowledge. *Content knowledge* involves knowing what must get done; *strategic knowledge* involves knowing how to get things done; and *implicit knowledge* involves understanding the relative place of the role within the organizational system.

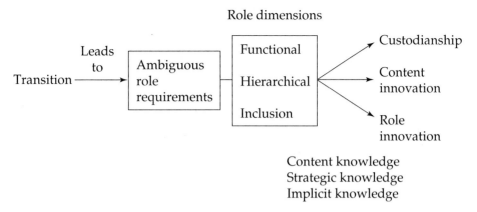

FIGURE 6-1. Creating the organization citizen

In response to the socialization attempts of the organization, according to Van Maanen and Schein, three forms of behavior are commonly adopted by the newcomer. The first is *custodianship,* which occurs when the newcomer simply accepts what he or she is given and performs according to the expectations expressed by the socialization agents. This is a passive stance by the newcomer and represents one end of a continuum. The second response, *content innovation,* occurs when the newcomer takes exception to some components of the role's content and works to change these parts. This is not tampering with the role requirements themselves, but with the content of the role. This is the middle of the continuum. The third response is *role innovation,* whereby attempts are made to reshape the entire role by rejecting most or all of the norms of that function. This is the most active stance by the newcomer and is at the end of the continuum opposite from custodianship.

Socialization, then, is an active process, composed of the behaviors of both the newcomer and the organization in its recruitment efforts. The importance of this process must be underscored. Without relying on any more terms, reflect for a moment upon what is happening here. Refer to Figure 6-1, and imagine that you have just graduated from college and taken an entry-level position in the sales department at a hypothetical company called CleanCo. You're the newest hire. You cover a territory that includes established clients in towns 80 miles away, as well as local clients. You travel about two days a week. Every morning is spent in the office making "cold calls," having sales meetings, and doing paperwork.

The description that I just gave you represents a list of *formal role requirements* in Figure 6-1. When you took the job you weren't sure what would be expected. After a brief time on the job these formal expectations are clearer and, let's assume, are acceptable to you. However, what if, on the first day in the office, your coworkers jokingly said that it was the new person's job to make the coffee and do a daily "doughnut run"? How would you respond? This is clearly not job related *(functional)*; yet, you might be willing to take on these tasks in order to be seen as a "good sport" *(inclusion)*, especially if you tend to think that the new people get stuck with all of the dirty jobs everywhere *(hierarchical)*.

So you decide to play along—to not rock the boat. You may believe that making the coffee is a small price to pay to be accepted into this group *(content and strategic knowledge)* and that you'll get your revenge on the next hire *(implicit knowledge)*. If you play along without questioning, your behavior is *custodianship*. *Content innovation* would happen if you agreed to make the coffee but not to get the doughnuts, or if you agreed to alternate with another person. With *role innovation* you would refuse altogether these informal role requirements.

From Figure 6-1, then, we can readily see the importance of socialization for both the organization and the newcomer. The results of successful socialization will profoundly affect the newcomer. They include understanding the workplace communication climate, demonstrating the preferred approaches to decision making, a degree of satisfaction with the work and one's coworkers, the ability to meet the demands of the role consistently, remaining a member of the organization, and becoming an innovative, cooperative member in the fulfillment of organizational objectives. Accomplishing these results, however, is tricky business, as we'll see later in this chapter.

- *Summarize Van Maanen and Schein's model, as well as the importance of effective socialization.*

The model and example also point out the complexity of socialization for both the organization and the employee. These two participants in the socialization process may have widely divergent goals in mind. The organization wants a cooperative citizen who identifies with its values and goals. The employee wants to be an individual—recognized as part of a team but rewarded for individual effort and initiative (Eisenberg & Goodall, 1993). The newcomer, then, faces quite a challenge in maintaining his or her identity while also participating in the process of organizational assimilation.

THE NEWCOMER EXPERIENCE

Just what is "the newcomer experience"? That is the question explored throughout this chapter. To help structure the presentation we'll open here by discussing the most common socialization model. After examining it, though, some rather severe problems will be noted. We'll then look at a more complete model of the newcomer experience, that of Meryl Reis Louis.

Stages of Socialization

The typical socialization process is portrayed as consisting of three stages or phases (Feldman, 1981; Jablin, 1982, 1987a): The first stage is *anticipatory socialization*, during which the potential employee forms expectations about what the job will be like, before actually getting the job. These expectations come from many sources, including family, acquaintances, and educational institutions. These sources tend to create inflated expectations about what life in organizations is like (Jablin, 1987a). The second stage is the *encounter period*, during which the newcomer's expectations are actually challenged by the working environment. The third stage is the *metamorphosis*, during which the employee adopts the expected values and norms of the work situation. It is important to note, as did Jablin (1982), that "regardless of the method of information exchange between applicant and employer . . . the typical outcome of this process is the emergence of inflated expectations by the recruit of what his or her potential job and organization will be like" (pp. 263–64). Thus, newcomers tend to enter their new jobs with unrealistically high expectations, making the challenges of the encounter period more harsh.

- *Summarize the three stages of the most common socialization model.*

Despite the simplicity and popularity of stage models, Louis (1980a) pointed out that the newcomer experience was more complex than stage models commonly portrayed. She focused her critique on the common conclusion drawn by stage theorists: that employee dissatisfaction with new work environments is primarily the result of unmet expectations accumulated during anticipatory socialization.

According to the stage model, the newcomer takes a new position but has unrealistic expectations. When these expectations are unmet, the result is voluntary turnover—withdrawal from the experience. Louis's criticism of this "turnover model" is that it is based on the presumption of rationality on the part of the newcomer and assumes that the newcomer enters the organization with certain expectations that, if met, will result in the newcomer's remaining. If these expectations are unmet, the newcomer leaves. Such expectations play only a small role in Louis's model.

Stage models, in emphasizing what the newcomer must absorb, overlook the active role that the newcomer plays in shaping the socialization experience him- or herself. They also downplay the significance of the cultural content—the values and belief systems that newcomers must understand to be fully integrated into the organization. Finally, much of the work from stage approaches has focused on identifiable behavior, rather than on the effect of the process on the individual at the cognitive level.

- *Summarize the "turnover" perspective of organizational socialization.*

Louis's Model of the Newcomer Experience

Louis (1980a) argued that newcomers initially experience change, contrast, and surprise as key features of the entry experience (see Figure 6-2). *Change* is understood as "an objective difference in a major feature between the new and old settings" (p. 235). The newcomer must adjust to the new situation. But this adjustment is not just passive absorption. It is, rather, the active identification of elements of the new environment that must be understood in order for the

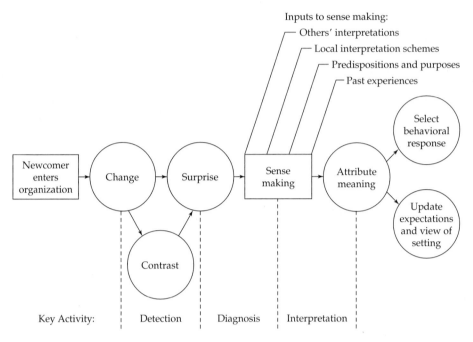

FIGURE 6-2. Louis's Model of newcomer sense making
(*Reprinted from "Surprise and Sense Making: What Newcomers Experience in Entering Unfamiliar Organizational Settings," by Meryl Reis Louis, published in* Administrative Science Quarterly, 25 *[June], p. 242, by permission of* Administrative Science Quarterly.)

newcomer to lower the amount of uncertainty inherent in the new position. This adjustment will be more or less difficult depending on the degree of difference between the old and new environments.

Contrast "is personally, rather than publicly, noticed and is not, for the most part, knowable in advance" (p. 236). Contrast is a degree of difference perceived between old and new ways, old and new situations. Thus, contrast will be specific to each individual, based on what the person holds as important. The person chooses elements of the new environment as different enough from the old environment to merit attention and, thus, adjustment. *Surprise* "represents a difference between an individual's anticipations and subsequent experiences in the new setting" (p. 237). Any dimension of a new work experience may be a source of surprise, and surprise may be positive or negative. Surprise may take the form of unmet conscious or subconscious expectations about the job or features of the job, unanticipated feelings about the work or the job, or the magnitude of cultural differences between the old and new. The point is, surprise requires adaptation. The individual must make sense of the surprise.

- *Define change, contrast, and surprise.*

The entry experience is a major source of personal disruption, filled with uncertainty and unpredictability. In an effort to make some sense of the situation, the newcomer will rely on four kinds of input: *others' interpretations* (this stresses the importance of insiders who will help the newcomer interpret uncertainty), *local interpretation schemes* (an interpretation of a situation by a member of the group, so that the interpretation is based on knowledge of the situation and other relevant information, rather than the newcomer's having to apply knowledge of other, perhaps quite different situations to the present one), *predispositions and purposes* (a person's personal characteristics and tendencies, such as how much accountability a person is generally willing to accept), and *past experiences* (drawing on similar situations from the past to help interpret the present). These sources of input, then, serve to clarify and thus lower the uncertainty of the experience. "Sense" is made.

Once sense is made, that is, once *meaning is attributed*, the newcomer must *select behavioral responses*, to determine how to act in accordance with the meaning developed and to determine if he or she has acted similarly in similar situations in the past. The newcomer may also need to *update expectations and view of setting*, if the meaning assigned calls for a reevaluation of initial expectations.

In short, Louis's model highlights the complexity of the newcomer experience. Becoming socialized into a new group is not the relatively straightforward process of being taught, learning, accepting, or leaving that might come to mind when thinking about it. It is the active process of coming to terms with the old and the new. The process is conducted by both the newcomer and the organization, both trying to tilt the result, if not in their favor, then at least toward maximum mutual benefit.

For example, consider the story told at the opening of this chapter by my colleague whose first teaching experience at a university found her facing two colleagues trying to use intimidation and power in some sort of odd, unfortunate "macho" attitude. My colleague's success in that organization had nothing to do with accepting that cultural component. Nor did she leave because her experiences did not meet her expectations. Rather, she negotiated her working circumstances until a balance was achieved that allowed her to work within that environment. Both she and the proponents of that attitude made changes. Clearly, in this case socialization was not one-directional. It was a joint process involving both organization and newcomer.

In terms of the model, my colleague experienced change as the difference between being a graduate student and being a faculty member. This change was not so great regarding teaching duties, though, as she had already taught for a number of years while obtaining her degrees. The contrast was greater than the amount of change. She had come from an environment in which people respected each other into one of hostility and derision. She brought the problem to the chair's attention, only to learn that he was part of the problem. She was surprised, to say the least. The behavior of her peers was unexpected and unwelcome. She quickly learned that she would have to adapt to an environment that was hostile to women.

My colleague sought the advice of other women in the department (others' interpretations), took stock of her personal desire to work there (predispositions and purposes), and looked at her own and others' past experience for guidance in dealing with this one. Once all the information was processed, and she realized that this experience was unique, she updated her expectations of working in that environment and adjusted her behavior accordingly.

A critical difference between Louis's approach and those of others to the questions of organizational socialization is that Louis does not overemphasize the "baggage" brought to the experience by the newcomer. This baggage (often referred to as the product of anticipatory socialization), including past experience, preconceived notions, and expectations, is important, but in itself is insufficient to explain why a newcomer survives or does not survive the entry experience.

Louis posits an active newcomer, someone who shapes the experience, rather than someone who simply responds and absorbs. Sense making is the active construction of the entry process. Individuals must go through such experiences many times in their lives. The next section explores this theme.

- *How does the vision of an active newcomer differ from that of a passive newcomer?*

Newcomer As Career Transitioner

It would be an error to assume too limited a definition of "newcomer." That label must apply equally to new hires, job changers, new students, individuals who have been promoted or demoted, and anyone who is making a significant change in "work" or "role" environment. Louis (1980b) used the term career transitioner to identify these varieties of types of newcomers. It is important to note that any type of career transition (CT), be it interrole or intrarole, is going to cause stress and expense for both the company and the individual. Understanding transitions can help reduce that expense.

At this point, four terms must be defined: role, transition, career, and newcomer. A *role* is a formal or informal position held by an individual, which carries with it certain expected behavior in light of the behavior of others. We all hold many roles, such as student, teacher, father, mother, and club president. We sometimes make dramatic role changes (interrole), such as the movement from student to full-time employee. More commonly, though, we make role revisions (intrarole), such as movement from high school to college student.

This movement can be referred to as a *transition*—simply, any change in one's roles. What is important to note is that a transition is a process without clearly identifiable beginnings and endings, in which the individual must resolve the tension between the old and emerging roles. Transitions are a common occurrence throughout one's life, as individuals progress through a career and move to new careers. A *career* should be understood as an extended period of role behavior (Louis, 1980b). So, just as attorney and doctor are careers, so are homemaker and student. A *career transition* (CT) is the passage from one role to another, such as when a student joins the full-time workforce, or when an employee joins the ranks of the retired. A CT is both an objective and a subjective role change. The amount of difference that is experienced between the old and new roles will influence how long the transition process takes. And, generally speaking, the greater the objective newness, the greater the subjective newness.

So, throughout one's life one can expect to be constantly faced with being a *newcomer*—an individual taking on an unfamiliar role. When faced with new circumstances, we tend to predict what the new roles will be like. When predictions are not realized, some cost is borne by the transitioner. These costs may be affective, such as frustration, sense of failure, and regret, and they may be objective, such as the cost of moving. Sense making, in Louis's model, is the process used by the transitioner to overcome the inconsistencies of unmet predictions.

- *Define role, transition, career, and newcomer.*

The career transitioner, then, should be understood in the same terms as the stereotypical newcomer. Career transitions result in degrees of change, surprise, and contrast that cause the transitioner to adopt any number of sense-making strategies. How the newcomer copes with the transition experience is of critical concern to the organization, for it affects the newcomer/transitioner's expectations (Jablin, 1984), satisfaction (Van Maanen & Katz, 1976), stress level, and overall effectiveness (Eisenberg & Goodall, 1993). Organizational strategies for facilitating socialization are the subject of the following section.

SOCIALIZATION STRATEGIES

To this point in the chapter we've seen the complexity of the newcomer experience and examined the importance of socialization. We'll now look at socialization strategies commonly used by organizations in their attempts to create good corporate citizens out of newcomers and transitioners; in other words, the efforts made (a reflection of culture) to create the cultures that the organization desires. After all, as Hess (1993) noted, newcomers cannot be expected to accept an organizational interpretation of reality if no composite reality is communicated to them. This summary begins by reviewing a seminal article by Van Maanen (1978), which concisely outlines some of the strategies organizations employ in their socialization efforts.

Definitionally, Van Maanen wrote that "organizational socialization or 'people processing' refers to the manner in which the experiences of people learning the ropes of a new organizational position, status, or role are structured for them by others within the organization" (p. 19). Strategies for people processing vary considerably both in their intent and in their results. The socialization strategies discussed by Van Maanen (see Table 6-1) differ in a number of critical ways and these differences go a long way in highlighting cultural variation among the socializing groups. When you read the descriptions below, think in terms of bringing newcomers into existing cultures. What will be the general advantages and disadvantages of each strategy?

Formal versus informal socialization refers to whether or not the socialization attempts are separated from the actual work environment. The formality level can greatly influence newcomer status. Van Maanen argued that formal processes prepare a status (level of importance), while informal strategies prepare a role. *Individual versus collective* socialization refers to whether members are socialized individually or collectively, in batches. With batch processing, members receive the same messages and commonly develop a sense of group identity.

Sequential versus nonsequential socialization refers to stages of socialization transition (sequential) versus nondiscrete stages, whereby individuals may be put into positions without an identifiable sequence. *Fixed versus variable* socialization refers to the level of certainty regarding the socialization and career progression timetable (that is, probationary employees tend to know the point at which they are off probationary status).

Tournament versus contest socialization refers to tracking (tournament) versus nontracking strategies, whereby the employee is given freedom to progress or move as his or her interests and abilities allow. *Serial versus disjunctive* socialization refers to the strategy of having the newcomer trained by the departing person (or the holder of a similar position—serial) versus the experience of taking a position without a predecessor available for training. Finally, *investiture versus divestiture* socialization refers to the degree to which the individual's past is valued (investiture) versus devalued (divestiture).

- *Define each of the socialization strategies discussed above.*

The socialization strategy chosen can have a profound effect on the ultimate goal: the integration of the newcomer and the organization. Each strategy, of course, calls for different tactics and aims at different newcomer needs and anticipated responses. Louis, Posner, and Powell (1983), for example, examined the relative effectiveness of various types of socialization strategies. In

TABLE 6-1. Organizational Socialization Strategies

1. Formal versus informal

2. Individual versus collective

3. Sequential versus nonsequential

4. Fixed versus variable

5. Tournament versus contest

6. Serial versus disjunctive

7. Investiture versus divestiture

Note: From Van Maanen (1978).

their poll of organizations, they found that the most common forms of socialization were formal on-site visits, buddy (mentor) relationships, off-site training sessions, socialization by other new recruits, socialization by secretarial and support staff, recreational activities, and daily interactions with coworkers. In a survey of new employees, the authors found that interactions with peers, senior coworkers, and supervisors were the most important socialization aids, the most important being interactions with peers. They found the on-site, formal orientation sessions were of tenuous value in successful socialization.

Zahrly and Tosi (1989) also examined the impact that specific forms of socialization had on newcomers. They argued that three components were common to all newcomers and could not be isolated: previous work experiences, the early experiences in the new setting, and personality characteristics. They found that a more formal mode of induction led to higher job satisfaction. The implication is that when organizations wish to create a given outcome in their workforce, their socialization strategy should not be left to chance. In this case, formal strategies wherein groups of newcomers were socialized together were effective in building job satisfaction.

- *Do you see the importance of having a socialization strategy?*

The Special Case of the Selection Interview

The one form of socialization that is common to all organizations is the selection interview. Unfortunately, for many organizations, as well as for many job candidates, the selection interview is overlooked as a significant form of socialization. However, the selection interview can play a critical role in the organization's overall socialization efforts. In the selection interview both the company (in the form of the interviewer) and the candidate get their first exposure to each other. So, even though the more "formal," official socialization may not occur until the person is actually hired, this interview serves as an important, early form of informal information sharing that may determine whether the formal process will even occur.

Jablin (1987a) reviewed the relevant literature and concluded that, unfortunately, the recruiter and applicant often leave the interview with contrasting understandings of the interview itself and of the potential work situation. Jablin's summary of that research, presented in Table 6-2, clearly highlights some important factors. First, the perceived credibility of the interviewer plays an important role in the interview's success. Second, the way the interview is structured and the types of questions asked are important. And third, although interviewee communication skills play an important role in the success of the interview, the interviews are often structured in such a way that the interviewer does most of the talking.

As a socialization device, then, the selection interview merits considerable attention by the organization. It offers the opportunity for early, interactive so-

TABLE 6-2. Selection Interview Research

1. Generally, applicants' interview outcome expectations (including likelihoods of accepting job offers) appear related to their perceptions of their recruiters as trustworthy, competent, composed, empathic, enthusiastic and well-organized communicators . . . .

2. Applicants do not particularly like or trust interviewers and appear hesitant to accept job offers if their only sources of information are recruiters; however, interviewers who are job incumbents are perceived as presenting more realistic job/organizational information than are interviewers who are personnel representatives . . . .

3. Interviewee satisfaction appears related to the quality and amount of organizational and job information the recruiter provides, the degree to which the recruiter asks the interviewee open-ended questions that are high in "face validity," and allows him or her sufficient talk time . . . .

4. Most questions applicants ask their interviewers are closed-ended, singular in form, typically not phrased in the first person, asked after interviewers ask applicants for inquiries, and seek job-related information . . . .

5. Applicants' perceptions of their interviewers as empathic listeners appear to be negatively related to the degree to which interviewers interject interruptive statements while the interviewees are speaking . . . .

6. Interviewees who display high versus low levels of nonverbal immediacy (operationalized by eye contact, smiling, posture, interpersonal distance, and body orientation) and are high in vocal activity tend to be favored by interviewers . . . .

7. Recruiters find interviewees more acceptable if they receive favorable information about them prior to or during their interviews; however, recruiters do not necessarily adopt confirmatory question strategies to validate their expectancies . . . .

8. Interviewers tend to employ inverted funnel question sequences (they begin with closed questions and then progress to more open-ended questions), thus limiting applicant talk time during the opening minutes of interviews . . . .

9. Interviewers tend to rate more highly and be more satisfied with applicants who talk more of the time in their interviews (though this talk is not necessarily in response to interviewers' questions), who elaborate on answers and whose discussion of topics more nearly matches interviewers' expectations . . . .

10. Applicant communication ability/competence (e.g., fluency of speech, composure, appropriateness of content, ability to express ideas in an organized fashion) is frequently reported by interviewers to be a critical factor in their decisions.

Note: From Jablin (1987a, pp. 691–92).

cialization between the recruit and the representative of the organization. How it is handled will be seen as a clear reflection of the organization by the recruit. And how the recruit conducts him- or herself may be the most important factor in determining whether or not he or she gets to become a newcomer.

- *What is the importance of the selection interview in organizational socialization?*

To this point in the chapter we've looked rather extensively at the organization side of the socialization coin. Let's now turn our attention more directly to the newcomer side.

THE INDIVIDUAL AS ACTIVE AGENT IN SOCIALIZATION

It is easy to view the individual as a passive participant in the socialization experience. After all, socialization appears to happen *to* the person; the newcomer is brought into the organization and the organization members teach the newcomer "the ropes." Gross (1975), for example, painted such a picture. He argued that newcomers are expected to develop a variety of skills in the process of socialization: technical skills (those mechanical skills necessary in the conduct of each specific job), tricks of the trade (labor- and time-saving tricks taught or picked up that help get the job done with less effort), and social skills (what it takes to get along in the informal power structure, the informal environment of the workplace).

Gross noted that beyond the acquisition of new skills, the result of socialization is a new self-image for the newcomer. The newcomer must learn to see him- or herself as a member of the organization. In short, then, the newcomer must shed the old self and adopt the image of the present. Part of that new image includes the values or ideology of the new organization.

Such portrayals of socialization make the process appear much more one-directional than it actually is. Louis (1990) did a nice job of pointing out the active role of the newcomer in the process. She argued that the newcomer experience is analogous to that of the ethnographic researcher (discussed in Chapter 3) in that both must experience new, strange work environments toward the goal of understanding the reality of the workplace from the point of view of the organizational members.

A realistic portrayal of socialization must present the newcomer as an active participant in the experience. Newcomers do not just assimilate the new organization framework; rather, they negotiate meanings with the other newcomers as well as with experienced members. This process of negotiating meanings is necessary for the individual to grow into the status of "competent group member."

So the newcomer must develop an awareness and appreciation of the normal way of doing and understanding things. Unfortunately, cultural knowledge is usually tacit and so is not likely to be explicitly taught. It therefore must be experienced to be understood. The newcomer must be attuned to the strangeness of the new environment to move away from a "thinking as usual" mode and into a more active stance of information processing (Louis & Sutton, 1991). Being a newcomer is not business as usual, and the person must be willing and able to adjust to the novelty of the situation in order to avoid relying too much on old cognitive maps that may result in interpretation errors.

Newcomers will be influenced primarily by three key socialization agents: peers (including other newcomers), supervisors, and mentors. Each of these groups contributes differently to the process and each brings different perspectives and offers different insights to which the newcomer will have to respond. Generally, peers offer insight into the daily life that the newcomer can expect. They also serve as models after which the newcomer is likely to pattern him- or herself. Supervisors offer insight into the formal organization, the distant, official point of view. A mentor's insight into the organization is less formal and gets at organizational values and visions, putting the organization into a historical context. (The importance of mentors will be discussed in the following section.) A fourth key source of acculturation is the customers and clients of the organization, particularly in the area of norms and values across organization lines.

Newcomers will progress through a series of "investigative roles" (Louis, 1990, p. 109) as they try to unravel the mystery of the organizational experience and their role in it. Many situational constraints will affect the newcomer's socialization strategy, including, the novelty of the situation and the amount of competing or overlapping subcultures, as well as the level of conflict between them. These will all increase the difficulty of the newcomer's socialization.

This view of socialization as two-way is, of course, consistent with the transactional perspective presented in Chapter 1 of this text. The one-way explanation portrays socialization as a linear process in which the individual is influenced by the structural configurations around him or her. The transactional view, on the other hand, treats socialization as two-way, holding that the individual shapes the sources that are reciprocally influencing him or her.

Recognizing this interplay between participants and context is important, for it reminds us that it is the individual and organization together that create situations that are challenging, threatening, inviting, rewarding, and so forth. Different individuals will have different strategies for dealing with what the organization serves up. These strategies will be based in large part on what the individual has experienced and what has worked or failed. Newcomers are likely to repeat previously successful coping strategies in new situations. So, it is individual differences more than situational differences that account for responses to socialization attempts.

- *What is meant by socialization being two-way instead of one-way?*

Of course, those newcomers fortunate enough to have a mentor working with them have many more opportunities for questioning and developing understanding. Mentors, as an important component in socialization, will be discussed next.

The Importance of Mentors

The vision of active newcomer stressed throughout this chapter is one of a new employee (or career transitioner) who participates in the construction of an overall interpretation of the working environment in which he or she finds him- or herself. One of the most important cocreators of this understanding, especially for women and minorities (Cunningham, 1992; Kalbfleisch & Davies, 1991), is a mentor. Indeed, participating in a mentor-mentee relationship may make the difference in keeping some new members from falling into the cracks of the organization and eventually leaving that company (Blank & Sindelar, 1992).

A *mentor* is an individual with some tenure in the organization who is willing to serve as advisor, friend, observer, giver of feedback, helper, teacher, sounding board, and encourager to a newer member. The *mentee* is the more junior member who is willing to be guided by the knowledge accumulated by the mentor. We should not assume from this description, however, that only the mentee benefits from the relationship. Kalbfleisch and Davies (1991) wrote that:

> Mentoring relationships bring encouragement, feedback, training, political guidance, interpersonal support, and visibility to the junior member of the relationship. . . . The senior member in the mentoring relationship also benefits through increased admiration, respect, possible workload support, and visibility in the institution. . . . In addition to benefiting the participants, mentoring relationships benefit the institution by maintaining commitment and enhancing the experience of its members. (p. 267)

Given the relative advantages of mentoring relationships, it would seem logical that they would be common in organizations. Unfortunately, such is not necessarily the case. Despite formal mentoring programs in such organizations as ATT, Johnson & Johnson, Federal Express, and the IRS, most mentoring is still informal and is dominated by white male to white male pairs.

Traditional hiring practices have created senior-level working environments conspicuously lacking the women and minority representatives who would be the likely candidates to act as mentors to new women and minority hires. These practices include filling positions by word of mouth, so that men who are part of the executive men's network get access to new jobs before those who are not members of the network; not holding senior executives accountable to affirmative action and equal opportunity hiring procedures; and not making career-building opportunities available to women and minorities early in their careers so that they can advance to the higher corporate levels (Cunningham, 1992, p. 21).

Without women and minorities in positions to offer themselves as mentors, the only option left is white males. There is nothing wrong with white males, of course, except that research shows that race plays an important role in the development of mentoring relationships. Kalbfleisch and Davies (1991), for example, found that for both the mentor and the mentee, race was the most significant factor in the development of a mentoring relationship. In other words, people of color wanted to mentor and be mentored by others like themselves.

There are many reasons mentees would want to be mentored by same-sex and same-race mentors. Society has created taboos or tensions around mixed-sex and mixed-race pairings. It also stands to reason that a woman, African-American, Hispanic, or any other racial or ethnic group member would understand the experiences and the organizational barriers they face better than even the most "sensitive" white male (Knouse, 1992). It is simply a fact that men don't experience life in the same terms as women; or whites as blacks; or Hispanics as Asians.

The mentor-mentee relationship is a winning combination for both the parties and for the organization, and is especially important for the success of women and minorities. Research consistently finds positive outcomes, including mentee perceptions of increased power, status, and greater access to important people (Fagenson, 1988). But the relationship must be one that is built on trust and respect. Organizations must work hard to create and encourage mentoring opportunities, and must promote women and minorities into senior-level positions in the company. By doing this, an organization can ensure that the mentoring relationship will become a significant component in socialization, a component that most likely will speak well for the company and will help retain newly hired or role-changing workers.

- *How might mentoring be seen as part of an organization's socialization program?*

THE GOALS OF SOCIALIZATION: COMMITMENT AND IDENTIFICATION

Commitment to and identification with the organization are two terms often used interchangeably in reference to the outcome of socialization (see Steers, 1977). However, it is not at all clear that the two concepts are the same. In this section I'll point out the subtle distinctions between commitment and identification, and show why both are necessary outcomes of the socialization efforts of organizations. It is important that we understand the value of separating the concepts.

In an important series of articles, Cheney (1983a, 1983b; Cheney & Tompkins, 1987) built a compelling case for the importance of identification in organizations and the differences between identification and commitment. Cheney's work is based on the writings of Kenneth Burke. According to Burke, identification is necessary for the individual in order to cope with highly abstract or ambiguous circumstances. The hierarchical nature of most organization structures, with their many ranks and roles, makes the individual uncertain what his or her identity is within the corporate structure.

Identification is necessary to give the organization member a meaningful relationship with the corporate "personality." This identification may take the form of group identification (for example, "Liberals don't support such policies"), or labels or titles (for example, "I'm a college professor," "I'm an IBMer"). Whatever form the identification takes, it serves to enhance the self-image of the individual by allowing that person to be affiliated with an identifiable unit.

Although the process of identification is personal—each person actively seeks the level of identification that he or she is willing to undergo—the organization also takes an active role in advocating identification. The organization's goal is to make the individual internalize the identification so that when he or she makes a decision or performs a certain task, that performance will automatically be what the organization would desire.

Cheney (1983a) outlined three identification strategies. The first, *common ground technique,* is found in attempts by the organization to convey to members that it shares their values and goals; the second, *antithesis technique,* occurs when the organization attempts to get its members to unite against a common enemy; and the third, the *transcendent "we" technique,* occurs through the use of the assumed "we" in communications.

Identification must be seen as a process rather than a product, whereby members link themselves to the value system of the organization. It is an important process because it opens the person to persuasion, as well as serving to anchor him or her within the organizational system.

- *What is organizational identification?*

Cheney and Tompkins (1987) also highlighted the distinction between identification and commitment. Identification refers to the development of "sameness" between individuals and groups. It is a process of symbol appropriation, whereby one entity (the individual or group) appropriates the symbols of the other entity.

Commitment, on the other hand, refers to an individual's pledge to conduct him- or herself in a certain way. Commitment is a rational expression for an individual, given a certain identification with a group. Identification and commitment are related; yet, while commitment narrows the focus of expression, identification highlights both the process and product of the individual-group relationship. Four relationships thus emerge: low commitment and identification, low commitment and high identification, high commitment and low identification, and high commitment and identification. Socialization efforts that aim at only commitment or identification are short-sighted. Strategies must be aimed at both.

- *What is the subtle difference between commitment and identification, and how are both important in organizational socialization efforts?*

Several studies have been conducted to further clarify this distinction between identification and commitment, including Allen and Meyer (1990), Buchanan (1974), Katz and Van Maanen (1977), O'Reilly and Chatman (1986), and Sass and Canary (1991). The results of these inquiries have consistently found a difference between the concepts.

A recent study by Bullis (1993b) offers us a fascinating look into just how complex the relationship between identification and commitment can be.

Bullis examined the question of whether organizations can be reasonably understood as single-value "containers," or whether they are more accurately understood as multivalued. The implications of these different perspectives are significant for our understanding of socialization.

If the organization is single-valued, the socialization effort will be aimed at getting newcomers to assimilate that value. As a multiple-valued context, the organization may attempt to bring members into a certain way of thinking and feeling, but those efforts may be made more difficult because newcomers may have well-developed value systems that they refuse to alter or relinquish just to work in that organization. In short, the multiple-value organization may have to settle for commitment rather than identification in its workers.

Bullis studied employees of the U.S. Forest Service, particularly the professional groups of foresters, engineers, and wildlife and fishery biologists. On the basis of the philosophy of *transorganizational pluralism,* Bullis wondered if the professional identification of each of these three groups would have given way to the overriding value system of the Forest Service. A transorganizational, pluralistic approach means, simply, that our value systems are formed by many groups and societal relationships, rather than by a sole or unified organization of which we become members. In short, the approach assumes that organizations, even those with theoretically "strong" or "unified" cultures, may actually be multicultural, based upon competing sets of values. The premises for decision making, then, come more from affiliations other than the primary organization.

Bullis found that, indeed, professional identity is a significant factor in the individual-organization relationship. Foresters were found to articulate values closest to the Forest Service's "ideal" set of values. Engineers articulated a vision of resource management that was more closely aligned to their previous professional training, while the biologists, as a group, articulated a vision that contradicted the "ideal."

Other than the obvious implication that the Forest Service is multicultural, in terms of this chapter Bullis's findings point out the importance of separating identification from commitment. The Forest Service will probably never succeed in getting its engineers and biologists to identify with its value system as strongly as do the foresters, because only the foresters will have been consistently trained in that way of thinking. The contrary values of the engineers and biologists will also have an impact on the Forest Service as an organization. Perhaps at some point, those values will replace the existing values.

SOCIALIZATION AND CULTURE

The position presented in this chapter is that anticipatory socialization plays an important, though commonly overstated role in the socialization of newcomers. The importance of what the individuals bring to the socialization experience lies in the degree to which it magnifies the degrees of change, contrast, and especially, surprise. The individuals' expectations are important, but focusing too heavily on them as the critical component of socialization diverts our attention from the active parts played by the individual and the organization in accomplishing the transition from newcomer to member.

This adjustment, organization to newcomer and newcomer to organization, is a deliberate process conducted toward a mutually agreed-upon goal: the creation of the organizational citizen. The stress of the transition is somewhat in the organization's control. How the organization deals with the stress is almost completely within its control. The type of citizen that the organization sets out to create is a question of the type of citizen that it wants. There is good reason to believe that organizations want citizens who are already like those it currently employs.

The Tendency toward Cultural Reproduction

Socialization can be understood as the strategic attempt by the organization to reproduce itself. The perpetuation of culture is easy to see: The existing culture is manifested in certain beliefs and behavior that become normative. Once commonplace, these beliefs and behavior become justifiable and are repeatedly justified in communications. The selection interview, as a form of cultural communication, has as one of its objectives the identification of individuals who demonstrate congruence with the existing culture. Those who show this congruence stand a good chance of being hired; those who do not will most likely be rejected.

As a socializing agent, the organization sets a variety of "traps" that both it and the newcomer should attempt to avoid (Sathe, 1985). The organization may oversell itself, making it seem too good for the recruit to pass up; it may seduce the recruit with flattery that goes beyond honest praise; it may jump to conclusions, making hiring decisions too early in the selection interview; and the interviewer's personal agenda should be of concern. Sometimes interviewers look for reasons to reject applicants, such as age, race, and sex, that should have no place in hiring procedures.

The recruit also controls part of the socialization process and is responsible for a variety of "traps" also. The most common trap is the tendency for recruits to oversell themselves. They might, for example, inflate their abilities beyond an honest portrayal, or collect job offers just to say that they were able to get them, or delude themselves, when the job search becomes discouraging, into thinking that alternatives are better than they really are.

Socialization, then, understood as the strategic integration of the newcomer and the organization, can be seen as the process whereby the organization, in concert with the newcomer, perpetuates the existing culture. The organization creates a system that excludes deviants, and the recruit, in an effort to get hired, behaves in a way that reinforces the image that the organization is putting forth.

The problems for the recruit and the newcomer are compounded by the fact that much of the cultural information necessary for the newcomer to make rational, informed decisions is tacit. It has to be inferred or actively uncovered.

Much of this tacit, normative information is hard to infer until the newcomer has been around long enough to understand what it is that he or she sees. Attempts at directly uncovering norms could easily be interpreted as suspicious in the recruit and naive in the newcomer. For example, a question about the "normal" working hours may be interpreted as showing an intention to get by with the minimum or as showing a fundamental lack of understanding of what it takes to "get the job done."

- *Do you understand the notion that socialization contributes to cultural reproduction?*

The most important point made in this chapter is that the newcomer plays an active role in socialization. Socialization is about cultural reproduction. But, when we see the newcomer as active instead of passive, the reproductive act can be seen as the process of negotiating meaning. Socialization can then become transactional, with the organization trying to establish a context for understanding, and the individual interpreting these messages in a way that makes the most sense for him or her.

The more that individuals identify with the existing culture, the purer the level of reproduction. But when newcomers and job changers reject certain cultural components, such as work-before-family expectations, harassment, or discrimination, the culture becomes available for modification by the newcomers.

SUMMARY

In this chapter we have looked at some of the complexity of the process of organizational socialization. The newcomer experience was discussed as being much more complex than traditional models indicated. Unitary stage models and turnover perspectives have too long given the impression that newcomers are passive recipients of socialization attempts.

Louis's (1980a) model was suggested as a more accurate picture of the socialization experience. In it, Louis suggested that newcomers experience surprise, change, and contrast, and in response, actively seek out information in order to make sense of the ambiguous situations in which they find themselves. In this model, the newcomer is an active participant in socialization.

"Newcomer" was discussed as a concept more far-reaching than the concept "new hire." A newcomer is anyone experiencing a career transition, making the newcomer experience a common event throughout individuals' lives. This makes understanding socialization all the more important. Portrayals of socialization as a simple, sequential series of acts was rejected in favor of more complex portrayals that included contributions by both the organization and the newcomer.

Socialization strategies were discussed, including an overview of research on the selection interview as a strategy. It was emphasized that the strategy will have a significant impact on the experience, for different strategies will tend to produce different results. The strategy must correspond with what the organization wants. The role of the individual as an agent in socialization was then considered. The active individual was seen as someone who affects the very process that is influencing him or her. This shaping takes the form of strategies for seeking information, as well as the inherent tendency of humans to filter information according to whatever perceptual biases they may have. Part of this active process is the use of mentors. Mentors were seen as part of an organization's overall socialization strategy and as an important part of the newcomer's repertoire.

The chapter also dealt with the goals of socialization: commitment and identification. It was argued that these two concepts are different goals, with identification the more overarching. Commitment is essentially behavioral, while identification is more of a psychological attachment that affects the decisions of the individual. Finally, the chapter dealt with the tendency of socialization attempts to serve the existing cultures. Through their socialization strategies, organization cultures tend to reproduce themselves, resulting in the acceptance of individuals who will not be different and rejection of those who are.

CHAPTER 7

Ethics and Organization Culture

Chapter Preview

In this chapter we will look at one of the most confounding of organizational issues: ethics. Throughout the chapter we'll face a variety of difficult questions, such as whether organizations can be understood as moral agents independent of the people who populate them, whether organizations have cultures with different sets of ethical parameters, making a general organizational stance on ethics impossible, and the ethical issues of sexual harassment, whistleblowing, and corporate social responsibility. As with the rest of the book, this chapter's focus will be presented in its relationship with culture.

The relationship between ethics and culture is difficult to specify, because, as we'll see throughout the chapter, in most respects they are the same thing. Ethical decisions, ethical parameters, ethical issues, are all culturally mediated. Like culture, ethics permeates all other organizational dimensions. Eisenberg and Goodall (1993) recognized this overlap. Their response was to insert "Ethics Boxes" into each chapter of their book, posing ethical questions raised by the chapters' topics. That was a good idea. What it sacrifices, though, is a detailed treatment of the complexity of ethics as an issue.

The approach that I've decided to take here is to devote a chapter to ethics. By doing so I hope to convey some of the depth of this difficult topic, while showing its interrelationship with culture at the same time. This chapter, then, like all of the chapters in this text, should be seen as an overlapping part of the whole vision, not as a separate organizational component.

The chapter progresses in a pretty straightforward fashion. I'll open with a variety of examples of potentially ethically questionable actions. These examples introduce the first major section of the chapter, on the importance of studying ethics. I'll then provide an overview of a number of approaches for defining and addressing ethics, followed by an examination of three of the most pressing ethical concerns from a communication and cultural perspective: sexual harassment, whistleblowing, and corporate social responsibility. Each of these issues strikes directly at questions of organization culture and the effect of culture on both internal and external ethical questions.

The chapter ends with a direct discussion of the overlapping of culture and ethics. We'll look at a perspective called narrative ethics to help account for why organization members behave as they do. We'll examine the controversies surrounding codes of conduct and look specifically at some of the organizational structural characteristics that may actually impede the development of a positive, healthy ethical environment.

Key Terms

nonrole acts	quid pro quo harassment
role failure	hostile working environment
role distortion	*Meritor* v. *Vinson*
role assertion	whistleblowing
ethics	corporate social responsibility
morals	homo narrans
sexual harassment	narrative ethics

Before venturing any further into this chapter, you might want to consider the following examples. In each case, ask yourself if, from your point of view, an ethical violation has occurred. Then ask, what does the example suggest about the organization?

Examples (media). (1) In *4-Wheel & Off Road* magazine (December 1980), an advertisement was run for a product line called "Brush Busters," a variety of "off-road accessories." This particular ad shows a smiling man, approximately 25 years old, leaning against a pickup truck, putting on his boots. The picture is framed through the spread legs of a woman. The framing features her crotch from about halfway up the zipper of her pants down to about midthigh. (2) The singing group Milli Vanilli won the Grammy for best new group in 1988. In 1991 they disclosed that it wasn't actually their voices on their albums and records. They were simply the faces; they mouthed the songs, which were sung by two other recording artists. (3) A 1988 Sears-Roebuck catalogue advertised a clothing line called "Disney Magic." The clothes were a sweatsuit-type material with a variety of Disney characters on them. The ad in question shows four little girls, between the ages of approximately 4 and 8. One girl is modeling a top and skirt outfit. The skirt, which in the picture comes down about halfway to the girl's knee, includes a black elastic suspender that hangs down from the waistband. The suspender clips to the hem, pulling the skirt up above midthigh. The description of the outfit reads, "Short and flirty skirt with ribbed yoke shirred to bottom. Black elastic suspender clips onto skirt hem for added interest."

Examples (politics). (1) In 1989, then-president Bush gave a speech about the drug problem in this country. During the speech he produced a bag of crack cocaine from behind his desk, describing it as one purchased by drug enforcement agents at a park across the street from the White House. As it turned out, though, the purchase was arranged after the president's speech had been written, to provide what the speechwriters felt would be a persuasive and exciting example. Agents arranged for a dealer, located at a school previously cited as drug-free by the White House, to meet them across from the White House. Not only did the 18-year-old dealer not know where the White House was, he thought that Ronald Reagan was still president. But he did show up, he did have the drug, and he was arrested in the first recorded crack sale in that park. (2) After receiving considerable public flak, Arne Carlson, governor of Minnesota, eliminated an advisory council in which individuals could become members and participate in quarterly meetings with the governor, in exchange for $5000 contributions to the governor's campaign account.

Examples (general organizational). (1) As a condition to their receiving financial aid and in line with the 1988 Anti-Drug-Abuse Act, most students throughout the country now have to sign a form certifying that they will not consume illegal drugs. (2) In 1991 the Minnesota Human Rights Department investigated the hiring procedures of the National Furniture Liquidators, Inc., of St. Paul. The company had given a newly hired African-American employee a "joke" application form that included a variety of racial slurs. (3) Any number of legal devices that are useful for invading the privacy of unsuspecting victims can now be purchased. These include wireless intercoms that, when placed in any electrical appliance, will transmit sounds, such as conversations, to receivers on the same electrical current; "spy" briefcases that allow the holder to take photographs by pressing a button in the handle; and infinity transmitters that, when attached to a telephone, turn that phone into a sound transmitter. The phone doesn't ring, but does become a microphone that picks up any sounds within 30 feet of it. (4) In 1991 it was reported that the United States ships 100,000 to 160,000 tons of toxic waste each year to other countries that have more relaxed dumping standards, with 75 to 90 percent of that total going to Canada. Also, in 1989 the United States exported $5 billion worth of tobacco products and $750 million worth of pesticides not approved by our government to countries with less rigorous standards.

There are no easy questions when studying ethics and no obvious answers. Despite those problems, however, ethics must still be discussed, especially in a book about organizations and communication. Ethics is, first and foremost, a communication issue. How we conduct ourselves in relationships of all kinds, personal as well as "business," always communicates something about us. Observers of our communication will make decisions about our character based on their assessments of the morality of our behavior.

The examples offered at the head of this chapter highlight the difficulty of ethics as a communication issue. We read the examples and, depending on our experiences and our attitudes, make decisions about the character of the offending agencies. However, we seem to use different criteria for judging each example. I might find the Sears-Roebuck advertisement using young children far more offensive than the truck accessories ad using the photo framed by the woman's legs. Or I might find the drug deal scripted for the George Bush speech less offensive than the shipping of hazardous waste into Canada.

The point is, our judgments about the companies and individuals in question will strongly shape our relationships with those companies and individuals. Intended and unintended communication happens. The meaning that results, in these cases, is bound up in the difficult issues of right versus wrong, good versus bad, just versus unjust, moral versus immoral. Given this significance, ethics is clearly an important focus of inquiry.

IMPORTANCE OF STUDYING ETHICS

There are many good reasons for examining ethics and organizations. Most of these, however, can be grouped under four headings: (1) the importance of ethics in the development of the organizational community; (2) the tendency to institutionalize ethics; (3) the ambiguity of legitimate behavior; and (4) the impact of organizations on the world.

Impact of Ethics on the Organizational Community

The central issue here was phrased by Deetz (1985), when he asked: *"If we innovate in this way, if we manage in this way, if we create this kind of product, what kind of people will we become?"* (p. 257; italics in the original). An organizational environment is often described as a complex composite of personal and situational forces, managed toward some goal, such as product development, family harmony, or profitability. Deetz asked about the result of this management effort. What will the organizational environment resemble in the absence of a focus on ethics?

The answer is that the organization would be a chaotic moral environment, composed of workers with differing and often contradictory senses of morality left to act in one another's best interests, but without a unified vision of "best." Organization practitioners and researchers alike have an obligation to discuss ethics because ethical behavior results in a type of community and a way of understanding life in the organization. To leave the formation of this community to chance would be foolhardy.

Each day the newspaper arrives it seems more and more as if unethical behavior has become the norm in organizational America. Authors such as Conrad (1993) and Eisenberg and Goodall (1993) have nicely pointed out this fact, as well as the difficulty of doing anything about it, especially when many organizations are structured in ways that actually reward, or at least encourage, unethical behavior.

The complexity of the moral environment of organizations was demonstrated in studies by Hegarty and Sims (1978, 1979) and Trevino and Youngblood (1990). Their basic question concerned whether unethical behavior was more the result of "bad apples" (unethical individuals) or "bad barrels" (unethical environments). The results (not surprisingly) showed that the moral environment of organizations is a combination of both. Unethical behavior was found to be more likely in individuals who were high Machiavellians (high need for control, willingness to use power and covert means of influence), while ethical behavior was more likely from individuals who felt that they were in control of their own behavior and those who were more highly morally developed. Situationally, competitive, financially bound contexts, especially those in which unethical behavior is rewarded, are more likely to produce unethical behavior, while situations that carry the threat of punishment and those governed by clear organizational policies regarding ethical conduct resulted in less unethical behavior.

The point of these studies was that if the moral environment of the organization were left to chance, the odds are good that it would decay to a level of conduct more unethical than would be seen in a more regulated moral environment. Our participation in organizations has a great impact on our lives. That moral impact can be positive or negative and is, to some degree, controllable by organizational members.

- *Why is talking about ethics important in terms of creating an overall ethical environment in the organization?*

This is not a small or insignificant point. *What is being suggested here is that within the organizational context, morality must be monitored and, to some degree, legislated.* This is a sad commentary, a cynical opinion that assumes that we cannot rely on individual integrity. Before you disagree too quickly, take another look at the examples at the beginning of this chapter, or read your newspaper or any magazine. Any examination will expose hypocrisy, half-truths, lies, cheating, misconduct, discrimination, and harassment in virtually all major societal institutions, including education, the church, the family, and industry.

On the other hand, attempts to legislate morality may be no less repugnant. A cultural standard of dishonesty, intolerance, or other forms of insensitivity may be the result of these attempts. One need only look at studies of student cheating, defense industry bilking, Wall Street insider trading, and legislative back-scratching to begin to see the depth of culturally ingrained immorality and the difficulty of doing anything about it.

Tendency to Institutionalize Ethics

Understanding intellectually that ethics should be talked about is one thing. Knowing when and how to discuss the subject is another matter altogether. The difficulty is compounded by the fact that ethics, as an act of communication, are amoral (Bradley, 1988). Ethics can be hard to talk about and understand because humans have the ability and often, it seems, the tendency to justify their behavior as legitimate given the "extenuating circumstances" that one faced. Thus, most behavior can be seen as ethical from one point of view or another.

This tendency must be curbed before individuals become full-time members of the workforce. Waiting until individuals are "formal" members of "formal" organizations and then confronting them with some "code of ethics" serves only to institutionalize ethics (George, 1988). If allowed to wrestle with questions of ethics at the college level, though, students may internalize ethical precepts and, thus, be predisposed to acting in ethically responsible ways when they gain employment beyond college. Ideally, of course, students at all grade levels will be exposed to questions that allow for the development of value clarification and the identification of ethical controversies.

Unfortunately, though many college students are being exposed to ethics courses, there is some reason to believe that the exposure is of limited value. Pamental (1989) argued that ethics courses must demonstrate the relationship between morality and business decisions. In order to accomplish this, three elements must exist: (1) The student must have some background in business, even if it is just a course or two, and some understanding of the business context; (2) the teacher must be competent in the area of business, so that the above relationship can be made clear, and so that relevant examples are available; and (3) case studies must be used.

On the basis of his study of the syllabi of ninety-nine business ethics courses, Pamental concluded that in 1989, business ethics courses were not meeting their challenges. They tended to be taught in philosophy departments, where, it may be presumed, the teachers are more experienced with ethical theory than with business practices. Though case studies tended to be used, the courses also tended to be taught at the freshman and sophomore levels, meaning that the students were less able to understand the complexity of the cases and will have had minimal if any exposure to business classes or experiences.

- *What does it mean to worry about institutionalizing ethics?*

Ambiguity of Legitimate Behavior

The third reason that ethics should be included in any discussion of communication and organizations is the ambiguity of legitimate behavior. In other words, within the organization (as well as within all communicative contexts) there simply exist few clear rules about what constitutes correct and incorrect behavior. Great insight into this issue was offered by Waters and Bird (1989). They argued that without a typology of unethical business practices, what is and is not ethical is often left to the statements of codes of ethics or CEO proclamations, which will often be too global to apply clearly to the many ethical issues faced each day by organization members.

Their typology identifies four types of unethical acts. The first are *nonrole acts*, in which the manager performs some behavior that is outside the manager's role. Such behavior might include embezzlement or stealing, acts that are directed against the firm. The second type are *role failure*. These acts are also directed against the firm, but consist of failure to perform the managerial role.

Examples of role-failure acts are inflating a poor performer's work record to make him or her look better to other organizations, or denying training opportunities to minorities.

The third type of unethical act is referred to as *role distortion*. These acts are performed for the firm in a distorted attempt to gain something for the company, usually to meet some organizationally mandated goal. Behavior such as bribery and price fixing would be examples. *Role assertion* is the fourth category. Such acts are also committed on behalf of the organization. They are cases in which public moral sentiment is vague, so the organization must assert its position. Examples include investing in South Africa or recalling potentially defective products.

Given this typology of unethical acts, the authors examined the focuses of management ethics in corporate codes of conduct. They found that nonrole and role-assertion behavior received the most attention in both codes of ethics and media attention to corporate ethical behavior. This was in contrast to the limited attention paid to role-failure and role-distortion acts, which are far more common in the day-to-day lives of organization members. Unfortunately, the standards for the two high-profile categories of conduct are often abstract and hard to apply at the everyday level of behavior. More attention must be paid, the authors argued, to the ethics of everyday behavior, for it is there that corporate ethics really lives.

- **Distinguish between nonrole, role-failure, role-distortion, and role-assertion acts.**

The Impact of Organizations on the World

The fourth reason that ethics should be talked about has to do with the impact of organizations on the world at large. It is not an overstatement to say that in a very real though hard-to-measure way, organizations shape the consciousness of every human being in the world. In western societies that impact might include the fact that most of us are born in a hospital, grow up in some sort of family environment, attend schools and churches, join clubs and teams, perform paid labor, and enter the full-time workforce. The effects of these experiences on human consciousness are impossible to fully estimate. Other effects, though, are more directly observable and available for comment.

The impact of organizations on the world economy is staggering. Yates (1991) reported that forty-seven of the top one hundred world economies are corporations, not countries. In other words, when measured by total revenues alone, in 1991 General Motors was the twentieth-largest country in the world. Ford was twenty-third, Exxon twenty-seventh, and IBM thirty-fourth. Such an enormous economic impact raises a host of ethical issues, including the politics of competition, plant and facility locations, influence on local and world markets, conflicts over incentives, wages, and hiring practices, power plays in where jobs are created and lost, and ethical concerns about how business is conducted.

The impact on the world, of course, is not important only during good economic times. In 1993, for example, IBM, Sears-Roebuck, Ford, and General Motors collectively lost about $17 billion. The resulting layoffs in these companies, and in their suppliers and related industries, will number in the hundreds of thousands. The total economic impact of the worldwide economic recession of the first years of the 1990s is not calculable, but is obviously enormous.

For four crucial reasons, then, ethics must be part of any organization-communication curriculum. The ethical conduct of the organization as a whole will affect the development of the internal community—the organization cultures—and, thus, the development of the individuals within the organization. Second, if "ethics" is left to the codes of conduct written to govern organization members' behavior, we might come to believe that ethics is relevant in a formal working domain only, but incidental in our everyday, away-from-work lives. Then too, these codes of conduct often fail to address the significant, everyday behavior that constitutes the majority of organizational events. Third, if we don't talk about ethics, we will continue to allow behavior to be seen as amoral—situationally right or wrong. Ethical ambiguity should be a significant cause for concern among organization members. And finally, the magnitude of the impact of organizations on the world community in both good and bad economic times mandates our attention. This impact, and the complexity of the internal and external ethical environments, can begin to be understood only when we clarify for ourselves our philosophical approach to ethics.

APPROACHING ETHICS

Issues of *ethics* focus on questions of values—degrees of right versus wrong, good versus bad, just versus unjust, in relation to others (Johannesen, 1975). This is as opposed to questions of *morals,* which are internal evaluations of right and wrong. Thus, we measure ourselves according to our own sense of morality; we measure others according to some social code of ethics. Ethical issues are, therefore, present in any social interaction.

- *Distinguish ethics from morals.*

There are a variety of approaches useful in studying ethics. Before actually commenting on them, however, we should remind ourselves why approaches to studying anything have value. An approach is a perspective. It allows us to frame both questions and answers; to reach conclusions that make sense to us. Whatever approach guides our inquiry will serve as the justification for the answers we give. For example, a cultural approach guides the presentation of material in this text. This means that both the questions and answers provided herein are biased toward a cultural orientation.

Regardless of the approach to ethics, the primary purpose of examining another's behavior is to draw evaluative conclusions. Johannesen (1975) offered the following guidelines for use in making ethical assessments, regardless of which specific perspective guides the inquiry:

1. Specifying exactly what ethical criteria, standards, or perspectives we are applying
2. Justifying the reasonableness and relevancy of these standards
3. Indicating in what respects the communication evaluated fails to measure up to the standards (p. 15)

So, for example, suppose I felt that the advertisement discussed at the beginning of this chapter—the one framed by the woman's legs—was unethical. I could strengthen the credibility of my assessment by stating that, first of all, women's bodies should not be dissected and then used to sell products, because, second, such a technique is demeaning to women. Because the advertisement in question does this, I can conclude that, according to my criteria, it is an unethical advertisement. Keep these criteria in mind when thinking about your own feelings concerning what is and is not ethical. To help guide your thinking, in Table 7-1 I've briefly summarized a variety of approaches useful in assessing ethics.

- *Take a moment and choose one of the opening examples that struck you as "unethical." Why did it hit you that way? Apply Johannesen's guidelines.*

Ethics and the Organizational Context

Whatever approach governs your understanding of ethics, ethics are basically about people, behavior, and situations. Organizing is also a combination of these three factors. Several researchers have made interesting inquiries into the relationship between individual character and organizational situations, and how the two intersect to result in "ethical" or "unethical" decisions. For example, Gellerman (1989) offered four conceivable explanations for why managers make patently unethical decisions. He noted that, given the long-term continuance of unethical, immoral, and illegal decision making, the explanation that all of the managers involved were simply immoral people makes little sense. What happens is that normal people get caught up in difficult situations and often make decisions that, in hindsight, they realize were bad. Unfortunately, "no one manages in retrospect" (p. 20). Gellerman put forth four rationalizations that often are offered as justifications for suspect behavior.

1. The behavior isn't really outside the limits of reasonableness.
2. The behavior is expected because it is in the organization's or the individual's best interests.
3. Nobody will ever find out, so the behavior is safe to perform.
4. The organization will approve of the behavior because the behavior helps the organization.

In contrast to those researchers who have tried to differentiate ethical and unethical behavior, fewer authors have offered specific recommendations for

TABLE 7-1. Approaches to Understanding Ethics

1. *Religious* perspective emphasizes the spiritual guidelines that govern the participants in the approach.

2. *Utilitarian* perspective advocates the course of action that accomplishes the most good for the most affected (while still considering and balancing the needs of minorities).

3. *Legal* approach simply measures behavior against the criteria of legality. That which is legal is ethical.

4. *Political* perspective measures behavior against the value system inherent within the ideology of the decision-makers. Values exist as desirable concepts, such as freedom and equality within democratic systems.

5. *Ontological* perspective measures communication against the criterion that it should enhance that which makes us uniquely human. Communication, then, should encourage our facility to think rationally, use symbols, and generate truthfulness, for example.

6. *Dialogical* perspective focuses on the attitudes that communicative participants have toward each other. These attitudes exist as a measure and a level of ethical commitment. Critical attitudes include genuineness, empathy, and unconditional positive regard (Johannesen, 1975, pp. 45–46).

7. *Situational* perspective focuses on the specific elements of the situation in order to determine what is and is not ethical. Thus, no predetermined criteria are allowed to apply across the board. Each situation must be evaluated according to its unique circumstances.

8. *Intuitionist* perspective argues that it is the intent of the source that determines the ethics of the situation. So, if a message source does not intend to deceive, the message is ethical.

what actual rights workers have within organizational systems. One such example is the work of Kreps (1990).

Kreps suggested that organizational members have the right to be treated ethically. Ethics, in this case, has to do with the communicative processes that characterize the organization. Kreps cited three principles for evaluating internal ethical organizational communication: members should be honest in their dealings with one another; members should not harm one another (physically or psychologically); and decisions should be made fairly, even though this may not be the same as equal treatment for all.

- *How does fairness differ from equality?*

External organizational communication ethics can be evaluated according to the principles of honesty (the information given must not purposely deceive), influence (organizations must not unduly restrict the ability of other organizations to engage in their own pursuits), and accountability (organizations are accountable to their stakeholders). Kreps suggested that the best way to ensure ethical practices was to establish clear ethical guidelines.

- *Summarize Kreps's principles for guiding internal and external ethics.*

In sum, each person needs to think long and hard about his or her approach to ethics. Humans have the capacity and the tendency to make quick decisions about the rightness and wrongness of others' behavior and character. We need to step back from these tendencies long enough to consider the following: (1) Do I use the same criteria to judge myself as I use to judge others? (2) Have I thought through the meaning and implications of the perspective that dominates my thinking about right and wrong? (3) What impact have my organizational affiliations had on my ethical outlook and my own behavior generally?

One place that organizations make a profound impact on us is in our conscious and unconscious beliefs about right and wrong. Our ability to justify our own behavior may in actuality be the result of organizational affiliations that we've internalized and no longer question. As noted earlier in this text, we are not simply the product of organizational designs, we actively shape our organizations. Thus, it would be hard to say that any given behavior is that of an individual or an organization alone. We must continually monitor our relationships with organizations to be sure that we're creating structures in sync with our own beliefs about right and wrong, just and unjust, moral and immoral.

The cultural implications of the first half of this chapter center on the metaphor of building. The issues raised thus far strongly suggest that individuals and organizations jointly construct the ethical environments that in turn affect the daily workings of both. Cultures are created by individuals trying to make sense of what's going on around them. Part of that sense-making process is reaching conclusions regarding right and wrong. Once the cultural foundation of rightness has been established, it will subtly influence future evaluations.

Because they are culturally ingrained, we must stop and evaluate our ethical points of view, to be sure that we're conducting ourselves in a fashion of which we approve. We must constantly question the sources of our values and be wary when we make judgments without thinking. We must always remember that, even though we are shaped by cultural influences, our behavior is part of the dialogue that creates and perpetuates the culture in the first place.

FOCUS ON ISSUES

In the next section of this chapter we're going to look briefly at three of the most critical ethical issues for the 1990s: sexual harassment, whistleblowing, and corporate social responsibility. The chapter will conclude with a discussion of culture as a reflection of a company's ethical environment.

The Problem of Sexual Harassment

Unfortunately, no one needs to look too long or too far to find an example of sexual harassment. The prevalence of the problem, of course, depends on how sexual harassment is defined (Lott, 1993). For our purposes, *sexual harassment* refers to situations in which one person persists in behaving in a way that offends the sexual morals of another or creates an expectation on the part of the harassed that his or her employment conditions are subject to change if the victim does not respond as the harasser desires. Harassment can also take the form of an overall working environment that is permeated with offensive behavior or materials. Sexual harassment may be physical or psychological, may occur between same- or different-sex individuals, may happen to both women and men, and is not a condition of hierarchical level.

In the fall of 1991, the country was able to observe firsthand just how difficult a subject sexual harassment is, especially when the harassment is psychological rather than physical. A University of Oklahoma law professor—Anita Hill—accused Supreme Court nominee Clarence Thomas of sexually harassing her when she was his law clerk some 10 years earlier. The accusations were played out on television while the case was conducted as a Senate investigative hearing over the course of a week. The "official" result was in favor of Judge Thomas. The "unofficial" result, however, was to bring the subject of sexual harassment into the homes of all Americans, with reverberations that included discussions, forums, publications, and consciousness raising across the world. In the winter of 1992, the discipline of Speech Communication opened the door of introspection by devoting a significant portion of one of its national journals to stories of sexual harassment experienced by professionals in the field (see Wood, 1992). This sort of action, especially at the national level, will encourage more reporting and research in the area of sexual harassment.

The issue of sexual harassment must be addressed, for the human costs of ignoring the issues are just too high, in terms of victim self-esteem, employer liability, employee morale, and productivity. If allowed to continue, ignored by the workplace generally, harassment will grow to the point that it will permeate a workplace in either real or perceived ways. *Harassment is about power and dominance,* and when these two issues become a wedge, a workplace may crumble and fall. At the heart of the matter, of course, is a basic question: "Why should anyone have to put up with such circumstances in the first place?"

There are two forms of harassment: *quid pro quo harassment,* or the sort of situation in which a supervisor gives some sort of favor to an employee in return for that subordinate meeting sexual demands, and a whole range of other, less obvious potentially harassing behavior that constitutes the vague category of *hostile working environment.* Such behavior might include staring, flirting, suggestive gestures, sexual remarks or jokes, hanging offensive calendars on the wall, brushing up against a potential victim, sexual propositions, and consensually agreed-upon sexual relationships. Regardless of the behavior, the key definitional variable is usually the term "unwanted." If the behavior is unwelcome to the recipient, it may be sexual harassment.

- *What is sexual harassment?*

Meritor v. Vinson

The landmark decision on what constitutes harassment was made in June 1986, when the Supreme Court decided the case of *Meritor* v. *Vinson* (Gilsdorf, 1990). Vinson had been an employee of Meritor Bank in Washington, D.C., and had originally filed the suit in 1978. The suit was filed on the basis of Title VII of the Civil Rights Act of 1964, which bars discrimination based on sex, religion, race, or national origin. The Equal Employment Opportunity Commission (EEOC), in 1980, when updating its policies regarding sex discrimination, declared that sexual harassment was a violation of Title VII. The Supreme Court referred to this reference by the EEOC in making its judgment in the *Vinson* case.

Vinson had worked for Meritor for four years. She had performed well, receiving a variety of merit-based promotions, eventually becoming branch manager. She was fired by her manager for what he described as abusing the sick leave policy (Vinson had requested indefinite sick leave). Vinson filed suit, claiming that she had been sexually harassed by Taylor over the course of four years. She claimed that she and Taylor had engaged in sexual relations over forty times, that he had raped her and exposed himself to her. Taylor claimed that no sex had occurred and that Vinson was provocative in both dress and talk. The suit was dismissed.

In 1985 the case was appealed, and the decision was reversed. The appeals court argued that Meritor, through its inaction, created a hostile working environment. The court also ruled that clothing and mannerisms did not serve as mitigating factors. The bank appealed to the Supreme Court and lost. The Court, however, declared that clothing and mannerisms might constitute mitigating factors.

- *Summarize the importance of Meritor v. Vinson.*

What Is and What Isn't Harassment?

What is and what is not harassment is the tough problem. Consider, for example, the following: touching nonintimate parts of a person's body, such as arms or shoulders; commenting on a person's morality; or claiming that a coworker received a promotion because he or she was intimate with the boss. Each of these examples might constitute part of a claim that a hostile environment exists. To what extent is consistency of behavior necessary? How much of a pattern of refusing is needed to constitute harassment?

To highlight the extreme complexity of this topic, consider the following:

> LaVigne (1993) reported that in Hennepin County court (Minneapolis, Minnesota), a harassment case was heard in which a female student filed against a male instructor. She had been harassed and had complained to three male administrators, who did nothing about it. The court found in favor of the woman, fined the harasser, and also fined the administrators more than the harasser himself.

Harassment in educational settings is far too common, especially between teachers and students. At some university-level institutions, codes of ethics have been adopted that actually bar romantic relationships between consenting students and teachers. The University of Minnesota takes a stance against teacher-student relationships, but falls short of barring them. It does state, however, that if a teacher and student engage in a romantic relationship that eventually breaks off, and the student then files a claim of harassment, the fact that their relationship was between consenting adults cannot be used by the teacher in his or her defense.

Schneider (1993) reported survey results compiled by the American Association of University Women, which found that 81 percent of eighth-through eleventh-grade boys and girls in this country report having been sexually harassed. Behavior included comments, jokes, touching, brushing in a sexual way, being "mooned," having clothes pulled, being the target of sexual graffiti, and being given unwanted pictures and notes.

Some courtroom battles are now being waged over the question of sexual harassment versus free speech. Croghan (1993) reported the case of Lois Robinson, who claimed that the pinups of naked women on the walls of the shipyard in which she worked constituted a hostile working environment. Robinson was represented by NOW's Legal Defense and Education Fund, and she won the case. However, the ACLU is now opposing the order in federal appeals court, arguing that the court should not be imposing overly general workplace restrictions that have the effect of stifling free speech. The ACLU argues that this is an issue to be decided by the workplace, not the courts.

Adding to the complexity of the issue is the uncertainty of what causes sexual harassment. Gilsdorf (1990) suggested that the abuse of power may be more a function of confusion than the deliberate acts of bad people. The causes of this confusion might be uncertainty concerning how men and women are supposed to act on the job, gender-based expectations, and misunderstandings about nonverbal male and female behavior. *But, whether confusion exists or not, harassment is, at its most basic, about power* (Ford & McLaughlin, 1988; Stringer et al., 1990).

- *Why can we argue that sexual harassment is mostly about power?*

Powell (1983) argued that definitional variation in studies, as well as on the part of receivers of potentially harassing behavior, serves to cloud the issue of when harassment is or is not occurring. Powell surveyed women from six New England organizations, allowing them to use their own definitions of harassment, rather than having them judge behavior according to the parameters of a researcher's definition. His results showed that 50 percent of the women surveyed had been harassed according to their own definitions. Seven types of behavior were identified as sexually harassing to greater or lesser degrees. In descending order (and with indications of the percentages of women who identified the behavior as harassment), they were: sexual propositions (81 percent), touching, grabbing, or brushing (69 percent), sexual remarks (51 percent), suggestive gestures (46 percent), sexual relations (46 percent), flirting (8 percent), and staring (7 percent).

Stopping Harassment from Occurring

The point is, despite the efforts at understanding harassment and stopping it from taking place, it still is occurring and affecting the lives of thousands of women and men. For many of these workers, the effects of harassment are devastating. To give some insight into the forms that this injury can take, I encourage you to read Case Studies 7-1 and 7-2. The stories of Carol Flower and Cheryl Turner will help put a face on what it feels like to be the victim of harassment.

Many researchers have offered suggestions for both the company and the victim to battle sexual harassment in the workplace. Some of those suggestions are listed in Table 7-2. After reviewing the table you will see much of the difficulty and controversy surrounding this whole issue. Researchers, like the legal system, are simply undecided about what distinguishes harassment from nonharassment, who is responsible, what is appropriate action, and what is the appropriate domain for organizational regulation.

Case 7-1:   The Case of Carol Flower

Carol Flower was a K-Mart discount store appliance department manager when, in 1983, she quit and filed a multi-million-dollar suit against the chain, claiming that she had been subjected to sexual advances as well as a hostile working environment. She accused her coworkers of making humiliating sexual remarks about her; her supervisor of imitating oral sex in front of her, propositioning her, commenting about her body, including her breasts and buttocks, and remarking at one point: "and this was hardly the worst of his remarks . . . 'You know Flower, I wonder what it would be like to screw you—whether it would be loose or tight'" (p. 54). Flower even walked into the employee lounge one day to find coworkers making a copy of an "X-rated" movie. Flower's appeals to upper management for remedy were ignored. She filed suit and, after four years in court, K-Mart was fined a total of $3.25 million. The case was appealed and settled out of court for an undisclosed amount.

The report of this case is basically straightforward and factual. One woman believed that she should not have to put up with the conditions of her surroundings and employment. No mention is made in the report of employment discrimination, inappropriate touching, or psychological harm. Ask yourself, then, where is the harassment? What should a working environment look like? What rights do employees have in their working surroundings? Should the company have been held liable, or just the individuals who performed the actions?

Note: This case was reported by Paige-Royer, M. (1987). Attention K-Mart managers. *Corporate Report Minnesota, 18* (10), 53–56.

Case 7-2:   *The Case of Cheryl Turner*

Cheryl Turner, at the time this report was printed, was working for $5.25 an hour as a clerk in a convenience store, a far cry from the $31,000 per year salary that she drew as a Minnesota State Trooper. Turner quit the force in 1988 after enduring years of harassment that ended with her having a nervous breakdown. Leading up to the breakdown, she suffered severe weight loss, difficulty eating and sleeping, confusion, anger, aggression, and self-doubt. Since she quit, Turner has endured the accusations of other troopers as well as opposing attorneys, flashbacks, nightmares, irritability, nausea, and shame, not to mention a $23,000 yearly pay cut. Turner was awarded a $200,000 settlement, but as of the printing of the report, she had not yet received any of the money. The amount is considered low by most standards, but represents the maximum that Minnesota law allowed for state employees.

An itemization of the causes of all this pain would include the following (accusations by Turner in her suit): a photo of a naked women in bondage, hung on the departmental bulletin board, with Turner's name written in at the bottom; a birthday sign posted at a gas station along Turner's route saying "Happy B Day! . . . T.T.T.T."—the four T's stood for "tiny tits trooper Turner"; explicit sex and nudity magazines strewn about the lounge areas of the sta-

tion house; continual references to women as whores, sluts, and bitches; "joke" essays such as "Why Beer Is Better than Women"; and "joke" slogans, such as a poster that read "Police Officers Like Big Busts." Additionally, Turner accused some of her male colleagues of making advances toward her.

Turner contended that about half the officers she worked with condoned such things. She argued that they cumulatively added up to a work environment that was nothing short of destructive. Her claim was that it caused her to question her own values and sense of propriety. Many of her coworkers accused her of being thin-skinned—if she wanted to make it as a trooper, she needed to play the game the "trooper way."

Again, as with the Flower case, we have a situation in which no touching has occurred. Here is one person who claims to have suffered psychological harm from being subjected to a certain working environment. Ask yourself again, where is the harassment? What should a working environment look like? What rights do employees have in their working surroundings? Should the state have been held liable, or just the individuals who performed the actions?

Note: This case was reported by McCarthy, K. (1991). Recovering from harassment. *Minnesota Monthly, 25*(8), 28–31; 88–91.

- *What are some recommendations for preventing harassment from occurring?*

Sexual harassment is one of the most pressing ethical issues of the 1990s. It is pervasive, easy to see, easy to find, and easy to define. Yet it is a complex and almost unmanageable legal concept. What is and is not harassment so often comes down to one person's word against another that the subject itself is minimized—its effects are overlooked in the hoopla over proof and legality and settlements.

TABLE 7-2. Stopping Harassment: Suggestions for Both Company and Victim

COMPANY ACTIONS

According to Bahls (1988):

1. Make a strong written statement against sexual harassment (should include a policy against dating).
2. Take complaints seriously.
3. Monitor the workplace.
4. Conduct exit interviews to determine why employees are quitting and if there is any hint that harassment is taking place.

According to Powell (1983):

1. Interviews should be conducted with both the accused and the accuser.
2. Personnel files should be checked to establish if a history of animosity exists between these parties.
3. The severity of the offense should be assessed.
4. The firm should make certain the offense occurred.
5. Appropriate action should be taken in light of the findings of the investigative steps described above.

VICTIM ACTIONS

According to Bahls (1988):

1. Act professional at all times (avoid flirting).
2. Give firm rejections in harassing situations.
3. Promptly report any harassing that does occur.
4. Keep a written record of all harassment.
5. Seek legal counsel if termination does appear sex-related.
6. Be prepared for a long, difficult process in following through with a harassment suit.

According to Terpstra and Baker (1989), who surveyed a population of undergraduate male and female business students to determine the range of reactions to sexual harassment:

1. Quit or transfer out of the area.
2. Report the behavior to some external agency such as the police or EEOC.
3. Report the behavior to some internal official.
4. Hit, kick, move the violator's hand, or physically retaliate in some way.
5. Alter the dress or environment in which the violations occurred.
6. Verbally attack or threaten, embarrass, or abuse the violator.
7. Ask the violator to stop, or explain why the behavior is offensive.
8. Ignore the behavior.

TABLE 7-2. *(Continued)*

9. Avoid the person or the area.

10. Other reactions, including being flattered, giving in, and enlist help.

Of these reactions (which were suggestions of what the person might do, rather than actual instances of what the person had done), three accounted for 60 percent of the responses: positive verbal confrontation (asking the violator to stop), internal reporting, and ignoring or doing nothing.

But the complexity of the subject cannot be a reason for disregarding it. Academia, the workplace, and society as a whole must come to terms with this insidious problem. Cultural allowances for power, dominance, and abuse cannot be allowed to control the workplace. Workers, students, kids on buses, and others should not have to put up with hostility and degradation; such things are not part of any job description.

A cultural analysis of sexual harassment centers on two primary domains: power and discourse. As noted above, harassment is primarily about power and control of one over another. A culture of power will inevitably subject some, usually women in the workplace, to the control of others. Steps must be taken to control the workplace value and belief systems so that sexual harassment is not allowed to be part of the everyday environment.

I doubt that anyone would disagree with the above statement. Perhaps more difficult to embrace is the cultural interpretation of harassment as the jointly created dialogue of men and women, abuser and victim, in the workplace. In short, how the victim responds may be part of the process that allows the abuse to continue.

This is not victim blaming. It is the recognition of the reality that organizations are often power hierarchies with men at the top. If harassment occurs, and the response by victims or onlookers is avoidance, trivialization, acceptance, silence, or other such responses, then the victims and onlookers are contributing to the oppressive dialogue (Clair, 1993).

Whistleblowing

Like sexual harassment, whistleblowing is a complicated ethical issue. The complexity of the issue is suggested in a listing of just some of the hard questions that surround the subject: "Does whistleblowing include internal disclosures of wrongdoing, or just external disclosures?" "Should there be legal protection for corporate whistleblowers, those who work in private industry?" "If organizations encourage the internal disclosure of controversial practices and policies, are they also encouraging their external disclosures?" "Is there a qualitative difference between disclosures of ethical misdemeanors and disclosures of illegal conduct?" We can't begin to answer the complex questions in this section, but we can take a look at some of the general issues and at the conclusions that have been drawn from this interesting and controversial area of research.

Whistleblowing refers to the disclosure of illegal or somehow illegitimate (unethical, immoral) business practices to individuals who can make a difference given knowledge of the incident(s) (Barnett, 1992). This definition includes disclosure to individuals who are internal to the business, in contrast to many others that prefer to define whistleblowing as an activity that exposes internal corruption to external audiences (see Stewart, 1980). Despite the definitional variation, though, researchers do seem to agree on three general areas: the process that whistleblowers go through in performing this behavior, the generally consistent attitudes that employees seem to hold about whistleblowing, and certain organizational characteristics that seem to predispose employees to whistleblowing.

- *What difference does the definitional distinction between whistleblowing to internal and whistleblowing to external sources make?*

In a seminal article on the subject, Stewart (1980) reported the results of her examination of fifty-one whistleblowing incidents. In this examination she was able to identify the most common order of steps taken by whistleblowers. In pure whistleblowing incidents, those in which the whistleblower was an active employee, rather than a former employee, during the whistleblowing process, the following order was followed 92 percent of the time, with the remaining examples showing the same behaviors, but in a different order.

First, the whistleblower becomes aware of the product or behavior that he or she feels is a danger to the public. Second, those concerns are shared with immediate superiors, but the whistleblower perceives that no action will be taken. Third, the whistleblower takes the concerns higher up, but has the same sense that no action will follow. Fourth, the whistleblower takes the concerns to a regulatory agency or to the public. Fifth, the whistleblower is ostracized by superiors. And, finally, the whistleblower is forced to resign or is expelled.

- *What is the general process followed by whistleblowers?*

Given the pervasiveness of this process, we might ask what employee perceptions of whistleblowing are. Callahan and Collins (1992) compactly summarized findings in this area. They reported that employees generally feel that there exists a "correct" hierarchy for reporting potentially unethical or illegal practices. They should be reported first to internal agents, then to law enforcement agencies, and only last to the media. Employees also support legal protection for whistleblowers, and this support was found at both managerial and nonmanagerial levels. Finally, employees report that a general fear of losing one's job is a significant deterrent to blowing the whistle.

- *Why would employee attitudes about whistleblowing be important to consider when developing a process to deal with such behavior?*

We can see, then, that the process followed by whistleblowers and employee perceptions of whistleblowing appear to be in sync. We can now look at organizational characteristics that might prompt whistleblowing. In a study of 240 companies nationwide, Barnett (1992) found that larger, unionized manufacturing companies may be more vulnerable to whistleblowing than their counterparts. Size becomes a factor because of increased bureaucratization that may make upward communication more difficult, prompting employees to go outside the organization to air problems. Unionization may play a role because the circumstances that prompt the presence of the union in the first place, such as unsafe working conditions found in many manufacturing organizational sites, may continue to exist after the union is in place, prompting reporting to such agencies as the Occupational Safety and Health Administration and the Equal Employment Opportunity Commission.

To offset the problems of whistleblowing, organizations will have to take steps to eliminate the conditions that prompt the whistleblower's behavior in the first place. This usually will mean much more deliberate and aggressive steps to ensure that employees at all levels are able to communicate their concerns to higher levels and be confident that those concerns will not be regarded as insignificant. Organizations must also understand that employees want protection for whistleblowers. Workers should not have to fear for their jobs just because they're exercising their consciences.

Whistleblowing, then, is a difficult organizational communication and cultural issue. How to ensure, even encourage healthy internal dissent and reporting of questionable activities and to protect employees' right to dissent, while at the same time not creating an atmosphere that encourages the needless reporting of insignificant disagreements with policy, and ensuring that dissent is not prompted primarily by the whistleblower's efforts to boost his or her ego, all increase the complexity of this action.

- *Why is whistleblowing a complicated cultural issue?*

Organizations must promote cultural expectations of openness and honesty. Employees must believe that they will be heard and their concerns will be addressed. They should not have to fear for their jobs because they have uncovered something that the organization would like to keep hidden. But the only way that this will happen is if organizations conduct their affairs honestly and ethically in the first place.

Ethics and Corporate Social Responsibility

Along with sexual harassment and whistleblowing, corporate social responsibility ranks as a third significant ethical issue that reflects the organization's culture. *Corporate social responsibility* (CSR) refers to how the organization treats its external environment. Like harassment and whistleblowing, social responsibility is a complex issue with many hard questions and few clear answers.

In the early twentieth century organizations were asked simply to contribute to the wealth of society, but they are now being asked increasingly to contribute to the social development of society (Dunham & Pierce, 1989).

These contributions may take many forms, including donating to the arts, investing in local economies, locating plants in high crime areas, avoiding certain world locations, and hiring emotionally or developmentally challenged individuals.

Although it would seem social responsibility would be self-evident, the issue is not nearly so clear-cut. Many argue that such a stance is actually a hindrance to the ultimate goal of social good and human growth (see Freeman & Liedtka, 1991). Andrews (1989) summarized the traditional argument against CSR as centering on the matter-of-fact contention that the organization's primary goal should be to maximize profit. If this is done in a nondeceptive, open way, in a free society, the corporate environment will police itself and society as a whole will prosper. Competition itself will regulate the corporate environment. Additionally, business people have little experience with social issues, they have their competitors to worry about, and it may actually be a violation of an individual manager's freedom of choice to force that individual to support social programs that his or her managers support. Table 7-3 outlines some of the arguments for and against social responsibility.

- *What arguments can be made both for and against CSR?*

Clearly, the majority of writers (see Andrews, 1989; Carroll, 1978; Fimbel & Burstein, 1990; Goodpaster, 1989; Mathews, 1988) argue that organizations do carry a level of responsibility to society at large. In these writings, two seminal issues are raised: How will an internal moral environment be created that will allow organizations to play the role of moral agent to the outside community? And where should organizations target their influence?

Nicotera and Cushman (1992) went a long way toward helping us understand the relationship between the organization's internal moral environment and its external ethical requirements. They argued from the perspective that organizations must be understood as actors, that is, as rational agents who behave in ways that can be evaluated as relatively moral or immoral. Organizations are ends-driven actors whose conduct is governed by the rule system (values) in place.

In their effort to construct a basis for evaluating an organization's moral and ethical actions, Nicotera and Cushman argued that these decisions should be based on two criteria: the extent to which the organization is true to its internal value system (culture) and the extent to which it conforms to the value system of the culture external to it (the national value system). They wrote: "Since the organization is a citizen of a culture, the organizational value system must uphold the national culture's value system before it can be used to judge the ethics of the organization's actions" (p. 440).

This perspective has obvious implications for multinational corporations. The operating assumption is that an evaluation of an organization's ethics must confront two guidelines: (1) Is the organization's behavior consistent with the organization's stated value system? (2) Is the organization's behavior consistent with the value system of the culture in which the organization is lo-

TABLE 7-3. Arguments for and Against Socially Responsible Organizations

FOR

1. It will balance corporate power with corporate responsibility.

2. Forced government regulation may be avoided with voluntary social responsibility.

3. The public will look approvingly upon those corporations that behave in this manner and, thus, contribute to the success of the organizations.

4. By conducting itself in these ways, the organization can help society solve its problems.

5. Social problems, such as pollution, that organizations tend to create can be dealt with by the organizations themselves.

6. Organizations tend to have the resources to deal with big problems.

7. Organizations are morally obliged to help society.

AGAINST

1. The costs of such behavior will lower a company's revenues, making its products more expensive for the consumer.

2. A company that bears more than its share of socially responsible conduct may be disadvantaged competitively against other companies.

3. The costs of social responsibility may take the form of lower wages, lower dividends, and higher prices.

4. Accepting social responsibility may confuse organization members about what the organization's primary goals are.

5. Accepting social responsibility may actually increase an organization's power.

6. Responsibility for social problems lies with individuals, not with corporations.

7. People who run corporations are not trained to solve societal problems.

Note: From Dunham and Pierce, 1989, pp. 108–11.

cated? The internal organization value system must not contradict the external cultural standards. An organization's ethics can only be judged according to its internal standard of right and wrong, but those internal standards must not violate the external standards, for if they do, the organization's actions will be judged unethical.

The authors reported two case studies—of GE and IBM—and their actions regarding plant closings, organizational downsizing, and protection of employees. They argued that, even though the two companies behaved quite differently—GE was aggressive, competitive, seemingly remote and uncaring, while IBM showed compassion, nurturing, protection, and humaneness—both responses must be judged as ethical, for both companies' actions were consistent with their internal value systems as well as with the American cultural value system.

- *Summarize Nicotera and Cushman's position on what constitutes ethical organizational behavior.*

The second seminal issue, much less discussed, is: Where should an organization target its social influence? The reason, of course, that this issue gets less treatment is that it could easily boil down to questions of opinion. I might favor contributions to the arts, you might favor economic development. Going beyond personal opinion, Andrews (1989) suggested that the areas targeted by any given business should first be those that the business most affects. For example, instead of donating large sums to a local museum, a paper mill would be acting more socially responsible if it turned its financial resources toward limiting its levels of toxic discharges into the local water supplies. When organizations have taken the large steps to address the issues of which they are a part, they then can turn their attention to the issues and causes of personal preference.

The issues that surround corporate social responsibility are no less straightforward than any of the other ethical issues discussed in this chapter. Profit and corporate stewardship are easily seen as competing goals. But, given the enormous influence that organizations have on society and the world at large, we urgently need to see a union of these goals. The difficulties of building moral communities that can contribute to moral environments may seem insurmountable. However, the problems associated with not creating these communities are far more daunting. They include the pollution of our air, water, and ground, discrimination in the workforce, suppression of employee rights, oppression of foreign labor forces, and tampering with local and foreign economies.

ETHICS REFLECTS CULTURE REFLECTS ETHICS

Are a "company's ethics" the reflection of the individual morality of its members, or is member behavior the result of a pervading organizational morality that is culturally embedded? This chicken-egg question will probably never be answered, but it lies at the heart of this section. To wrap up our discussion of ethics, we now turn directly to the relationship between culture and ethics. In this section I'll present the work of Walter Fisher and others, in an attempt to outline a perspective on ethics that argues that each subculture will reflect its own unique ethical sense, so individual behavior will most likely be the product of cultural influences. The problem for the organization, then, is to identify the critical ethical components and control them. The difficulty of that task will be addressed after an overview of Fisher's work.

Narrative Ethics

Fisher (1978, 1984, 1985, 1987) argued that human decision making is as much value-directed as it is "logic-directed." For the human being, reasoning is a process of symbol using, rather than the creation of formal ("logical") structures that guide thinking. It occurs in the process of narration, or storytelling.

He used the term *homo narrans* (1984, p. 6) to describe the fundamental character of humans as storytelling beings. The reality of our experience is translated into narratives. In that narrative form, experience takes on meaning, decisions are justified, and reasons are embedded. The content of these narratives is inherently value-laden and the validity of the stories lies in their probability and their moral implications (see the discussion in Chapter 1 of symbolic convergence theory for a reminder of the importance of storytelling in creating shared understanding).

All discourse, Fisher argued, is imbued with the narrator's version of a life experience. We build stories that account for our experiences, and these stories offer us a logic for gaining understanding. Sometimes this logic is viewed by others as rationalization. The point is, they offer the narrator a device for making sense of conditions that sometimes seem senseless. In other words, moral and ethical behavior becomes that behavior which is justified in the story created to account for organizational life. As an example, consider what happened in northern Minnesota a couple of years ago.

Unionized construction workers called a work stoppage at a paper mill expansion project to protest what they believed were unfair management practices. The strike was lengthy and bitter, prompting management to call in out-of-state, nonunion labor to work on the project. One day a few months into the strike a mob of strikers suddenly turned violent, attacking the temporary living quarters of the workers who were crossing the picket lines. They knocked down chain-link fences, overturned and burned mobile homes, and simply went on a rampage of seemingly random destruction, to the tune of millions of dollars in damages.

What could account for such violent behavior from normally honest, peaceful individuals? According to the narrative paradigm, such behavior is easily understood. Workers get together over a period of time and share experiences in the form of stories. The stories grow and grow, become shared, take on legitimacy and, as legitimate, become "truthful" justifications for actions. The violent acts, then, become justifiable within the story-based culture of the striking workers.

- *What is narrative ethics?*

Many researchers agree with Fisher's basic premises (see Cullen, Victor, & Stephens, 1989; Pettit, Vaught, & Pulley, 1990; Zey-Ferrell, Weaver, & Ferrell, 1979). When applied to the organization, the notion of *narrative ethics* means that ethics are the culturally mediated visions of right and wrong; that the ethical environment is a combination of internal morality, group construction (storytelling), and upper-management influence. Interactions with other humans play a greater role in shaping behavior than do interactions with institutions or agencies, such as the "church" or "school." These institutions are composed of people, and it is these people who shape the ethical conduct of those who come in contact with them. Any attempt to change an individual's unethical conduct, then, should be geared at the reference or peer group of that individual. This once again reinforces the notion that ethics cannot be seen as a per-person sort of concept.

This notion of internal ethical environment has been the focus of a number of researchers (e.g., Cooke, 1991; Murphy, 1988; Szwajkowski, 1989; Waters, 1978). These researchers tend to agree that ethics is both a formal and an informal variable. Efforts to understand the ethical environment must identify both formal and informal dimensions. Murphy (1988), for example, argued that the organization should develop a code of ethics that is specific, public rather than private, blunt and realistic, and revised periodically. This code should be conveyed through committees, conferences, training, ethics audits, and questions. Informally, the culture of the organization should be open and candid, and management should take a strong and explicit leadership role in modeling the ethics of the corporation.

In implementing the code, the organization should rely on top-management leadership, delegation to get ethics down the line, communication about ethics, and employee motivation to do the "right" things. So, the organization must show just how much ethics matters to it. A code that goes largely ignored does not demonstrate this notion. Only an adequate implementation program will show commitment.

- *What cautions should be noted about codes of conduct?*

Very few researchers would disagree with Murphy. Codes of conduct, however, will always be of limited value if not written with a recognition of what the current ethical situation is and what ethical environment is desired. Surveying the ethical landscape, then, is a critical step in creating and influencing organizational ethics. Cooke (1991) identified fourteen danger signs of corporate ethical risk. They included an overemphasis on short-term goals over long-term, routinely ignoring professional codes of ethics, the constant search for simple solutions, allowing an internal environment that discourages ethical behavior or encourages unethical behavior, penalizing or discouraging whistleblowing, and the tendency to see ethical problems as legal problems. These read, of course, like a partial checklist for any culture researcher.

Once the problems have been identified, the organization must move toward the sort of ethical environment it desires. Waters (1978) argued that rather than focusing on the individual as the immoral agent in cases of unethical conduct, we might be well advised to look at organizational variables—blocks—that predispose individual behavior. He highlighted seven such blocks. The first block, "strong role models," is the suggestion that many times, new employees are socialized into an unethical system and thus learn to copy the behavior of unethical managers and leaders.

The second block, "strict line of command," is a realization that without an open communication environment, the exposure of unethical behavior is unlikely. The third block, "group cohesion," suggests that highly cohesive groups may reinforce unethical behavior among their members. The fourth block, "ambiguity about priorities," is the concern that unclear management-level priorities will result in employees making their own determination regarding the acceptability of many acts, and often these determinations will violate the organization's preferred code of conduct. The fifth block, "separation of decisions," regards the difficulty of complying with the expectations of one work group when you have been accustomed to the procedures of another work group. The new work group presents the worker with procedures that he or she had no part in developing, but now must abide by. The sixth block, "division of work," concerns the fractionation and divisionalization that occurs in most large companies. In such an environment, an individual in one area may suspect unethical practices in another area, but because of limited access to their information, he or she cannot gather sufficient evidence to make the accusation. The seventh block, "protection from outside intervention," concerns the fact that any time a company undertakes an examination of its past practices and uncovers questionable ethics, it opens itself up for public scrutiny and investigation. So the organization becomes hesitant to look at itself too closely for fear that it may find something of interest to outsiders.

To unblock the organization, Waters suggested techniques such as opening the lines of communication, making discussions of ethics and morality commonplace, loosening up overly rigid patterns of communication, making access to top management easier, providing ways for whistleblowers to act within the organization, and clarifying priorities. All these suggestions are cultural concerns.

- *What are some of the structural blocks that make intervention in the organization's ethical environment difficult?*

SUMMARY

In this chapter we have seen some of the complexity of organizations understood as ethical environments. We began by looking at a number of examples that, most likely, were at different points on different readers' ethical-unethical continuum. Then we examined the idea of ethics as a communication issue. In this context, ethics was seen as amoral—most behavior can be justified in one way or another. This ability to justify ourselves allows us to view behavior as neutral—amoral—until it is evaluated by some other person as right or wrong.

The chapter then turned to the importance and the difficulty of studying ethics, including the impact of organizations on human development. Because of this impact, the ethical nature of organizational conduct must become the focus of communication researchers. Any focus will be guided by an approach or perspective for viewing ethics. A number of such approaches were discussed. The chapter then turned its attention to the complex, disturbing issues of sexual harassment, whistleblowing, and corporate social responsibility. A variety of explanations, examples, and views of these problems were discussed.

The overall point of the chapter was to demonstrate the interplay between the development of shared ethical understandings and the ethical ambience of the organization. I suggested a narrative approach to ethics as the most reasonable explanation for the development of the cultural ethical stance. If such an approach is legitimate, it means that the organization will create its own justification for its behavior, and its behavior will be justifiable within the storytelling context of the organizational environment.

Ethics as narrative suggests that organization members construct their own social reality, which includes understandings of right and wrong, just and unjust. This reality may be contrary to what outsiders consider reasonable, but it will exist as a sensible guideline for the organization members who constructed it. This implies that the imposition of a code of ethics from cultural outsiders may be of limited value in shaping the attitudes and behavior of members of a culture. Perhaps the only way to affect a culture's ethics is to change the culture itself.

CHAPTER 8

Culture and Communication Networks

Chapter Preview

In this chapter we'll look at a subject that may not seem totally appropriate to a text that takes a cultural view of organizations. The examination of communication networks is the study of communication flow via formal and informal links. It explicitly focuses on structure, and we've already seen that structure is less central to a communication explanation of organizations than is meaning.

However, understanding organizations as communicative networks actually is in sync with the general approach taken in this text to explain organizations. From both network and cultural approaches the organization is viewed as the construction of the organizational participants. A network approach puts more emphasis on structure, while a cultural approach puts more emphasis on the meaning that constitutes those structural links.

Merging these structural and cognitive approaches offers the researcher a clearer picture of the complex communicative organizational environment than either offers alone. For example, if researchers focus only on communicative structure as defined by the network data, they may overestimate the influence of certain network members on the overall network belief systems, while underestimating the influence of other, less central network members.

Salancik's (1986) study of twenty-four organizational research journals made this point exactly. He argued that earlier analyses of this type relied too much on primary citations, ignoring secondary links and, thus, secondary dependencies. In other words, relying only on the direct links, in this case articles cited in reference sections, ignored the impact of those works that informed the authors who were actually being cited. Salancik demonstrated the importance of these secondary links for the impact they had on the primary sources.

All organizations consist of systems of relationships, wherein one member's output is another member's input. Network research does a good job of ferreting out these structural links. But only cultural studies help us understand how two people, who may be part of the same network, when faced with the "same event," can interpret it in totally different ways (see Dunn & Ginsberg, 1986).

Those differences come from competing assumptions, attitudes, beliefs, paradigms, points of view, frames of reference, whatever you've come to understand as the basis of culture. At their simplest, understanding and interpretation have little to do with whether you're part of a communication pathway. So network research reminds us of the importance of information flow and relational links. But only when network researchers devote as much energy to content as they do structure, as did Bullis and Bach (1991), who are discussed later in the chapter, will they make significant contributions to a cultural understanding.

The network literature is vast and often exceedingly complex. The complexity lies in the mathematical difficulty of representing, studying, and reporting communicative relationship building. In this chapter I will try to avoid much of that complexity, focusing on four specific contributions that network research offers to a cultural orientation. This chapter will begin with an overview of network theory, terminology, and methods. Network research, more than any other focus in organizational studies, has a unique and precise language. A variety of examples of network studies will be offered to indicate the diversity of focuses and results that can be obtained by network researchers, as well as the overlap between cultural and network approaches.

The chapter will then move to the examination of boundary spanning and the controversial study of corporate interlocking—overlapping boards of directors. We'll see the boundary spanner as intercultural communicator, playing an important role for both the organization and external stakeholders. Too much boundary spanning, however, as in the case of much corporate interlocking, may result in closed value systems.

The chapter then reviews network contributions to the issue of just how big the world is. You may be surprised later when you see just how connected you are to me interpersonally, as well as to any randomly chosen person in this country. The small-world research is full of surprises of this sort. Finally, the chapter highlights the networks of superior-subordinate working relationships and closes with a discussion of the various ways that network and culture research inform each other, resulting in a more complete picture of the organization.

Key Terms

network	size
emergent structure	grapevine
clique	network multiplexity
dyad	direct interlock
boundary spanner	indirect interlock
bridge	corporate elite
density	

Before venturing any further into this chapter, you might want to consider the following question: "How close are you to me?" I don't mean, of course, how close are we physically, but rather, how close are we communicatively? This question is not as far-fetched as it sounds. If you wanted to get a message to me about this book, for example, what steps would you take?

Obviously, you might simply call me on the phone, or drop me a note in the mail. Each of these responses would demonstrate that communicatively, we're quite close. But what if we changed the question a little? Instead of asking how quickly we can engage each other's attention, what if we asked, "How many known, familiar intermediaries stand between you and me?" In other words, suppose that you couldn't call me or send me a note in the mail. Suppose that you had to contact me through a series of message exchanges between people who are acquaintances of one or the other of us. Now how close would we be?

From a "network" perspective, the question I'm asking here is, "How linked are our acquaintance networks?" We don't know each other, but what individuals might we know who do know each other? You might be surprised just how close we actually are.

For example, you might be a student who lives in a dormitory at a college campus in Texas. You might know a student who comes from Minnesota. You assume that student has a better chance of knowing someone who knows me, so you give your message to your Minnesota friend—acquaintance number one. That person doesn't know me personally, but does know a person who attends the University of Minnesota, Minneapolis campus. On a visit to Minnesota, acquaintance number one hands the message to acquaintance number two, who happens to live in Duluth, Minnesota. On a visit home, person number two hands the message to a friend who happens to be a major in my department, and one of my students. Person number three, then, walks over to my office, introduces him- or herself, and delivers the note. In this example, only three acquaintances separate you from me.

Similar questions were raised by a group of researchers discussed later in this chapter. This group, sometimes referred to as "small-world" researchers, asked the very same question: "How small is the world?" "How linked are any two randomly chosen people?" This is one example of a network question. The results, reported later, are very interesting. The implications of this and other network research are important and far-reaching.

Networks are the day-to-day relationships of organization members. They are those formal and informal ties we have with others that influence such things as how and where we find jobs, how much power we have, who gets to control our affairs, and with whom we tend to come in contact. In short, it would be a great error for us to discount the importance of our networks, for to do so would be to minimize the importance of our formal and informal relationships and how those relationships develop into distinctive subgroups within the larger organization (Van Maanen & Barley, 1985). This subcultural variation represents many networks of relations among groups that, even though composed of participants in the same organization, are often in conflict with each other.

This point, that organizations are composed of overlapping, often competing subgroups, highlights the importance of joining network and culture theory and research. The two inform each other, resulting in a more complete, rich-ly detailed understanding of the organizational environment. A cultural per-spective is the position that organizations are constituted in the belief and be-havioral systems constructed by organization members. Network theory explicitly focuses on the development of social relationships. So, even though most network theory is less concerned with the cognitive dimensions that are of interest to culture researchers, the contributions of network studies in help-ing us understand the importance of formal and informal communicative groupings cannot be discounted.

NETWORK THEORY, METHODS, AND RESEARCH

Many useful overviews summarize network research and philosophy (Blair, Roberts, & McKechnie, 1985; Dansereau & Markham, 1987; Jablin, 1987b; Monge & Eisenberg, 1987; Richards, 1985; Rogers & Kincaid, 1981). A sam-pling of these and other reviews indicates apparent unanimity among authors about the purposes, procedures, and content of network analyses. *Network analyses focus on representing structure in terms of relationships of various types and patterns.* The analysis of these relationships supplies information on issues of overall structure, clustering within networks, and individual member roles.

With few exceptions, network researchers are concerned with structure, because structure is assumed to have the primary impact on individual behav-ior within the network (see Monge & Contractor, 1988; Rogers & Kincaid, 1981; Tichy & Fombrun, 1979). This "structure," however, must be understood as dynamic, evolving, or in Galaskiewicz's (1979) terms, as *emergent structure.*

Galaskiewicz argued: "Social structure emerges out of the purposive ac-tion of social actors (whether they be individuals or organizations) who seek to realize their self interests and, depending on their ability and interests, will negotiate routinized patterns of relationships that enhance these interests" (p. 16). These emergent structures could be affected by beliefs (Sproull, 1981), val-ues and ideologies (Beyer, 1981), systems of interpretation (Dunn & Ginsberg, 1986), and overlapping communication networks (Roberts & O'Reilly, 1978).

Structure as emergent simply represents a moment in the process of orga-nizing. Networks, then, are momentary clusters of individuals. This clustering is sometimes formal (prescribed) and sometimes informal (emergent). Within these clusters, content flows in a variety of forms, including information, goods, expressiveness, and influence or power.

• *What are communication networks? What is emergent structure?*

A Network Approach

It is important to understand that network analysis is an approach, a method for viewing organizations, rather than a theory of organizations. Methodologi-cally, the theoretical driving force behind the complex statistical manipulations of most network inquiries is system theory (Fombrun, 1982). A network analysis focuses on relationships and interrelationships that emerge during the data analysis. In other words, they are not artificially prescribed before the research according to categories such as age, income, and sex. Organizations are understood as stable relationships within a process of change. It is argued that network analysis provides a means for uncovering the emergent nature of the apparently static organizational system.

On the surface at least, network analysis seems quite congruent with a cultural interpretation of organizations. Keep in mind, though, that networks are systems of behavioral relationships, defined by information flow rather than meaning. This clearly may cue the culture researcher to look for a subcultural grouping, but an identifiable communicative link is not a culture, as we've discussed culture in this text.

- *How might a culture researcher use network theory to help uncover organization cultures and subcultures?*

At this point I'd like to turn your attention to Case 8-1: Leadership Changes at IBM. The case highlights a variety of issues to be discussed throughout this chapter, including the already mentioned notions of emergent networks, as well as the forthcoming issues of boundary spanning, interlocking directorates, and the strength of weak ties, which will be discussed later.

Case 8-1 offers a glimpse at the importance of networks when the stakes are high. In the example, the process of choosing a new CEO for one of the largest, most prestigious, most technologically advanced firms in the world boiled down to relationships. Who did the board know who knew someone who knew something about . . . ? The players in the search were individuals whose responsibilities and organizational affiliations overlapped and who often represented competitors. Choosing John Akers's successor was a question of who was a member of the relational network, the power network, the prestige network, the IBM network, the industry network, and the headhunter network. Louis Gerstner was that person, the only one of the sixteen finalists who did not have a technical background.

As an organization, IBM changed. It got bigger. The people who became part of the search also became part of the company. The media became involved in the search, as did the observers. The boundaries of the company expanded to include these groups, the communication flow within the company changed to accommodate the new dialogues, and employee interpretations of the company changed to make sense of the drama.

Network Language

Thus far in this chapter you've probably run into a number of unfamiliar terms. Part of understanding network research and the importance of communicative networks generally is becoming fluent in the language. This section will present some key network language and focus specifically on a number of the most important concepts.

Case 8-1:   Leadership Changes at IBM

IBM was in trouble. Between 1987 and 1993 the giant computer manufacturer had lost 70 percent of its stock value. A big change was needed, and on January 26, 1993, the official start of that change was announced. John Akers, IBM chief executive officer, announced his resignation, effective as soon as a successor could be found. This search for a successor is a story of unbelievable effort, power, wealth, and networking, as the search committee attempted to discover the next chief officer of one of the largest companies in the world.

The key players in this story are Akers, the outgoing CEO; James Burke, retired CEO of Johnson & Johnson, IBM board member and chair of the search committee; Gerry Roche, a top executive "headhunter" with the firm of Heidrick & Struggles; Tom Neff, a top executive headhunter with the firm of SpencerStuart, an executive placement firm on whose board of directors Burke sits; and Louis Gerstner, ex-CEO of RJR Nabisco, and now the newly appointed CEO and chairman of IBM.

This search is remarkable for more than a few reasons. First, it was conducted in only about three months, when the "normal" search for a CEO takes about six months. Second, it was a joint effort between the search committee itself, internal to IBM, and two competing headhunter firms. The committee insisted on these two firms because an industry code of ethics prevents a firm from approaching executives of client companies for two years after those executives have been placed. To use only one search firm would have eliminated many of that firm's clients from competition. Going with the two largest firms made virtually every CEO around the world a possible candidate for the IBM job. Third, the committee looked seriously only at outsiders. IBM's problems were considered so difficult that only an outsider with a "non-IBM" mentality could solve them. As Cauley (1993) put it:

The search was not that of a typical company looking quietly for a new CEO among its own executive ranks. This was arguably the most important U.S. company of the 20th century announcing it would replace its CEO and then scouring the globe for a new one. Never before had a company so prestigious, so proud and so private acted this way. (p. 2B)

The financial cost of this effort was straightforward: $500,000 for each headhunting firm, plus expenses. Gerstner's compensation package included a $2 million yearly salary, up to an additional $2 million in bonuses, $5 million in compensation for lost potential income from RJR, and stock options over the next four years that could add an additional $25 million. Of greater interest than the financial compensation, however, is the process that resulted in the hire itself.

The network of players in this process read like a who's who of American industry. Other than Burke, the search committee consisted of the chairman emeritus of the Bechtel Group, Stephen Bechtel, Jr., a counselor at the Center for Strategic and International Studies, Harold Brown, the CEO of Hos-

Case 8-1: *(Continued)*

pital Corporation of America, Thomas Frist, Jr., the president of Wellesley College, Nannerl Keohane, retired CEO of Time-Warner, Richard Munro, and the chairman of Capital Cities/ABC, Thomas Murphy. Neff and Roche created a list of one hundred possible candidates within a week of getting the assignment. In a 90-minute meeting with the search committee, the list was pared down to the top sixteen choices.

Those choices included Paul Alaire, CEO of Xerox, Lawrence Bossidy, CEO of Allied-Signal, John Clendinen, CEO of BellSouth, Charles Exley, CEO of NCR, George Fisher, CEO of Motorola, Bill Gates, CEO of Microsoft, John Young, retired CEO of Hewlett-Packard, John Sculley, CEO of Apple Computer, Jack Welch, CEO of General Electric, and Charles Knight, CEO of Emerson Electric. Of the sixteen finalists for the position, Gerstner, who actually was the fourth choice, was the only person without a significant technical background.

The search included interviews and discussions about the candidates themselves with about seventy-five people over a two-month period. In interviews with the candidates a wealth of information about IBM was disclosed, and an equally impressive amount of advice for IBM was offered. Included in discussions were Sculley's plan to merge IBM and Apple; considering soliciting the help of President Clinton to persuade Bossidy to accept the position; and Gates's insights into IBM's failings in the software product lines. Gates was so impressive that he became an important player in the overall search.

For the most part, executives declined because they didn't want to leave successful companies to take on one of the biggest headaches in the world. Some took themselves out of the running, some were never actually seriously considered. The one who got the job was the fourth pick. Welch had been offered the job, but turned it down because he didn't want to leave GE; Bossidy turned the job down out of loyalty to Allied-Signal and worries over the ethics and image of accepting a huge compensation package while cutting jobs; and Young turned down the job both because of IBM's problems and because he didn't want to move to the East Coast.

In the end, IBM got what most consider a good pick. Gerstner is a former consultant with McKinsey, one of the largest and most prestigious strategic consulting firms, ex-CEO of American Express, and now ex-CEO of RJR Nabisco. Also, as Cauley (1993, p. 2B) put it, "The people who knew Gerstner liked him. He was one of them: rich, successful, intelligent. He lives in Greenwich, Conn., where many IBM executives live. Another plus: Gerstner's brother, Richard, 54, worked at IBM for 30 years." The offer, like much of the search itself, was ultimately made at Roche's vacation home in Hobe Sound, Florida. The announcement was made on March 26, 1993, by Akers himself, as he introduced the first outsider in IBM's history as the next chairman and CEO.

Note: This information is drawn from Cauley, L. (1993, April 26). The search for a new CEO: IBM. *USA Today*, pp. 1B–3B.

Some of the language of network research is summarized in Table 8-1. When reviewing the terms, notice the strong thread that ties most of them together: the concept of "relationship." *Network research is about the identification and explication of communicative relationships.* Some of these relationships are hierarchical; some are more informal than formal; some are between groups rather than individuals; all concern information. The key point is that a "network approach" to organizing is a specific focus on relationship building and maintenance.

- *What is the importance of relationship in network theory?*

Six of the concepts in Table 8-1—clique, dyad, boundary spanner, bridge, density, and size—should be examined more closely, for they shed considerable light on the value of network study to a cultural representation of organi-

TABLE 8-1. Network Glossary

Acquaintance volume:	The total number of individuals any given person knows.
Boundary spanner:	An individual whose role puts him or her in contact with those outside the group's or organization's boundaries.
Bridge:	Individuals who connect clusters and are members of one or more of those clusters.
Clique (cluster):	A group of individuals who are in contact with each other more frequently than with others outside of the group. A clique, then, represents an identifiable and distinct set of relationships.
Communication network:	Individuals linked by information.
Connectedness:	The degree to which network members are linked to one another. These links can be direct or indirect. Connectivity also refers to the length of the connections (long versus short, direct versus indirect).
Density:	Represents the proportion of the organization's membership that is a member of a given network. Density, then, represents the measure of actual network membership against potential membership.
Distance:	The number of links between any two members of a clique.
Downward communication:	Communication that flows from someone at a rank hierarchically higher than that of the receiver of the message.
Dyad:	Two individuals.
Formal channel:	Information spreading via the official chain of command.
Gatekeeper:	An individual who is both a primary member of a cluster and the cluster's link to external clusters.
Grapevine:	The pattern that informal messages travel.

zations. Of these six concepts, clique is the most central. A *clique* is a "culture" of relationships, a "culture" of contact. It is important for us to note the extreme differences between the approach to culture taken in this text—culture as beliefs, values, attitudes, and so forth—and cliques, which are societal much more than they are cultural. It stands to reason that a culture might develop within a clique, but we must remember that cliques are structural, cultures are not. In other words, a clique may form more as a result of spatial proximity than of shared beliefs.

The second key term to note is dyad. A *dyad,* two people, is the minimal unit necessary to have a network. One cannot share information with oneself. So, just as we noted earlier in the text that the dyad was the minimal unit necessary for organizing, we now see why: without the dyad information exchange and coordinated action are unnecessary.

TABLE 8-1. *(Continued)*

Hierarchy:	Usually, a prescribed assignment of positions within a group.
Informal communication:	Messages that flow without regard to the formalized chain of command. Rather, personal relationships more often account for where and why these messages are transmitted.
Interorganizational relationship:	Any situation in which two or more organizations exchange resources.
Isolate:	An individual dissociated from the cluster.
Liaison:	An individual who connects two or more clusters but is a member of none of them.
Link:	A communication relationship.
Multiplexity:	The degree to which members of a relationship play different roles within those relationships. The greater the number of roles (for example, I may be both a father and a friend to my daughter), the stronger (more intense) the link. Multiplexity also refers to the diversity of content experienced in a communication link.
Reciprocity:	The degree to which each member of a communication relationship perceives the other as a member of that relationship.
Relational demography:	Demographic characteristics of individuals who interact regularly.
Size:	Total membership within a network.
Stability:	The changes within a network over time.
Star:	The most connected member of a network.

The final four terms are all interrelated and understandable given an understanding of clique and dyad. *Boundary spanners* are individuals who journey back and forth between groups. They are sojourners, of sorts, and must be skilled intercultural communicators. *Bridges* are actual members of more than one cluster and thus serve the important role of offering contrary cultural points of view. *Density* and *size* are both measurements. Density is a measure of proportional representation. Size is an actual measurement. For example, suppose that your department has 400 majors. Your communication club, however, has only twenty members. The size of the club would be twenty; the density of the club would be 5 percent of the majors. Assuming a unified club culture, there would be some doubt, based upon the density figure, that the club represented the average communication major.

- **Define each of the six key terms highlighted above and discuss their importance from a cultural perspective.**

The language of network research, then, points us to system theory with its focus on the relationships between system members. Though clearly not the language of culture theory, network terminology helps the culture researcher remember to keep his or her attention on the emergent patterns of relationships within the group and on how those relationships might result in the sharing of experiences that will become the focus of a cultural explanation.

Communication networks can be shown visually. Some of the common network patterns are diagramed in Figure 8-1. The illustrations highlight some important points about networks. First, groups may demonstrate equal or unequal information flow. Groups with unequal flow, in which certain members have greater control, are called *centralized.* Both the wheel and chain configurations show centralization. Individuals A (wheel) and C (chain) control more information than their comembers. Groups that demonstrate equal flow, in which no member exerts greater control over information, are called *decentralized.* The circle and all channel networks are examples.

Methods

Three serious methodological problems face any network researcher: information overload, especially when examining large networks; sampling, gaining access to the participants within the network; and boundary specification—deciding where the network begins and ends. Each of these three issues will be explored briefly below.

Information Overload

The examination of communication networks is the attempt to show the interdependence between the macrolevel and microlevel of understanding and information flow (Shrader, Lincoln, & Hoffman, 1989). As the researcher moves further and further from the microlevel, he or she will be faced with the challenge of handling data that grow at an exponential rate.

Consider, for example, a two-person relationship. In the dyad, one network relationship is possible. Add a third person, though, and the number of

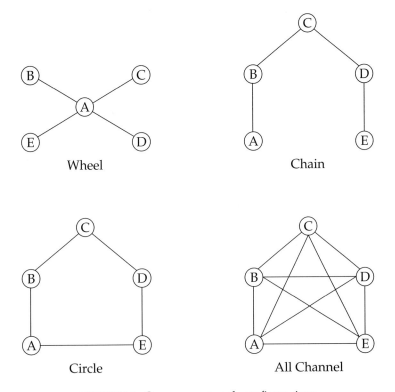

FIGURE 8-1. Common network configurations

potential ties increases to three; a four-person group has six potential ties; a five-person group, ten ties; and a six-person group has fifteen potential ties. Carry the math up to a group of 5000 and you'll find about 12.5 million one-directional ties (Granovetter, 1976). If you define a network tie as two-directional, as did Rogers and Kincaid (1981), a 5000-person group has roughly 25 million potential communication relationships!

This sort of figure is far more relevant for each of us than we might at first realize. For example, consider the problem of finding a job after college. We all know that most jobs are not found by looking in the want ads. This means that most people find work through their personal contacts. So how many people do you know? How many people's names could you come up with if you saw their faces?

If you think hard you can probably come up with a lot of names—let's say 1,000 people. And let's assume that each of these 1,000 people knows 1,000 people, also. This would make your acquaintance network nearly one million people [n × (n − 1), or 1,000 × 999]. Assume for the sake of argument that there is a 50 percent overlap in the networks (not everyone knows different people; friends know friends). This still gives you about a quarter of a million (500 × 499) possible job contacts!

This sort of huge data set mandates the use of computers, for only computers can handle the bulk of information, highlight hidden or hard-to-see aspects, and standardize the determination of network structure. This is why we didn't see much large-network analysis before the widespread use of computers.

- *What does information overload refer to in network research?*

Network Sampling

Basically, there are three general sampling techniques in network research. The first is sometimes referred to as survey sociometry: the respondents are simply asked to identify all those from a given list with whom they have communicated on a given issue. A variation of this technique, called the roster method, consists of giving respondents a list of all network members and having them identify links. Some sort of survey or roster method is necessary for any large network and, indeed, these name-eliciting methods are by far the most popular in network research (Granovetter, 1976; McCallister & Fischer, 1978).

The other two techniques are appropriate for smaller networks. The second method—observation—consists of the researcher observing and recording communicative behavior. The third method, unobtrusive observation, has the researcher gathering information through sources such as public records or telephone logs.

Boundary Specification

Regardless of the approach or method, the network researcher must always face the problem of boundary specification. Network research is about the specification and delineation of communicative links. Specifying exactly where these links begin and end, however, can be a mammoth headache. Network inquiries are system inquiries and systems, by definition, are composed of interdependent components. This complexity is even more confounding when we remember that any organization is composed of systems of subsystems (Freeman, 1978; Rogers & Kincaid, 1981).

Fombrun (1982) and Laumann, Marsden, and Prensky (1983) suggested that boundary definition choices seem divided between realist and nominalist approaches. A *realist* approach uses the network participant point of view of boundary. In other words, the network exists to the degree that the individuals being examined believe that it exists. With the *nominalist* approach, the network is defined by the researcher to suit his or her own needs. For example, the researcher might specify that the organizational boundaries include the members' home lives, even though the members don't necessarily count their homes as part of their work boundaries.

Theory and Methods Examples

In this section I'll briefly review four network studies. The theory discussion that has dominated this chapter thus far will make more sense when you can see some results, especially as they are interpreted from a cultural perspective.

In a now-classic article, Davis (1953) reported a study of the communication grapevine at Jason Company. For the research he used a method referred to as "ecco analysis," in which he located a piece of information, then traced it to its original source. Davis reported four interesting findings regarding the *grapevine:* (1) It is fast, much faster than the formal channels of communication. (2) Rather than being unwieldy and random, Davis found the grapevine quite selective, with only certain individuals targeted for information sharing. (3) The grapevine was a workplace phenomenon, not operating away from work; (4) The grapevine and the formal communication channels were not independent of each other. When one was humming, so was the other, and when one was silent, the other tended to be silent, also.

The most common form of grapevine transmission found at Jason was the "cluster" chain. This type of information sharing is illustrated in Figure 8-2. As shown, *A* sent a message to *B* and *C*. *B* passed it along to *D* and *E*, while *C* sent the message to *F*. *D* and *F* sent the message to *G*, *H*, and *I*, who sent it along to *J* and *L*, and this pattern of message transmission continues. What is important to note in Figure 8-2 is that the message sending is inconsistent, with some receivers passing it on and others not sending it along, and the condition necessary for sending the message along has to do with relationship rather than formal position. In other words, inclusion in the grapevine has more to do with who you know than with your position in the formal organizational hierarchy. Davis advocated increasing the use of managerial liaisons to act as the receivers of such messages in an effort to keep management up to date with what's going on around the company.

FIGURE 8-2. Communication grapevine

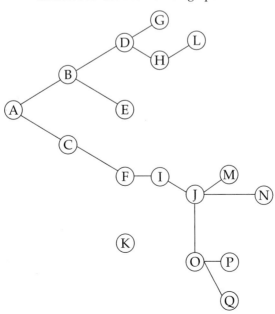

The most obvious cultural implication of the Davis results is that informal information flow will most likely be culture controlled. In other words, members of the same subcultures will share interests, beliefs, and interpretations of experience, resulting in common interpretations of organizational events. There will be a greater tendency to share these interpretations with individuals who we assume also share our viewpoints—that is, members of our cultures.

- *What is the communication grapevine?*

In our second study summary, Bullis and Bach (1991) attempted to overcome one of the key criticisms of much network research: that it tends to emphasize structure rather than communication content (p. 181). Their study correlated *network multiplexity* with organizational identification. In this case, multiplexity referred to those instances when more than one content or relation was present within a dyad. Identification referred to the individual's sense of belongingness to the organization. The authors' assumption was that individuals with more multiplex links would demonstrate greater levels of organizational identification.

They studied a group of twenty-six new graduate students over the course of one year. Their results showed a definite influence of multiplex relationships on organizational identification. In other words, as the students developed more complex relationships with others, beyond work-related content, they developed a stronger sense of identification with their departments.

The cultural implications of this study lie to a large extent with managerial attempts to control culture. If Bullis and Bach are correct, organizations should encourage their employees to socialize and to be together away from work. This is exactly the strategy reported by Van Maanen and Kunda (1989) in their analysis of emotional control of Disneyland employees.

In our third study summary, Lincoln and Miller (1979) set out to examine the differences between "instrumental" (work-related) and "primary" (friendship) network ties. Their goal was to shed light on intraorganizational structure by contrasting situational and personal characteristics in the formation of communication networks.

The authors surveyed members of five organizations. Members were asked to name five close friends and five individuals with whom they had worked closely in the past month. The characteristics examined were authority, education, sex, and race (skin color).

They found three interesting results. First, the ties within instrumental networks tended to be relatively even, while ties in primary networks were unpredictable; second, central members in one kind of network tended to be identified as central members in the other kind; and third, sex and race had a greater impact on primary network composition than instrumental network composition. Their overall finding was that the measured characteristics tended to be status determinants: "White males with high education in formal positions of authority have high probabilities of occupying the most central locations in the network space" (p. 193). In short, it appears that certain attributes will predispose those holders to be central members in both instrumental and primary networks.

The cultural implications of this study remind us of the error of viewing organizations as overly "rational" information processors. This means that we have come to view organizational decision-makers as data-collecting machines, of sorts, who gather pertinent information and use it to make sound, unbiased decisions. This vision is seriously questioned by these results. Because friendship ties influence decision making probably as much as formal ties, the composition of primary networks indicates a significant influence on organizational decision making. And, given that the results indicated that sex and race played a role in the makeup of primary networks, the results would imply that white males are playing a more significant role in organizational decision making than either women or minorities.

In our fourth study summary, Brass (1985) looked at men's and women's interaction patterns within a newspaper publishing company to try to draw conclusions about how network centrality affected perceived influence of men and women. The study proceeded on the assumption that women tended to be less central figures in critical informal influence networks. This lack of centrality may be a contributing factor in the difficulty women face in being promoted to managerial levels. The study looked at centrality in each worker's department, in the entire organization, and within the all-male and all-female interaction networks. Three types of networks were examined: workflow, communication, and friendship.

The results indicated that when the entire organization was the reference group, women occupied a more central role than men in the workflow and interaction networks. However, when focusing on the upper management level, men were found to be more central in the informal network of individuals who constituted the dominant group of top-level management. Thus, even though the number of men and women in this organization was about equal, and even though both the men and the women appeared skilled in building communication networks, participation (real and perceived) in the more powerful informal network was reserved mostly for men. This finding was demonstrated by the record of promotions within the company. Promotions were directly related to centrality in men's and the dominant group's interaction networks. This study also corroborates Lincoln and Miller's (1979) results, reported earlier. And its results once again reinforce the notion that organization cultures, beliefs, and value systems, play a prominent role in decision making and interpretations of organizational events.

CROSS-BOUNDARY NETWORKS

A great deal of network research has focused on the relationships between members of different groups. How these links come about and their impact on the abilities of both groups to function are serious questions with sometimes disturbing answers. This work is often discussed under the heading of "interlocks." In this section I'll offer an overview of some of this work, including some of the interesting results regarding how interlocking networks result in an uneven, some would say unnatural, amount of power in a small number of hands. Before discussing interlocking, however, we must remind ourselves of who it is that is responsible for performing the interlocking behavior. That function is performed by those individuals known as boundary spanners.

Boundary Spanning

All interlock research depends on the examination of boundary spanners. Boundary spanners are individuals who represent the group or company outside its boundaries. To customers and other organizational outsiders the boundary spanner is their link to the company, and to the organization, the boundary spanner is the source of information about those outsiders. In short, a boundary spanner is an individual whose work within an organization includes coming in contact with the environment outside the organization's boundaries. To intraorganizational groups, boundary spanners represent the groups' interests to other groups. In Case 8-1, reported earlier, James Burke is a good example of a boundary spanner.

It is important here to remember that "boundary," as used throughout this book, has little to do with walls and desks and rooms and doors. An organization's boundary, in most of the boundary-spanning research, has more to do with activities than with structures (Adams, 1980). Organizations are linked to their environments through the activities of their members, and that link is the domain of the boundary spanner.

- *What is a boundary spanner?*

Boundary spanners perform two general functions: information processing and external representation (Aldrich & Herker, 1977). Within these two functions they perform five important activities: (1) They present organizational information to the outside environment and bring environmental information into the organization; (2) they filter both organizational outputs and environmental inputs; (3) they scan the environment and decide what information to bring into the organization; (4) they buffer the organization from external threats; and (5) they represent the organization.

Given these five activities, the boundary spanner is easily seen as a key communication player in the organization. According to system theory, any system needs negative feedback in order to grow and adapt to environmental changes. If the boundary spanner fails to accurately scan a hostile environment, or inaccurately portrays the inner organizational environment to the outside, the organization could easily find itself in serious trouble.

- *What functions are fulfilled by boundary spanners?*

The more turbulent the environment, the greater the need for boundary spanning (Adams, 1976). Interaction with the environment is necessary to obtain critical input and to dispose of goods and services. Common examples of boundary spanners are marketing and sales persons, purchasers, dispatchers, personnel recruiters, admission and placement staff, public relations workers, negotiators, and bargaining agents.

The cultural implications of boundary spanning are quite important. The boundary spanner as intercultural communicator will play a critical role in the transmission of cultural meanings from one group to another. The boundary spanner will be looked to for information regarding the environment, will take the group's message to other groups, and must function successfully in both worlds. The boundary spanner, as resident of multiple, sometimes competing cultures, takes on a role of immense power and importance.

Interlocking Corporate Directorates

One of the most powerful boundary-spanning activities occurs at the level of organizational boards of directors. This point was illustrated clearly in Case 8-1. In the United States a board of directors is required for publicly traded corporations (Baysinger & Hoskisson, 1990). The board is responsible for a wide range of duties, including the evaluation of overall managerial performance. On the other hand, CEOs generally are given the right to choose the members of their company's board of directors. When an individual sits on two or more boards, he or she is performing a boundary-spanning function at the highest organizational level. The result is that the boards become interlocked.

It is necessary to identify two forms of interlocks: direct and indirect. A *direct interlock* occurs when one person sits on two boards of directors. An *indirect interlock* exists when two directors sit on the board of a third company. Their two organizations, then, are indirectly linked through the third company. Legally, there are few restrictions on indirect links. Direct links, however, are governed primarily by the Sherman Antitrust Act of 1890 and the Clayton Act of 1914. The intent of the Sherman Act was to restrict efforts that would impede open market competition. Section 8 of the Clayton Act, addressed specifically to the issue of interlocking directorates, "prohibits an individual from being a director in two or more companies that are competitors. It also prohibits any employee of a financial institution from being a director of another financial institution" (Schoorman, Bazerman, & Atkin, 1981, p. 248).

- *What is corporate interlocking?*

Interlocks present a controversial issue for organizational observers and participants. Most authors agree that interlocks are a way for organizations to cope with uncertain environments (Bazerman & Schoorman, 1983; Schoorman, Bazerman, & Atkin, 1981). Interlocking offers four key advantages for the corporations: The first is horizontal coordination, in which individuals with knowledge of the industry can combine that knowledge toward mutual advantage in areas such as pricing, research and development, and advertising. The disadvantage, obviously, is one primarily for the consumer, who loses the possible advantage of an open, competitive market. The second advantage is vertical coordination. In this case, the uncertainty of suppliers or distributors can be reduced. The third benefit is the knowledge and skills brought to one board by those who may be members of other boards. The varying ranges of experiences may prove invaluable in decision making. The fourth benefit is prestige. A company may gain status by having its board composed of high-profile individuals both within and outside its industry.

- *What advantages does interlocking offer?*

How common is interlocking? Bazerman and Schoorman (1983) reported a 1978 study of 130 of the largest American companies. The study found 530 direct and 12,193 indirect interlocks. A 1980 study of 797 American companies found 1572 interlocks. Allen (1974) studied 50 of the largest financial and 200 of the largest nonfinancial corporations, as defined by assets, in 1935 and 1970. Results showed not only that significant amounts of interlocking occur, but also that corporate interlocking is becoming more pervasive and more centered on financial institutions (banks and insurance companies).

Mariolis (1975) specifically addressed the question of whether banks exert undue corporate influence because of interlocking directorates. He found, using the 1970 *Fortune* list of the top 500 industrials, top 50 banks, insurance companies, retailers, and utilities, and top 47 miscellaneous companies, that 92 percent were interlocked at least once, while 84 percent were interlocked at least twenty-five times. Of these, Mariolis found, "Banks are far and away the heaviest interlockers" (p. 431).

Useem on Interlocking

In contrast to the relatively sympathetic or neutral studies above, Useem (1982) took a much more critical look at the impact of interlocking. Useem addressed the relationship between business and government and the role that interlocking directorates play in that relationship. Useem's question revolved around trying to understand how government policies come to reflect business interests in the United States and Great Britain. He built his explanations on the behavior of a group identified as the *corporate elite*, that group of upper managers or power holders whose first and foremost concern is the profitability of their companies.

Three explanations that have been offered as ways of accomplishing this profitability were contrasted. The first is the *upper-class principle*. This explanation asserts that business is a way of continuing the wealth of the few most preeminent, wealthy families. The corporate elite is composed of the wealthiest families who wield great power in the largest and most influential organizations. The second explanation is referred to as the *corporate principle*. With this explanation, the corporate elite is defined by position in the organization, not by family lineage. Those who hold the highest positions in the most influential organizations will wield the greatest amount of influence. The third explanation, and the one that Useem most favors, is the *classwide principle*. With this explanation, membership in the corporate elite is dependent on being a player in the network of associations (friendships, directors, owners) that links all organizations. And, within this network, some players will have greater potential than others. Useem argued that the classwide principle is the most reasonable explanation for the influence of business on government policy. The relationship between government and industry is presented as one in which government becomes part of the industrial network of associations, via the influential interlocking of powerful members of the elite.

Useem offered data from a large sampling of corporate executives in both England and the United States. The data analysis suggested that organizations do not enter into interlocking directorates in an effort to meet mutual concerns, but rather, that interlocking is a business strategy to accomplish influence. The strategy of inclusiveness was demonstrated convincingly in Useem's findings regarding corporate ownership of other businesses. In Britain, for example, 38 percent of company shares in 1975 were held by other companies. Additionally, Useem reported that of a sample of eighty-five British manufacturing and financial firms surveyed in 1970, more than four-fifths were interlocked. In the United States, a 1969 report identified a greater than nine-tenths interlock among the largest 797 corporations.

Thus, Useem's work stands in stark contrast to more sympathetic explanations of interlocking, which justify it as an attempt to predict and respond to an uncertain environment by pooling knowledge. For Useem, interlocking has more to do with control, power, and influence than with anything else.

- *What are Useem's criticisms of interlocking?*

Corporate interlocks nicely demonstrate the real value of a cultural analysis. Interlocking means that a relatively closed value system will dominate the most powerful decision-making level of corporate America. The lack of diversity of thought on boards of directors will be guaranteed by the cultural overlap brought about through the members who sit on multiple boards.

THE SMALL WORLD AND THE STRENGTH OF WEAK TIES

Small-world questions, such as the one that opened this chapter, have profound implications for areas such as obtaining employment and achieving influence within organizations and social groups. If influence is your communicative goal, reaching the right person will be the crucial determinant of success. Most people greatly underestimate their acquaintance, and thus their influence, networks (de Sola Pool & Kochen (1978/79). The result of this misrepresentation is the perception that one has little or no ability to influence events. The critical influence question that we each need to ask is: "How small is the world?"

Milgram (1967) pioneered the "small-world" research agenda by asking, "How many links separate any random person 'A' from person 'B'?" The question is prompted by the common occurrence of finding yourself meeting someone in an unlikely place who "just happens" to be an acquaintance of an acquaintance of yours. Such a meeting often results in the saying, "It's a small world, isn't it?" Milgram set out to find out just how small the world (United States) was.

In two studies, one initiated in Omaha and one in Wichita, Milgram "invented" small-world research. He asked participants to mail a folder of documents to a person that they knew on a first-name basis who might be more able than themselves to deliver the folder to a randomly selected stockbroker in Sharon, Massachusetts. His findings were interesting. The median number of exchanges necessary to connect random pairs in Kansas and Nebraska and Massachusetts was 5.5. Milgram also found a pronounced tendency of males to send the folders to other males, and of females to send them to females. Interestingly, the stockbroker's primary link to these outside acquaintances was a local clothing merchant, rather than his work associates.

In a related study, Korte and Milgram (1970) looked at whether racial differences would affect the size of acquaintance networks. They performed the small-world exercise using whites and blacks located in Los Angeles (starter persons were all white males) and New York City (target persons were half white and half black males). The method called for the starter individuals to send the informational folder on to another person who they felt would have a better chance to deliver it to the target person. Each link in the process recorded his or her name and certain demographic characteristics and sent the folder on. The target person's occupation, address, name, and organizational memberships were included, but not his race.

The results showed again that only between five and six exchanges were necessary to link any two random persons in Los Angeles and New York City. The researchers further found that both network size and network efficiency were important variables in completing the task. They found that more of the white-to-white chains were completed than of the white-to-black chains. Their reasoning was that perhaps the whites had a less extensive black network established, thereby reducing the probability of a successful transfer of information.

The cultural implications of small-world research lie in the possibility of overlapping value and belief systems. If de Sola Pool and Kochen (1978/79) are correct, the average acquaintance network is 1000 individuals. Carrying out the math, this links any two randomly chosen individuals in this country by two to four intermediaries. The unknown and exciting factor in this equation is the amount of overlap in the networks. In other words, How many of my 1000 acquaintances will also be among your 1000 acquaintances? And, given that we tend to associate with people who think the way we do, at what point do our belief and value systems overlap?

- *What has small-world research shown us about the size of our acquaintance networks?*

SUPERIOR-SUBORDINATE COMMUNICATION

One of the most heavily studied network relationships is that between organizational superiors and subordinates, and for good reason. The superior-subordinate relationship is one of the most common in organizational structures as well as one of the most important. Successful communication between these levels is crucial to the effective functioning of any organization as well as to the effective performance of workers. Unfortunately, a variety of causes obstruct the effective flow of information between superiors and subordinates.

Katz and Kahn (1978, p. 440) offered a concise summary of the sort of information that tends to get sent up and down the formal hierarchy in organizations (Table 8-2). Despite the difficulties of facilitating this sort of communication, active steps must be taken to ensure that information flows between hierarchical levels. This is especially true in the case of upward communication (information sent from subordinates to superiors). According to Pace and Faules (1994, pp. 130–31), upward communication should be encouraged and valued in the organization because it provides information for those who must make decisions, it gives supervisors a sense of how well subordinates are receiving and understanding information, and when they're ready for more information, it opens the door for the handling of concerns and conflicts and allows the subordinates to contribute potentially good ideas.

Unfortunately, valuing upward communication and getting it are two very different things. Employees may hide their thoughts and concerns, may feel that their supervisors don't care about their ideas, may see their supervisors as inaccessible, and may work in a system that offers no reward or incentive for sending information upward. (You've no doubt noticed that these are cultural obstacles obstructing structural links.) Also, subordinates may offer misleading information in an effort to please superiors by giving them the sort of information they think the superior "wants," or the subordinate may offer incorrect information in an effort to make him- or herself look good, or in an effort to subvert the superior's position.

- *What are the reasons for encouraging and the problems in facilitating upward and downward communication?*

TABLE 8-2. Content of Three Primary Types of Formal Communication

Downward (From Superior to Subordinate)	Upward (From Subordinate to Superior)	Horizontal (Across Same Hierarchical Level)
Job instructions	Information about the subordinate	Task coordination
Job rationale	Information about the subordinate's peers	Socioemotional support
Procedural information	Communication about policy	
Feedback	Questions and comments about work	
Indoctrination efforts		

Many studies have been done to determine the factors that most affect superior-subordinate communication, sometimes with contradictory results. In Table 8-3, which highlights a number of these studies, you can see that the superior-subordinate relationship is complex and subject to many forces, including trust, mobility aspirations, gender, and openness. Its importance is evi-

TABLE 8-3. Factors that May Affect Superior-Subordinate Relationships

1. *Trust:* Subordinates who trust their superiors are less likely to distort information (Glauser, 1984; O'Reilly, 1978; Roberts & O'Reilly, 1974), and are more likely to offer greater amounts of information than subordinates who distrust their superiors (Roberts & O'Reilly, 1974).

2. *Subordinate mobility:* The impact of high mobility aspirations of subordinates on upward information flow (whether subordinates withhold or contribute greater amounts of information) is not clear. Results seem to depend on the study (Jablin, 1979; O'Reilly, 1978; Roberts & O'Reilly, 1974). However, supervisors spend from one-third to two-thirds of their time in face-to-face interactions with subordinates, superiors initiate most of these interactions, and superiors are less satisfied generally with such encounters than they are with interactions with their superiors (Jablin, 1979).

3. *Superior's upward influence:* Greater amounts of less distorted information are offered by subordinates who perceive their superiors as exerting upward influence. These subordinates are also more satisfied with their relationships with their supervisors (Jablin, 1979; O'Reilly, 1978; Roberts & O'Reilly, 1974).

4. *Openness:* Both superiors and subordinates prefer open communication relationships, as defined by message content and appropriateness (Jablin, 1979).

5. *Overload, underload, and channels:* Because of the greater number of members at lower levels, there may be less channel availability for message sending. The sheer volume of information that those at upper hierarchical levels are expected to process may result in much being overlooked (Glauser, 1984). Network isolates commonly report information underload. Underload tends to correlate with both lower job satisfaction and higher performance, while overload correlates with higher satisfaction but lower performance ratings by superiors (O'Reilly, 1980).

6. *Gender:* Women may direct more information upward and may tend to distort more upward information (Glauser, 1984). In mixed-gender dyads, subordinates were rated as performing more poorly and reported higher levels of role conflict and role ambiguity than subordinates in same-sex dyads. They were also less well liked than subordinates in same-sex dyads (Tsui & O'Reilly, 1989).

7. *Power:* Unequal relationships need not be assumed to cause poor communicative relationships. The context of the relationship has a greater impact than the relationships themselves. Specifically, assistance and supportiveness are both greater in cooperative conditions than in individualistic or competitive conditions (Tjosvold, 1985).

8. *Message clarity:* The greater the gap between what the message source intended and what the receiver actually understands, the greater the negative impact on the relationship. Even with this knowledge, there is a tendency for managers to overestimate the clarity of their messages as well as the amount of knowledge possessed by their subordinates. Gaps are frequent between superiors and subordinates (Jablin, 1979).

dent. All of us will spend significant portions of our lives participating in these networks.

Unfortunately, offering definitive conclusions about the superior-subordinate relationship is hard, if not impossible, to do. The relationship is potentially affected by so many variables that perhaps the most accurate conclusion that can be drawn is that the superior-subordinate relationship is a complex network defined by real or perceived status differential. The relationship will be influenced by personal characteristics of the participants, as well as by situational characteristics.

NETWORKS AND ORGANIZATION CULTURES

A number of points have been stressed about the fit between network and culture theory. While it was apparent from the outset that the two perspectives emphasize different issues, we have also seen that the two approaches usefully inform each other in important ways. First, both network and culture theory argue that groups are communicative constructions, always evolving, based upon information exchange and sense making. A network approach views the construction from primarily behavioral terms (Who comes in contact with whom?), while a cultural view emphasizes cognition (who shares beliefs with whom?).

Second, despite the differing orientations, merging these approaches offers us a more comprehensive understanding of organizations as overlapping subgroups. Network research shows these overlaps through quantitative representation, mapping lines of interaction and clique formation. A cultural explanation understands these subgroups less as direct links than as shared value systems. Thus, a person may be part of a subculture without being aware of it.

The third important insight offered by the chapter is the importance of culture in controlling the flow of both formal and informal communication. Evidence cited showed clearly that as relationships grew among organization members, those members identified more strongly with the organization, and that friendship ties and network centrality were important components in power and advancement. This led to the conclusion that organizations are not rational agents, that decision making was as likely to be informed by friendship ties and informal networks as by data and "facts."

The final issue highlighted in the chapter deals with intercultural networking and the importance of the boundary-spanning role. As structural networks interlock, cultural stagnation may occur through the perpetuation of closed value systems. On the other hand, when monitored closely, interlocking may produce innovative ideas (as may ultimately be the case with the IBM choice of Louis Gerstner as CEO). Network research has shown that the world is, truly, very small. Though small, our world seems to be marked more by subcultural variation than by similarity. However, by tracing our acquaintance networks we may be able to better understand the points where our value systems diverge. Understanding these points may help us come together as group members, organization members, and participants on the planet as a whole.

SUMMARY

This chapter has approached the subject of communication networks in an uncommon way. I've chosen to discuss a few of the network issues that demonstrate the potential overlap between network and culture theory and research. This discussion showed that the two are not necessarily incompatible.

The chapter began by looking at network theory, methods, and research. We saw that network theory is about structure: communicative relationships and clique formation. However, despite the appearance, we also saw that theorists approach this structure as emergent, evolving, to the point of understanding the network as a form of temporary stability in a developing organizational form. This is very much the reasoning offered throughout this text. The chapter examined key methodological issues and offered a summary of selected research to highlight both the interesting nature of network theory and the relevance of the study.

The chapter then went into boundary spanning and corporate interlocking. Through this examination we saw that organizations often merge their knowledge in an effort to predict the environment as well as gain control. The boundary spanner is the key player in all of this, moving back and forth between groups, representing each group to the other. The chapter wound up with examinations of small-world research and superior-subordinate communication.

CHAPTER 9

Organization Cultures, Politics, and Conflict

Chapter Preview

In Chapter 7 we took a long look at sexual harassment and noted that it is less about sex than about power. Power, organizational politics, and conflict will be focused on throughout this chapter, allowing us to examine one of the most frustrating and troublesome cultural reflections: the organization as political process.

To understand the organization as a political arena we have to first understand the basic nature of politics. Little good is served by turning away from politics as if it were a dirty word. The connotations of "organizational politics" and "politics as usual" have caused us to be wary of political systems and the application of political analysis to contexts such as organizations.

Such an aversion, though understandable, is certainly inadvisable. Approaching the organization as a political system helps us clarify some of the most fundamental components of organizations: power, rule systems, governance, and conflict. These are significant variables in all organizations and must be confronted and understood. By directing our attention to these issues we can gain a clearer picture of the development and role of organization culture.

We'll begin our discussion by looking at organizations as political arenas, which revolve around an intimate relationship among politics, power, and control. Politics and the political system will be seen as rules, which often result in the creation of power structures or derive from existing power structures. Many of the rules developed within the political arena are created to preserve the existing systems of control, by those who want to hold on to whatever forms of power they have.

We'll see during this discussion how power permeates organizational life, and how it is both overt and covert. Covert power is unobtrusive, affecting us without our knowledge until it is even passed into the actual structure of the organization itself. The discussion of power concludes with a reminder that power tends to belong to the already powerful, so gaining power has much to do with aligning oneself with power holders.

The chapter then turns to the inevitable result of power and political relationships: conflict. Conflict is understood as an important and pervasive part
of any political environment. We'll look at the role of communication in conflict, conflict style, and the effect of gender on conflict management. We'll see
that women are perceived differently than men in conflict situations. We'll
also examine the role of women as informal organizational peacekeepers.

Two perspectives on managing conflict are discussed—principled negotiation and the 5A model—followed by an overview of Linda Putnam's work with
bargaining and negotiation. The chapter concludes with a discussion of labor
negotiation and a summary of politics as a reflection of organization culture.

Key Terms

power	structuration
reward power	conflict
coercive power	conflict style
referent power	peacekeepers
expert power	principled negotiation
legitimate power	coorientational accuracy
covert power	bargaining
politics	bargaining frame
unobtrusive control	reframing
juristic person	negotiation power

Before venturing any further into this chapter, I'd like to relate a story about
an organizational experience I once had. After reading it, try to think about
any similar experiences that you have had. Also, think through the nature of
politics in that work group and how power was developed and demonstrated.

I was employed for about a year as a commission-based sales clerk for a
large retail store. I was one of three part-timers in this department, which was
a combined department that housed outdoor supplies, such as lawn mowers,
snow throwers, and shovels, along with "big-ticket hardware," such as table
saws, drill presses, and lathes. Also in the department were two full-timers,
who worked the day shift, and a department manager and assistant manager.

One of the first things I noticed when joining that department was the
way that the full-timers and the part-timers who had been there a while treated the manager. There was a clear sense of distrust and lack of confidence. The
full-timers decided what signs announcing sales were appropriate, interacted
with the manager in a patronizing fashion, gave us part-timers our work assignments, and performed other roles commonly reserved for management. I
soon learned that the manager, who was about fifteen years younger than either of the full-timers, was perceived as "just moving through," on his way to
bigger promotions. This perception caused the full-timers and part-timers to
resent the manager, suspect his sincerity, and question his competence.

Within this context I had a significant run-in with this manager. The manager decided work schedules a week in advance. Two weeks before my wife's

birthday, I approached him with a note requesting the day of her birthday off so that we could attend a concert. "No problem," was his response. Imagine my surprise, then, to discover the next Monday that I was scheduled to work the Thursday that I had requested off. I approached the manager with his mistake and was told that there was nothing he could do about it. I should arrange to switch days with another part-timer.

Unfortunately, none of the other sales clerks who weren't scheduled for that night could switch with me. As I stood there on the sales floor cursing the manager, one of the part-timers who had been there about two years longer than me asked why I was so upset. I explained that I had really wanted the night off and now would be unable to celebrate my wife's birthday. Her response was: "Just take it off. Don't show up. Nothing will happen to you."

I didn't take her seriously, but she pressed on, explaining that this manager had no power over us; that he was afraid of us and would do nothing if I broke the rules. I thought about it for a couple of days and, on Thursday, enjoyed a wonderful concert with my wife. I returned to work the next Saturday, my next scheduled workday, fully expecting to be fired. About an hour after I arrived I ran into the manager in the storeroom. He asked me where I had been on Thursday. I told him, honestly. He looked frustrated and angry, told me not to do it again, and walked away.

ORGANIZATIONS AS POLITICAL ARENAS

A political approach to organizations is neither new nor radical. What the political approach opens up to the researcher was encapsulated nicely by Bacharach and Lawler (1980):

> Organizations are neither the rational, harmonious entities celebrated in managerial theory nor the arenas of apocalyptic class conflict projected by Marxists. Rather, it may be argued, a more suitable notion lies somewhere between those two—a concept of organizations as politically negotiated orders. Adopting this view, we can observe organizational actors in their daily transactions perpetually bargaining, repeatedly forming and reforming coalitions, and constantly availing themselves of influence tactics. . . . Survival in an organization is a political act. Corporations, universities, and voluntary associations are arenas for daily political action. (p. 1)

Given this statement, reflect on the example at the head of the chapter. What sort of order was negotiated between the sales clerks and the manager? How would you describe the political environment, even with only the limited information supplied?

Communication is at the heart of organizational functioning, being the means of negotiation and coalition formation in the political arena. And power, through its link to communication, is the constant in all political-organizational life (Conrad, 1994, p. 267). Power and politics are intertwined; approaching one forces the realization of the other, moving back and forth between rules, influence, tactics, intent, and a host of other dimensions of this complex perspective.

A cultural explanation of organizations as political systems must begin, then, with the nature of politics, in an effort to understand why power is an inherent feature of political systems. Then, after reviewing the nature of political order, we'll turn our attention directly to power itself.

The Nature of Political Systems

Political systems are most simply understood as forms of governance. Underlying any governmental system is the assumption that without a form of control over the mass of people, chaos will rule. *This control comes in the form of rules, making political systems governance via rules.*

Rule systems, of course, come in many forms. Some organizations are governed by the rules of bureaucracy, some by autocracy, some by technocracy, some by democracy. Whatever the form that the rules take, the goal in each case is the same: control. A bureaucracy controls through formal, codified rule systems; in an autocracy control is exercised by a recognized authority who has the power to dictate to followers; in a technocracy control is given to those with the greatest amount of technical expertise; and in a democracy, control is exercised through the joint participation of the masses and those chosen to represent the masses.

Rule systems are designed to control things such as people, resources, chaos, the environment, and products. The rules may be formal and codified or informal and covert. Either way the rules for control are the foundation of the political-ethical environment and are manifested in the conflicts and power struggles within these environments.

- *Why are rules important in our understanding of organizations as political systems?*

Because political systems are about rules and rule enforcement, conflict is inevitable. At some point in any ruled environment, disagreement will occur, and this disagreement may prompt the use of power, as power is validated by the political process, or the conflict may be the result of the use of power, again as validated by the political process. Either way, the conflict-power relationship will define the ethical environment, making the ethical-political environment hard to distinguish as two separate organizational components. The complex relationship between politics and power will be explored in the next section.

Politics and Power

When we talk about power, we're not referring to influence only. Influence is relatively neutral. It refers to persuasion and voluntary conformity on the part of the influenced. *Power,* on the other hand, refers to control and a potential to coerce. Power often refers to involuntary submission rather than voluntary compliance (Bacharach & Lawler, 1980, p. 12).

In this section we will examine four claims about power: first, that power is inherent within political structures; second, that power permeates organizational life; third, that power is both overt and covert; and fourth, that power is relational and developmental. These four issues are especially important to an understanding of organization culture.

Power Is Inherent within Political Structures

Earlier in the chapter I wrote that organizations are systems of rules. We should ask now: "Who made the rules, and why?" The answer, of course, is that the rules of the organization are made by those with the power to make rules, in an effort to maintain their power. Rules are generally guidelines for the maintenance of the status quo (Clegg, 1989). If these rules are not reproduced, that is, if steps are not taken by those with power to maintain their powerful positions, some sort of transformation is likely. New rules will be offered to take the place of the existing rules; political transformation will occur.

Rules will always reflect the strategic interests of organizational members. Strategic interests will always be protected by the creation of power differentials between those with power and those without. Thus, we can see that power is inherent within political structures, as people try to define and control their relationships with others and with self.

Power Permeates Organizational Life

Power is a pervasive fact of organizational life. This is not to say that everyone wants power "over" others; indeed, such a conceptualization defeats a thorough understanding of power and its value in the first place (Conrad, 1994). The pervasiveness of power is reflected in the fact that we all want some. We don't all want to have control over others, but we do all want to have some control over ourselves. Not having power leaves one feeling dependent, trapped, and frustrated. Hagberg (1984) suggested that the powerless in organizations suffer from a "victim mentality." They are dependent upon others to make things happen. Because of their dependence upon others, the powerless must resort to manipulation of those with power.

Ashforth (1989) studied the effect of perceived feelings of powerlessness on newcomers' work expectations and experiences. Specifically, Ashforth examined the impact of a discrepancy between expectations and a work environment that likely would not meet those expectations. Powerlessness was defined as "a lack of participation and autonomy" (p. 207). Ashforth studied 206 workers from a telecommunications company, representing all hierarchical levels, with less than two years tenure. His results showed that powerlessness led to feelings of frustration, helplessness, and lack of commitment. Conversely, a sense of power was related to the absence of such negative feelings.

- *What is the effect of powerlessness on workers?*

We should note, then, that the answer to the question of why people want power is so that they're not powerless. Wanting to avoid the feelings of helplessness that go along with powerlessness is very different from wanting to dominate others. Unfortunately, in many political systems power and domination are not so separate.

Power Is Both Overt and Covert

One of our biggest problems regarding power is the mistaken assumption that power is something that people can see. This notion of overt power is a real fact of organizational life. Legitimated power hierarchies exist, in which some individuals have power over others. This perspective on power was popularized by French and Raven (1959) as existing in five forms: reward, coercive, referent, expert, and legitimate.

With *reward power,* I have power over you if I can control something that you want. With *coercive power,* my power over you stems from your fear that I may punish you for your failure to perform adequately. With *referent power,* my power over you comes from your appreciation of me as a person; you find me charismatic or enjoy my personality. With *expert power,* my power comes from my greater competence. And with *legitimate power,* my formal position gives me the right to control your behavior.

Though the above five forms of power have made an important contribution to our understanding of power "over," their limitations as an adequate explanation for the complexity of power within organizational structures has been questioned in many places (see Bacharach & Lawler, 1980; Eisenberg & Goodall, 1993). To develop a more complete understanding of power we must go beyond the overt level and examine the covert nature of power.

Covert power refers to power that is being exercised out of the awareness of the individuals being affected. Power is so much a part of organizational life, operating at the very deepest, structural levels, embedded within the very nature of the organization, that its impact on organizational behavior is easy to overlook (Frost, 1987).

Politics is the form that power and power relations take in the organization. Politics is about rules and rule systems, power relationships and influence groups, coalitions and dominance. It is a legitimate form of organizational enterprise that sometimes is used illegitimately. The important point about organizational politics is that it is power in both action and conception (Frost, 1987). *This means that the organizational system can be developed to favor some over others (conception) and, when functioning, political action is the demonstration of power relationships (action).*

Power at the covert level should be of greater concern to organizational researchers and members. Referred to as the "deep structure" of power (Conrad, 1983), power at the covert level is more difficult to understand because its influences are tacit. When the organization's norms or rules serve as the premises used by an individual to make decisions, then in essence, power has achieved its greatest potential: it is reified (Clegg, 1989), meaning that the individual being influenced is unaware of the influence and, hence, cannot resist it. This influence may be in the form of rules, rituals, rites, stories, artifacts, and so forth.

This is not to say that all behavior is political. Viewing organizations as political arenas sometimes results in this incorrect assumption. Much behavior is not aimed at increasing one's power or political effectiveness (Mayes & Allen, 1977). Showing up to work in the morning, for example, is certainly a neutral behavior. However, consistently coming in to work early may be viewed by coworkers as political maneuvering.

- *What is the relationship between politics and power?*

Unobtrusive Control

When control resides within the very structure of the organization it is understood as unobtrusive. *Unobtrusive control* results when individuals identify with the organization so strongly that the organization's values become the workers' values. The organization in this case is personified as the "juristic person" (Tompkins & Cheney, 1985). The *juristic person* is an entity, such as an organization, in contrast to natural persons, that exerts power over workers.

Tompkins and Cheney argued that in contemporary organizations, power has been transferred from natural to juristic persons. This transfer is the result of organizations' exerting concertive control: control via the inculcation of organizational values and beliefs into the worker. This control works by supplying the worker with bases for decisions—premises—that are in accordance with organizational goals. The organization strives to instill within its workers such a level of identification that the worker will make decisions that are in the best interests of the organization, because the worker identifies so strongly and unconsciously with the organization. The worker will see the decisional premises as "factual," directing that actor to a course of action that is "natural" given the understanding of the worker. Finally, communication sets the premises. Organizational identification and concertive control, then, are communication processes.

- *What is unobtrusive control?*

These assumptions about concertive control were tested by Bullis (1991) and Bullis and Tompkins (1989). Bullis and Tompkins conducted a longitudinal examination of changes in the forms of control used by the U.S. Forest Service, an organization recognized as having a "strong culture," capable of controlling it members' ways of thinking and believing. They examined the culture of the service and then measured their results against predictions about organizational identification suggested by Cheney and Tompkins's earlier works. What they found was a definite shift in forms of control. Whereas the "old" Forest Service relied on unobtrusive, concertive control, this study found that the contemporary Forest Service relies more on obtrusive, explicit, bureaucratic control mechanisms. The result has been a decrease in member identification with the organization.

In an interesting followup study of concertive control, again with the Forest Service, Bullis (1991) found support for the prediction that unobtrusive control does affect member decision making in organizations. The implication, of course, is that the organizational value system comes to serve as the premises upon which decisions are made, possibly supplanting reasoned, critical thinking.

Power Is Relational and Developmental

It is a great error to equate power with individual characteristics, such as height and weight. Power is not a component of individual makeup. Rather, power is a dimension that exists between entities, be they people, groups, or individuals and organizational structure, that is developed over time. Power refers to an interaction that is characterized by influence tactics and dependency, through which one of the partners directs the other's outcome (Bacharach & Lawler, 1980). In short, power would be a relatively uncomplicated, straightforward concept if it were not relational. A cultural view of power focuses extensively on the relational character of the concept, looking specifically at the developmental events that lead to the emergence of the "power relationship."

As relational, then, power is created and sustained by the partners in the relationship, through the exercise of the rules of interaction and the resources that the participants bring into the interaction. This process is often referred to as *structuration* (Clegg, 1989; Conrad, 1983; Poole & McPhee, 1983). The creation and maintenance of a power relationship leads to the notion of "duality of structure" (Conrad, 1983), in which structure is created by the participants and then serves to influence the relationship. As this form takes shape, it takes on a level of rationality (Clegg, 1990), in which it justifies its own character and existence. Power becomes a property of the relationship, constituted in the rules of production and maintenance. The source of the power is resource dependency—the unequal distribution of resources, so that what one partner needs, and does not have, the other partner controls.

To say that power refers to relational influence should not be construed to mean that it exists only in interpersonal relationships. Often power is argued to be a *structural* component of organizations, with relational implications. Kanter (1977) offered a concise summary of many of the structural dimensions. She noted that system size and complexity can affect power as the ability to work through others. For example, how centralized or decentralized the workplace is can affect members' ability to build and nurture power-based relationships.

Structurally, power is "accumulated as a result of performance—the job-related activities people engaged in" (Kanter, 1977, p. 176). But these activities must fulfill three criteria: They must be extraordinary, visible, and relevant.

First, activities must be extraordinary, for the performance of routine jobs doesn't give their performers any advantage. If the job is predictable, expected, then no matter how well it is carried out the performer will derive little in the form of power. This is the lot of the factory assembler, workers low in the organizational hierarchy, custodians, and so forth.

Second, visibility is crucial for an activity to enhance power—not just visibility to anyone, but visibility to those with influence of their own. The most visible performers in organizations are boundary spanners (discussed in Chapter 8). The ability to participate in multiple structural configurations is a quick route to visibility, influence, and power.

Third, the key to the importance of extraordinary performance and visibility as sources of power is relevance. Activity for activity's sake is no more interesting to the organization than lack of activity. For activities to enhance power, they must be relevant to identifiable issues and problems.

What is extraordinary, how to be visible, and what is relevant are all structurally determined elements that individuals must understand in their efforts to derive power from the workplace itself, rather than from other workers. Clearly then, power is relational. But we must generalize our understanding of relationship to include those with personal bases, such as friendships; those with structural bases, such as alliances with peers, sponsors (such as superiors and mentors), and subordinates; and those with organizational structure itself.

- *Summarize the conceptualization of power as structural.*

GAINING POWER

Now that we have a feel for what power is and where it resides in the organization, the next question is "Where can I get some?" The answer seems to be "by belonging to an already powerful group." In two important reports, Pfeffer and Salancik (1974) and Kelly (1976) demonstrated convincingly that power belongs to the powerful.

Pfeffer and Salancik studied the effect of departmental politics on a university's resource allocation process. Noting that the budget process may be constrained by at least two sets of forces, universalistic (everyone shares equally) and particularistic (resource allocation is unequal), the authors studied the budget process in an attempt to identify the relative impact of these two forces. They found that subunit power had a direct impact on resource allocation. The actual work load of the departments studied had much less impact on their budgets than did their power within the university relative to other departments.

Similarly, Kelly presented the argument that the success of any organizational innovation attempt depends on the degree to which the innovator manages to "seduce" the elites—those individuals who, by the legitimacy of their positions within the company, have the ability to make or break a program. This is a political model of organizational innovation. In it, organizations are presented as arenas of competing interest groups that go at each other like gladiators in a ring. Indeed, Kelly talks in almost these terms:

> The elites seldom enter the organizational arena: they are, instead, the spectators. They watch clashes between coalitions of technocrats over policy and programs, usually supporting the winner. . . . The elites do not enter the arena and become bloodied; they instead act as prerequisites to action, controlling support that may be withdrawn at any time. The essential nature of

the elite is to be fickle. So the innovator must woo and seduce these fickle elites at critical junctures in the innovative process, to insure the success of the project. (p. 67)

Because of their power, then, these coalitions of elites have enormous influence on the ultimate success of any new venture the organizational innovator advocates. Those programs that stand the best chances of succeeding, according to Kelly, are those viewed as the most conservative—the least departure from the status quo. The elite dislikes change.

SUMMARY: CULTURE, POWER, AND POLITICS

We need to pause here and summarize the points that have been made thus far, so that we don't lose track of their cultural implications. What I've said to this point can be encapsulated in a few succinct statements: Organizations are political arenas composed of rule systems created to control the flow of activity; inherent within any system of control will be a distribution and use of power; power permeates organizational life; everyone wants, at a minimum, the power to control his or her own affairs; power is both overt and covert; power is often shifted from natural to juristic persons; power is relational and developmental; and gaining power has much to do with belonging to or aligning yourself with already powerful groups.

This isn't a very pretty picture of organizational life, is it? However, a more important question than whether we like the picture is: "Is it accurate?" I'd say "yes." The reason that this is an accurate overall picture has to do with culturally biased value systems and some primary components of typical western organizations: scarcity, hierarchy, the ladder of success, and competition. Allowing these components to guide our thinking, we create rules to enforce their legitimacy.

For example, we have come to believe in this country that organizations are contexts of limitation: limited resources, limited opportunities, limited options, and so forth. This scarcity mentality has become virtually a structural parameter, accepted by almost all individuals as a fact of their employment. As a culturally embedded operating assumption, it goes unquestioned by organization members as they struggle from workday to workday.

The hierarchical nature of most organizational design reinforces the scarcity mentality. Workers can see the limited opportunity above them, forcing them to compete harder to climb that ladder of success. Within this competitive environment, we use power, seek power, resent power, and become victims of power. Our own thoughts and behavior become influenced by the assumptions that surround the relationships among power, control, success, and scarcity.

Consider how different life is in organizations that don't reinforce a scarcity metaphor. How different would it be to participate in a culture of abundance, where employees were treated as an unlimited resource, where advancement included job enlargement rather than filling positions of power over others, and where potential was considered unlimited? The point is that our organizations are products of our culture, not the other way around. We participate in the dialogues that create the organizations, which then turn around and help shape the dialogues.

In other words, if we are victims of power relationships that we find unfulfilling, or we are participating in rule systems that we disagree with, we must remember that we have options. We can help to reshape the rules, we can actively work to call the unquestioned assumptions out into the open for discussion, we can leave the system. Ultimately, we can have power over ourselves, and we must never be willing to relinquish that.

CONFLICT AT WORK

Power, politics, unequal distribution of resources, powerlessness, influence, control—these are the cultural variables that constitute the organizational political environment. It is no surprise, then, that conflict and conflict management play such an important part in understanding organizations.

The Importance of Understanding Conflict

Conflict plays a significant role in how people understand and play out their organizational lives. Thomas and Schmidt (1976) drove home that point when they found that managers spend about 20 percent of their time dealing with conflict, with CEOs reporting the least amount of time spent, and middle managers the most. This pervasiveness of conflict in the workplace has been noted by most conflict researchers, including Hall (1993), Kolb and Putnam (1992), Putnam and Poole (1987), Putnam and Roloff (1992a), and Rahim (1985).

Communication is the dominant characteristic of conflict, for it serves as the vehicle of conflict transmission and the source of conflict management. The importance of communication is highlighted in most definitions of conflict. For this text, we'll use Folger, Poole, and Stutman's (1993) definition (adapted from Hocker & Wilmot, 1985) of *conflict:* "Conflict is the interaction of interdependent people who perceive incompatible goals and interference from each other in achieving those goals" (p. 4).

This definition brings several significant features of conflict to the surface. First, *conflict involves interdependence and incompatibility.* These are two of the most crucial definitional components in identifying conflicts. Interdependence means that if two individuals are in disagreement, but are not dependent upon each other, conflict doesn't exist. Likewise, even if the participants are dependent on each other, but their goals are not incompatible, even though the goals differ, then conflict does not exist.

For example, consider the situation in which two roommates decide to go to a fast food restaurant for supper. They take one car and at the intersection where they must turn they realize that one of them wants to turn right to dine at the pizza place, while the other wants to turn left to dine at the burger joint.

Clearly, since they are in the same car the participants are interdependent. Just as clearly, however, their goals are not incompatible, for they can easily go one direction, pick up the food, and swing back in the other direction to satisfy the hunger of the other.

- *What is the importance of interdependence and incompatibility in identifying conflict?*

The third significant component of the definition is interaction. *Conflict must be an interactive communicative event.* This means that one cannot have a conflict with oneself. Conflict is not about inner choices, such as, "Should I go to class or stay in bed an hour longer?" This is an example of a decision, not a conflict. Conflicts are dependent on the behavior of conflict partners. A conflict is a dynamic, evolving communicative relationship based upon the actions and reactions of the conflict parties.

The importance of conflict and the seminal role of communication in conflict was summarized by Folger, Poole, and Stutman (1993). They offered the following five properties of conflict interaction (Chapters 3 and 9): (1) Conflict consists of the moves and countermoves of the participants; (2) conflict behavior tends to be repetitive (both productive and unproductive behavior, once introduced, tends to perpetuate itself); (3) conflict episodes are communicative interactions embedded within the larger framework of overall relationships; (4) although conflicts may appear chaotic, they do have direction and movement that can be understood; and (5) conflict always has an effect on relationships.

- *Summarize the importance of communication in conflict.*

We must also remind ourselves that conflict is, in and of itself, neither good nor bad. Rather, the way that conflict is managed can lead to either positive or negative outcomes. Some of the positive effects of conflict include increased stimulation among workers, better ideas and idea generation, recognition of flaws in the system, cohesiveness among conflict partners as they work toward a common goal or purpose, and adjustment of the balance of power. We hardly need to remind ourselves of some of the negative consequences, including destroyed relationships, hurt feelings, anger, frustration and resentment, and physical illness from stress. Is it any wonder that we so often work to avoid conflict, forgetting that it carries a host of potentially valuable outcomes!

KENNETH THOMAS AND CONFLICT STYLES

Kenneth Thomas's work has played a profound role in our overall understanding of conflict—particularly in the area of *conflict style.* Since the 1970s, Thomas (1976, 1988; Kilmann & Thomas, 1978) has worked to demonstrate the importance of style in the management of conflicts. Though widely discussed and adopted, Thomas's work is also subjected to a fair amount of criticism.

Most of the criticism revolves around his articulation of a two-dimensional model to depict five conflict styles (Figure 9-1). Critics argue that two-dimensional scaling, such as that used by Thomas and many others, may not be representative or exhaustive of the actual conflict process (Knapp, Putnam, & Davis, 1988).

As shown in Figure 9-1, Thomas maps five conflict styles along two axes, depending upon one's general desires to satisfy self and other. A high desire to satisfy self coupled with a low desire to satisfy other results in a *competitive* conflict style. This win-lose orientation is typical in much of our discussions of conflict as well as our general societal infatuation with sports. A low desire to satisfy both self and other results in an *avoidance* style. Of the five styles discussed, avoidance is potentially the most destructive, for it rests on the assumption of a lose-lose orientation. Nobody's needs are met and the conflict itself in not addressed, often resulting in additional conflicts.

A high desire to satisfy other coupled with a low desire to satisfy self is referred to as *accommodation*. This is a lose-win style in which the individual yields to the conflict partner. This is a style of passivity, and the accommodating person is easily and often taken advantage of. A moderate desire to satisfy both self and other is a *compromising* style. It is hard to specify compromise as win-win, lose-lose, or win-lose. It is win-win in that both parties get some of their needs met; it is lose-lose in that the "rules" of compromise are such that both parties prioritize their needs so as to surrender those less important; and it is win-lose in that the more powerful or skilled negotiator easily wins concessions from the less skilled negotiator.

Finally, a high desire to satisfy both self and other is called *collaboration*. This is the only true win-win style on the grid, for collaboration, by definition, means mutual need fulfillment.

- *Summarize the five conflict styles discussed by Thomas and plot them on the grid used in Figure 9.1.*

FIGURE 9-1. Thomas's five conflict styles

Assertive	Competitive	Collaborative
Desire to Satisfy Self	Compromise	
Unassertive	Avoidance	Accommodation
	Uncooperative	Cooperative

Desire to Satisfy Other

It is important to note that none of these five styles is appropriate to every conflict situation. Style must be adapted to circumstances. For example, avoidance is necessary if physical harm might occur and is useful for issues of no real consequence to the participants. Competition is useful in situations in which the partners have limited time to make decisions, or in which one partner is clearly more knowledgeable than the other. Accommodation is valuable in situations in which one partner wants to please the other, or the issue is less important to one than the other. Collaboration is important in those situations in which much time is available to make the decision, or shared commitment is necessary. Compromise is useful in situations in which conflict partner needs can be rank-ordered, and less important ones sacrificed for those more important.

CONFLICT AND GENDER

The importance of conflict communication is especially apparent when dealing with perceived gender differences in organizations. A number of studies have clearly pointed out that women tend to be perceived differently as conflict managers than are men, even when these perceptions are not congruent with reality. For example, Conrad (1991) found that men and women managers accurately predicted which conflict management strategies they would use in first iterations of conflict management attempts, but when those strategies were unsuccessful, predictions of subsequent strategies were less accurate. Conrad found that both men and women managers shifted to coercive styles at the second (men) or third (women) iterations of management efforts. This shift occurred for managers who opted for both prosocial and antisocial initial styles. The bottom line, then, was that threat can be predicted to be used by both men and women managers. For women, threats may come somewhat later, but they still come.

Monroe et al. (1990) looked at the relationship between gender and difficult personalities—the difficult subordinate, specifically. They cited earlier research that sorted difficult subordinate behavior into four categories: avoidance (tendency of difficult subordinates to avoid conflict), apparent compliance (saying that they will comply, but then falling back into old behavior patterns), alibis (blaming others or circumstances for the problem), and relational leverage (reinterpreting negative feedback as a form of confrontation). The study relied on descriptions by superiors of conflicts with difficult subordinates.

The results showed a definite gender impact. What was found was that the gender of either of the participants was less important than the gender relationship between the participants. When the supervisor was male and the difficult subordinate was female, that subordinate was described as using avoidance, but when the supervisor was female, no such reported tendency with female subordinates was reported. When the supervisor was female and the subordinate was male, the behavior reported was a tendency toward confrontation. But when the supervisor was male, this reported tendency disappeared.

Women As Peacekeepers

Though most of the formal research on conflict in organizations is concerned with public, overt conflicts, resolved through formally sanctioned methods (Martin, 1992), an increasing number of researchers are looking into the other world of conflict—that which is played out behind the scenes. One interesting example is the work of Kolb (1992), who researched the role that women play as informal peacekeepers in organizations. Kolb argued that women may play a prominent part in organizational conflict management as the informal *peacekeepers* who engage in behind-the-scenes efforts at promoting harmony and peace in the organization. Women are more likely than men to perform this role because of their generally lower hierarchical positions and their large representation in support functions. Society may also expect women to perform these roles.

The informal peacekeeping role differs greatly from the formal, mediational conflict management role. Peacekeepers are insiders with intimate knowledge of the workplace and the conflict participants. Their presence within the organization makes their intervention in the conflict timely and private. Also, because the peacekeeping role is behind the scenes, it may often lead to more formal, public conflict management.

There seem to be three personal reasons for women to engage in the peacekeeping role. First, loyalty to the organization may prompt them to want to help smooth over conflicts. Second, women may genuinely be motivated to help the conflict participants. Third, women may be more motivated than men to avoid conflicts and thus desire to have them resolved. Regardless of their motivation for becoming peacekeepers, four activities seem to characterize the role.

First, *the peacekeeper provides support for the parties in conflict.* By allowing the participants a sympathetic ear the peacekeeper is offering support and reassurance that the conflict is legitimate and will be managed effectively. Second, *the peacekeeper reframes the conflicts.* As a third party the peacekeeper is able to help the conflict participants reframe the conflict in such a way that more creative resolutions or interpretations may appear. This reframing function may be the most important from a conflict management perspective. Successful conflict management is often the process of reframing or changing the partner's field of vision. The frame is the basis upon which the conflict participant will evaluate information. It is the influence of the person's past in current understanding. Thus, tendencies such as competitiveness, biases against certain individuals, and preferred modes of conflict management all form part of the person's frame (Putnam & Holmer, 1992).

Third, *the peacekeeper translates the perceptions of the conflict participants.* This occurs as the peacekeeper listens and interprets or carries messages back and forth between the conflict partners. Finally, *the peacekeeper orchestrates*, by providing the means through which these private conflicts can become publicly resolved.

Clearly, then, the peacekeeping role is an important one in organizations. It helps the organization keep going in a relatively smooth fashion by helping the participants get along better with each other. Unfortunately, even though these benefits are clear, the peacekeeping role is seldom rewarded by the organization. It is behind-the-scenes work that often goes unnoticed by superiors and those charged with promoting and rewarding. Peacekeeping is not part of a job description nor is it part of the formal reward structure. Thus, even though the peacekeepers may find the role rewarding, and even though the organization derives value from the peacekeepers, performing the role will seldom result in tangible organizational rewards.

We should also note, in closing this section, that the informal peacekeeping role may also serve to help escalate conflicts. The peacekeeper is a third party, increasing the interpretations and chances of misinterpretation of intent. Additionally, peacekeepers must internalize much conflict in which they are only secondarily involved. This internalization may eventually exact a psychological toll on the peacekeeper.

- *What is the peacekeeping role in organizational conflict? Why is it important? What are the implications of the tendency of women rather than men to play this role?*

MANAGING CONFLICT

Conflict management is a combination of perspective and action. How conflict is conceptualized will usually have a direct bearing on the actions taken to manage conflict. For example, overestimating the tendencies or abilities of conflict participants to behave rationally may result in a model of conflict that is more mechanistic or linear than the actual process (Louis, 1977); valuing competitive behavior or not being aware of one's competitive nature may result in the conflict participant not being receptive or not seeing alternatives (Filley, 1978); and seeing conflict as bad or as something to be avoided may result in the inability to use conflict to generate positive outcomes in relationships or in the workplace (Rahim, 1985). In this section we'll look at two models of conflict management. Each offers guidelines for behavior based upon overarching conceptualizations of what conflict is.

Principled Negotiation

Fisher and Ury (1981) discussed a process for conflict management called "principled negotiation." The process stems from their recognition that most participants in conflicts argue over positions: "I'm right, you're wrong." Posi-

TABLE 9-1. Principled Negotiation

Principled negotiation depends on four rules.

1. *People:*   The partners must separate the participants in the dispute from the problem itself. The focus should be on the problem.

2. *Interests:* The participants should focus on their mutual interests. It is more common for participants to focus on positions, rather than interests or needs.

3. *Options:* They should try to create a variety of options that would meet each other's needs.

4. *Criteria:* They should measure the quality of their solutions against some objective, commonly agreed-upon criteria.

Note: Based on Fisher and Ury (1981).

tional bargaining only leads to painting oneself into corners that are difficult to get out of. *Principled negotiation,* on the other hand, is a technique for dispute management that moves the focus of the dispute away from the participants themselves and onto the problem. The process of principled negotiation is outlined in Table 9-1.

The behavioral options suggested by the philosophy of principled negotiation are very much in step with that philosophy because, quite simply, the philosophy and the behavior are the same thing. Principled negotiation is a process of conflict management in which the rules that govern behavior are the evidence of the philosophy itself. For example, principled negotiation relies on the conflict partners moving away from positional bargaining—arguing one's position instead of finding and meeting mutual needs. If the conflict partners are arguing positions, their behavior is inconsistent with the philosophy of principled negotiation.

- *What are the components of principled negotiation?*

Borisoff and Victor's 5A Model

Borisoff and Victor (1989) presented a five-step model for conflict management based on the importance of interaction management and mutual understanding. Their model is presented in Table 9-2.

The model is deceptively complex. Like Fisher and Ury's model, Borisoff and Victor's offers a number of philosophical and behavioral guidelines, meaning that the conflict participants will be demonstrating their understanding of conflict management by their use of the suggested behavior. However, unlike Fisher and Ury's model, Borisoff and Victor's model might be too easily interpreted as a stage model. Stage models are linear, sequential presentations that oversimplify complex processes. The reader should be cautious not to interpret Table 9-2 in a way that it was not intended to be seen.

- *Summarize Borisoff and Victor's 5A model of conflict management.*

TABLE 9-2. 5A Model of Conflict Management

Step 1: Assessment (the determination of an initial level of understanding)

Step 2: Acknowledgment (of the other party's concerns and the legitimacy of those concerns)

Step 3: Attitude (must have a willingness to work toward resolution)

Step 4: Action (the actual verbal and nonverbal behavior)

Step 5: Analysis (a review of the process to be sure that both parties' needs have been met, and that the solution found is acceptable and can be implemented)

Note: Based on Borisoff and Victor (1989).

This model is particularly compelling in light of recent research by Papa and Pood (1988). Papa and Pood examined what conditions might be necessary to keep conflict episodes from degenerating into negative, counterproductive experiences. The authors suggested that *coorientational accuracy* might be a significant factor in determining the difference between satisfactory and unsatisfactory conflict. It might also predispose tactic selection by the conflict partners. Coorientational accuracy refers to having a sense of the views of the conflict partner. Knowing the views of the partner should put the conflict participants in a better position to constructively manage the conflict toward mutual goal and need satisfaction.

The authors studied eighty employees of an insurance company office that was undergoing heated discussions concerning the use of a more participatory decision-making approach in the office. The subjects were paired and observed during conflict discussions, which were coded for tactic selection, and all participants were surveyed for satisfaction and coorientational accuracy. The results confirmed the authors' hypothesis. High coorientational accuracy (CA) positively affected participant satisfaction with both the process and the outcome of conflict episodes, as well as tactic selection. Furthermore, in high CA pairs, discussion time was significantly less than in the low CA pairs. Tactic choice in the high CA pairs moved from friendliness and bargaining to reason and assertiveness (forceful). On the other hand, in low CA pairs the participants preferred assertiveness, followed by reason, bargaining, coalition building, and friendliness.

LINDA PUTNAM: BARGAINING, NEGOTIATION, AND CONFLICT MANAGEMENT

In this section we'll look at some of the contributions of Linda Putnam, particularly to our understanding of bargaining and negotiation as communication events. This section, then, completes our overview of the theoretical and applied value of conflict research.

Putnam has written widely on the topic of bargaining and conflict management (including Kolb & Putnam, 1992; Putnam, 1988; Putnam & Geist, 1985; Putnam & Holmer, 1992; Putnam & Jones, 1982a, 1982b; Putnam & Poole, 1987; Putnam & Roloff, 1992a, 1992b; Putnam, Van Hoeven, & Bullis, 1991). In this section we can only review briefly some of Putnam's work on bargaining as conflict management.

Bargaining, as conflict management, "focuses upon the moves and countermoves, concessions and counterproposals in quest of a zone of reasonable outcomes for both parties" (Putnam & Jones, 1982a, p. 263). Bargaining is central to negotiation (discussed in greater detail later). Negotiation is distinguished by the fact that, unlike the participants in problem solving or decision making, the participants in negotiations may have incompatible goals and may work to actively obstruct the process of reaching resolution (Putnam & Roloff, 1992b).

Clearly, communication plays the central role in the success of bargaining and negotiation. A communication focus approaches negotiation from the examination of messages and communicative behavior. Communication researchers attempt to uncover meanings through focusing on the elements of message (such as verbal and nonverbal components, channels, and form) and the features of message exchange (such as tactics, strategies, goals, and sequences).

Putnam and Jones (1982a) argued that bargaining is the most common mode of conflict resolution in today's businesses. Bargaining is a rule-governed form of communicative behavior that resembles a game. Bargaining can lead to both integrative (win-win) and distributive (win-lose) outcomes. Thus, it is unreasonable to consider bargaining a select communication event, restricted to management-labor contract disputes. Suppliers bargain with buyers, students with teachers, spouses with spouses, and so forth. The common theme in these contexts is that each of the participants has an aim for the outcome that differs from that of the partner. These different aims produce the tradeoffs that characterize bargaining. Communication facilitates the information exchange necessary to produce a successful outcome.

- *What is bargaining?*

Putnam and Jones (1982b) studied how reciprocity (matching the tactics of the partner) affected both integrative (win-win) and distributional (win-lose) bargaining outcomes. They matched graduate and undergraduate male and female students role-playing labor or management positions and found that the role played by the bargainer had an effect on the types of strategies employed. Those in the distributional management role engaged in far more defensive behavior than did those in the labor role, who engaged in offensive tactics. Thus, reciprocity played a limited part in distributional bargaining. The opposite was found in integrative situations, in which both labor and management reciprocated efforts to cooperate or not cooperate. The sex of the bargainer had no effect. Putnam and Jones concluded: "In particular, escalating conflicts appear to evolve from the mismanagement of distributive communication rather than from the ineffectual use of problem-solving behaviors. But when integrative acts are emitted, individuals reciprocate these problem-solving approaches" (p. 191).

Finally, in a fascinating study of two teacher-administration collective-bargaining efforts, Putnam, Van Hoeven, and Bullis (1991) found that bargaining can facilitate the process of symbolic convergence (see Chapter 1 for a discussion of symbolic convergence theory). Bargaining was viewed as a symbolic and interpretive process, rather than as a game or an economic activity. The focus, then, was on stories, rites, rituals, and so forth, rather than on winning and losing. Symbolic convergence is a reasonable theoretical framework here because the assumption is that the two sides work to unite values, visions, interpretations, attitudes, and so forth.

The researchers found that the participants in the bargaining did indeed cast themselves and their opposition in terms of heroes and villains. The fantasy themes that emerged served to unify the teams as well as isolate the enemies. Although the specific content and nature of the two districts' fantasy themes varied, separate analyses showed the prevalence of fantasies as well as the value of this sort of interpretive approach to understanding the bargaining process.

Putnam's work has particular relevance to negotiation. So before concluding this chapter, we'll take a quick look at one of the more complex negotiation contexts: the labor-management dispute.

LABOR-MANAGEMENT NEGOTIATIONS

When labor and management sit down at the negotiating table, it sets off one of the most complex of organizational communicative scenes. Hierarchy, working conditions, communication style, conflict management skills, roles, norms, the history of working conditions, expectations, gender of participants, and a host of other variables play themselves out in the difficult process of reaching contractual agreements.

The situation has become even more complicated by recent changes in the environments in which both employers and unions find themselves (McKersie, 1993). These changes include the impact of foreign competition, the situations faced in labor markets, deregulation, and a general decline of unions throughout the country. Employers increasingly have used a number of strategies to weaken the bargaining strength of unions in general, including pulling assets out of unionized plants and subcontracting work out to nonunionized workers who work for less pay.

These environmental and strategic changes have forced employers and unions to reframe the labor contract bargaining context. A *bargaining frame* refers to how the bargainer understands the negotiation context, usually based in large part on past experiences (Putnam & Holmer, 1992, p. 129). *Reframing,* then, refers to developing a new set of expectations, a new perspective or frame of reference to help the negotiators bargain toward achieving their goals. An interesting example of the framing-reframing process, and how symbolic convergence can affect it, was reported above (Putnam, Van Hoeven, & Bullis, 1991).

- *What is the importance of framing and reframing in successful conflict management?*

The importance of framing can be seen by a quick reminder of some of the basic variables that affect it: past experiences, goals, personal characteristics, perceptions of loss and gain, and risk seeking. One of the more important reframing necessities that has been recognized recently has to do with perceptions of women as negotiators. Gender issues may affect the ability of women to negotiate successfully. Kolb (1993) argued that women's voices may be silenced at the negotiating table for a number of reasons. The first is that women tend to view themselves as interrelated with others. This approach to life as relationship may be contrary to the male approach of independence and self-reliance and may result in women making concessions in negotiating in order to preserve their relationships with the other participants at the table.

The second reason has to do with differing conceptions of time and place in reference to the conflict event. Women tend to conceive of events as situated in time, following and preceding other events. Men are more likely to see events as discrete, so conflict becomes a matter of immediate resolution. This could lead to a conflict "resolution" before a woman fully realizes that a conflict is being played out.

The third reason that women may be seen as less successful negotiators is that women tend to approach power as something held jointly with conflict partners. Empowerment is the term that best describes their approach. Men, on the other hand, tend to view power as something held over others. The female tendency to empower may result in their loss of negotiating effectiveness. Finally, women tend to prefer dialogue and reasoned discussion over the traditional language of negotiation: debate and argument.

- *How might women differ from men as negotiators?*

To wrap up this discussion of bargaining, negotiation, and framing, we need to bring back the issue of power. Negotiation will always be about power. Bargaining is characterized by disputants with different goals, and power plays a significant role in achieving one's goals. Fisher, Ury, and Patton (1993) did a good job of summarizing the difference between resources and power in negotiation.

They noted that often one negotiator is discouraged, believing that he or she holds too little power to move the bargaining opponent. Fisher, Ury, and Patton suggested that bargainers should worry less about who holds what amount of power, and think more about how to increase their own *negotiation power*—"the ability to persuade someone to do something" (p. 4). Several strategies were suggested for increasing negotiation power: Improve the quality of your working relationship with the negotiation partner; understand your partner's interests; invent elegant solutions; use external standards to judge the legitimacy of the proposed solutions; have a good "walk-away" alternative (your option if the negotiation fails); and have a clear commitment to the process and the partner. Each of these suggestions should improve your negotiating position and ability.

- *What are some strategies for increasing negotiation power?*

POLITICS AND ORGANIZATION CULTURE

Cultural assumptions about conflict, power cliques, competitive subcultures, and so forth, are the sorts of issues addressed by a merger of culture and politics. A cultural approach to understanding organizations from the political metaphor will allow the researcher to zero in on issues such as the communicative structure that favors some cultural groups over others, the importance of role playing in conflict tactic selection, and the emergence and importance of concertive control as opposed to alternative, more overt forms of control. The organization becomes understood as sets of competing interest groups, formed around shared interpretations of an environment of scarcity, power, conflict, domination, and inequality. This may not be the picture of organizational life that we wish to see, but it is it very much a real part of the organization.

As rules-based systems of competing interests, the organization becomes an arena of unequal power distribution. The rules will favor some at the expense of others. The result of this unequal distribution of power will be the creation of subcultural power networks. Clegg (1989, 1990) uses the term *network embeddedness* to describe the creation of organized power networks within the dominant organizational structure. Viewing the organization from this perspective forces us away from a notion of organization as an overall singular belief system. In its place we find a fragmented set of relationships built around the premise that wealth, success, advancement, and so forth are scarce resources that must be won.

Because of this embeddedness, we can see how subcultural variation could survive and prosper. The segmentation of the larger power structure into smaller networks allows for overall organizational survival because of subnetwork design and efficiency that is appropriate to their niches within the overall structure.

From the political perspective, then, culture is constituted within the power networks of organizational members. *Ideology* is a way of seeing things, a perspective, a point of view that establishes the logic that a group or individual applies when making decisions. Organizations as forms of government, exercised through the creation of rules, demonstrate their ideology in the development of influence strategies. The more structurally embedded the ideology, of course, the more difficult it is for organization members to realize that they're being influenced.

This final point concerning ideology is very important. As ideology, these powerful perceptions become the bases for decision alternatives and organizational understandings. They serve as the justification for action, and the actions performed then justify the ideology. This is concertive control.

Concertive control is beyond the conscious awareness of organization members, and thus is seldom called up for comment and discussion. Member understandings, then, as the basis for the development of culture and subcultures, will be tainted by organizational representations of reality. This doesn't mean that these representations can't be called into question; it just means that they operate at a tacit level, making them harder to recognize.

SUMMARY

In this chapter we looked at a variety of issues that surface when discussing organizations as political arenas. We began by examining the intimate relationships among politics, power, and control. Politics and the political system were discussed as rules and rule systems, which tend to be created to preserve existing power structures. We then looked at the pervasive nature of power, in both its overt and covert forms. Covert power was seen as unobtrusive, affecting us without our knowledge. The discussion of power concluded with a reminder that power tends to belong to the already powerful, so gaining power has much to do with aligning oneself with power holders.

The chapter then turned to the inevitable result of power and political relationships: conflict. Conflict was shown to be an important and pervasive part of any political environment. We looked at the role of communication in conflict, conflict style, and the effect of gender on conflict management. We saw that women are perceived differently than men in conflict situations, and we also examined the role of women as informal organizational peacekeepers.

Two perspectives on managing conflict were discussed—principled negotiation and the 5A model—followed by an overview of Linda Putnam's work with bargaining and negotiation. The chapter concluded with a discussion of labor negotiation and a summary of politics as a reflection of organization culture.

CHAPTER 10

Organization Culture and the Multicultural Workplace

Chapter Preview

In this chapter we look at the complexity of the multicultural workplace. The chapter addresses some of the concerns of Asian-Americans, Hispanics, Native Americans, and African-Americans in their quests for employment and equal opportunity. After discussing a variety of issues of concern, the chapter focuses on the experiences of women in the workplace. By the end of the chapter we will have a good overall feeling for the complexity of the multicultural workplace.

This chapter is about discrimination, both overt and covert. We'll see compelling evidence that women and minorities are not receiving fair and equal treatment. However, in order to build a reasonable case that discrimination exists, we need to draw heavily on numerical data, and the only group that has been researched adequately to build a compelling argument is women. So I will use data on women employees to make my claim that discrimination, rather than characteristics of women or minorities, is the cause of their underrepresentation.

In the remainder of the chapter, I'll offer an overview of the "minority experience" in the workplace. By drawing on recent summary data I'll review the current employment circumstances of Asian-Americans, Hispanics, Native Americans, and African-Americans. I'm forced to keep this review brief because of the lack of reliable summary data. Perhaps, as the 1990 census continues to be deciphered, more up-to-date information will soon be available.

The chapter then goes into much greater detail on the American female experience. There is no shortage of information showing clearly that women, despite their numerical representation, are as undervalued as most minority groups in the workplace. We'll look at labor force participation, occupational representation, and income. The only conclusion that can be reached, after reading the minority and female experience data, is that discrimination is a fact of corporate America. The chapter then turns to discrimination. We look at arguments that discrimination doesn't exist, theories of discrimination, and antidiscrimination legislation.

The final portion of the chapter deals with difference. Discrimination is about punishing difference. But a cultural approach to organizations values difference. First, we'll look at whether there are significant differences between men and women, and the effects of perceived difference. We'll then look directly at the importance of embracing difference, building it into the workplace, to accomplish a truly healthy, fair, multicultural organization.

Key Terms

minority
person-centered argument
race
ethnicity
Hispanic
Chicano(a)
marriage bar
labor market discrimination
rational bias
personal prejudice
statistical discrimination
monopoly power discrimination
Equal Pay Act of 1963
Title VII of the Civil Rights Act of 1964

affirmative action plan
individual sexism
organizational sexism
gender role spillover
uniform group
skewed group
tilted group
balanced group
token
career-primary orientation
career-and-family orientation
marginality
marginal persons

Before venturing any further into this chapter, I want you to take the following quiz. Answer each of the questions honestly. The basis for this quiz is an article by Peggy McIntosh (1989), which had an interesting effect on me in my preparation to write this chapter. Get the article, read it, discuss it. Here are the questions:

1. Is your race privileged in comparison to other races?
2. Is your race widely represented in the nightly news and the daily newspapers?
3. When you accept a job can you be relatively sure that your race was not a factor in your receiving the job offer in the first place?
4. Can you easily buy "flesh" color makeup or bandages that actually match the color of your flesh?
5. Do you feel safe when you go out for the evening alone? Safe from harassment? Safe from being followed?
6. Are you confident that your race will not work against you in your applications for loans? Your search for medical help? Your choice of housing?
7. Do you feel as though your word is often taken as representative of your entire race?
8. Can you easily find food, music, and entertainment that fit your cultural heritage? Can you find a hair stylist who knows how to cut your hair?
9. When you ask to speak to the "person in charge," do you anticipate facing someone of your own race?

The issue addressed in this quiz is *white privilege:*

> I have come to see white privilege as an invisible package of unearned assets which I can count on cashing in each day, but about which I was "meant" to remain oblivious. White privilege is like an invisible weightless knapsack of special provisions, maps, passports, codebooks, visas, clothes, tools and blank checks. (McIntosh, 1989, p. 10)

White privilege is about unearned dominance because of the assumption that white is "normal," and normal is "right." It is a dominance system that excludes nonwhites and pertains mostly, though not exclusively, to white men.

How did you answer the quiz questions, and what do you think of the notion of white privilege? Discuss your thoughts with others before you begin this chapter. Your thoughts will help you understand the material you're about to read.

THE MINORITY EXPERIENCE

In this section I'm going to try to characterize what I'll simply call the minority experience in the American workplace. *Minority* is defined as a group that is numerically less represented than another group. In this country whites represent the majority. Discussing a single minority experience is impossible to do, and I won't even try. Each minority group represents a diverse population with different experiences. However, we can enter this section by recognizing the one common denominator of all minorities in the workplace: they are underrepresented in comparison to the majority.

The question with which we must wrestle, of course, is why these numerical differences exist. The two most common explanations are that the difference is natural, given the differences between whites and nonwhites and that the differences are the result of discrimination. I reject the notion that there are important racial or ethnic differences between groups that would account for the numerical disparities that I'm about to report. There simply does not exist a reliable source of data that supports such a claim. Those who do advocate such a position are making what is called a *person-centered argument*—that discrimination is caused by inadequacies of those who are discriminated against (Morrison & Von Glinow, 1990).

If the underrepresentation isn't the "fault" of the underrepresented, how can we account for it? Throughout this chapter we'll see that discrimination is the cause. Before getting to that argument, however, we need to look at the minority experience. As we do, let's remember one fact. By the year 2000, 15.5 percent of the workforce will be composed of minorities (Luzzo, 1992). If we allow discrimination to occur or continue, this means that soon we will be losing the talents, skills, and expertise of almost one of every six workers. And if women, a group that constitutes half the workforce, are discriminated against also, the whole American workplace takes on a perverted, distorted image.

At present (according to the 1990 census), there are about 121 million men and 127 million women in this country. Of that total, about 12 percent are black, about 0.8 percent are American Indian (including Eskimo and Aleut), about 3 percent are Asian/Pacific Islanders, and about 9 percent are Hispanic.

The remainder of this section explores, to various degrees, the work experiences of these four ethnic and racial minorities. *Race* refers to a distinct group marked by genetically transmitted physical characteristics, such as skin color. Blacks are a racial group, for example. *Ethnicity* refers to a much broader category, wherein members distinguish themselves according to variously defined traits, such as national origin or religious affiliation. Thus, African-American is both a racial and an ethnic category, whereas Hispanic and Jewish are ethnic markers. The groups to be discussed in this section are Asian-Americans, Hispanics, Native Americans, and African-Americans.

One note before going into the rest of this chapter. You're about to wade through a lot of tables, which might leave you wondering why they weren't collapsed into just a few large, summary tables. The answer is that the various researchers who compiled the data often used different categories or reported altogether different figures. To collapse data into summary tables would have risked misrepresenting the data, which would be unacceptable. So please tolerate the tables as the most honest, simple form of presentation.

The Asian-American Experience

A very limited but increasing body of research is available that examines the Asian-American work experience. Part of the problem of making a coherent statement about this group of workers is that it represents an extremely diverse population of individuals, with really quite different experiences. On the one hand, the Asian-American population includes refugees from countries such as Vietnam, Cambodia, and Laos. Among this group, the Vietnamese is the only subgroup to have been analyzed in any detail. On the other hand, Asian-American also includes immigrants from China, Taiwan, Hong Kong, Japan, Korea, and the Philippines. In this section I'll offer an overview of this diverse group of people to try to give some understanding of both the diversity among them and the challenges they face as part of the American workforce. I'll begin with the refugee population.

By 1981, over 560,000 Asian refugees had come to the United States (Kelly, 1986). The first wave of immigrants from Vietnam represented exceedingly well-educated, professionally elite citizens of that country. The group was composed largely of doctors (7 percent), lawyers, technicians, managers, university teachers (24 percent), clerical workers (12 percent), service professionals (8 percent), farmers (5 percent), and skilled crafts and construction workers (11 percent). However, 65 percent of this group did not speak English.

The first wave of refugees, arriving from the mid-1960s to the mid-1970s, settled in urban areas around the country. There, the general employment trend for the Vietnamese was underemployment, unemployment, and the

American welfare system. By 1978, close to 95 percent of Vietnamese refugees were employed, with 82 percent full-time, but with less than one-third earning more than $200 per week. Mean income stood at $9600 per year, the U.S. poverty level (Kelly, 1986). Occupational representation for this group in 1982 was a distinct change from what they had experienced in their homelands. According to Kelly (1986), over 29 percent of these professionally trained, skilled refugees worked in crafts, 24 percent worked in unspecified blue-collar labor, over 18 percent in clerical and sales, over 11 percent in transportation, over 7 percent in unskilled labor, and only about 9 percent as professionals or managers.

A very different story is told of the Asian immigrant population. Like the refugees of the 1960s and 1970s, 46 percent of the Asian population lives in central cities, and 82 percent live in urban areas (Wong, 1986). In 1986, 44 percent of the total number of immigrants came from Asian countries, primarily as immigrants, but also as refugees. As of 1986, 52 percent of the total Asian population lived in the western United States.

Generally speaking (again, this is a very heterogeneous group), Asian male immigrants are better-educated than their U.S. counterparts, and have a higher level of labor force participation. Educationally, almost twice as many Asian immigrants have college degrees and postgraduate training, especially those groups from China, Japan, Korea, and the Philippines.

Occupationally, Asian immigrants have a slightly higher labor force participation rate than the U.S. average. According to Wong (1986), Asian immigrants are heavily represented in white-collar (62 to 77 percent) and professional (22 percent) occupations. Comparatively, when looking at Asian representation to U.S. population representation, the following figures show the 1980 occupational distribution: executive manager or professional, 39 percent to 28 percent; technical worker, 8 percent to 3 percent; sales and administrative support staff, 15 percent to 15 percent; service and farm workers, 15 percent to 12 percent; crafts workers, 12 percent to 21 percent; and operative, 12 percent to 21 percent.

Finally, while Asian male immigrants earn less than European-Americans, on the whole Asian immigrants earn slightly more than their American counterparts. On the other end, though, more Asian immigrants than Americans live below the poverty level.

- *Can you characterize the Asian-American workforce?*

The Hispanic Experience

In 1991, Hispanics represented 9 percent of the U.S. population (Knouse, Rosenfeld, & Culbertson, 1992). Still, despite this large number, surprisingly little research has been done on the Hispanic experience in the workplace. Perhaps the reason is that, like the Asian population, the Hispanic population is diverse, including Mexicans, Puerto Ricans, and Central and South Americans. Indeed, many people are confused about what the specific labels refer to.

Hispanic generally refers to that group which identifies with Spain, its language, and its people. *Chicano(a)* refers to a U.S. citizen or inhabitant of Mexican decent. For the most part, in this chapter (as in much of the literature on the subject) we will use Hispanic as the identifying term for those individuals of Spanish, Mexican, Cuban, and South and Central American, descent and identification.

This diversity makes the group as a whole hard to define and account for as a unified workforce. Because of birth rates and immigration, Hispanics will most likely become the largest U.S. minority group by the early twenty-first century (Cervantes, 1992; Knouse, Rosenfeld, & Culbertson, 1992), overtaking African-Americans. With this large representation, visibility and power will accrue, meaning (most likely) more research into the groups.

Fortunately, unlike the case for Asian-Americans and Native Americans, some systematic research has documented the occupational representation of the U.S. Hispanic population. As of 1989 (according to Cresce, 1992), 7.4 percent of the civilian labor force was Hispanic, and this percentage is expected to rise to 10.2 percent by the year 2000.

In 1989, 7.8 percent of Hispanics were unemployed, compared to 4.6 percent of white non-Hispanics. Occupationally, Hispanic males have the highest concentrations as operators, fabricators, and laborers (28.6 percent), while white non-Hispanic males concentrated in management and professional occupations (29.1 percent). Among women, Hispanics were concentrated in service, operator, fabricator, and laborer positions, while white non-Hispanic women were clustered in management, professional, technical, and sales positions.

Compared to their white, non-Hispanic counterparts, Hispanics are much less educated. About 45 percent of Hispanics have less than a high school education (Cresce, 1992), compared to about 12 percent of white non-Hispanics. This lack of formal education may account for some of the large earnings disparities between the two groups. The 1988 median year-round, full-time earnings for Hispanic men and women were $17,851 and $14,873 respectively, compared to $28,259 and $18,115 for white non-Hispanic men and women respectively (Cresce, 1992).

- *Can you characterize the Hispanic workforce?*

The Native American Experience

Of all of the minority groups discussed in this chapter, none is less researched or more difficult to generalize about, regarding occupational representation, than American Indians. The Native American population is well discussed from cultural and artistic perspectives. But little information can be found about the day-to-day, work-related status of this group. The best that can be done at this point is to offer some information about the economic standing of this group.

One of the biggest problems for occupational research is the heterogeneity of the Native American population. For example, in 1989 most of the American Indian population in Arizona and New Mexico lived on reservations and spoke their native languages, while the majority of American Indians around the country lived in urban areas (Red Horse, Johnson, & Weiner, 1989). As we will see, these two factors seem to result in much of the research being more about unemployment than about employment.

As of 1980 (Martin, 1991), 46 percent of Americans Indians lived on "identified Indian areas," including reservations and tribal trust land. In 1987, Indians on or adjacent to reservations lived with a 33.5 percent unemployment rate. In the twenty-eight states with the largest American Indian populations, the average unemployment rate was 43 percent in 1985. Indeed, American Indians represent some of the lowest numerical indicators of "success" and "opportunity": high unemployment, low education, low per capita income, and poor housing.

Again, according to the 1980 census (Cornell & Kalt, 1990), 14 percent of reservation households had yearly incomes less than $2500; 45 percent of reservation Indians lived below the poverty level; 25 percent of reservation households got food stamps; 21 percent of reservation households had no indoor toilets; 16 percent of reservation households had no electricity; 54 percent of reservation households had no central heating. And in 1989, the reservation unemployment rate averaged 40 percent.

However, the above figures do not tell the complete story. Amazing differences exist among reservations. Some of them thrive, some of them don't. And, while most of the available data is for reservation Indians, most American Indians don't live on reservations. Rather, like Hispanics and Asian-Americans, they live in large urban areas. Unfortunately, at this writing, the 1990 census data that may shed light on nonreservation American Indian employment is not yet compiled.

The African-American Experience

Unlike American Indians, Asian-Americans, or Hispanics, African-Americans have received considerable attention as a workforce (see, for example, Cox & Nkomo, 1986; Hecht, Collier, & Ribeau, 1993; Jaynes & Williams, 1989; Morrison & Von Glinow, 1990). Much of this research can be categorized under one of two headings: that aimed at identifying race bias and that aimed at clarifying the effects of bias on the earnings of black Americans. In this section I'm going to briefly review some of the arguments that contend that race is a significant factor in the African-American working experience. We'll then look at specific occupational representation.

Even a cursory review of the literature leads to the inevitable conclusion that race is a very real factor in the economic potential of African-Americans. For example, Cox and Nkomo (1986) found that the criteria used to measure overall performance when making promotion decisions differed for blacks and whites. For blacks, social behavior was weighted more heavily, resulting in a form of covert discrimination, allowing blacks to rise only to a certain level of the organizational hierarchy.

The biggest concern for James, Cox and Nkomo, and others is the covert, often unconscious discrimination that keeps good workers from being recognized purely because of their skin color. Blacks find themselves in a double bind. If a low-level black manager complains that he or she has been discriminated against in a promotion decision, he or she is perceived as a troublemaker. But to not complain leaves one feeling stagnant, frustrated, and abused. Discrimination, both overt and covert, has resulted in a dramatic underuse of talent. In 1988, only one African-American headed a *Fortune* 1000 company. In 1986, less than 9 percent of all managers were minorities.

Education is one factor that affects income. However, the 1984 earnings ratio of college-educated black men to college-educated white men was still at 74 percent. Although the numbers are changing, as of the early 1980s, about 80 percent of blacks and 90 percent of whites completed high school. In 1980, 12 percent of black women and 11 percent of black men, compared to 22 percent of white women and 25.5 percent of white men, had finished college. Much of this disparity may be due to precollege living and schooling conditions. In 1985, blacks earned only about 3 percent of the advanced degrees (Ph.D., M.S., B.S.) in engineering, hard sciences, and computer programming (Leinster, 1988). As a result, blacks often end up in human-relations-oriented positions, which rarely lead to top management. Thus, blacks are excluded from the networks necessary to rise to the most advanced levels of the company (James, 1986; Leinster, 1988). Most likely, however, changes will be forthcoming. Hecht, Collier, and Ribeau (1993) reported that between 1985 and 1990, black enrollment in colleges had increased to 33 percent.

The occupational representation of African-Americans is shown in Table 10-1. As you can see, black men are most represented in craft, operative, and service occupations, while black women are most represented in clerical and service professions. Of the two, African-American women had (as of 1984) made the greatest gains in obtaining professional and managerial stature.

As with each of the minority groups discussed in this chapter, generalizing about the African-American population is difficult because of the great diversity within the group itself. One of the biggest reflections of that diversity is in income levels. In 1985, 31 percent of black families, as compared with 11 percent of white families, lived below the federal poverty line. In 1984 the per capita income ratio of blacks to whites was 57 percent. A large income disparity exists within the black population itself. Jaynes and Williams (1989) reported that in 1984, the lowest-earning 40 percent of black men generated only 5 percent of the total amount of black earnings, while the highest-earning 20 percent generated 60 percent of the total. And, while the African-American middle class grew in the 1980s, so did the African-American poor. Mean earnings for black and white men and women are reported in Table 10-2. You can see that, whereas black women fare almost as well as white women, black men are still struggling at about 65 percent of the annual earnings of white men. Lest we applaud the comparison figures of black and white women too quickly, we do need to remember that white women are still not even close to economic parity with white men.

TABLE 10-1. Occupational Representation for African-American Men and Women (percent): 1984

	Men	Women
Professional	8.0	13.9
Proprietors, managers, officials	6.3	5.2
Clerical/sales	13.1	33.1
Craftpersons	15.8	2.6
Operatives	22.6	12.0
Domestic service	0.1	5.9
Other service	18.3	24.8
Farmers/farm workers	4.9	0.5
Nonfarm labor	11.0	1.8

Note: From Jaynes and Williams (1989).

One big reason for the lack of wealth in the African-American community has been the considerable growth in female-headed families. In 1969, 58 percent of all poor black children lived in female-headed households, compared to 36 percent of white children. Those numbers grew in 1984 to 75 percent of black children and 42 percent of white (Jaynes & Williams, 1989). In 1985, 44 percent of all black children lived in poverty, compared to 16 percent of white children. Additionally, 57 percent of black poor, compared to 34 percent of white poor, live in central cities, meaning that to a much greater degree, black poor interact mainly with other black poor.

- *Summarize the African-American workplace experience?*

Interpreting the Minority Experience

Summarizing the minority experience in the American workplace isn't hard. Such key terms as lack of opportunity, underemployment, unfair wage prac-

TABLE 10-2. Mean Earnings by Race and Sex: 1984

	Black Men	White Men	Ratio Black/White (percent)
Weekly earnings	$289	$429	67.4
Annual earnings	$13,218	$20,457	64.6

	Black Women	White Women	Ratio Black/White (percent)
Weekly earnings	$227	$233	97.4
Annual earnings	$10,252	$10,354	99.0

Note: From Jaynes and Williams (1989).

tices, frustration, and resentment are descriptive of these groups as well as the general experience of women, discussed in the next section.

The Asian-American experience stands out because, unlike other minorities, this group is better-educated and, as a whole, is making as much money as their white counterparts. Still, on the whole, more Asian-Americans live in poverty than Americans generally. Why?

The answer is complex. The Asian-American group is a combination of refugees and immigrants, who bring differing levels of language and technical skills into the workplace. We've seen in the case of refugees that those technical skills were devalued; immigrants fared somewhat better.

In both cases, though, this group is centered geographically in large cities, as are blacks, Hispanics, and nonreservation Indians. Our surroundings play an important role in the development of attitudes about work. Being located in the middle of a large urban environment may result in narrow perceptions, or in feelings of limited occupational possibilities. Reservation Indians fare no better. According to Martin (1991), American Indians on reservations have less mobility, less job tenure, less exposure, and less job variability than Indians or non-Indians off the reservation.

Beyond different perceptions of self and options, blacks, Hispanics and Native Americans also suffer from less formal education than white Americans. All of these factors work against minorities in the workplace. Minorities may also have to deal with language problems, identity issues (integrating into a white population without losing their ethnic identity), and "colorism" (Jones, 1986)—the tendency of people to act differently with those of their own skin color than they do with those of different skin color.

This is a gloomy picture, indeed, but one which the data support. Minorities face an uphill battle, that's for sure. It is a battle that must be fought by both the minority and majority members of society, for the good of all. We'll look at the reasons for insisting on progress in this area toward the end of the chapter. For now, though, we'll take a detailed look at a majority that is accorded minority status: women.

- *What general conclusions can be drawn about the minority workplace experience? What is the prognosis for improvement?*

THE EXPERIENCE OF AMERICAN WOMEN

By far the most examined "disadvantaged" group in the workforce is women. We'll capitalize on the wealth of data available to take a long, careful look at women and work. Although women do not represent a minority in raw population numbers or in actual labor force representation, many have long argued that they are accorded minority status: low pay, discrimination, artificially imposed achievement ceilings, and tracking into low-status professions.

In this section I'll present information on labor force participation, where women work, and what women earn. On the basis of those findings, we can then look more directly at the issue of discrimination.

Labor Force Participation

The numerical "facts" of participation lead to only one conclusion: Anybody who believes that most women don't work in some income-earning occupation is, simply, wrong. To help you see why, consider the following points.

First, participation by women in the labor force has grown from 19 percent of all women in 1890 to 60 percent in 1990. During that same period the percentage of married working women has increased from 5 percent to 60 percent—about 56 percent of white women and 64 percent of nonwhite women (Goldin, 1990).

- *What are some implications of the increases in labor force participation by married women?*

Second, labor force participation among American Indian, Chicana, European-American, African-American, Japanese-American, and Chinese-American women has changed from a 1920 men/women ratio of about 4:1 to a 1980 ratio of about 1.5:1 (Amott & Matthaei, 1991, p. 305).

Third, while women have seen about a 200 percent increase in labor force representation over the last 100 years, the percentage of men employed in the same period of time has remained relatively stable (about 78 percent). Still, there continues to be enormous segregation in the types of work that men and women do. In 1981 over 61 percent of the workforce would have had to change jobs in order to eliminate occupational segregation (Powell, 1988, pp. 73–74).

Fourth, by the year 2000, 85 percent of the new workers in this country will be women and minorities. So, whereas today about 47 percent of the workforce is native white male, over the next decade only 15 percent of new entrants to the workforce will be from that category (Betters-Reed & Moore, 1992; Haslett, Geis, & Carter, 1992).

Fifth, women held 42 percent of managerial and specialty (includes lawyers, physicians, and teachers) jobs in 1990, as compared with 31 percent in 1980 and 19 percent in 1970. In 1990 women represented 46 percent of the overall labor force and held 40 percent of the management jobs overall. However, in 1990 women held only 7 percent of the vice-presidential and higher positions in 94 of the nation's largest firms; only 19 of over 4000 women were among the highest-paid executives in the 799 largest companies in the country. On the other hand, women represent 68 percent of the administrators and managers in education and related fields, and 67 percent of the accounting and auditing managers. Finally, only 3 percent of the over 47,000 directors from boards of directors nationwide in 1988 were women. Seventy-eight percent of those boards had no women members at all (Legislative Commission on the Economic Status of Women, 1992).

- *Summarize some of the trends and data regarding women in the workforce.*

Obviously, despite some of the small differences in actual numbers above, women constitute at least half the paid workforce in this country, and indications are that their numbers will increase in the future. This fact alone carries interesting implications for the workplace. If the organization is composed mostly of women, managers and compensation professionals will need to address the question of satisfaction. In short, they'll ultimately have to ask if women are motivated by the same concerns as men, if they derive value from work in the same way as men, and if their criteria for a positive, healthy workplace are similar to men's criteria.

Where Women Are Working

We should now look more closely at where women are working. Table 10-3 gives a longitudinal perspective of occupational distribution for women generally from 1900 to 1980. The table shows an interesting shift from predominantly "blue-collar" to "white-collar" work. The table also shows an emphasis on service professions and generally low-paying occupations.

A more specific numerical breakdown of occupational representation is offered in Table 10-4. That table gives a percentage of representation in a variety of occupational categories for six racial and ethnic groups of women during three periods: 1900, 1960, and 1980. Two points leap out of Table 10-4. First, in terms of occupational representation, women of these six groups are remarkably similar. The table would seem to support such qualified global statements as, "Women are significantly underrepresented in managerial and administration professions." I say "qualified global statements" because the other point that the table raises is that not all women are alike. The history of Chinese- and Japanese-American women has not been the history of European-Ameri-

TABLE 10-3. Female Occupational Concentration: 1900 and 1980—Highest to Lowest Concentrations

1900	1980
Servants	Secretaries
Farm laborers	Teachers (elementary school)
Dressmakers	Bookkeepers
Teachers	Cashiers
Laundry work	Office clerks
Farmers and planters	Managers
Farm and plantation laborers	Waitresses
Sales workers	Sales workers
Housekeepers and stewards	Registered nurses
Seamstresses	Nursing aides

Note: This information is from Sapiro (1986, p. 387).

TABLE 10-4. Occupational Distribution of Six Racial/Ethnic Groups of Women (in percent): 1900, 1960, and 1980

	American Indian			Chicana			European-American			African-American			Chinese-American			Japanese-American		
	00	60	80	00	60	80	00	60	80	00	60	80	00	60	80	00	60	80
Agriculture	47	11	1	21	4	3	10	2	1	44	4	.5	7	.7	.3	58	7	1
Manufacturing	25	18	17	25	29	26	33	19	13	3	16	18	41	24	21	8	19	13
Private household service	13	17	1	33	12	2	30	4	.8	44	39	5	36	2	.8	29	8	1
Service (not private household)	12	26	24	4	17	20	4	13	15	8	23	24	9	9	13	4	13	16
Sales	.2	4	8	8	8	10	4	9	12	.1	2	6	1	8	10	.2	7	11
Clerical	.1	14	27	3	22	26	7	35	32	.1	8	26	.5	32	25	.1	31	32
Professional and technical	2	9	15	3	6	8	10	15	18	1	8	15	1	18	20	.3	12	18
Managerial and administrative	.4	2	7	4	3	4	3	4	8	.5	1	5	4	6	10	1	4	8

Note: Definitions of occupations include the following: Agriculture includes laborers, farmers, planters, florists. Manufacturing includes carpenters, miners, dressmakers, tailors, tobacco and cigar factory operatives. Private household service includes housekeepers, servants, laundresses. Service (not private household) includes barbers, hairdressers, bartenders, janitors, nurses, soldiers, firefighters. Sales includes sales men and women, porters, helpers (in stores), and transportation agents. Clerical includes bookkeepers, accountants, clerks, stenographers, typists, telephone operators. Professional and technical includes professional specialty occupations, health technologists, physicians, teachers, writers, artists. Managerial and administrative includes managers, administrators, executive officers.
Note: Condensed from Amott and Matthaei (1991).

can or American Indian women, for example. These differences should be noted and much more work must be done to document the differences.

- *What general conclusions can be drawn about where women work?*

Even a cursory reading of these tables and figures leads the reader to see that women are disproportionately represented in certain occupational categories—overrepresented in clerical, teaching, low-status white-collar, and low-level managerial positions, and underrepresented in executive and technical areas. What is not yet clear is whether this representational discrepancy is mirrored in income. Unfortunately, as the following shows, the income of women has not kept pace with their advancement in the workplace.

What Women Earn

Table 10-5 summarizes U.S. Census data on both seasonal and year-round full-time median incomes for men and women. You'll note that women fare the worst in sales, the best in professional specialty and clerical. On the whole, according to Table 10-5, in 1987 the median income for women was $0.65 for every $1.00 that men made. What the table also shows is that women make less money than their male counterparts. This income discrepancy might be the result of discrimination, it might reflect different hierarchical positions within the same occupational categories, or some other explanation might be offered. The point is, the numbers don't speak for themselves.

Table 10-6 takes the median income of the same six groups analyzed in Table 10-4, and then compares those incomes with those of men of the same groups, and with those of European-American women. The results of these in-

TABLE 10-5. Median Earnings for Men and Women, 1987: Selected Occupations

	All Workers		Year-Round Full-Time Earnings		Ratio: W/M
	Women	Men	Women	Men	
Total	$10,618	$19,878	$16,909	$26,008	.65
Executive, admin., and managerial	19,134	33,408	21,874	36,155	.61
Professional specialty	19,634	32,891	24,565	36,098	.68
Sales	6,268	21,624	14,277	27,880	.51
Administrative support, including clerical	12,220	18,512	16,346	23,896	.68
Machine operators, assemblers, inspectors	10,050	17,363	13,028	20,821	.63

Note: From U.S. Bureau of the Census, *Statistical Abstract of the United States: 1989* (109th ed.), Washington, D.C., 1989, p. 408.

TABLE 10-6. Women's Median Incomes, by Racial/Ethnic Group, 1980

	Median Income	As Percent of Men of Same Racial/Ethnic Group	As Percent of European-American Women
American Indian	$4,247	53	79
Chicana	4,556	51	85
European-American	5,378	41	100
African-American	4,676	60	87
Chinese-American	6,064	56	113
Japanese-American	7,410	49	138

Note: From Amott and Matthaei (1991, p. 310).

come and occupational distribution tables show that men clearly dominate the income power of the workplace. In every racial and ethnic category, men fare better than women. Even in 1980 dollars the income figures for women are often barely above the poverty level. Finally, note in Table 10-6 that Chinese- and Japanese-American women were making more money than their European-American counterparts. This is quite interesting when you note from Table 10-4 that in terms of occupational representation, the three groups are remarkably similar.

Hybrid tables and summary data such as those presented above are useful in gaining global understanding. But their value is limited because they don't make clear whether men and women who perform the same work are making the same income. Table 10-7 does provide this information. As you can see from Table 10-7, men and women who are in the same occupations clearly do not enjoy the same incomes.

All the way down the line, with the exception of one occupation (mechanics/repairers), men make more than women performing the same work. Although numbers don't speak for themselves, Table 10-7 makes it very hard to not draw the conclusion that discrimination plays a role in the income differential between men and women. Those who doubt the legitimacy of the data tend to fall back on four general arguments to account for the income disparities. Each of those arguments will be reviewed briefly below.

- *What conclusions can you draw at this point about how much money women make compared to men? Compared to other women?*

Maybe It Isn't Discrimination?

First, some people argue that when considering opportunity, women haven't been discriminated against. They could have worked if they had wanted— they didn't want to participate in the workforce and did so only when they had to. We might address that argument by noting one of the most interesting and confounding tangents in the history of women and work: marriage bars. A *marriage bar* was a formal or informal proscription against hiring or keeping married women as employees (Goldin, 1990). Marriage bars were in place for many professions, including teaching, clerical work, medicine, and law, since before the turn of the century.

Amazingly, as late as 1942, about 78 percent of school districts reported that they would not hire a married woman, while 70 percent said they would not retain a single woman when she married. Those figures were reduced to 19 percent and 9 percent respectively by 1951. In short, married and single women wanted to work. Men wouldn't let them!

The second argument against the accusation of discrimination is that women have only recently become as educated as men, and thus, their lower wages are a reflection of educational attainment rather than discrimination. It is true that by a small margin (and becoming smaller every year: Schwartz, 1992), men have more advanced degrees.

However, income and education data show clearly that even when educational level is held constant, women make much less than their male counterparts. The average yearly income for women college graduates in 1990 was $21,000, compared to $40,000 for men. As a matter of fact, college-educated women were making less than men with only high school diplomas (U.S. Bureau of the Census, Current Population Reports, No. 462, 1992, p. 5). The only way to account for this disparity is to identify the level of work performed by men and women in the same occupational categories. We've already seen that men and women in the same job categories make different amounts of money. Men and women of equal educational level also tend to enter the same professions in roughly comparable numbers. Therefore, we can only conclude that education is not a satisfactory explanation of the earnings disparity.

The third argument commonly offered against the accusation of discrimination is that women have only recently entered the workforce, and therefore, it stands to reason that their earnings would be below those of men of longer tenure. All of the data presented thus far show this to be far from the case. Representation of women in the workforce has increased about 200 percent over the last 100 years. Women have always been part of the workforce. And over half of the white-collar workforce is women. Finally, when compared with male counterparts doing the same work, women make less. It would appear that the earnings disparity has less to do with tenure in the workforce than with the relative value society places on the types of work that men and women commonly do.

The final argument often offered against the accusation of discrimination is that women tend to enter lower-paying professions. Clearly this tends to be the case. However, (1) even when men and women work in the same professions at the same levels, men make more; (2) the status of the profession tends to change (with the amount of money the profession offers) when the makeup of the profession becomes female rather than male (one need only chart the

TABLE 10-7. Median Weekly Earnings for Full-Time Wage and Salary Workers by Selected Characteristics: 1987

	Median Weekly Earnings
All Workers	$373
Male: 25 yr. & Older	$477
Female: 25 yr. & Older	$321
White: Male	$450
Female	$307
Black: Male	$326
Female	$275
All Other Races: Male	$306
Female	$251
Women who maintain families	$300
Men who maintain families	$399
Occupation, male	
Managerial/professional	$636
Executive, admin., managerial	$647
Professional specialty	$625
Technical, sales, admin., support	$453
Sales	$479
Admin. support, incl. clerical	$402
Service	$296
Private household service	$—
Precision production	$431
Mechanics/repairers	$423

history of clerical and secretarial work and teaching, as they moved from "male occupations" to "female occupations," to notice this change); and (3) it makes less sense to suggest that women enter lower-paying professions than it does to notice that even when women enter higher-paying professions they're kept at the lower end of the pay scales.

In short, from a "data point of view," *the income differentials can't be explained away by focusing on the women who are doing the work.* They can only be explained by focusing on the biases of both women and men. The male, the masculine model still reigns supreme in our society (Powell, 1988).

- *Summarize the numerical response to the question: "Are women discriminated against in the workplace?"*

TABLE 10-7. (*Continued*)

	Median Weekly Earnings
Occupation, male	
Construction trades	$416
Operators, fabricators, laborers	$344
Machine operators, assemblers, inspectors	$353
Farming, forestry, fishing	$219
Occupation, female	
Managerial/professional	$441
Executive, admin., managerial	$416
Professional specialty	$458
Technical, sales, admin., support	$293
Sales	$246
Admin. support, incl. clerical	$294
Service	$199
Private household service	$130
Precision production	$302
Mechanics/repairers	$456
Construction trades	$—
Operators, fabricators, laborers	$231
Machine operators, assemblers, inspectors	$227
Farming, forestry, fishing	$191

Note: From the U.S. Bureau of the Census, *Statistical Abstract of the United States: 1989* (109th ed.), Washington, D.C., 1989, p. 406.

IS IT DISCRIMINATION? A THEORETICAL RESPONSE

Thus far in this chapter we've used the term "discrimination" very loosely, allowing each reader to interpret data and information according to his or her own understanding of the term. It is time now for us to settle on a more specific definition, which will help us account for the findings above. For our purposes, we'll use the term labor market discrimination.

Labor Market Discrimination

Flanagan, Smith and Ehrenberg (1984) suggested that discrimination be differentiated from "premarket" factors that may lead to discrimination but do not actually affect an employee's wages or advancement in the workplace. The definition of discrimination we will use in this chapter is from Flanagan, Smith and Ehrenberg, who define *labor market discrimination* as "the valuation in the labor market of personal characteristics of the worker that are unrelated to productivity" (p. 291). This definition allows us to focus our discussion on employer activities that affect the worker's income or chances for advancement (or chance of becoming an employee at all). This definition, then, distinguishes between discrimination and premarket factors that may or may not be discriminatory.

- *Define labor market discrimination.*

Four sources of labor market discrimination can be contrasted to help explain what is happening in organizations. The first source of discrimination is called *rational bias* (Larwood, Szwajkowski, & Rose, 1988). According to rational bias theory, a manager acts on behalf of his or her own self-interest in making hiring and promotion decisions, even though those decisions may not be in the best interests of the company or the person being discriminated against. This is a logic of self-interest; a subjective rationality.

When faced with a promotion decision, for example, the manager will scan the organizational environment to get a reading of what the operating norms are. If the norms favor discrimination, the manager will likely find political advantage in allowing the norm to continue by discriminating in the promotion decision. External biases, then, exert a form of covert pressure (discussed in Chapter 9), which biases the personal decision making of the manager.

Some of these covert pressures may actually be built into the structure of the organization itself (Acker, 1992; Mills, 1992/1988). Cultural values such as rationality, bureaucracy, the suppression of emotion, the separation of work from the home, with work as the foremost concern, are stereotypically seen as "male" traits. When these values inform organizational decisions, they can lead to unconscious gender discrimination.

The second source of discrimination is personal prejudice. *Personal prejudice* as a source of labor market discrimination occurs when an employer satisfies a preference for one group over another at the expense of what might be best for the organization. Examples include a preference for males in management positions and an aversion to hiring "young" people for certain jobs. A second form of personal prejudice comes from customers who prefer to obtain service from one group rather than another. Restaurant customers may prefer waitresses, patients may prefer male doctors. The result is a barrier for entry into those occupations by members of the less-preferred groups. A third form of prejudice comes from employees themselves. Some employees may prefer to be managed by a man or a white person, for example, or they may prefer to delegate typing or keeping of the minutes to a woman.

The third model of discrimination is called *statistical discrimination*. This occurs when employers assign assumed group characteristics to individual applicants, resulting in a subjective evaluation of applicant potential. This is common in jobs where some sort of evaluative or "objective" test is given to screen applicants. Employers commonly mistrust the projective validity of such measures and supplement them with their own judgment.

Suppose, for example, that an employer has "reason" to believe that graduates from a certain school are better educated than those from another school, or that blacks are more aggressive than Italians, or that women will take more sick leave than men. The result of assigning such assumed general tendencies to any individual will be the exclusion of some good applicants as well as the inclusion of some weak applicants.

The final model of discrimination is referred to as *monopoly power discrimination*. In this model is it assumed that organizations, in either an overt or a covert fashion, have worked to build a segregated workforce. The result is a noncompeting labor caste system in which some workers (white, male, educated) get better than equal access to high-paying, interesting careers with plenty of advancement potential. On the other hand, the remaining workers (minority, women, less educated) have access primarily to dead-end, low-paying, limited-advancement work. And these workers have limited access to the top end of the caste system.

- *Explain the four models of discrimination offered above.*

We're now in a better position to answer the question, "Does discrimination occur?" To judge from the material presented thus far, the answer can only be, "Yes." Remember, we're not talking here about prejudice. Discrimination goes beyond prejudice to affect an individual's ability to earn income and advance in an organization. Prejudice may or may not play a role in discrimination.

For whatever reason, personal prejudice, statistical discrimination, monopoly power discrimination, or rational bias, discrimination is a predominant feature of the workplace. Women and minorities are occupationally segregated; they make less money then white men on the average and less than white men in the same occupations; they confront more entry and advancement barriers than white men; and women and "feminine characteristics" are perceived more negatively than men and "masculine characteristics." The arguments given in response to the accusation of discrimination seem hollow and contrived. What all of these data boil down to is that the history of women, minorities, and work is marked by discrimination and the general failure of relying on individual initiative to overcome the tendency to discriminate. It is little wonder that the government had to turn to federal legislation in an attempt to mandate equality. Obviously, though, even federal mandates have failed to eradicate workplace inequality. The next section reviews some of the most pertinent antidiscrimination legislation.

ANTIDISCRIMINATION LEGISLATION

Discrimination has persisted in spite of the efforts of the federal government to halt it. In this section I'll briefly review some of the most important antidiscrimination legislation. This overview will point out some of the most apparent reasons that legislating equality has not erased inequality. The reader interested in studying more about these laws is encouraged to check Carr-Ruffino et al. (1992), Farley (1979), Maynard (1993), and McKee (1993). In chronological order, here are some of the most significant pieces of equality legislation.

The *Equal Pay Act of 1963* was designed to prohibit paying men and women different wages when they perform work that calls for the same or similar skills, in similar working conditions. "Equal work" was defined using four sets of conditions: skill, effort, responsibility, and working conditions. The act allowed exceptions in systems that rewarded differences based on things such as seniority, merit, or piece-rate pay.

The act was deficient as an antidiscrimination tool because it said nothing about equal opportunity. It also suffered from a virtually unsolvable problem in defining comparable worth. The act left open the interpretation of the "intrinsic worth" of jobs. How were employers to determine if the work of a secretary (primarily a low-paying job held by women) was comparable to that of a janitor (primarily a well-paying job held by men)? What would employers do about tenure in the organization? Or about different educational attainment?

Title VII of the Civil Rights Act of 1964 barred employers from discriminating against employees on the basis of race, sex, religion, or national origin. Title VII resulted in the creation of the Equal Employment Opportunity Commission (EEOC). It also banned advertisements for jobs that indicated discriminatory preferences.

What the EEOC is all about is using fair and fairly applied standards in hiring and advancement decisions and in working conditions. It is about fair and intelligent recruitment practices that offer the same options to all potential employees, regardless of color, sex, race, national origin, or other non-job-related criteria. At its simplest, what equal opportunity is all about is finding and choosing the best people for the jobs. Affirmative action is not about quotas. Nowhere in the legislation are quotas mandated. What is required are programs to allow equal access to employment. This is not the same as a lowering of standards. Employers are encouraged to review their standards to be sure that they're legitimate and nondiscriminatory.

These strengths of the law were obvious. Its weaknesses, however, were substantial when the law was measured as a device for ending discrimination. First, it was not retroactive. It did not mandate special treatment to overcome existing discrepancies in a workforce. Second, the law allowed exceptions in cases where religion, sex, and so forth could be shown to be bona fide occupational qualifications. And third, the law allowed preferential treatment in cases of seniority systems if it could be shown that there was no intent to discriminate in the seniority system.

The *Office of Federal Contract-Compliance Programs* was established in 1965 to oversee the hiring and promotion practices of companies with federal contracts. The office was to evaluate the practices of these companies in regard to the composition of their workforce and to help them develop affirmative action plans. Such plans are a requirement for a company to continue to do business with the government. An *affirmative action plan* is a hiring and promotion plan designed to accomplish a balance in the workplace, between white males and minorities and women, that reflects the balance in the pool available outside the workplace. Affirmative action is not a "quota" system. Rather, it is about making good faith efforts to include women and minorities in the hiring and promotion policies of the company.

Affirmative action plans and laws suffer from a number of problems, including the fact that organizations are sometimes situated far from where given minority populations may live; the law prohibits the firing of existing employees of one race to make room for new employees of another race, meaning that any quick remedy to a workplace imbalance will most likely not be seen; and it is not clear if the firm should base its hiring decisions on the actual number of minorities (for example) in a given geographical area, or on the number of potential applicants actually qualified for a given position, or even on the number who might be interested in a position.

The *1990 Americans With Disabilities Act* requires employers to make accommodations for people with disabilities. The "public access" component, in which business establishments must be made accessible to the handicapped, was activated in January 1992, and as of July 1992, companies must make accommodations for employees with disabilities. In 1994 the cutoff will be companies that employ more than fifteen workers. This law protects people with disabilities from discrimination in recruitment, pay, hiring, benefits, leaves of absence, and job assignments.

Finally, the *1993 Family and Medical Leave Act* requires that U.S. businesses that employ more than fifty people must allow up to twelve weeks of unpaid leave per year for childbirth, adoption or foster care, and care for self, child, or spouse with health problems. The law covers employees with twelve months' tenure and 1250 hours worked and requires that employers continue to provide health benefits as well as guarantee the employee an equivalent job when he or she returns. The employer is allowed to exempt the highest-paid 10 percent of the workforce from the program and can require periodic status reports from employees on leave.

- *Summarize the Equal Pay Act of 1963, Title VII of the Civil Rights Act of 1964, and affirmative action.*

Regardless of what laws exist, the difficulties of overcoming discrimination are daunting. Still, difficult or not, employers have both a legal and a moral obligation to act fairly in hiring, firing, and promotion. The first step in overcoming discrimination against women and minorities is to identify what form of discrimination is occurring. For example, Haslett, Geis, and Carter (1992) identified two forms of sexism: individual and organizational. *Individual sexism* occurs when an individual or group behaves in a deliberate or non-deliberate way toward a woman that is discriminatory, dominating, exploitative, and so forth. *Organizational sexism* is sexism that is built into the very structure of the company—part of the rules and policies of interaction. One must have an understanding of the type of discrimination one is facing if it is to be overcome.

Beyond this first step, employers can do a number of other things to act fairly (Farley, 1979): (1) Determine the sex/race composition of the current workforce. (2) Determine the availability of those groups (usually women and certain minority groups) underrepresented in the national workforce. (3) Determine the degree to which the groups of interest are underrepresented in the company. (4) Set goals and target dates for accomplishing "adequate" representation. (5) Monitor progress in meeting goals. (6) Correct job advertisements so that underrepresented segments of the potential workforce have access to the postings. (7) Develop and encourage training programs.

- *What steps should be taken to act more affirmatively in hiring practices?*

ARE THERE DIFFERENCES THAT MAKE A DIFFERENCE?

At the center of the discrimination issue is the question of differences. Are there differences between men and women, blacks and whites, Hispanics and Japanese, and so forth that make a difference? Regarding sex-based differences, the only category to have been examined, the answer is yes, at least according to the efforts of many well-intentioned researchers and publications. For example, the interested reader might check *Working Mother* (1992) magazine's list of best companies in America for working mothers. Baird and Bradley (1979) and Tannen (1990) also report substantial differences between the sexes. On the other hand, many researchers are finding either little to no difference (see Canary & House, 1993; Correa et al., 1988; Harper & Hirokawa, 1988), or more variation within sexes than across sexes (see Mulac et al., 1988; Pearson, Turner, & Todd-Mancillas, 1991).

In short, on the question of difference, the jury is still out. However, whether real or not, difference is a common perception in the workplace. Haslett, Geis, and Carter (1992) presented results of literally dozens of studies that demonstrate time and time again the negative effect of perceived gender differences. From identifying men as leaders because of where they sit at tables, to evaluating essays attributed to men as of higher quality than when those same essays are attributed to women, to evaluating job candidate resumes attributed to male candidates as worthy of higher positions than when those same resumes are attributed to female candidates, the studies continue to demonstrate the power of human perception to defy reality. Recent work is beginning to show some shifts in these perceptual biases, but the overwhelming body of research points out clearly that men and women are perceived differently.

Men are given more opportunities to succeed. Their success is usually attributed to ability and internal resources, whereas women's successes are often attributed to external causes, and women's failures to a lack of ability. "Masculine" characteristics are more highly valued in descriptions of "good managers" than are "feminine" characteristics. Men's leadership is often described as better than women's, even when their contributions are objectively the same. In both laboratory and field studies stereotyped beliefs about both men and women abound.

The finding that virtually all researchers seem to agree on is that whether real or not, when differences are perceived, the perception will prompt the discrimination. The discrimination will be "caused" by the perception of differences that must be factored into the income and advancement equation.

- *What are the implications of the perceptual tendency to see differences that may not be real? What difference would it make if there were more differences among men as a group, and among women as a group, than between the general groups of men and women?*

Gender Role Spillover

A big part of the breakdown of our perceptual apparatus when it comes to men, women, and work is the idea of gender role spillover (Haslett, Geis, and Carter, 1992). *Gender role spillover* is the confusion that occurs when men (or women) rely on stereotypical assumptions about women (or men) that are unrelated to the work environment when making determinations and evaluations of work roles and responsibilities. Gender role spillover is the cause of much of the confusion and perceptual bias in the organization.

Our perceptions are developed throughout our lives and, though they can be called up to consciousness for evaluation, tend to affect our judgments unconsciously. Gender stereotypes serve as a form of subconscious knowledge about people and their roles in the world. These stereotypes, no matter how accurate or inaccurate, often become self-fulfilling prophecies.

Such stereotypes will be one of the most difficult problems to address and may be the reason that only legislation can eliminate discrimination in the workplace. What happens is an insidious process whereby a societal preference for a gender, such as men, or a race, such as white, leads to a division of labor and control that favors the preferred groups. When the dominant group is consistently seen in the privileged positions, we lose track of the fact that the position is the result of societal miscue, rather than of the sex or physical makeup of the individuals. It becomes easy for us, then, to mistake privileged position for natural order. Nowhere are the problems of gender role spillover and stereotyping more apparent than with the experience of being a token in the workplace.

- *What is gender role spillover?*

Tokenism

In her now-classic study of the organization called Indsco, Rosabeth Moss Kanter (1977) discussed the significance of numerical proportions for both work effectiveness and cultural understanding. Kanter identified four types of groups on the basis of the ratio of men to women within the group. (This ratio could also be applied to racial or ethnic composition.) The four types were *uniform groups* (all one sex), *skewed groups* (a dominant-token situation in which one group vastly outnumbered the other, for example by an 85:15 ratio), *tilted groups* (around a 65:35 ratio, identifying a majority-minority relationship), and *balanced groups* (a basically even distribution, up to 60:40). The skewed group is the most problematic, for that is the unbalanced form that results in the presence of token-dominant relationships.

Tokenism has a profound effect on working relationships, as well as on the performance and self-concept of the tokens. As Kanter used the term, *token* refers to an individual whose group is underrepresented, not to a person who is unqualified to fill a position. Kanter argued that tokenism results in three outcomes: visibility, contrast, and assimilation. *Visibility is the result of the fact that tokens are noticeable.* They get a larger share of attention than others. This increased attention creates performance pressures on the token (Kanter, 1977, p. 212). *Contrast is the tendency of the dominant group, because of the conspicuous presence of the token, to focus more attention on their differences than they would in a more evenly balanced group.* This focus on differences may actually heighten or exaggerate the perceived differences, further isolating the token. *Assimilation refers to the perceptual tendency of people to stereotype.* Tokens are easily lumped into their general category, be it race, gender, or whatever, allowing the dominant group to overlook whatever unique characteristics a person might bring to the group. Thus, assimilation reduces the range of behavior that the dominant group perceives as available to the token.

- *What are the ratios that identify uniform, skewed, tilted, and balanced groups, and what are the three outcomes of tokenism?*

The results of tokenism leave tokens in no-win situations. The token can react to the pressures and stereotypes by trying to overachieve or become socially invisible. Tokens may have to accept and even contribute to the boundary-heightening attempts of the dominants, participating in self-deprecating humor, for example, as a way to show loyalty and similarity to the dominants. Tokens may have to put up with formal and informal isolation from the dominant group. They may have to demonstrate their loyalty to the dominant group by rejecting their own category. And, because they are always being stereotyped, tokens will always have to battle the assumptions generated by those stereotypes.

EMBRACING DIFFERENCE

Are men and women, blacks and whites, Hispanics and Chinese, and so forth different, and are they different in significant ways? I've asked this question throughout the chapter and we have seen evidence that supports both yes and no responses. A large part of this chapter has focused on what might be called the legislation of sameness. Federal attempts to guarantee discrimination-free work environments have, in essence, tried to eliminate perceptions of differences or, if not eliminate them, at least compensate for their potentially harmful effects.

A variety of authors have advocated a more aggressive campaign of recognizing differences and working to build cultures of acceptance and tolerance, rather than cultures of sameness, built upon somebody's contrived criteria. At the center of this movement is Carol Gilligan. Gilligan (1982) argued that women and their experiences represent a "different voice" from that of men. There does not exist a single social experience and it is foolhardy to proceed as though there were. By embracing differences we will arrive at a fuller, richer understanding of the relationships between men and women, blacks and whites, language and thought, equality and fairness. Gilligan's work has spurred controversy because it advocates the recognition and acceptance of difference. One of the controversial sequels to Gilligan's ideas that nicely illuminates the problems of legitimizing difference was Schwartz's (1989, 1992) work on a phenomenon dubbed the "mommy track."

Capitalizing on Differences: Felice Schwartz and Women's Careers

In a very controversial article, Schwartz (1989) identified two key work-related differences between men and women: those related to maternity and those related to expectations of the sexes. The most critical juncture between the two occurs when men perceive family as the province of women and work as the province of men. This sort of thinking only reinforces stereotypes and makes capitalizing on differences more difficult. Organizations must learn to value differences. Schwartz predicted that over the next decade, about 80 percent of the new entries into the workplace will be women and minorities (p. 68). What this means, of course, is that companies that still carry a bias in favor of hiring white men will have to look harder and harder to find good ones, passing up potentially superior women.

She recommended that employers begin by changing their attitudes about women. They must understand that women, like men, are not all alike. Basically, women should be understood as having a "career-primary" or a "career-and-family" orientation. Women with a *career-primary orientation* should be identified from the beginning of their careers and advanced through the ranks as quickly as their male counterparts. Artificial barriers to their advancement hurt not only them, but the company as well, which will suffer from their underuse and their loss of productivity. These women can offer their abilities to the company as well as serve as mentors for other women. These women must be included in the same activities and given the same opportunities as their male counterparts.

Schwartz argued that most women have a *career-and-family orientation* (dubbed the "mommy track" by journalists). "The career-and-family woman is willing to trade off the pressures and demands that go with promotion for the freedom to spend more time with her children. She's very smart, she's talented, she's committed to her career, and she's satisfied to stay at the middle level, at least during the early child-rearing years" (Schwartz, 1989, p. 71). This person, in other words, is no less valuable as an employee. She simply performs her work from a different set of assumptions than the career-primary woman.

Schwartz recommended job sharing as the best solution for retaining these women. Job sharing would allow them the flexibility they need and desire to balance home and work demands. It would allow them to continue to work, be involved, keep their motivation high, and lessen the amount of time it would take for these women to "reenter" the workforce after maternity leave. Flextime, family support, and most important, child care are what this group of employees needs. Meeting these needs means that the company can hold on to a valued, valuable employee, trained and successful, rather than lose this person for no good reason.

- *What is the difference between career-primary and career-and-family women?*

Building Differences into Career Development

While Schwartz's ideas were given the unfortunate and unfair title of "mommy track," Larwood and Gutek (1987) put forth ideas that were very similar, no less controversial, but subjected to far less popular media scrutiny. They suggested that a model of women's career development should look different from one for men's career development, because women do not experience their careers in the same way. Men's career development can be generalized as having three parts: education/exploration, identification/establishment, and maintenance/stagnation. Clearly there are exceptions, especially to phase three. Many men continue to grow in their work.

A model of women's career development would have five parts: preparation; opportunities available; influence of marriage, pregnancy, and children; timing; and age. This more complex model may help in understanding men who do not fit the traditional male career model. It also better accounts for the female experience. Women have traditionally been less educated, though that is changing; they have had fewer opportunities, both formal and informal; and marriage, pregnancy, and children have been seen as career hindrances and disadvantages. These factors have forced women to put off certain career decisions, and the result is an older employee at the earlier stages of a career. Only a model that recognizes the social differences between men and women will adequately and equitably facilitate career planning and progression.

- *What are the advantages and disadvantages of viewing men's and women's careers differently?*

In short, Schwartz and Larwood and Gutek advocate that organizations work to incorporate into their thinking and decision making the social experience of being female. These authors suggest that we stop regarding the organization as a separate entity, distinct from society, and work to understand it as a part of the social experience of men and women. Societal expectations and influences don't stop at the office door for either men or women. They can't be legislated away. They must be recognized, some of them overcome and some of them embraced. Either way, recognition is the first crucial step.

- *Summarize the above recommendations regarding recognizing difference.*

OVERCOMING THE OBSTACLES

Extending this theme of recognizing and embracing difference to minorities leaves us wondering what would happen if organizations worked harder to incorporate the minority experience into their career planning.

Currently the underuse of minority talent is both shameful and illogical. Organizations might begin by capitalizing on some of the unique attributes of minority groups. For example, Martin (1991) argued that the Native American tendency to value family and community first might be channeled into corporate loyalty. And Foeman and Pressley (1992/1987) suggested that blacks possess a number of attributes desirable in the workplace. First, they tend to be positively assertive; second, they are forthright and straightforward; third, they have a clear sense of justice, of right and wrong; fourth, they are active and responsive; and fifth, they have a clear sense of community and loyalty to family groups.

The key first step in overcoming obstacles faced by minorities is more research. Until we get a clearer, more consistent picture of the various minority situations, any solutions will be guesswork.

Haslett, Geis, and Carter (1992) offered a variety of suggestions for overcoming the obstacles faced by women in the work environment. These suggestions include the following, and many of these read equally well as advice for minorities.

1. Rather than letting their work speak for itself, women need to take advantage of the appropriate means of self-promotion.
2. Realize that men will have trouble reorganizing their thinking about women as sisters, mothers, daughters, and so forth to allow for a category of women as coworkers, bosses, and so forth.
3. Determine what type of image or role you want to project, and work to project that. *Don't let your image be chosen for you.*
4. Keep in touch with the informal communication network. It often supplies accurate information about what's going on around the company, as well as opportunities that are or may become available.
5. When confronting both men and women coworkers, develop a win-win strategy so as not to leave the other feeling belittled.
6. Don't let others determine your feelings about yourself or your decisions. For example, if you are comfortable with the day-care arrangements that

you have made for your children, don't let others convince you that you should feel guilty.

7. Try to understand the source of negative reactions toward you. They might be the results of perceptual misunderstandings, language differences, emotional responses, and so forth.

- **What are some of the things that women can do to overcome obstacles to their advancement?**

DISCRIMINATION AND CULTURE

Discussions of minorities and women and work seem constantly to center on the question: Are they at the top yet? Are they managers? This attitude is apparent in the many articles that end with a statement something like: "However, in spite of all these efforts, women are still at the bottom of the managerial ranks in corporate America." This is an unfortunate attitude, for it puts a peripheral issue at the center of a complex communication problem. A cultural approach to understanding discrimination is less about tops and bottoms than it is about the communicative construction of an environment of fairness and equality.

A useful concept in understanding a cultural approach to discrimination is *marginality* (see Bullis, 1993a; Buono & Kamm, 1983). Marginality, as a sociological construct, refers to individuals who are "between groups." In other words, they have left one group to join another, but find acceptance into the next group slow, strained, and conditional. Marginalized others represent dominated, oppressed outsiders forced to stand on the edge of dominant systems, excluded from life within. By all indications in this chapter, *we may actually create and perpetuate cultures of marginality.*

Women and minorities in the workplace can profitably be understood as *marginal persons.* The marginal person suffers the consequences of having no firm footing. The lack of a peer or reference group, coupled with the hostility or rejection or conditional acceptance of the desired reference group leaves the marginal person feeling as though he or she is only a peripheral participant.

Marginality offers an interesting clarification, if not a replacement, for existing theories that attempt to explain the slow progress that minorities and women have made in the workplace. Rather than relying on explanations like differences in socialization, or patriarchal organizational environments, the theory of marginality is a communication-based explanation for discrimination. It is predicated on the assumption that the marginal person, an intercultural sojourner of sorts, will continually have to wrestle with the rejection of the group left behind and the resistance of the group desired. The resistance from the desired group has been a fixture in many studies, including early ones going back to 1965, in which it was found that women had to be exceptional, even overqualified to succeed in management (Bowman, Worthy, & Greyser, 1965).

- *How does the concept of marginality help explain the female and minority experience in the workplace?*

This book has emphasized over and over again that the organizations of today and tomorrow are multicultural environments. This means that the most necessary managerial skill will be the ability to manage diversity. And managing diversity means the ability to recognize and overcome marginality.

Organizations as multicultural environments will be filled with marginal persons, with those in transition, and with individuals suspicious of and even hostile to the efforts of the marginal person to be fully and successfully integrated into the desired group. Managing this process of acceptance will mean that organizations, organization members and managers alike, will have to begin anew the process of learning to understand and accept difference.

Efforts at homogenizing the organization are contrary to an understanding of culture and subcultural variation. We don't need to legislate equality, we need to work harder to create belief systems of tolerance and understanding. Subcultural variation is a strength of the workplace, not a weakness. The continued presence of women and minorities in the workplace offers the organization of tomorrow a much more complete understanding of the world outside the organization, a world to which the organization must adapt and understand.

Unfortunately, we seem to be far from succeeding in the integration of marginal persons into the dominant culture of organizational America—one of discrimination, power, fear, and mistrust. Women and minorities face an uphill battle to infuse the dominant cultures with new ideas, beliefs, values, and understandings. But from an organization culture point of view, this effort must come from the women and minorities themselves, for there is little chance of real cultural change happening when it is "forced" by the dominant culture itself.

SUMMARY

In this chapter we have looked at the experience of being a member of a minority within a majority system. We looked specifically at Asian-American, Native American, Hispanic, and African-American occupational issues. Though a very brief overview was provided, a sense was gained of the frustration that must be felt by these minority groups when faced with unequal access to opportunity and organizational success. The chapter then turned to the American woman's experience and found it strikingly similar to the minority experiences summarized earlier. By all measurements—labor force participation, occupational representation, and income—women were found to be treated differently from men.

In an effort to explain the data, we looked at explanations other than discrimination, as well as at theories of discrimination. The chapter then turned to antidiscrimination legislation and concluded that fairness cannot be legislated. We then looked at the question of differences, noting that there doesn't seem to be much good evidence for the claim that men and women are all that different from each other. However, in this case, perceptions speak louder than reality.

The chapter then turned to the issue of embracing difference. A cultural approach to diversity is one that values difference as positive and energizing. It is not afraid to build difference into career planning and our understanding of coworkers. The key to overcoming the obstacles created by discrimination, then, is the recognition and acceptance of diversity.

CHAPTER 11

Organization Culture, Decision Making, and Environmental Uncertainty

Chapter Preview

In this chapter we review some of the complexity of decision making. This is an important chapter because, given the enormous impact of organizations on our lives, we would hope that decision-makers are making the best decisions possible. Unfortunately, as you will see, the pervasive influence of culture and human limitations make the decisional world of organizations suspect.

I'll first present the notion of organizations as decision environments and describe the role of culture in those environments. We'll immediately see the complexity of the issue: Do individuals make decisions or do organizations make decisions that transcend individuals? And, ultimately, who is responsible?

To help make sense of such questions, as well as offer a theoretical explanation for the idea of organizations as decision environments, the chapter then turns to the work of Karl Weick. This review will give us a global understanding of the various decisional constraints and the organizational decision-making and sense-making processes. This discussion includes a review of tight and loose coupling, the sociocultural evolution model, and strategic ambiguity. We then look at Herbert Simon's work on rationality, and at a number of researchers who extend Simon's ideas to get a clearer sense of the frailties of the human decision-maker, outlined by Weick's ideas.

The chapter then turns to decision making in crises. Crises, more than the commonplace activities of daily organizational life, highlight the decision-making process and the important role of culture in establishing the decisional environment. Through several case studies we'll examine the issues of crisis communication, product liability, and executive moral responsibility. The chapter closes with an overview of how culture constrains the decision-making process.

Key Terms

decision
tightly coupled
loosely coupled
change
enactment
selection

retention
retrospective sense making
strategic ambiguity
bounded rationality
Abilene Paradox

Before venturing any further into this chapter, you might want to consider the following question: How certain is the world? Don't laugh, this question is not nearly so rhetorical as it might seem. Suppose that you were one of the employees, owners, presidents, customers, or citizens affected by one of the following: In 1980 Toxic Shock Syndrome was linked to the use of Procter & Gamble's Rely tampons; in 1982 and 1986, eight people died (seven in 1982, one in 1986) after taking poisoned Johnson & Johnson Tylenol capsules; in 1985, during a bitter labor strike, razor blades were found in Hormel meat products; in 1986 glass pieces were found in Gerber baby food products; in 1979 the world came close to experiencing a total meltdown at the Three Mile Island nuclear reactor; in 1984 toxic cyanide gas escaped from Union Carbide's plant in Bhopal, India, killing thousands; in 1985, skywalks collapsed inside the Hyatt Regency Hotel in Kansas City; in the first six months of 1988, fourteen terrorist acts were committed against U.S. firms; in New York bombings occurred at IBM offices in 1984, at Motorola and Honeywell offices in 1983 and 1984, and at the World Trade Center in 1993; between 1980 and 1985, about 6900 chemical accidents occurred in the United states, injuring 1500 people, and killing 135; on March 3, 1974, DC-10 Ship 29 crashed, killing all 346 people aboard. The cause of the crash was a faulty cargo door that had been reported corrected when in fact the corrections were never made; in 1979 Life Savers' Bubble Yum chewing gum was rumored to contain spider eggs; and, in 1985, both Procter & Gamble and Sears were rumored to be in collusion with the devil—P&G because of its logo, and Sears because its credit cards began with the numbers 666. Consider one more example of uncertainty. It is now generally accepted that somewhere between one million and two million men, women, and children in the United States, mostly between the ages of 18 and 40, are HIV positive. With no cure on the horizon, most, if not all, of these people will die of AIDS-related diseases within seven years of this writing. And many, if not most, of these individuals will hold jobs somewhere.

So how certain is the world generally and the world of work specifically? And, how should organizations conduct themselves in the face of this uncertainty? Can organizations predict the future? Should they be able to? How should they respond to crises of the sorts listed above? What decisions should be made and what factors should guide those decisions?

This chapter is about culture and decision making. The premise of the chapter is that organizations are decision environments and culture plays a primary role in the shaping of the decisions made by organizations and organization members.

To begin our examination we need to unpack what was just said. Three key questions are implied in the above paragraph: (1) What is a decision environment? (2) How would culture play a role? (3) Can "organizations" make decisions or must decisions be attached, ultimately, to a single person?

ORGANIZATIONS AS DECISION ENVIRONMENTS

A *decision* is the outcome of reasoning. Decision making is part of problem solving and conflict management. A decision becomes a problem when the decision must be made in light of disagreement about alternatives. A problem becomes a conflict when the disagreement is between interdependent individuals who must decide between incompatible alternatives (see Chapter 9). Without much exaggeration, it may be said that making decisions, solving problems, and managing conflict are the primary activities of organization members. Since organizations are the communicative constructions of organization members, and since the primary activity of those members concerns decision making, the organization easily becomes a decision environment.

THE ROLE OF CULTURE IN SHAPING DECISIONS

Throughout this text culture has been referred to as the beliefs, assumptions, values, expectations, paradigms, frames of reference, and so forth that are both the product of sense making and the key factors in forging the sense made of organizational events. In other words, cultural assumptions are the premises that underlie the logic applied by organizational members, as well as the result—the conclusion of sense-making activities. Culture is both a product and a process.

This dual role that culture plays has a profound impact on decision making. Culture will predispose individuals to make certain decisions at the expense of others. Organizationally relevant decisions, once made, will continually reinforce the existing cultural premises, resulting in a cyclical, self-perpetuating process.

In other words, since culture exists largely out of the conscious awareness of organization members, its influence on their decision making will be subtle and unseen. Culture will exist as the status quo—the result of past and present practices. It will serve as the logic for making future decisions, resulting in a tendency to "not rock the boat." So, culture tends to reproduce itself in the decision making of organization members who seek to maintain the way things are.

ORGANIZATIONS AS DECISION-MAKERS

Ultimately, organizational decision making is a question of accountability. Is an identifiable, isolated individual ultimately responsible for "organizational decisions," or can we talk about decisions that go beyond individuals and are attributable only to an organizational entity? Many, if not most, readers would like to say that only individuals are responsible; but a cultural explanation of organizations would suggest otherwise. Culture is a pervasive influence, subtle, tacit, out of awareness. The cultures of which we are members will lead us to make certain assumptions at the expense of others, will force us to see the world according to given parameters. Because of this influence of culture and because of an overwhelming amount of evidence demonstrating the vulnerability of individuals to peer and cultural influences, it will be assumed here that many decisions are beyond the control of any specific, single individual.

- *Explain the complexity surrounding a portrayal of organizations as decision environments.*

We need to understand that this is not a "copout" on the responsibility issue, nor is it a suggestion that individuals cannot be held accountable. Indeed, society and organizations demand accountability. Just ask Michael Milken (jail and about a billion dollars in fines for insider trading on Wall Street), Ivan Boesky (jail and about a hundred million dollars in fines for insider trading on Wall Street), Jim Bakker (prison for fraud surrounding the PTL ministry), or Robert Stempl (removed as CEO of General Motors because the board of directors perceived too much caution and too slow a turnaround in the giant auto maker). All that I'm suggesting here is that *a cultural interpretation of organizations will force us to look beyond the decisions in an effort to ascertain if there were cultural premises that promoted decisions that might now be condemned.*

We'll be referring to these theoretical preconditions throughout the following discussion. First, though, we'll look at the vision of organizations offered by Karl Weick. Weick's work has had a profound influence on the field of organizational communication, and he, more than any other theorist, has offered a foundation for our overall understanding of organizations as decision environments. After spending some time on a wide-angle picture of the organizational decision environment, the chapter will turn directly to the individual as decision-maker and the individual-culture relationship as it pertains to decision making.

KARL WEICK AND ORGANIZATIONAL DECISION ENVIRONMENTS

Offering a simplified explanation of Weick's (1979a) discussion of organizations as organizing is no small task.[1] The best place to start is with his definition of organizing, from which we will progress to his model of the process. Weick defined organizing as a *"consensually validated grammar for reducing equivocality by means of sensible interlocked behaviors.* To organize is to assemble ongoing interdependent actions into sensible sequences that generate sensible

[1]For a discussion of experimental examinations of Weick's model, the interested reader should see Bantz and Smith (1977), Kreps (1980), and Putnam and Sorenson (1982).

outcomes" (p. 3, italics in original). In other words, organizing is about two or more individuals agreeing upon a set of rules (consensually validated grammar) for understanding environmental ambiguity (reducing equivocality) through a system of exchange with one another. The goal of organizing is the accomplishment of understanding.

This organizing process is the organization. As such, the organization is seen as a temporarily managed moment in a stream of activities. The structural permanence that we like to call "the organization," then, is built upon the fragile foundations of the interlocked communicative behavior of organizational members as they try to make sense of the world around them (see Chapter 1 of this text). This notion of organization as behavior, as action rather than substance, seems hard to grasp and harder to "do anything with." It is much easier, after all, to visualize the organization as a container in which are offices, desks, telephones, workers, and all the other nouns of organizing.

- *Explain Weick's definition of organizing? Do you see why organizing is the organization?*

But the reduction of process into parts results in our overlooking what is most important about organizing in the first place: the communicative actions of members. For example, the tragedy summarized in Case 1-1 is a sad example of organization members who didn't recognize that organizations are always in the process of becoming. In the case we can see that the participants forgot that "flight safety" is about communication much more than it is about planes, towers, radar, pilots, weather, and all the other nouns of airline organizations. The organization became both the product and the act of creating. The pilots and the control tower crew were faced with uncommon organizational dimensions, including changes in the normal routine, scripted behavior, thick, low clouds, language differences, inadequate lighting, the stress of fearing a terrorist attack, the stress of being diverted from original destinations, and for the Dutch crew, the stress of approaching their monthly allotment of flight time.

All of these contributed to an emergent organizational form that was simply the momentary realization of a continuing process. The organization was unstable, the rules were changed; it was not business as usual. The organization truly became a series of decisions made in an effort to reduce uncertainty. The premises that guided the decisions were past practices—cultural assumptions.

The most important quality of this organization-building process is the interdependence between the parts, for it is there that we are reminded that the constructive process is not linear, but circular. An event near us may prompt recognition but that same recognition serves to reconstruct the event, leading to interpretation, which includes further construction, and so on. For example, suppose that you're traveling through a highway tunnel at a speed of 55 miles per hour, knowing that the speed limit is 45 miles per hour. Upon clearing the tunnel you spy a police car parked about a quarter mile up the road on your side. You immediately slow down in response to the environment and your in-

---

Case 11-1:   *The Tenerife Air Disaster*

One of the worst air disasters in history occurred on March 27, 1977, when 583 people died as a result of the collision between their two aircraft 13 seconds into takeoff from Los Rodeos airport at Tenerife. The collision was between Dutch (KLM) and American (PanAm) 747s that had both been diverted to Tenerife when their original destination in the Canary Islands was closed because of terrorist activities. Weick (1991) built a compelling argument that the tragedy resulted from a variety of factors that changed a relatively straightforward, linear organizational environment into a complex, ambiguous environment characterized by levels of equivocality that, when left unaccounted for, resulted in tragedy and death.

The context of the disaster demonstrates how a series of apparently small decisions and events can cumulatively add up to a large effect. Among the contributing causes are the following: In one transmission, the KLM aircraft requested two clearances from ground control; the ground controller gave a response at one point that may have been intended to refer to an after-takeoff procedure, but may have been interpreted by the KLM aircraft as takeoff clearance; a number of controller-to-aircraft transmissions violated procedure or were garbled; both aircraft had been diverted from their original destinations; transmissions were sent to the control tower that were unexpected and ambiguous; the KLM cockpit crew was under pressure to complete its flight before a given monthly work time allotment had expired, which put severe limits on time worked per month and set severe penalties for violating these rules; the KLM crew was required to maneuver a 747 into a 180-degree turn on a 150-foot-wide runway (142 feet are necessary to make the turn); the Tenerife air traffic control crew was shorthanded, had little experience handling 747s, was working with no ground radar, was working in English (a second language),

---

terpretation that the environment is hostile. You and the police car created both an environment and a hostile relationship. The organizing process was reciprocally interlocking, not linear.

- **What does it mean to say that the organizing process refers to reciprocal interlocking?**

Tight and Loose Coupling

Interlocked behavior constitutes the organizational structure that is in actuality the communicative balancing of organization members. If the systems in transaction share many variables, or if an impact on one causes a significant strain on the other, the systems are said to be *tightly coupled*. The less the systems have in common or the more independent they are, the more *loosely coupled* they're said to be (Orton & Weick, 1990; Weick, 1976). The notion of loose coupling is in contrast to the more common vision of organizations as rational-

Case 11-1: (Continued)

and at the time the centerline runway lights were not operating; finally, a large cloud (not fog) was hovering 1300 feet above the PanAm runway. The collision occurred in that cloud. The planes could not see each other, the ground control crew did not see the collision, and indeed, the cloud was so thick that when the fire crew began dousing the flames they weren't aware that two planes were involved.

The point of describing this incident in such detail is that it points out how vulnerable human systems are to the cumulative complexity of the external environment. When faced with such complexity, Weick argued, we fall back upon what we know, what has worked in the past. The stress of the environment created unknown and uncomfortable levels of equivocality for all parties. The KLM pilot was head of flight training for KLM and his copilot was a recent graduate of the KLM program. "He was a training captain which meant that the flights he was most familiar with were those which followed a script, had fewer problems, and were shorter in duration. . . . Giving clearance is what he had done most often for the last 10 years when sitting at the head of a runway and is the response he may have reverted to as pressures mounted at Tenerife" (Weick, 1991, p. 123).

From an organizing perspective we must note that the communicative events at the airport were part of the organization construction process. The various conversations within the cockpits, within the control tower, between the tower and the planes, and between the KLM plane and its home base all contributed to the communicative construction of organizational reality. The distortion that occurred resulted in a distorted organization structure. The appearance of unity and coherence was actually a mask covering distortion and confusion.

Note: This summary is based on Weick (1991).

ly (tightly) planned and coordinated activities. The loosely coupled system is one in which the units or members are both connected and somewhat autonomous. Thus, they retain their sense of independence while at the same time they are identifiable as elements of the organization as a whole.

Coupling is a useful term to describe a relationship, such as that between attitudes and behavior. If behavior naturally follows from attitudes, the two are said to be tightly coupled; if not, then loosely. Similarly, the counselors, principals, teachers, students, and parents of a given school are said to be loosely coupled, as are elected officials and voters. According to Weick (1976, pp. 6–8), loose coupling offers an organization several advantages. Loose coupling allows the organization to persist, rather than respond to every environmental shift; it provides the organization with a method for sensing the environment; it allows for small-scale, or "localized" adaptation; because of the independence of units, a loosely coupled system can achieve greater variation within its units than can a tightly coupled system; weaknesses or breakdowns in one part of the system have less effect on the system as a whole; because of the potential of greater independent growth, participants in a loosely coupled system may experience greater fulfillment and power than otherwise; and a loosely coupled system is less expensive than the alternative because it is unnecessary to constantly monitor all of the parts.

- *What are the differences between tightly and loosely coupled systems?*

Weick argued that we tend to believe that our organizations are more tightly coupled than they actually are. In the face of loose coupling, individuals must engage in a greater amount of sense making and socially constructing meaning. In Case 11-1, the participants engaged each other as though they were part of a loosely coupled system (which an airport cannot be), when in actuality, their tight coupling should have been recognized. Had it been recognized and had steps been taken to actually tighten the process, the tragedy might have been avoided.

Weick's Sociocultural Evolution Model

The above discussion is diagrammed in Weick's Sociocultural Evolution model of organizing. The model revolves around four key components: change, enactment, selection, and retention (see Figure 11-1). *Change* refers to discontinuity within the external environment. It supplies the raw material for enactment. Change represents a level of equivocality (uncertainty) that must be reduced for the organization to maintain a sense of stability. *Enactment* is the most abstract of the processes. Enactment is more than recognizing a change in the environment. It is the active process of defining that change. Enactment creates a level of equivocality that must be interpreted. Noticing a police car is only part of enactment; seeing that car as the law, as a rule system, as a form of safety and punishment, as something to be respected and feared are also enactment. Enactment is the activity of directly engaging the environment. This direct engagement is filtered through our perceptual apparatus and, thus, is not neutral.

From enactment comes selection. With enactment, the organization is importing a given level of ambiguity and uncertainty. *Selection* is the process of reducing this equivocality. The puzzle of enactment is shaped and formed by the interpretive process of selection. Through selection the environment is stabilized. Finally, *retention* refers to information storage. It refers to the organization's capacity to call upon previously used selection strategies and to store new ones. Because of retention, the organization is not continually facing uncertainty as though each uncertain situation were brand new. With retention

FIGURE 11-1. Weick's Sociocultural Evolution model

Change ----► Enactment ----► Selection ----► Retention

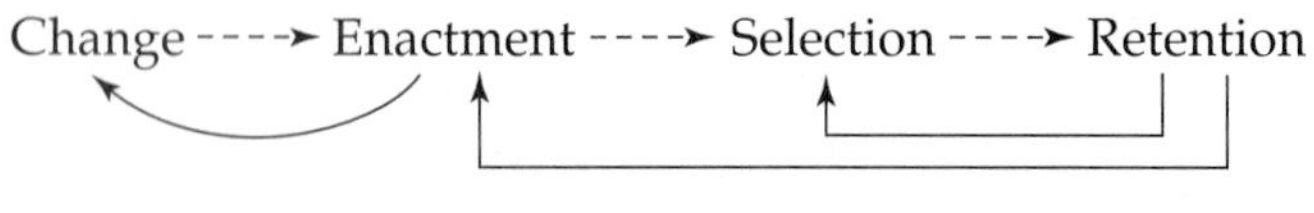

the maps of the past can be imposed on the present to make sense of new input.

The process, then, progresses as follows: Change is enacted by the organization, resulting in a level of uncertainty that must be lowered through selection, often by drawing upon the past as stored in retention. Thus, enactment affects the environment, and retention affects both enactment and selection. Finally, the process of selection is referred to as a series of *assembly rules*. These simply mean the number of interpretive cycles necessary to reduce equivocality. Or, to put it differently, we could describe assembly rules as instructions for interpreting the result of enactment.

If the organization enacts a fairly common portion of the environment, it stands to reason that it will have experienced this "new" input in some fashion in the past, so it will have a number of successful interpretation schemes available. It will remember how it interpreted in the past and will draw upon these interpretation options in the present.

On the other hand, a higher ambiguity input would mean a greater chance that the organization would not have an existing stock of interpretation schemes, and would have to go through more assembly series in order to make sense of the input.

- *Explain the process of enactment, selection, and retention, and the importance of assembly rules.*

An example will help demonstrate the process outlined in the model. Read Case 11-2: Nestle Baby Formula Controversy. The case shows a company that found an outlet for its product and, without breaking any laws, successfully marketed that product. The decisions that Nestle made, rather than the product itself, prompted a backlash in public opinion that had a significant effect on the company and its image.

In Weick's terms, we can view Case 11-2 as follows: The organization scanned the environment for its products and noticed a segment of that environment called "mothers who breast feed their babies." It redefined these women as potential users of infant formula (enactment). The process of redefinition is crucial here, for it points out the important role that enactment plays in setting up the environment for interpretation. *Enactment is a creative process, segmenting or bracketing a portion of the environment for further attention.*

Once the portion of the environment had been isolated, it then had to be interpreted (selection). The portion of the environment chosen was a relatively clear, low-ambiguity (low-equivocality) element, meaning that a sufficient stock of rules of interpretation already existed in organizational memory (retention). These rules were applied as interpretation, resulting in the relatively straightforward understanding of the environment as potential consumer, rather than as breast-feeding mother. As a consumer, the target was available for standard marketing techniques, which included authority appeals and free samples.

The backlash occurred because social interest groups offered a contrary version of what the environment actually "was." They suggested a vastly

Case 11-2:   Nestle Baby Formula Controversy

Nestle has sold baby formula to Third World countries since the 1920s, but did not encounter controversy until the early 1970s when it began an intense marketing campaign that promoted baby formula instead of breast feeding. Marketing techniques included the use of "mothercraft nurses"—lay women dressed in white so that they appeared to be professional nurses. They would visit mothers of newborn infants in hospitals and give them free samples of baby formula. Often these practices made the mothers dependent on baby formula because their breast milk would dry up.

Strong criticism developed against Nestle, even though its marketing practices were legal and its formula was nutritionally sound. Critics said that baby formula was inferior to breast feeding. Baby formula cannot provide the natural immunities of breast milk. Critics said that sanitation, illiteracy, and poverty created dangerous situations for infants that could lead to death. Many times, contaminated water diluted the formula and poor sanitation prohibited sterilization of bottles. Illiterate mothers could not read the instructions. Poverty caused mothers to overdilute the formula, which made the nutritional value inadequate.

Interest groups began an aggressive publicity campaign against Nestle in 1971, specifically against the company's marketing practices. Nestle countered by coordinating with other industries and formed the International Council of Infant Food Industries (ICIFI). ICIFI created a code of ethics and professional standards, which provided guidelines for self-regulation.

This did not satisfy Nestle's critics. They demanded that Nestle cease mass media advertising, free sample distributing, and mothercraft nurse promotion of its product. These terms were unacceptable to Nestle and it continued its marketing techniques. In 1974, the Infant

more complex (high-equivocality) interpretation, which included the categories of illiterate mothers, unknowing women, women willing to trust authority, and unethical treatment through misrepresentation. These highly ambiguous forms of interpretation meant that the company had had less chance to experience them in the past, meaning less chance for already existing rules of interpretation.

Figure 11-2 illustrates Nestle's interpretation according to Weick's model. In the figure you can see that mothers who breast feed their babies existed as a degree of environmental equivocality, recognized and defined by Nestle as potential users of infant formula. With that recognition, Nestle both defined and changed the environment. The definition offered by Nestle was a common one, resulting in the interpretation of potential customer, an interpretation easily available in company memory, which demonstrated that new mothers are susceptible to persuasive infant care messages. Thus, the Nestle interpretation was well within its experience. We would have been surprised to see any other.

Case 11-2: (Continued)

Formula Action Coalition (INFACT) called for a boycott against Nestle until the marketing techniques changed. Nestle decided not to comply and responded with an aggressive program of counter publicity. The company released many advertising campaigns, publicized literature and pamphlets, and lobbied government agencies involved in the issue.

In 1981 the World Health Organization (WHO) became involved and created a code regulating infant formula marketing. The code recommended that infant formula marketing provide safe and adequate nutrition, promote breast feeding, ensure proper use of infant formula, and market and distribute infant formula properly. In 1982, Nestle responded by unilaterally implementing the WHO code and formed the Nestle Infant Formula Audit Commission (NIFAC). The stated purpose of NIFAC was to examine marketing complaints and to ensure that Nestle honored its commitments to the WHO code. Measures taken to ensure NIFAC's independence from Nestle included appointing Senator Edmund Muskie as chairperson and offering membership on the committee to critics of Nestle.

However, INFACT said that the WHO code and NIFAC were ineffective and continued criticizing Nestle. Finally, in 1984 Nestle and INFACT agreed to a joint press conference and resolved their differences. INFACT suspended the boycott for a trial period of six months. At the end of that period, it was found that Nestle was complying with INFACT demands and the boycott ended. Critics said that they would closely monitor Nestle's marketing techniques to make sure that they complied with the WHO code.

Note: I am grateful to Ms. Diane Anderson for this case study. The summary is based primarily on Gerber (1990), Gerber and Short (1986), and Greenhouse (1989).

ORGANIZATIONS AS THOUGHT PROCESSES

In cultural terms, organizations can be viewed as bodies of thought (nouns) and thinking practices (verbs) (Weick, 1979b). When viewing organizations as thought processes we must examine the predispositions and biases of those

FIGURE 11-2. Nestle's demonstration of Weick's model

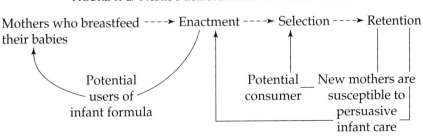

thinking actors. The standard operating procedures and business-as-usual traditions (tacit cultural assumptions) that often guide behavior in the examination of the environment might just lead the organization to make wrong or woefully inadequate choices. The search for good outcomes must begin with an understanding of the decisional premises guiding the search.

Organizations are not only thought processes, they are also interpretation systems (Bougon, Weick, & Binkhorst, 1977; Daft & Weick, 1984). It is the organization's ability to interpret the environment that distinguishes it from lower systems. Interpretation refers to assigning meaning to environmental events. The two primary factors that affect the organization's ability to interpret the environment are the level to which it intrudes into the environment and the level to which it believes that the environment is interpretable. If the organization sees the external environment as relatively clear, interpretable, then interpretation is seen as a process of finding the correct answer. However, the more fluid the environment, the more likely that it will shape the interpretation process. The environment itself will drive the questioning. The interpretations of the organization become forced onto the fluid environment, resulting in a level of equivocality (certainty).

One result that often occurs is that the organization behaves before it understands and then justifies the behavior. This is called *retrospective sense making* and can be seen, for example, in a parent who disciplines a child and justifies the discipline as an appropriate response to the child's behavior, or in a company that responds to a downturn in profits by laying off workers and justifies the layoffs after the fact as the necessary and only course of action. Retrospective sense making is largely a result of the organization's retention system, which allows it to explain and justify its past rather than inspire its future.

- *What is retrospective sense making? Why is it an important concept when viewing organizations as thought processes?*

Strategic Ambiguity

One additional issue to consider when explaining organizations as bodies of thought is the degree to which organizations encourage a given level of internal ambiguity: *strategic ambiguity.* Eisenberg (1984) argued that often in organizations, information is used to avoid clarity, rather than to accomplish the greatest amount of clarity possible. Remember, here, that clarity and ambiguity are relational variables, rather than message attributes (meanings do not reside in messages). The level of clarity of any given message is actually a perception on the part of message senders and receivers.

Strategic ambiguity is essential and useful within the organizational context for the following reasons. First, it promotes unified diversity by allowing organization members to be exposed to the same message, believe in the same symbolic construction, and yet interpret it in vastly different ways. Eisenberg used the example of academic freedom to illustrate. The varying interpretations of "freedom" help ensure creativity and diversity. Second, strategic ambiguity facilitates organizational and interpersonal change. At the organizational level, ambiguity offers alternatives to the dominant organizational image, allowing new insights and ways of understanding to emerge. At the interpersonal level, ambiguity allows the source to offer messages that the receiver then has to "fill in." This filling in may increase attraction among the participants, as the receiver will see the source as more similar. Third, strategic ambiguity preserves privileged positions by allowing distortion by receivers. More highly credible message senders may find themselves credited with more important communications as a function of their credibility more than of their messages. Ambiguity allows for message deniability by sources. The less ambiguous the source is, the harder it is for the source to deny intent or meaning.

There is one additional reason that organizations may desire internal message ambiguity: because key policymakers may decide that little purpose would be served by being totally open. An obvious and very controversial example concerns plant closings. Many argue that workers should be given notice of closings, as much as six months' warning. Organization executives, on the other hand, fear that warning may prompt low morale, inefficiency, poor product quality, and even sabotage. Some companies go so far as to tell their workers of layoffs only 10 minutes before closing, and then have a guard help them clear their desks of personal belongings and escort the workers to the door.

Consider a second, possibly less controversial example. Suppose that the dean of your college had decided to respond to financial pressure by retrenching the faculty of your communication department. This would mean the termination of all communication faculty and staff and the elimination of the degree program over the course of one to two years. The faculty has been told and, not surprisingly, is going to fight the decision. The question here is, should the students in the department be told? They are key stakeholders, after all. And, of course, the students (like the employees in the case of plant closings) would appreciate knowing. The question with which the faculty would have to wrestle is: "Would greater good be derived from telling the students (before the absolutely final word had been given) than from not telling them?"

As a cultural issue, strategic ambiguity involves the degree to which the organization encourages silence as a value. Silence may be seen by management as a strategic tool in a humane workplace. Silence may be seen by soon-to-be-laid-off workers as the manipulative tactic of a nontrusting managerial regime. These two contrasting interpretations are reflections of subcultural variation within the same workplace.

Cultural perspective, then, allows one to see that strategic ambiguity is not necessarily an insidious device used by management to control workers through selective ignorance. It is simply a fact that workers (or students) don't need to know every detail of the organization, don't want to know every detail, would be overburdened by trying to keep up with every detail, and are unprepared to understand every detail. Strategic ambiguity is about selective information flow, upward, downward, and horizontally.

The contrary cultural view would argue that such notions are overly paternalistic, don't give workers enough credit, and set the stage for manipulation. Clearly strategic ambiguity is a controversial subject in a cultural approach to organizations.

- *What is strategic ambiguity and what are some justifications and criticisms of the process?*

At this point we need to move away from the broad understanding of the organization discussed thus far and turn our attention directly to the decision-makers themselves. We've seen so far how organization culture serves as the premises behind the decisions that members make, which in turn usually reinforce the cultures. In the next section we'll use Herbert Simon's discussion of rationality to frame our understanding of the subtle influence of culture on the individual decision-maker.

HERBERT SIMON AND THE LIMITS OF RATIONALITY

We can look to the work of Herbert Simon (1976) to get a better understanding of rationality, identification, and how a decision-maker's reasoning will affect organizational levels of enactment, retention, and especially selection. Simon argued that any choice an individual makes will be subjected to any number of conscious and unconscious influences. In making the choice, the individual will reflect on those influences of which he or she is aware and arrive at a "rational" conclusion. No decision ever perfectly fulfills all the goals or objectives possible; it is, rather, a best decision at the time of decision making. Simon gave us the term *bounded rationality* to refer to this notion that clear, critical thinking is subject to many extraneous forces.

By participating in an organization, individuals relinquish some of their decision-making autonomy. Their organizational roles will put pressure on them to make decisions in accordance with their role demands (as explained by rational bias theory in Chapter 10). In this way, organizations apply unconscious pressure on their members to make decisions that meet organizational ends (see Chapters 6 and 9). Individual decision making, then, is informed primarily by individual predispositions and organizational authority. The organization hopes that the decisions made will be in accordance with its best interests over the interests of the worker. The organization works to instill a sense of loyalty—identification—in the worker. When this happens, the worker will make organizationally "correct" decisions. However, this worker might also make decisions that, while organizationally correct, are not in the best interests of the individual or society at large.

- *What is bounded rationality?*

Simon wrote:

It is impossible for the behavior of a single, isolated individual to reach any high degree of rationality. The number of alternatives he must explore is so great, the information he would need to evaluate them so vast that even an approximation to objective rationality is hard to conceive. Individual choice takes place in an environment of "givens"—premises that are accepted by the subject as bases for his choice; and behavior is adaptive only within the limits set by these "givens." (p. 79)

The myth of objectivity or objective rationality relies on the capacity of the individual to have access to all available information, the ability to preview this information in the context of the whole process and then choose a best option. Actual behavior does not approximate this ideal (see Zey, 1992, for an excellent critique of the limitations of rational choice models). *One of the greatest limitations on objectivity is the amount of organizational identification felt by the decision-maker.* This identification or loyalty results in the individual being predisposed to see decisional options from the organization's point of view. The organization creates the role filled by the worker, who assimilates this role and the expected behavior. Value is assigned to that role, along with facts, alternatives, and so forth that become the bases upon which decisions get made. Decision making, then, clouds when the decision-maker must decide in a way that pits organizational correctness against societal correctness. A decision can easily be organizationally correct and contrary to the best interests of society at large.

- *How does identification affect decision making?*

It is simply a fact, then, that there are limits to the human ability to make judgments. One could even carry this reasoning a step further and suggest that organization leaders and members behave in ways that are the result of underlying psychological tensions, childhood traumas, and various other nonobvious maladies (Kets de Vries, 1991). And if it is true that managers and leaders must battle underlying psychological tensions, the result is a potentially neurotic or psychotic organization!

In short, it clearly is in the organization's best interest to try to control the decision-making process by encouraging cultural values that support the overall corporate goals. Organizations attempt to accomplish this through many techniques discussed throughout this book, including socialization strategies, codes of ethics, power tactics, unobtrusive control efforts, and the use of symbols and stories. All these efforts contribute to limiting the ability of individual decision-makers to make unbiased decisions.

In the remainder of this section I'd like to emphasize two additional limitations of the individual decision-maker. The first is referred to as the Abilene Paradox—the problem of individuals' agreeing because they think everybody else agrees. The second is a confrontation with the very notion of "rationality" as a preferred goal. An increasing amount of work is questioning the legitimacy of the claim that rational is superior to emotional.

The Abilene Paradox

The *Abilene Paradox* refers to a situation in which members agree to something with which they actually disagree, under the mistaken impression that their comembers agree (Harvey, 1974, 1988). It is a problem of managing agreement rather than disagreement. The label was coined from a story in which a family disrupts a pleasant afternoon in Texas in order to undertake a long, hot, dusty trip to eat at a restaurant in Abilene. Only upon returning at the end of a ruined day do the family members realize that none of them had actually wanted to go—all of them had agreed to go because each assumed that the others desired the trip.

The paradox is seen as a problem of managing agreement rather than disagreement because it explains those situations in which an organization finds itself in a position that actually contradicts its intentions. Disagreement is relatively straightforward and, thus, easy to address. Agreement, on the other hand, when offered as a substitute for disagreement and discussion, will become a source of organization dysfunction.

The paradox explains, for example, the Watergate fiasco that toppled the presidency of Richard Nixon (see Gouran, 1984; Harvey, 1988). Advisors privately disagree with the hierarchical supervisor, fail to voice that disagreement, and allow a group decision that gives the appearance of consensus. The cycle repeats itself, and disagreeing becomes more and more difficult because members refuse to deal with the issue of failure to voice opinions. The limits of rationality are easily seen on trips to Abilene.

- *How would the Abilene Paradox affect decision making?*

There are six clues that a group or organization is taking the Abilene turnoff: Privately, the members are in agreement about the nature of the problem or issue; privately, the individuals know what should be done to address the issue; when opinions are put forward, members not only fail to voice objections (which they hold privately), but go so far as to actively voice support; the individual affirmations lead to a collective decision that appears to be a consensus when, in actuality, none of the members actually supports the ideas; the result is a counterproductive decision that frustrates the members, resulting in finger pointing, name calling, and coalition building to distance themselves from responsibility; and finally, the cycle will repeat itself if the members fail to address the issue of false agreement among themselves.

Watergate is an extreme case. Another example would be a company that continues to pour money into a developing product that the product managers know will be obsolete before it hits the market. A third example would be a couple that continues to spend money frivolously even though it is deeply in debt. Or consider a group of which I am a member: the board of governors of a statewide association. The association was considering a change in its logo and asked a local artist to offer some alternatives. At the meeting at which the alternatives were to be presented we waited in anticipation. The artist came and gave us his offering. The nonverbal response of the group members was less than overwhelming.

The artist was asked to leave the room so that the group could discuss the new logo. Nobody was pleased with the work, but when the artist came back in, the work was praised and accepted with only the request that it be darkened so that it would copy better on the stationery. We were all quite tired after that trip to Abilene.

The cultural implications of the Abilene Paradox are profound. Trips to Abilene are more likely in cultures that discourage risk taking, cultures that discourage disagreement and confrontation, and cultures "molded" or controlled by extremely charismatic or powerful leaders. The values of agreement, consensus, group harmony, togetherness, and teamwork may actually lead the group off its course and into unanticipated problems.

The Rationality-Emotionality Split

Simon's theory of bounded rationality and Harvey's Abilene Paradox both presume that "rational" is the preferred mode of decision-makers. Researchers such at Etzioni (1992) and Mumby and Putnam (1992) have called that presumption into question. Etzioni argued that decision-makers are guided more by normative-affective factors (values and emotions) than by information and reason. Indeed, values and emotions are the basis of the kind of reasoning advanced by rationalists as the superior method of decision making.

As rational decision-makers, humans are usually described as having a clear goal in mind and processing the information pertaining to that goal in a straightforward, neutral fashion until the most reasonable solution is found. Such a vision, however, ignores the fact that many, if not most, of our decisions, are "self-evident," and thus not in need of information processing, or are based on very value-laden factors. For example, because of my allergy to shellfish, my choice of steak over lobster is a self-evident choice. I have no options. Or a student may choose to study for an examination instead of going to a party because he or she values the image created by getting good grades, and this value may drive the decision as much as the student's goal of getting an *A* in the class (the rationalist explanation).

The important point is that we must not discount the importance of values and emotions in our discussions of decision making. To do so is to devalue those factors and, by association, to devalue those associated with letting their values and emotions "get in their way." The "rational man" of traditional organizational theory must be redefined to account for the inherent emotionality of decision making.

Mumby and Putnam (1992) offered a "feminist deconstruction" of Simon's notion of bounded rationality. They argued that the concept itself perpetuates the masculine vision of organizational life: orderly, rational, straightforward, goal-directed. But, like Etzioni, Mumby and Putnam argued for the merging of emotion and reason, so that the process of decision making does not remain separated from the product. So emotional experience, commonly associated with the feminine, becomes regarded as equal to cognitive experience, associated with the masculine.

The result of the merging of emotion with reason is the idea of "bounded emotionality." Individuals bounded emotionally are limited by their interrelatedness with others (rather than with the organization), by a tolerance for ambiguity (rather than need to reduce ambiguity), by heterarchy of goals and values that allow for flexibility (rather than hierarchy), by community in which work is a method for understanding self (rather than the sense of fragmentation and alienation of the rational system), and by relational rules (rather than gendered rules) (Mumby & Putnam, 1992, pp. 474–77).

The essence of this feminist deconstruction of bounded rationality is that the very term limits our conception of the decision-making process, biasing us toward a masculine orientation. In actuality, the stereotypically feminine reliance on emotions, feelings, and values plays an integral part in the process. In response to that fact, we need to rethink our understanding of the role of values and emotions, as well as our biases in constructing models of organization form.

- *How does including values and emotions in the process of decision making change how we think of bounded rationality?*

Culturally speaking, bounded rationality, the Abilene Paradox, bounded emotionality, emotions, and feelings all add up to an ambiguous, uncertain decision-making context. A culture that encourages "rationality" fools itself into believing that humans can gather all pertinent information and process it in a neutral fashion. They can't. All data analysis is subject to interpretations, which are flawed by the inability of humans to have access to all relevant information and to screen out all extraneous influences.

A culture that rejects the "traditional" model as masculine and overly rationalized fools itself into thinking that values are less rational than logic. They aren't. They're simply an alternative form of rationality, based on experience, "gut feelings," instinct, or whatever. But the bases of value-based decisions make every bit as much sense as the verifiable, empirical data used to support most logical decisions.

Groups must learn to encourage the strengths of the two alternative forms of decision making. The strengths of rationality are clarity of vision, goal-directedness, and the critical application of criteria. The strengths of emotionality are the realization of interdependence, the appreciation of style differences, and the recognition of human frailty and diversity. Cultures that reflect the union of these two realizations tend to encourage decisions that allow risk taking in the pursuit of goals, reward initiative even in the face of failure, and never assume that having facts in hand equals control over the environment.

The remainder of this chapter will focus on a number of the most important decision-making challenges that organizations have faced over the last few years. While studying them, keep Weick's notions of tight and loose coupling, enactment, selection, and retention in mind, as well as bounded rationality, the Abilene Paradox, and bounded emotionality. These ideas go a long way toward explaining why organizations respond the way they do to crises.

DECISION MAKING IN CRISIS SITUATIONS

Perhaps the most explicit way to demonstrate the effect of culture on decision making is to use examples from crises, for nowhere will culture be more felt than when the organization must respond to the unexpected. This section, through the use of case studies, will focus on crisis management and the importance of crisis management plans (CMPs).[2]

When Crisis Hits

Whether a company survives a crisis has a lot to do with whether it has a crisis management plan ready to go, and whether it conducts itself in a fashion to which the public will respond favorably. For example, Johnson & Johnson responded well in both 1982 and 1986 when tampering with their Tylenol capsules resulted in a number of deaths, and both times regained their market share. The company attributed much of its success in those crises to its prevailing culture and corporate value system. On the other hand, Gerber in 1986 and Audi in 1987 both responded negatively to customer complaints: Gerber denied accusations that baby food had glass fragments in it, and Audi denied that the Audi 5000 was prone to runaway acceleration. In fact, Audi blamed the problem on reckless drivers. Case 11-3: The *Exxon Valdez* Crisis offers a glimpse into a company that apparently had no crisis management plan and suffered the wrath of consumer groups for this failure and for its consistent efforts to deflect responsibility for what at that time was the largest oil spill in history.

The reader can easily see the differences between the Exxon cultural parameters and those of Johnson & Johnson. In Exxon's case, deception, blaming, denial, and defensive posturing painted an image of an uncaring, guilty (even if, in actuality, the company was not guilty of negligence) corporate goliath in the minds of the American public. Oddly, in Exxon's case, only the environment took a beating, whereas in Johnson & Johnson's case, people died. Still, Johnson & Johnson emerged virtually undamaged.

The primary difference in the two companies came down to their cultures. A crisis management plan reflects the prevailing cultural values in the case of unplanned events. In both cases the companies could have anticipated the disasters. If we're going to ship oil by tanker, sooner or later one is going to sink. And, in the case of the second Tylenol incident, one had already happened. Companies must learn from their own and others' experiences; history must become part of their retention systems. And the result of this learning must become part of the overall corporate value system, so that decision-makers can respond in such a way that the problem is not made worse by the corporate response.

Given the business environment of today it just doesn't make sense for any company not to have a crisis management plan (CMP). Unfortunately, for

[2]A complete discussion of crisis communication and crisis management, including risk assessment and aversion, is beyond the scope or purpose of this chapter. The interested reader should see Fischhoff et al. (1981); Milburn, Schuler, and Watman (1983a, 1983b); and Smart and Vertinsky (1977).

Case 11-3:   *The* **Exxon Valdez** *Crisis*

On March 24, 1989, after the Exxon oil tanker *Valdez* struck a reef, eleven million gallons of crude oil spilled out of the ruptured hull into the apparently pristine Prince William Sound off Alaska. The accident angered several publics at once, including the Alaska fishing industry, environmentalists, the state government of Alaska, and much of the general population of the United States. In the aftermath of the crisis, Exxon demonstrated an amazing lack of understanding of crisis communication. It was clearly reactive rather than proactive and too little was done too late to restore public confidence in the company. Beyond the environmental magnitude of the crisis, Exxon endured a financial backlash from the accident. By April 26, 1989, 31 lawsuits and 1300 claims had been filed against the company, for amounts from $500 to $4 million (Williams & Treadaway, 1992). Exxon could end up paying over $1 billion to the state of Alaska and various constituencies over the next ten years.

Exxon committed at least three critical communication errors in its treatment of the crisis. Because of its reactive stance, it was slow to issue any clear, decisive statements about the magnitude of the problem. Indeed, the company's initial statements were gross underestimations if not outright lies. The company continued to play down the severity of the accident for at least three days, until it was clear to the general population that the spill was much worse than was being claimed. The second key error occurred when the company attempted to shift the blame for the crisis to another company. It argued that the Alyeska Pipeline Service Company was primarily responsible for oil spill cleanup in that area, and its negligence resulted in the accident becoming larger than was necessary. Alyeska Pipeline Service is the industry consortium created by Exxon and other oil companies and charged with running the trans-Alaska pipeline. The general public rejected this strategy. However, evidence does seem to exist that suggests that Alyeska was indeed unprepared for a crisis of this magnitude.

Third, Exxon tried scapegoating. The company suggested that the blame for the accident rested with the unlicensed third mate who was actually piloting the ship at the time of the acci-

most companies the assumption is that business will go on as usual. However, as Wisenblit (1989) wrote: "The very nature of a crisis indicates a situation which cannot be handled by old or existing rules" (p. 33). In Weick's terms, the retention process of the organization may actually be an obstacle to the organization's response to crisis, because it predisposes the company to use old methods to deal with new problems. Organizations must be proactive when thinking and dealing with crisis.

Wisenblit (1989) surveyed 166 U.S. firms. The results showed that size of firm was the strongest predictor of the presence of a plan. The largest companies (over $10 billion in sales or over 50,000 employees) were the most likely to have plans (88 percent). Less than 50 percent of nondurable con-

Case 11-3: (Continued)

dent. Furthermore, the company released information that suggested that the ship's captain, Joseph Hazelwood, may have been drunk at the time. Hazelwood had a five-year drinking problem and, the company argued, since it was against company policy to have alcohol aboard ship, Hazelwood and the pilot should be held accountable. Again, the public rejected this strategy, condemning Exxon for allowing Hazelwood to continue to captain ships after his drinking problem was known.

An additional result occurred in the wake of *Valdez* accident. The *Valdez* principles were created by environmentalists and other social activists as a code of environmental conduct. They are a set of voluntary guidelines that its creators hope will guide the environmental actions of corporations that believe that accidents such as occurred with the *Exxon Valdez* should not occur again. Unfortunately, as of 1991, only twenty-one companies had confirmed their adherence to the principles.

The *Valdez* principles exist as ten broad guidelines:

- Companies agree to work hard to protect the biosphere.
- Companies will plan carefully so as to sustain and preserve the natural resources that they consume.
- Companies will work to reduce their total amounts of waste.
- Companies will reduce the amount of risk to which their workers and communities are exposed.
- Companies will produce and market environmentally safe products.
- Companies will maximize energy efficiency.
- Companies will take responsibility for any harm that they cause, including financial responsibility.
- Companies will publicly disclose incidents of harm to workers and the environment.
- Companies will create a position charged with the responsibility of adhering to the *Valdez* principles.
- Companies will annually assess their performance according to the principles. (From Sanyal & Neves, 1991)

Note: This summary is based on information found in Sanyal and Neves (1991), Williams and Treadaway (1992), and "Firms must hand over" (1992).

sumer goods companies, industrial materials companies, and electronics, computers and measurement instruments companies had CMPs. Of course, most companies are not "large" as defined above. On the basis of the findings, Wisenblit recommended that a CMP have seven components, summarized in Table 11-1.

Of all the components listed in Table 11-1, the most important is the first. A CMP is a device for reading the environment in an effort to ferret out potential disasters. Standard operating procedures are by definition inappropriate to dealing with crises. A good example of a company that had a plan ready that was able to meet all Wisenblit's criteria is Johnson & Johnson and its response to the second Tylenol incident (Case 11-4).

TABLE 11-1. Components of a Crisis Management Plan

1. The plan must be able to determine the nature of the crisis.

2. It must identify the audience affected.

3. Exact procedures should be specified clearly.

4. The plan should include business contingency plans so that business can continue during the crisis.

5. The plan should include and specify a crisis management team.

6. The plan should include details of crisis communication.

7. The plan should be evaluated and revised periodically, especially after its use.

Note: Based on Wisenblit (1989, pp. 38–39).

The Particular Problem of Product Liability

In the 1990s it seems evident that product tampering should be part of any organization's internal thought processes. Obviously this hasn't always been the case, nor is it the case today. Thoughts about product liability, however, which often includes tampering issues, do play a large role in planning. According to McGuire (1989, p. 1), in a survey of over 500 U.S. corporations regarding product liability, the following results emerged:

1. Forty percent of the corporate CEOs claimed that product liability issues affected how they plan and do business.
2. Fifty percent of the CEOs suggested that product liability had a major impact on the ability of U.S. firms to compete internationally.
3. Two-thirds of the CEOs expected the impact of liability issues to grow in significance in the future.

Liability considerations factor heavily in the planning and conduct of U.S. business. The impact includes discontinuing products and abandoning research into areas prone to litigation. The business costs of liability are staggering. McGuire (1989, p. 2) reported that:

> 30 percent of the price of a stepladder, 33 percent of the price of a small airplane, 95 percent of a childhood disease vaccine, and 25 percent of the cost of a bus ride are attributable to the costs of product liability. In 1987, physicians and hospitals paid $8 billion in malpractice insurance premiums. It is estimated that an additional $20 billion was spent on unneeded test procedures designed to guard the doctors and hospitals against claims of malpractice. . . . The costs imposed by liability amount to a tax on the American economy estimated, in 1988, to have added $80 billion to the costs of U.S. goods and services. That amount is equal to the total profits made by America's top 200 corporations.

From 1960 to 1986 the number of product liability cases in U.S. courts doubled to almost 42,000, with plaintiffs winning more than half.

Case 11-4:   The Second Tylenol Tampering Incident

On February 8, 1986, Diane Elsroth, a 23-year-old woman from the Bronxville, New York, area died after ingesting two Extra Strength Tylenol capsules. Within two days, Johnson & Johnson, makers of Tylenol, had removed Tylenol from the shelves of stores in the Bronxville area, as well as suspended all advertising. On February 11, Johnson & Johnson held a press conference in which it noted that potassium cyanide was found in a Tylenol capsule and that it was this cyanide that caused the woman's death. Johnson & Johnson recalled all twenty-four-capsule bottles of Tylenol from lot ADF 916 the next day. On February 13, potassium cyanide was found again in another bottle of Tylenol in the Bronxville area. That day, Johnson & Johnson urged all consumers nationwide to avoid its product. On February 14, Johnson & Johnson announced a suspension of the production of the capsules, offered consumers a refund or exchange for capsules already purchased, and offered a $100,000 reward for information leading to the arrest of the person(s) responsible for the product tampering. On February 15, the FBI announced that the capsules had been tampered with before they left the production facility, not after. On February 17, Johnson & Johnson held its third news conference and announced that it was stopping production of all Tylenol capsules.

Halting production of the capsules must not be seen as a simple decision for Johnson & Johnson. Benson (1988) reported that the 1982 production halt

(prompted by the deaths of seven people in the Chicago area) and subsequent development of tamper-resistant packaging and market reclaiming cost the company $300 million. Though expensive, it clearly was seen as the right thing to do.

The success of Johnson & Johnson's responses to its two product-tampering crises is generally attributed to its proactive crisis management teams. Proactive teams anticipate the possibility of crisis, as occurred during the second tragedy. Reactive crisis management, on the other hand, responds to other interpretations of crises. Reaction is retrospective. Proactive stances allow the company to create the communicative environment to which it then responds.

Benson (1988) identified four key proactive strategies used by Johnson & Johnson during the second crisis. First, the company came forth with quick initial communication about the crisis and the company's response. Second, the company kept key corporate personnel available and visible during the crisis. Third, the company continued to assert its position. In other words, it continually put forth its interpretations of events. Fourth, the company continually interpreted itself and its motivations for behaving the way it did. This allowed it to put forth and maintain an image of caring and compassion. By all measures, the efforts were successful. Within five months after the second crisis, Johnson & Johnson had recovered over 90 percent of its previous market share.

Note: This summary is from Benson (1988).

Most product liability claims revolve around four issues: (1) improper manufacture of the product; (2) proper manufacture but improper design, where some alternative design improvement would have made the product less hazardous; (3) a lack of offered information about the proper use of the product; and (4) lack of foresight by the manufacturer in predicting that a product might be used in a hazardous way and warning against such misuse.

Thus, product tampering and product liability have become part of the ambiguous external organizational environment. Such issues must be part of organizational planning. Crisis communication plans must extend from before the crisis occurs to long after it has been neutralized. Crisis preparedness must not be seen as primarily an internal process of dry runs and planning documents. This limited thinking fails to emphasize the need of the organization to enact the environmental potential before the crisis materializes, and it fails to remind organizations that the purpose of a crisis management plan (beyond assuring public safety) is to maintain public goodwill.

This is a process that must be begun before crisis and must continue after the crisis is resolved. The crisis communication plan, then, should be understood as a foundation that ensures movement through a period of turmoil, rather than as the response to a catastrophe. Thus, the crisis communication plan must be part of the cultural attitude of foresight, accountability, and stability. Unless these values are ingrained in the organizational persona, the company will continue to make ill-informed crisis decisions.

- *What is a crisis management plan and why would a company want one?*

As good as this advice sounds, it ignores the fact that sometimes an organization is its own worst enemy when it comes to crisis management. NASA was a classic example, as seen in Case 11-5.

In NASA's case, we find a clear example of the difference between theoretically "strong" culture and theoretically "healthy" culture. NASA's was a strong culture, sure and confident. Unfortunately, it was also sick, full of self-denial and unclear about its own limitations. Its "culture of infallibility" was discovered only after tragedy occurred. Its crisis prevention program turned out to be a reflection of this false sense of security. The perception of shuttle missions as routine lulled the organization into the false belief that its image of itself was true.

Crisis and Executive Moral Responsibility

Are senior executives morally responsible for accidents that cause injury and death to employees, customers, and others? Clearly the trend in our society is to say, "Yes." But upon what grounds can this case be made? First, consider why we might argue that senior management is not responsible. The manager might argue that he or she did not have access to the information necessary to foresee the accident, or if such information was known, that it was never communicated to the manager.

Neither of these arguments works very well. Senior executives accept pay for their companies performing well. Why should they not be held accountable when their companies fail? The capacity to predict the future is a communication question. If the necessary information is being withheld, it is the executive's responsibility to create the communicative environment that will ensure access to that information. Information blockage, especially of critical safety information, can easily become a cultural assumption. When it becomes embedded in the culture, the senior manager must take active steps toward cultural change.

The executive in any company exists in a position that goes beyond a contractual obligation. As Bishop (1991) pointed out, if a customer buys a pair of pants that don't fit, he or she can simply return them and, upon receipt of a refund, feel satisfied that the company has fulfilled its professional and moral contract. But when an operation is botched, or a plane crashes, or toxic gas escapes from a plant, when people die or are seriously injured, a simple refund is not enough. Both professional and moral responsibility extend beyond the contract to ensure that lives are not lost in the conduct of business. The only way that executives can perform according to these responsibilities is to encourage a culture in which information flow is open. Case 11-6: Union Carbide and the Bhopal Tragedy illustrates the complexity of moral responsibility.

The case of Union Carbide and Bhopal is one that includes a culture of complacency and a company with a confused sense of morality. Regarding culture, Union Carbide's history (Weick would say its retention system) was its own worst enemy here. The company had a good safety record and counted on that record more than on clear thinking to protect it and its workers from industrial accidents. Regarding morality, Union Carbide couldn't decide who to blame or where to place authority. Its chair, Warren Anderson, was put forth as the compassionate representative, a stance rejected by India. The company wanted authority to control which courts heard liability suits but at the same time rejected responsibility for the accident.

In the case of the Bhopal tragedy, Union Carbide's cultural parameters and value system are glaringly apparent in its response to the disaster. The fact that it responded, rather than foresaw, is telling in itself. And that its response looks remarkably like Exxon's in the *Valdez* incident indicates a culture similar to that of the big oil company.

CULTURE AND DECISION MAKING

This chapter has been about the limits of rationality. It is an unsettling chapter because its premise is that individuals are flawed decision-makers. In these days when organizations are increasingly complicated, when toxic waste and nuclear potential and human lives are the issue we would like to think that decisions will be based on sound reasoning and clear thinking. Unfortunately,

Case 11-5:   NASA and the Challenger Tragedy

Technically, it was the failure of the O-rings in the right solid-fuel booster that caused the space shuttle *Challenger* to explode after takeoff, killing all seven of the astronauts aboard. However, to truly understand the tragedy, we need to look at the circumstances that allowed the shuttle to be launched in spite of the fact that all parties knew of the risks involved. There is no doubt that NASA was aware of the potential of O-ring failure. Engineers at Morton Thiokol Corporation (manufacturers of the O-rings) had consistently pointed out the risks of low-temperature launches and O-ring performance. O-rings had been identified as high-criticality items, meaning that their failure could result in loss of mission and life. Therefore, it would be an error to say that the decision-making and risk-assessment methods of NASA were insufficient in isolating problems.

What should be understood is that the space program operates in a highly uncertain, ambiguous environment. The uncertainties are profound and everywhere. NASA, as an organization, accepts operation in these risk conditions. Unfortunately, the organization had built a tradition of successes that made it begin to define shuttle flights as routine, as existing within environments less complex that they actually were. Culturally, NASA evolved into an organization that began to fear loss more than risk. When flight became routine, the decisional premises shifted from a concern for risk to a concern for loss. Their decision-making style forced Morton Thiokol engineers to prove that launching the shuttle would result in its loss (and, therefore, the loss of astronauts, money,

reputation, funding, confidence, and so forth.) Because they could not, "a launching of Flight 51-L under high-risk conditions was guaranteed" (Renz & Greg, 1988, p. 73).

Seventy-three seconds into launch, on January 28, 1986, *Challenger* exploded, killing all astronauts aboard and sending NASA into a tailspin of public scrutiny and self-analysis beyond what virtually any organization will ever experience. It appears clear that the decision making that led to the launch was as much responsible for its outcome as was the failure of the O-rings. Indeed, given the fact that Morton Thiokol advised against the launch, the actual decision to launch perhaps was the primary cause of the disaster.

Gouran, Hirokawa, and Martz (1986) highlighted five factors that led to the decision to launch in the face of technical reservations. First, the parties who made the decision perceived pressure to convince the O-ring engineers to concur with a launch decision; second, the formal structure of NASA and Morton Thiokol obstructed the decision-makers' ability to cross perceived role boundaries; third, the actual reasoning used by the decision-makers was questionable; fourth, the actual language used clouded the risk; and fifth, the decision-makers simply failed to ask important questions.

Beyond the loss of life, the crisis resulted in a loss of legitimacy for NASA, which, ironically, "was, in part, precipitated by NASA's attempts to enhance legitimacy" (Seeger, 1986, p. 147). Seeger made the point that the more dynamic the environment, the more susceptible

Case 11-5: (Continued)

the organization to crisis. The explosion of the *Challenger* was a significant crisis, costing $1 billion, killing all the astronauts aboard, including the first teacher to be an astronaut, and casting doubt on both the space program and the agency itself.

The government took four steps to reestablish the legitimacy of NASA. First, it conducted public hearings at which detailed accounts were given of the breakdowns in decision making in the organization. Second, responsibility was dispersed to parties other than NASA, specifically to Morton Thiokol (a relatively unsuccessful shift) and to senior NASA officials, who were replaced. Third, the decision-making process itself was realigned to include astronauts, engineers, and revised decision-making structures. Fourth, NASA shifted its goals away from making the shuttle program commercially profitable, to redefining it in terms of military uses.

Schwartz (1991) argued that NASA had simply lost touch with reality. The organization was living in a self-imposed fantasy world. Consider the example, cited by Schwartz:

That study found that NASA's planned $37 billion space station would require 3,800 hours of outside maintenance per year, as against the 130 hours NASA had estimated for the job. Moreover, it was learned that the space station would require 6,000 to 7,000 hours of maintenance *even before becoming permanently manned.* (p. 287, italics in original)

The problem, of course, is that there is nobody up in space to do this maintenance.

Schwartz offered the theory of the organization ideal to account for NASA's jump from grandiosity to fantasy. It is the unconscious drive for success that leads to power and control over self and others. The problem is that the ideal never happens. The drive of success-oriented management can lead the organization into a continuous cycle of bad decision making. Product development and testing may become premature in an effort to get products to market (or into space in this case), resulting in continued failures and further retreat into fantasy. Managers with one foot still in reality end up being replaced by those more comfortable with fantasy. The result can be total tragedy, as occurred with the *Challenger.* The fantasy-based "culture of infallibility" can actually have believed that the O-rings had been tested and that reasonable confidence could be assumed given the testing. Schwartz wrote:

Yet not only did NASA management decide to launch the *Challenger,* but those responsible for the decision did not even give any indication to their own superiors that there had been a disagreement over the issue and, indeed, even after the explosion, continued to defend it as correct. . . . [The only possible explanation for this is that] NASA officials believed that they, as NASA, the organization ideal, having made the decision to launch, had made it correctly. (p. 300)

Note: This summary is derived from Gouran, Hirokawa, and Martz (1986), Renz and Greg (1988), Schwartz (1991), and Seeger (1986).

Case 11-6: Union Carbide and the Bhopal Tragedy

On December 3, 1984, at a Union Carbide pesticide production facility in Bhopal, India, pressure built up inside a storage tank filled with methyl isocyanate (roughly, cyanide gas). The pressure caused a relief valve to open, sending a cloud of poisonous gas "escaping one hundred twenty feet into the air" (Trotter, Day, & Love, 1989, p. 441) over the surrounding villages. During a period of about 40 minutes this toxic product escaped, covering an area of about 25 square miles.

As the gas spread, weak and elderly people died within moments. Incoming trains were diverted, halting the most effective means of escape. The affluent fled in their cars. Approximately half of the 1,000,000 inhabitants of Bhopal fled on foot, victims of the worst industrial accident in history. (Trotter, Day, & Love, 1989, p. 441)

The result of the leak is a human tragedy of immense proportion: 3000 dead (perhaps as many as 8000), over 300,000 injuries, including burned lungs, charred eyes, damaged nervous systems, sterility, kidney and liver infections, tuberculosis, vision problems, brain damage, and still unknown long-term effects.

In terms of restitution, the results are a confused mass of legal wrangling and perceived moral responsibility. In India, according to Trotter, Day, and Love (1989), as of 1989 there had never been a wrongful death settlement over $40,000. Indian law and custom are not U.S. law and custom. Obviously, in this case, Union Carbide would benefit by having all court proceedings happen in Indian courts. In 1986, the Indian government made temporary benefit payments to victims in the amount of $766 for each family of a victim who died and $115 for the families of those injured. The government also filed a variety of homicide and negligence charges against the company, amounting to over $35 billion.

The company, in its defense, argued that it had an impeccable safety record, logging an average of four injuries per 100 workers less than the national average. On the other hand, it is clear that the company was trying to sell the Bhopal plant. It allowed the management of the facility to fall off. To decrease expenses Union Carbide had cut back the workforce and lowered the standards for qualified personnel. The Indian government and Union Carbide

---

the "soundness" of the reasoning and the "clarity" of the thinking are usually defined by the reasoners and thinkers who, as we've seen, are subject to many influences beyond their understanding and control.

Fortunately, this is not the death knell of good decisions and quality decision making. This book has stressed over and over again that we need to move away from the myth of organizations as stable, rational, logical, predetermined structures in order to understand the dynamic and evolving nature of organizational reality. Part of that dynamic nature is the decision-making process.

Perhaps the most serious myth that clouds our understanding of decision making is that it begins with the problem. After all, we reason, there has to be

Case 11-6: *(Continued)*

had allowed an entire shantytown to be built next to the plant, as workers moved to the location when it was learned that work was available.

Again, according to Trotter, Day, and Love (1989):

In weighing all strengths, weaknesses, opportunities and threats of the Union Carbide–Bhopal tragedy, it is evident that the external threats, and internal weaknesses far outweighed the company's strengths and opportunities. Therefore, in hindsight, these difficulties obviously contributed significantly to the Bhopal tragedy. However, even more significant is the fact that the situation audit would be almost the same today because nothing has changed as a consequence of the Bhopal tragedy. Furthermore, the legal complications appear to be a disaster of equal or greater proportions. (p. 444)

In short, it might be argued that the company should have enacted the significant portions of its environment that might have allowed it to redirect resources to prevent the tragedy. The company survived just fine, although some have criticized the company's crisis management response. The company reacted to the crisis with a posture of concern. Warren Anderson, Union Carbide chairman of the board, immediately flew to India to assess the situation. This, of course, meant a lack of reliable information to news outlets in this country. The chaotic situation in India, exacerbated by the lack of experience with this sort of event, resulted in an even greater lack of reliable information. With no central spokesperson and little reliable information the company opened itself up to media criticism. Upon arriving in India, Anderson was arrested and told to leave the country for his own safety.

On another front, the company has been criticized for its legal handling of the situation. It has done all it could to be sure that the case was heard in Indian courts. Still, though, it denies that India has the jurisdiction to make good on its arrest warrant for Anderson, issued in 1988. In short, this is a story of a company with a good record that relied on that record to be its future. No crisis management team and the apparent lack of accountability combined to make it a focus of criticism in the handling of one of the worst industrial accidents in history.

Note: This summary is derived from Trotter, Day, and Love (1989) and Wilkins (1989).

---

a problem about which we make decisions, doesn't there? Actually, decision making begins with the preparation (Fritzsche, 1991). And preparation is subject to any number of cultural influences. Culture, then, the value and belief systems of organization members, lays the foundation for the reasoning that results in the decisions that get made, and that more often than not reinforces the status quo.

Why would this cyclical process happen? The reason is that culturally based expectations predispose the reasoning process to advocate certain decisions, and to allow certain logic and justifications, at the expense of other decisions and justifications. As culturally based logic becomes more entrenched, the decisional premises become more out of awareness, resulting in regular decisions that support the status quo, and that are seen as "logical" and "natural" given "the way things are around here."

The task, then, becomes understanding how the rules that guide decision making are developed and applied. What effect is culture having? What beliefs and values are we demonstrating through our decisions? How are we contributing to the value system of the past, or the value system desired for the future?

For example, consider the case of an executive group that is charged with deciding which new products will be funded for development. On its table are two proposals. The first is for an experimental product that is not yet tested, but that offers a huge profit if successful. The second is yet another modification of the same product that the company has put out for years. The product promises the same steady, comfortable profit, far less than the potential of the alternative proposal, but virtually guaranteed. Which proposal would the group choose?

Obviously, in determining your answer you would ask such questions as: Is this a high-risk company? Is this a high-risk group? Has the company taken chances in the past? Is the business one that expects innovation? Is the company profitable? Is there a strong leader in the group who favors one proposal over the other? Notice here that the questions being asked are less about the products themselves than about the preparation to make the decisions regarding the products. These are questions of values and beliefs and past practice. These are questions about decisional preconditions. These are culture questions.

Let's make the example more concrete. Suppose that you have been called in to observe the above group at M&M/Mars Candy Company. The group is deciding the following question: Should they invest in a "radical" innovation of M&Ms? The innovation would call for fruit flavoring of the hard candy shell. Given the experience of Coca Cola a couple of years ago, the group is proceeding cautiously with the idea. What do you think you would observe in the meeting?

The above examples are relatively simple because they involve only money. Look back on some of the examples throughout the chapter, such as that of the *Challenger,* the *Exxon Valdez,* and Union Carbide. Then reconsider our questions of cultural preconditions, rationality, and responsibility. I think you'll see clearly that we cannot separate culture from decision making, for the two are intimately and reciprocally intertwined.

SUMMARY

In this chapter we've reviewed some of the complexity of decision making within organizations, including defining organizations as decision-making environments. Decision making was discussed as the primary activity of organization members, and those decisions are shaped both consciously and unconsciously by prevailing cultural influences. Culture establishes the premises by which decisions are measured and judged.

We looked at Karl Weick's arguments that organizations be understood as composed of individuals who agree upon certain rules for the reduction of equivocality. This enactment process was shown to be the biased reconstruction of the external environment into a level of certainty that the organization could then interpret and respond to. The organization, then, is seen as an active process of interpretation, as a thought process and interpretation system.

Decision making, the primary activity of organization members, was shown to be bounded by both conscious and unconscious influences. The "rational" decision-maker is actually subject to culturally embedded logic, value-laden justifications, and corporate value systems. All of these forces are most apparent when the organization confronts a crisis. A variety of crisis case studies were used to demonstrate the importance and impact of corporate values and the difficult issue of corporate morality.

CHAPTER 12

Epilogue:
The Culture-Leadership
Conundrum

Chapter Preview

To conclude this book I would like to invite you to join me in an exercise. The topic of our excursion is the relationship between culture and leadership. Specifically, we're going to explore the issue of whether leaders have a more profound impact on the development of organization culture than other organization members.

I have saved this topic for the end because, quite frankly, I'm not at all sure what to do with it or say about it. I have a pretty firm opinion, of course: I would state that a leader's role is no greater than anyone else's in the cultural development of a group. After all, if culture is the product of shared sense making, a leader's "sense" is just part of an overall process. Isn't it?

Despite what I consider the reasonableness of this opinion, many others in the disciplines of both communication and management disagree. Indeed, it would be fair to say that there is currently no issue that is vaguer or sparks more heated debate than the importance of leadership in establishing and maintaining organization culture. It is in recognition of this debate that I offer this epilogue. Debate is healthy and I encourage you to join in. Read the chapter, roll the issues around in your mind, discuss them. Culture research is all about making decisions about the relative importance of this versus that.

To help guide our thinking, this chapter will be structured straightforwardly. I will open with the argument that leaders do play a seminal role in the creation and maintenance of culture and explain why this role should be recognized. This will be followed by the opposing position. The chapter will conclude with a brief recap of the implications of each point of view. Enjoy the debate!

This chapter will also read a little differently than the rest of the book. Too often in textbooks information is presented as though it were the end of the author's thinking. This leads readers to conclude that the ideas are self-evident, and the author is simply reporting what is clear from the research. Such clarity is the exception rather than the rule, and is certainly not the case when looking at the issues addressed in this chapter.

So, instead of reporting "results" here, I'm going to report thoughts. We're going to engage in some inductive research, looking at the ideas of a number of proponents of two sides of a controversial argument. You, then, can make up your own mind.

Before venturing any further into this chapter, I want you to imagine for a moment that you are an organization culture and communication consultant, called in to give advice to the BagCo organization, a hypothetical company that manufactures plastic lunch and storage bags. BagCo's biggest seller in the competitive lunch bag market has been its "Zipper" bag, a reusable plastic bag that has a zipperlike reclosable seal. This seal helps keep sandwiches and other food products fresh longer.

Recently, though, BagCo's market share on this product has been diminishing. Increased competition has hurt, but not nearly so much as the fact that consumers are no longer using the bags once and then throwing them away. Instead, they're washing and reusing the bags over and over again. This recycling is made possible by the quality of the zipper seal. The bottom-line result is decreased profits and flat sales.

You enter the scene and are confronted by the CEO and senior management team, who offer you three options to explore to skim the tide of declining sales and profits. They want your opinion, from a "cultural point of view," about whether they can anticipate an effect on their company's culture from the implementation of one of these options. The choices presented are: (1) Change the manufacturing process so that the "zipper" is less efficient, making future uses of the bag less satisfactory. This should lead to increased consumer purchasing. (2) Design a campaign around additional nonfood uses of the bag, thus broadening the market of potential consumers. (3) Promote the company as the environment-friendly folks, absorb the lost profits, and hope that the goodwill created by this campaign will promote sales.

What do you think? Will any of these strategic options change the existing "corporate culture"? How will you answer their questions about the interplay between management decisions and organization culture? Is there a direct line between the CEO, upper management, and organization culture? Is culture created and changed by large (or small) decisions made by management? Should management even be concerned about "culture"? Shouldn't they simply worry about market share?

The dilemma faced by the officers of the BagCo organization is not uncommon in industries the world over. Questions of product improvement, image, and market share have always been and will always be considered in organizational boardrooms. But concern over how the decision may affect company culture is a relatively recent development, complicating the already complicated process of making good decisions.

In turning to the culture consultant, the executives are essentially asking what impact their decisions will have on the employees' beliefs and values.

What they would like is a clear, manageable answer. They would like to hear that the decisions won't have an effect, or that if an effect does occur, it can be handled, in the same way that a change in benefits might be handled. Such words would be comforting because, even though most executives would probably prefer not to have to deal with employee beliefs and values, at least they are being told that these factors can be controlled.

But what if their culture consultant gives them the opposite impression? What if the advice is that culture is beyond their direct control and, indeed, that it is wrong for them to even consider "managing" beliefs and values? Two points of view: culture is part of the manager's domain; culture is not part of that domain. Who is more right, who is less right?

The remainder of this chapter will be devoted to outlining these two contrasting points of view. The first, discussed in the next section, suggests that leaders have a significant impact on organization culture. With this suggestion is the argument that culture is a variable that can and should be controlled by leaders. After that perspective is put forth, we'll look at the alternative position: that culture is not an organizational variable to be controlled and there is good reason to stop considering it as such.

This chapter, then, is not about leadership. There are many fine books about that subject, which explore in detail the history of leadership research and the various and interesting complexities that surround the leadership issues in organizations (see Hackman & Johnson, 1991). Instead, this chapter is about a critical issue that culture researchers have begun to probe, only to discover levels of complexity and ambiguity that may never be unraveled.

THE CASE FOR LEADER INFLUENCE

Many researchers have argued quite convincingly that leaders play a central role in the management of organizational symbolism. Hackman and Johnson (1991) summarized this perspective when they presented organizations as symbol systems. They suggested that one of the most important functions of leaders was to control the symbol system, making leaders critical to the creation and maintenance of organization culture. The foundations of that argument were laid only recently.

Founding Visions

The fascination with leader/manager effort can be traced to three primary sources: Peters and Waterman's *In Search of Excellence* (1982), Deal and Kennedy's *Corporate Cultures* (1982), and most important, Schein's *Organizational Culture and Leadership* (1985). Peters and Waterman gave us the idea of unified, single organizational cultures, nurtured by founders and CEOs of amazing charisma, such as Tom Watson of IBM and Sam Walton of Wal-Mart. After reading this book, an executive would want to create an "excellent" culture.

Deal and Kennedy's book was more systematic in its treatment of exactly what culture is and how it varies from organization to organization. They argued that, "Whether weak or strong, culture has a powerful influence throughout an organization; it affects practically everything—from who gets promoted and what decisions are made, to how employees dress and what sports they play. Because of this impact, we think that culture also has a major effect on the success of the business" (p. 4).

Like most culture researchers, Deal and Kennedy put values at the center of culture. They considered values important because they help define the corporate character and affect performance. Strong values imply certain risks as well as certain strengths and result in four general types of cultures: (1) the tough-guy, macho culture of individualists (as in police departments, construction, advertising, and entertainment); (2) hard-work, hard-play culture of sales (for example, Mary Kay cosmetics, McDonald's, and Xerox); (3) bet-your-company culture of high-stake, long-term investments (for example, oil and aircraft companies and NASA); and (4) process culture of the bureaucracy (for example, banks, insurance companies, and government agencies). These four cultural types will be distinguished in many ways, including dress, housing, sports, language, greeting rituals, and coworker rituals.

As important as Peters and Waterman and Deal and Kennedy have been in defining the leader's role in managing the corporate culture, the seminal characterization that has sparked the greatest amount of research and defined the greatest amount of thinking has been Schein's (1985) argument that leaders create culture, that "the only thing of real importance that leaders do is to create and manage culture" and that "the unique talent of leaders is their ability to work with culture" (p. 2).

Schein argued that there are three levels of culture: (1) artifacts, or the physical, visible level, (2) values, and (3) basic, underlying assumptions (the most important level). He wrote that the basic and most important function of culture is to aid in adaptation to the environment and the integration of internal processes. Founders of an organization lay the groundwork for culture. The underlying assumptions of the group, established by the founder and carried on by the organization's leaders, serve as the most basic, most crucial dimension and reflection of culture. Schein (1985) wrote:

> The most powerful primary mechanisms for culture embedding and reinforcement are (1) what leaders pay attention to, measure, and control; (2) leader reactions to critical incidents and organizational crises; (3) deliberate role modeling, teaching, and coaching by leaders; (4) criteria for allocation of rewards and status; (5) criteria for recruitment, selection, promotion, retirement, and excommunication. (pp. 224–25)

Proving the Theory

Interest in managing and controlling culture is easy to understand when looking at the results and case studies offered by authors and researchers such as Davis (1984) and Kotter and Heskett (1992). Kotter and Heskett conducted four studies on over 200 firms and drew the following four conclusions about the relationship between culture and economic performance: corporate culture does have a significant impact on performance; over the next decade the impact of corporate culture on performance will be even greater; cultures that diminish performance are common; and, though it is difficult to do so, a culture that discourages performance can be changed. An example of a culture that discourages performance would be a work group that ridicules a new worker as being a "rate-buster" until he or she slows his or her performance to meet the slower group standard. Another example would be when a company closes plants and lays off hundreds or thousands of workers, while its senior managers accept huge year-end bonuses. A third example would be a company that creates quality circles but ignores most of the results and advice directed upward by those circles.

Kotter and Heskett distinguished between two levels of culture. The visible level is that of behavior and is relatively easy to change. The more difficult level to reach is that of shared values. This is virtually invisible and resistant to change. However, the two levels clearly influence each other.

They also argued that "strong" cultures begin with and are perpetuated by charismatic founders and leaders who put the values forth as business strategies. They wrote: "The single most visible factor that distinguishes major cultural changes that succeed from those that fail is competent leadership at the top. In all ten of the cases we studied, major change began after an individual who already had a track record for leadership was appointed to head an organization" (1992, p. 84).

Some corporations identified as having a strong corporate culture over the last decade were Wal-Mart, Procter & Gamble, Northwestern Mutual Life, Dow Chemical, Du Pont, and IBM. Some that were identified as having a weak or nonexistent corporate culture over the last decade were American Motors, Eastern Airlines, PanAm, Unisys, Honeywell, and Firestone.

Having a "strong culture," a unified value system, and control over both is a tempting goal for organizational management. This goal is especially pertinent given findings such as those by McDonald and Gandz (1992). They argued that a focus on values is an imperative for the executives of the 1990s, a change from the mindset of the executives of the 1960s, 1970s, and 1980s who "managed by objectives, not values" (p. 64). McDonald and Gandz conducted interviews with forty-five private- and public-sector managers, executive recruiters, and consultants to identify the importance of values in the organization today and to identify the values important to today's workers.

Generally, they found a workforce that now demands to be involved with its work and to derive meaning from that work. These different demands from today's workers call for different control and motivation techniques from managers. Their interviews resulted in the identification of twenty-four key values most relevant in today's organization. The importance of these values, of course, may vary from one organization to another.

The analysis of the values resulted in the identification of four general value-based organizational forms: relationship-oriented, change-oriented, task-oriented, and status-quo oriented. Each of these forms will reward and encourage different sorts of values. The *relationship-oriented* form (clan) will encourage values such as consideration, forgiveness, humor, moral integrity, and social equality. The *change-oriented* form (adhocracy) will encourage values such as adaptability, experimentation, creativity, and development. The *task-oriented* form (market) will encourage values such as aggressiveness, initiative, and diligence. And the *status-quo-oriented* form (hierarchy) will encourage values such as cautiousness, formality, logic, and orderliness. Finally, in examining the process of value formation, McDonald and Gandz found three forces to be key: the founding legacy, the current administration, and significant events in the organization's history.

But can leaders and managers control the organization's culture and values? Various researchers, such as Denison (1990) and Quick (1992), have found exactly that. For example, Quick argued that Herb Kelleher crafted a distinctive culture that allowed Southwest Airlines to prosper when other airlines were failing. Indeed, Quick suggested that Kelleher's leadership over corporate culture can be credited with saving the airline.

Such a contention is a bold one, but is reasonable given the perspective that Quick takes on culture. He wrote:

> Thus, cultural values become the platform for specific and concrete actions designed to meet difficulty and challenge. We cannot think of organizational culture as a substitute for responsible, problem-solving behavior on the part of leadership. Culture becomes the vehicle through which problems and challenges become addressed, defined, reframed, and ultimately solved. When cultural values do not work in this fashion, they must be modified or jettisoned. The culture is not the end or goal but rather the means. (1992, p. 54)

Culture, thus, is viewed as an organizational variable, not unlike inventory practices, technology, or merchandising strategies. As a variable, it is more reasonable to think it can be manipulated, controlled, and so forth.

Less bold, though certainly no less convincing research results that demonstrate the leader's influence on culture have been found by many others (see Davis, 1984; Feldman, 1988; Morley & Schockley-Zalabak, 1991). For example, Morley and Schockley-Zalabak (1991) set out to determine the relationship between founder and organizational member value systems. They collected data from 174 members of a computer corporation, including the founders and all managers. They found support for the contention that founders play a significant role in the formation of the corporate value system, shaping the culture from which come the rules that shape both correct and incorrect behavior.

Davis (1984) argued that the organization's belief and value systems are created and spurred by the founder or leaders (primarily the CEO). He argued that it is risky for a company to ignore its culture, but it can be done. He also suggested that if a change in culture appears too difficult, it may be better to just "manage around it" (p. 88). Davis wrote:

> During all my work on corporate strategy and culture over the last five years, I have learned that guiding beliefs are invariably set at the top and transmitted down through the ranks. Also, any effort to change them must be led by

the chief executive officer (CEO). These are not judgments, but observations.
. . . The significance of this observation for setting and implementing strategic direction in a company cannot be overstated. Culture, and therefore strategy, is a top-down affair. If the CEO ignores culture, he will be formulating
strategy without its being grounded in what the company stands for, and he
will be attempting to implement it without taking into account the major force
for its success or failure. (p. 7)

To summarize, the argument presented thus far boils down to the assertion that culture is relatively straightforward. You have one or you don't. You
insert the one you need and, if the one you have isn't working, it is withdrawn
in favor of an alternative. Because culture is important, it should be of concern
to top management. Those individuals at the "top" have the power and responsibility to infuse the correct culture into the workplace.

We'll now take a look at the other side of the coin. Not surprisingly, many
researchers feel that culture is much more complicated than the image offered
above.

ON THE OTHER HAND: CULTURE AS BEYOND
THE LEADER'S CONTROL

Despite what many view as the inherent validity of the above arguments, others have presented an opposing viewpoint, one that suggests that culture is
not easily available to management manipulation and, indeed, that to suggest
such manipulation is in itself unethical. The best place to begin this counterar-
gument is with Hatch (1993), who targeted Schein's (1985) seminal work for
criticism.

Hatch presented a model that extended Schein's arguments that culture
was a composite of artifacts, values, and assumptions. She argued that
Schein's portrayal discounted the importance of symbols and processes in the
construction and interpretation of culture. Her model, called "cultural dynamics," extends Schein's by demonstrating the active part played by organizational members in the everyday symbolic construction of organization culture.

Her primary argument is that Schein's model would be more useful if it
accounted for four key processes: manifestation, realization, symbolization,
and interpretation. These processes, which are articulated in the everyday life
of organization members, underlie the cultural assumptions and values of the
organization. These processes become links, a focus discounted in both
Schein's and others' discussions of culture, in their focuses on key elements of
culture (artifacts, values, assumptions). In other words, the culture is manifested in these four processes, which work to both perpetuate and change the existing culture. For example, whereas Schein presented artifacts as tangible representations of culture, the cultural dynamics model would focus on the
process of realization as bringing about the tangible quality of the artifact. Discussed as "proactive realization," the activity of bringing about meaning becomes constituted as a meaningful artifact.

Expectations become represented in artifacts. However, the interpretation of that artifact is what gives it meaning, not the intent of the creator. For example, consider the case of cubicles in place of traditional offices. Have the cubicles been created to offer a more open work space, or have they been created to more closely monitor laggards? These are two very different intentions, but neither is relevant when compared with the interpretations of the recipients. Hatch wrote:

> The cultural significance of an artifact is not set for all time at the moment of its production or importation. True, the artifact at this moment is infused with the assumptions and values that led to its proactive realization, but these are localized in the realization processes of the producing members. Other members, who participated in the production indirectly, if at all, when exposed to the product may accept, reject, or ignore it. In any case, the product itself becomes available to a much broader interpretation process than the one that formed the context of its inception. (1993, p. 669)

Thus, we may be exposed to a message that is presented as a person's expectation of how things should be. But when received by others, that message may be seen both as a symbol of intention and values and as a reflection of what has always been. Thus, the same message may alter cultural understanding just as easily as it confirms such understanding.

Whereas Hatch (1993) suggested that it is patronizing to assume that managerial intent is easily and automatically transferable, others have made a less philosophical, more direct attack on the contention that culture is manageable. Much of this argument centers on the question of what culture is and what it is that is being managed. For example, Fitzgerald (1988) pointed out that we must not mistake managing behavior as managing culture. The two are different and though one may reflect the other, until we are sure about the relationship between values and behaviors we cannot be sure if a change effort is behavioral or cultural.

Finally, change attempts usually begin with work on top management's value system, on the argument that any change must be supported by the top. Though the move to reorient top management's thinking makes sense, it does not take into account that workers at the lower levels have value systems of their own, forged throughout their lives and just as rational as those of upper management.

Not only, then, will management have to contend with nonmanagement belief systems, but they may be faced with extraorganizational factors beyond the control of either management or workers. Gordon (1991) suggested just this in his argument that certain industry requirements will lead to similar cultural development within organizations in the same industry. These assumptions and values are taught to new organization members. And certainly, differences in assumptions and values can exist within the company, as long as they do not conflict with the basic industry-wide assumptions. What happens is that industry assumptions drive the development of value systems that in turn keep the company from conducting itself in contradiction to industry values (see Chapter 2).

Other authors go so far as to suggest that the very notion of focusing on leaders is erroneous, for it sets up a false conclusion. Martin, Sitkin, and Boehm (1985) made such a point:

> Even when researchers or employees give a leader credit for having influenced the culture creation process, that credit may be misplaced. Two social cognition biases, salience and attribution, make it particularly likely that retrospective accounts overestimate a leader's impact on events. . . . Rather than creating a culture in his or her own image, the founder is cast into a system molded by forces beyond his or her individual control. (pp. 101–02)

The point here is that leaders are an obvious focus of attention and are thus more likely to play a large part in the remembrances of others as they attempt to account for events in the organization. This salience will likely lead to the attribution to the leader of an impact that may have been less the product of the leader's efforts than of circumstances or others' efforts beyond the leader's control.

The desire to find a starting point for culture, a causal agent, may have something to do with the western tendency to find dichotomies between things that really have no clear demarcation (Foo, 1992; Smith & Peterson, 1988). Smith and Peterson (1988) made the point that in western societies we tend to want to split the notion of culture between the individual and the group, organization, or society. Such a split is probably artificial. They also state that "the creation of changes in organizational culture may not depend so much upon externally administered programs of training and consultancy as upon the cumulative impact of day-to-day events" (p. 121). Thus, culture emerges more than it is imposed.

Foo (1992) examined the differences in approaches to productivity improvement between western-owned and domestically owned companies in Singapore. This study looked at the effect of culture on organizational attempts to increase productivity. He compared productivity improvements in thirty-two Singapore-owned firms and thirty-five foreign-owned firms. Both tended to put the most importance (in terms of employee training) on middle management. Foo found evidence to support his claim that western companies used training as a mechanical device aimed at increasing efficiency and productivity. Training was a "hard" strategy intended to produce hard results. Eastern companies, on the other hand, more fully integrated training into overall human development. This is a more organic approach, less strategic than that of the western companies, aimed more at the internal belief systems of the employees than at the overall efficiency strategy of the company.

Finally, there are those researchers who rebel at the suggestion that we should even look to cultures in an effort to manage productivity. Siehl and Martin (1990), for example, argued that such an approach promotes a managerial bias in culture research, which does little more than justify another means of control of the worker by the manager. And Smircich and Calas (1987) criticized the notion that culture is a tool available to managers in their efforts to control the workplace. This is an overly simplistic, mechanistic model in which symbols, which represent culture, are manipulated in such a way that workers are led into integrating managerial belief systems. It is a premise that defies the idea of culture as an emergent set of values and meanings that result from the dialogue engaged in daily by workers as they go about making sense of their surroundings.

IMPLICATIONS

This chapter has raised a number of difficult questions in its presentation of the relevance of leadership in the creation and maintenance of organization culture. In this section I'll summarize a variety of those implications and leave it up to you to decide whether leaders play a more significant role than nonleaders in this issue.

Implication 1: Certainly all of the research reported above, as well as all of the data known to me, that links culture with improved financial performance does not make it very clear if what is being reported is culture or good management. In other words, when does good management end and culture begin?

The data reported by Kotter and Heskett (1992), Davis (1984), Peters and Waterman (1982), and others, and the theories of Schein (1985) and others are based on research aimed at assessing managerial value systems. Period. No mention is made nor is any apparent systematic account taken of nonmanagement values. It is simply taken for granted that managerial values are transmitted to nonmanagers and embraced as the dominating set of cultural assumptions. This research must be understood as conclusions about management, not nonmanagement. This research argues for good leadership, not culture.

Implication 2: Many proponents of the argument that leaders and managers play a central role in culture creation use the term "culture" in two contradictory ways. On the one hand, researchers like Davis (1984) argue that it is risky for a company to ignore its culture, but it can be done. He also suggests that if a change in culture appears too difficult, it may be better to just "manage around it" (p. 88). This culture as variable perspective contrasts rather sharply with the contention made by the same authors that culture is an internalized value system crucial to the success and performance of the organization.

The obvious question is: Is culture superficial and thus available to be ignored and managed around? Or is it a key dynamic of the workplace, affecting every worker from the inside, at the level of beliefs and values? The answer given will depend on how one approaches the concepts of culture and climate. Most who say that culture is manageable use the two terms interchangeably. Those who argue the contrary suggest that climate is a superficial organizational component, such as level of openness and trust, that can be managed, while culture is less available to direct manipulation.

Kopelman, Brief, and Guzzo (1990) made a useful distinction between the two concepts. They argued that organizational culture refers to member value systems, embedded within societal value systems. Climate refers to the goals, means, rewards, task, and emotional support systems of the organizations. These dimensions may be manipulated by management, resulting in changes in behavior that affect productivity. But organizational culture probably plays less of a role in productivity than either societal culture or climate.

Implication 3: With regard to those who suggest that culture can be ignored, we should point out that the attempt to "ignore" the values of organizational members is a telling cultural statement in itself.

Implication 4: In contrast to the position taken in this book, those who favor the approach to culture as manageable usually assume culture is monolithic. Even when they agree that there may be some subcultural variation, their primary assumption is that the company is unified by a shared value system. This is the assumption of the early "popular" management books (for example, the search for "excellent" cultures), as well as much of the scholarly research accused of demonstrating a "managerial bias." This reasoning even implies that culture can be "nonexistent" (Kotter & Heskett, 1992).

Implication 5: Suggesting that leaders and managers play an important role in developing the corporate culture advances a behavioral vision of what constitutes culture (see Thompson & Luthans, 1990). Such a vision, identifying culture as the behavior of organization members, certainly simplifies and clarifies culture. The question, of course, remains: Is culture really that simple?

Behaviorists argue that it is behavior that leads to the development of culture. Behavior is learned and reinforced through feedback, leading to an understanding of what is culturally acceptable and unacceptable. Feedback, then, transmits culture. When the behavioral perspective is added to the cognitive, the following definition emerges: "The socially constructed realities come about through patterns of direct and vicarious interactions involving the cognitive matching of antecedents-behaviors-consequences that reinforce accepted norms of behavior" (Thompson & Luthans, 1990, p. 328). So, though culture is a cognitive construct, it can only be changed through changes in the behavior of members, which will then act to change attitudes. This is a structural definition of culture—causal and one-way.

Implication 6: Linking leaders and managers with extraordinary cultural influence forces a potentially false dichotomy between individuals and their beliefs. Many argue that individuals cannot be separated from their social contexts—the processes that influence their value and belief systems.

CONCLUSION

This chapter isn't about answers. It was offered in the spirit of questioning. A cultural approach is a philosophy of understanding organizations. We've seen that throughout this text. In developing that approach we must tackle both the difficult and the easy issues for, as you can see, even those issues which to me seem pretty clear are full of controversy and contradictions.

Every argument has at least two sides, and most of the time, each side represents some amount of "truth." You have read this chapter and now must decide for yourself which side is the most right. Do leaders and managers play a more significant role in culture creation than nonleaders and nonmanagers? Is culture usefully conceptualized as monolithic—organizationwide? Should culture be linked to financial performance? Are organization member belief and value systems a legitimate domain for managerial influence tactics? Is culture about behavior as much as it is about beliefs?

Think about it. Talk about it. Enjoy the process.

References

Acker, J. (1992). Gendering organizational theory. In A. J. Mills and P. Tancred (eds.), *Gendering organizational analysis* (pp. 248–60). Newbury Park: Sage.

Adams, J. S. (1976). The structure and dynamics of behavior in organizational boundary roles. In M. D. Dunnette (ed.), *Handbook of industrial and organizational psychology* (pp. 1175–99). Chicago: Rand McNally.

Adams, J. S. (1980). Interorganizational processes and organizational boundary activities. In L. Cummings and B. Staw (eds.), *Research in organizational behavior* (vol. 2, pp. 321–55). Greenwich, CT: JAI Press.

Aldrich, H., & Herker, D. (1977). Boundary spanning roles and organization structure. *Academy of Management Review, 2*, 217–23.

Allen, M. P. (1974). The structure of interorganizational elite cooptation: Interlocking corporate directorates. *American Sociological Review, 39*, 393–406.

Allen, N. J., & Meyer, J. P. (1990). The measurement and antecedents of affective, continuance and normative commitment to the organization. *Journal of Occupational Psychology, 63*, 1–18.

Amott, T. L., & Matthaei, J. A. (1991). *Race, gender & work: A multicultural economic history of women in the United States.* Boston: South End Press.

Andrews, K. R. (1989). Can the best corporations be made moral? In K. R. Andrews (ed.), *Ethics in practice: Managing the moral corporation* (pp. 257–66). Boston: Harvard Business School Press.

Ashforth, B. E. (1989). The experience of powerlessness in organizations. *Organizational Behavior and Human Decision Processes, 43*(2), 207–42.

Atkinson, P. (1992). *Understanding ethnographic texts.* Newbury Park, CA: Sage.

Bacharach, S. B., & Lawler, E. J. (1980). *Power and politics in organizations.* San Francisco: Jossey-Bass.

Bahls, J. E. (1988). Stopping sexual harassment. *Business Credit, 90*(7), 53–55.

Baird, J. E., Jr., & Bradley, P. H. (1979). Styles of management and communication: A comparative study of men and women. *Communication Monographs, 46*(2), 100–11.

Bales, R. (1970). *Personality and interpersonal behavior.* New York: Holt, Rinehart and Winston.

Bantz, C. R. (1983). Naturalistic research traditions. In L. L. Putnam and M. E. Pacanowsky (eds.), *Communication and organizations: An interpretive approach* (pp. 55–71). Beverly Hills: Sage.

Bantz, C. R. (1989). Organizing and the social psychology of organizing. *Communication Studies, 40*(4), 231–40.

Bantz, C. R. (1993). *Understanding organizations: Interpreting organizational communication cultures.* Columbia, SC: University of South Carolina Press.

Bantz, C. R., & Smith, D. H. (1977). A critique and experimental test of Weick's model of organizing. *Communication Monographs, 44,* 171–84.

Barley, S. R. (1983). Semiotics and the study of occupational and organizational cultures. *Administrative Science Quarterly, 28,* 393–413.

Barnard, C. I. (1938). *The functions of the executive.* Cambridge, MA: Harvard.

Barnett, T. (1992). A preliminary investigation of the relationship between selected organizational characteristics and external whistleblowing by employees. *Journal of Business Ethics, 11*(12), 949–59.

Barnett, G. A. (1988). Communication and organizational culture. In G. Goldhaber and G. Barnett (eds.), *Handbook of organizational communication* (pp. 101–30). Norwood, NJ: Ablex.

Bastien, D. T., & Hostager, T. J. (1988). Jazz as a process of organizational innovation. *Communication Research, 15,* 582–602.

Bastien, D. T., & Hostager, T. J. (1992). Cooperation as communicative accomplishment: A symbolic interaction analysis of an improvised jazz concert. *Communication Studies, 43*(2), 92–104.

Baysinger, B., & Hoskisson, R. E. (1990). The composition of boards of directors and strategic control: Effects on corporate strategy. *Academy of Management Review, 15*(1), 72–87.

Bazerman, M. H., & Schoorman, F. D. (1983). A limited rationality model of interlocking directorates. *Academy of Management Review, 8*(2), 206–17.

Benson, J. A. (1988). Crisis revisited: An analysis of strategies used by Tylenol in the second tampering episode. *Central States Speech Journal, 39*(1), 49–66.

Berlo, D. K. (1960). *The process of communication: An introduction to theory and practice.* San Francisco: Rinehart.

Betters-Reed, B. L., & Moore, L. L. (1992). Managing diversity: Focusing on women and the whitewash dilemma. In U. Sekaran and F. T. L. Leong (eds.), *Womanpower: Managing in times of demographic turbulence* (pp. 31–58). Newbury Park: Sage.

Beyer, J. (1981). Ideologies, values, and decision making in organizations. In P. Nystrom and W. Starbuck (eds.), *Handbook of organizational design* (pp. 166–202). New York: Oxford University Press.

Bice, M. (1990). Culture can make or break a restructuring. *Hospitals, 64*(18), 60.

Bishop, J. D. (1991). The moral responsibility of corporate executives for disasters. *Journal of Business Ethics, 10*(5), 377–83.

Blair, R., Roberts, K. H., & McKechnie, P. (1985). Vertical and network communication in organizations: The present and the future. In R. D. McPhee and P. K. Tompkins (eds.), *Organizational communication* (pp. 55–77). Beverly Hills: Sage.

Blake, R. R., & Mouton, J. S. (1964). *The managerial grid.* Houston: Gulf Publishing Company.

Blank, M. A., & Sindelar, N. (1992). Mentoring as professional development: From theory to practice. *The Clearing House, 66*(1), 22–26.

Boje, D. M. (1991). The storytelling organization: A study of story performance in an office-supply firm. *Administrative Science Quarterly, 36,* 106–26.

Borisoff, D., & Victor, D. A. (1989). *Conflict management: A communication skills approach.* Englewood Cliffs, NJ: Prentice-Hall.

Bormann, E. G. (1972). Fantasy and rhetorical vision: The rhetorical criticism of social reality. *Quarterly Journal of Speech, 58,* 396–407.

Bormann, E. G. (1980). *Communication theory.* New York: Holt, Rinehart and Winston.

Bormann, E. G. (1983). Symbolic convergence: Organizational communication and culture. In L. L. Putnam and M. E. Pacanowsky (eds.), *Communication and organizations: An interpretive approach* (pp. 99–122). Beverly Hills: Sage.

Bormann, E. G. (1990). *Small group communication: Theory and practice* (3d ed.). New York: Harper & Row.

Bormann, E. G., & Bormann, N. C. (1992). *Effective small group communication* (5th ed.). Edina, MN: Burgess.

Bormann, E. G., Howell, W. S., Nichols, R. G., & Shapiro, G. L. (1982). *Interpersonal communication in the modern organization* (2d ed.). Englewood Cliffs, NJ: Prentice-Hall.

Bougon, M., Weick, K. E., & Binkhorst, D. (1977). Cognition in organizations: An analysis of the Utrecht Jazz Orchestra. *Administrative Science Quarterly, 22,* 606–39.

Boulding, K. E. (1956). *The image.* Ann Arbor: University of Michigan Press.

Boulding, K. E. (1968/1956). General system theory—The skeleton of science. In W. Buckley (ed.), *Modern systems research for the behavioral scientist: A sourcebook* (3-10). Chicago: Aldine.

Bowman, G. W., Worthy, N. B., & Greyser, S. A. (1965). Are women executives people? *Harvard Business Review, 43*(4), 14–28; 164–78.

Bradley, B. E. (1988). *Fundamentals of speech communication: The credibility of ideas* (5th ed.). Dubuque, IA: Wm. C. Brown.

Brass, D. J. (1985). Men's and women's networks: A study of interaction patterns and influence in an organization. *Academy of Management Journal, 28*(2), 327–43.

Brown, M. H. (1985). That reminds me of a story: Speech action in organizational socialization. *Western Journal of Speech Communication, 49*(Winter), 27–42.

Brown, R. H. (1977). *A poetic for sociology: Toward a logic of discovery for the human sciences.* Cambridge, Engl.: Cambridge University Press.

Buchanan, II, B. (1974). Building organizational commitment: The socialization of managers in work organizations. *Administrative Science Quarterly, 19*(4), 533–46.

Bullis, C. (1991). Communication practices as unobtrusive control: An observational study. *Communication Studies, 42*(3), 254–71.

Bullis, C. (1993a). Organizational socialization research: Enabling, constraining, and shifting perspectives. *Communication Monographs, 60*(1), 10–17.

Bullis, C. (1993b). Organizational values and control. In C. Conrad (ed.), *The ethical nexus* (pp. 75–102). Norwood, NJ: Ablex.

Bullis, C., & Bach, B. W. (1991). An explication and test of communication network content and multiplexity as predictors of organizational identification. *Western Journal of Speech Communication, 55*(2), 180–97.

Bullis, C. A., & Tompkins, P. K. (1989). The forest ranger revisited: A study of control practices and identification. *Communication Monographs, 56*(4), 287–306.

Buono, A. F., & Kamm, J. B. (1983). Marginality and the organizational socialization of female managers. *Human Relations, 36*(12), 1125–40.

Byrne, J. A. (1993). The virtual corporation. *Business Week, 3304*(Feb. 8), 98–103.

Callahan, E. S., & Collins, J. W. (1992). Employee attitudes toward whistleblowing: Management and public policy implications. *Journal of Business Ethics, 11*(12), 939–48.

Canary, D. J., & House, K. S. (1993). Is there any reason to research sex differences in communication? *Communication Quarterly, 41*(2), 129–44.

Carroll, A. B. (1978). Linking business ethics to behavior in organizations. *S.A.M. Advanced Management Journal, 43*(3), 4–11.

Carr-Ruffino, N., Baack, J. E., Flipper, C., Hunter-Sloan, K., & Olivolo, C. (1992). Legal aspects of women's advancement: Affirmative action, family leave, and dependent care law. In U. Sekaran and F. T. L. Leong (eds.), *Womanpower: Managing in times of demographic turbulence* (pp. 113–57). Newbury Park: Sage.

Cauley, L. (1993, April 26). The search for a new CEO: IBM. The inside story. *USA Today*, pp. 1B–3B.

Cervantes, R. C. (1992). Occupational and economic stressors among immigrant and United States–born Hispanics. In S. B. Knouse, P. Rosenfeld, and A. S. Culbertson (eds.), *Hispanics in the workplace* (120–33). Newbury Park: Sage.

Cheney, G. (1983a). The rhetoric of identification and the study of organizational communication. *Quarterly Journal of Speech, 69*(2), 143–58.

Cheney, G. (1983b). On the various and changing meanings of organizational membership: A field study of organizational identification. *Communication Monographs, 50*(4), 342–62.

Cheney, G., & Tompkins, P. K. (1987). Coming to terms with organizational identification and commitment. *Central States Speech Journal, 38*(1), 1–15.

Clair, R. P. (1993). The use of framing devices to sequester organizational narratives: Hegemony and harassment. *Communication Monographs, 60*(2), 113–36.

Clegg, S. R. (1989). *Frameworks of power.* London: Sage.

Clegg, S. R. (1990). *Modern organizations: Organization studies in the postmodern world.* London: Sage.

Conrad, C. (1983). Organizational power: Faces and symbolic forms. In L. L. Putnam and M. E. Pacanowsky (eds.), *Communication and organizations: An interpretive approach* (pp. 173–94). Beverly Hills: Sage.

Conrad, C. (1991). Communication in conflict: Style-strategy relationships. *Communication Monographs, 58*(2), 135–55.

Conrad, C. (1993). The ethical nexus: Conceptual grounding. In C. Conrad (ed.), *The ethical nexus* (pp. 7–22). Norwood, NJ: Ablex.

Conrad, C. (1994). *Strategic organizational communication: Toward the twenty-first century* (3rd ed.). Fort Worth: Harcourt Brace College Publishers.

Cooke, R. A. (1991). Danger signs of unethical behavior: How to determine if your firm is at ethical risk. *Journal of Business Ethics, 19*(4), 249–53.

Cornell, S., & Kalt, J. P. (1990). Pathways from poverty: Economic development and institution-building on American Indian reservations. *American Indian Culture and Research Journal, 14*(1), 89–125.

Correa, M. E., Klein, E. B., Stone, W. N., Astrachan, J. H., Kossek, E. E., & Komarraju, M. (1988). Reactions to women in authority: The impact of gender on learning in group relations conferences. *Journal of Applied Behavioral Science, 24*(3), 219–33.

Cox, T., & Nkomo, S. M. (1986). Differential performance appraisal criteria: A field study of black and white managers. *Group & Organization Studies, 11*(1&2), 101–19.

Crabb, S. (1990). Ringing in the changes. *Personnel Management, 22*(8), 38–41.

Cragan, J. F., & Shields, D. C. (1981). *Applied communication research: A dramatistic approach.* Prospect Heights, IL: Waveland.

Cresce, A. R. (1992). Hispanic work force characteristics. In S. B. Knouse, R. Rosenfeld, & A. L. Culbertson (Eds.), *Hispanics in the workplace* (9-28). Newbury Park: Sage.

Croghan, L. (1993, May 16). Sex harassment, free speech rights collide in case. *Duluth News-Tribune*, p. 7B.

Cullen, J. B., Victor, B., & Stephens, C. (1989). An ethical weather report: Assessing the organization's ethical climate. *Organizational Dynamics, 17*, 50–62.

Cunningham, J. P. (1992). Fostering advancement for women and minorities. *Public Management, 74*(8), 20–25.

Daft, R. L., & Weick, K. E. (1984). Toward a model of organizations as interpretation systems. *Academy of Management Review, 9*(2), 284–95.

Daft, R. L., & Wiginton, J. C. (1979). Language and organization. *Academy of Management Review, 4*(2), 179–91.

Daniels, T. D., & Spiker, B. K. (1994). *Perspectives on organizational communication* (3rd ed.). Madison: WCB Brown & Benchmark.

Dansereau, F., & Markham, S. E. (1987). Superior-subordinate communication: Multiple levels of analysis. In F. M. Jablin, L. L. Putnam, K. H. Roberts, & L. W. Porter (eds.), *Handbook of organizational communication: An interdisciplinary perspective* (pp. 343–88). Newbury Park: Sage.

Davis, K. (1953). Management communication and the grapevine. *Harvard Business Review, 31*(5), 43–49.

Davis, S. M. (1984). *Managing corporate culture.* New York: Harper & Row.

de Sola Pool, I., & Kochen, M. (1978/79). Contacts and influence. *Social Networks, 1*, 5–51.

Deal, T. E., & Kennedy, A. A. (1982). *Corporate cultures: The rites and rituals of corporate life.* Reading, MA: Addison-Wesley Publishing.

Deetz, S. (1985). Ethical considerations in cultural research in organizations. In P. J. Frost, L. F. Moore, M. R. Louis, C. C. Lundberg, & J. Martin (eds.), *Organizational culture* (pp. 253–69). Beverly Hills: Sage.

Denison, D. R. (1990). *Corporate culture and organizational effectiveness.* New York: John Wiley & Sons.

Dickson, W. J., & Roethlisberger, F. J. (1966). *Counseling in an organization: A sequel to the Hawthorne researches.* Boston: Harvard University.

Duncan, W. J. (1989). *Great ideas in management: Lessons from the founders and foundations of managerial practice.* San Francisco: Jossey-Bass.

Dunham, R. B., & Pierce, J. L. (1989). *Management.* Glenview, IL: Scott, Foresman & Company.

Dunn, W. N., & Ginsberg, A. (1986). A sociocognitive network approach to organizational analysis. *Human Relations, 39*(11), 955–76.

Eisenberg, E. (1984). Ambiguity as strategy in organizational communication. *Communication Monographs, 51*(3), 227–42.

Eisenberg, E. (1990). Jamming: Transcendence through organizing. *Communication Research, 17*, 139–64.

Eisenberg, E. M., & Goodall, Jr., H. L. (1993). *Organizational communication: Balancing creativity and constraint.* New York: St. Martin's Press.

Emery, F. E., & Trist, E. L. (1973). *Towards a social ecology: Contextual appreciations of the future in the present.* London: Plenum.

Etzioni, A. (1992). Normative-affective factors: Toward a new decision-making model. In M. Zey (Ed.), *Decision making: Alternatives to rational choice models* (89–111). Newbury Park: Sage.

Fagenson, E. A. (1988). The power of a mentor: Proteges and nonproteges' perceptions of their own power in organizations. *Group and Organization Studies, 13*(2), 182–94.

Farley, J. (1979). *Affirmative action & the woman worker: Guidelines for personnel management.* New York: AMACOM.

Fayol, H. (1949/1916). *General and industrial management.* (Trans. Constance Storrs). London: Sir Issac Pitman and Sons Ltd.

Feldman, D. C. (1981). The multiple socialization of organization members. *Academy of Management Review, 6*(2), 309–18.

Feldman, S. P. (1988). How organizational culture can affect innovation. *Organizational Dynamics, 17*(1), 57–68.

Filley, A. C. (1978). Some normative issues in conflict management. *California Management Review, 21*(2), 61–66.

Fimbel, N., & Burstein, J. S. (1990). Defining the ethical standards of the high-technology industry. *Journal of Business Ethics, 9*(2), 929–48.

Firms must hand over spill tapes. (1992, November). *Duluth News-Tribune*, p. 4C.

Fischhoff, B., Lichtenstein, S., Slovic, P., Derby, S. L., & Keeney, R. L. (1981). *Acceptable risk.* Cambridge: Cambridge University Press.

Fisher, R., & Ury, W. (1981). *Getting to yes.* New York: Penguin.

Fisher, R., Ury, W., & Patton, B. (1993). Negotiation power: Ingredients in an ability to influence the other side. In L. Hall (ed.), *Negotiation: Strategies for mutual gain. The basic seminar of the Harvard Program on Negotiation* (pp. 3–13). Newbury Park: Sage.

Fisher, W. R. (1978). Toward a logic of good reasons. *Quarterly Journal of Speech, 64*(4), 376–84.

Fisher, W. R. (1984). Narration as a human communication paradigm: The case of public moral argument. *Communication Monographs, 51*(1), 1–22.

Fisher, W. R. (1985). The narrative paradigm: An elaboration. *Communication Monographs, 52*(4), 347–67.

Fisher, W. R. (1987). *Human communication as narration: Toward a philosophy of reason, value, and action.* Columbia, SC: University of South Carolina Press.

Fitzgerald, T. H. (1988). Can change in organizational culture really be managed? *Organizational Dynamics, 17*(2), 4–15.

Flanagan, R. J., Smith, R. S., & Ehrenberg, R. G. (1984). *Labor economics and labor relations.* Glenview, IL: Scott, Foresman & Co.

Foeman, A. K., & Pressley, G. (1992/1987). Ethnic culture and corporate culture: Using black styles in organizations. In K. L. Hutchinson (ed.), *Readings in organizational communication* (pp. 404–16). Dubuque, IA: Wm. C. Brown. Originally published in *Communication Quarterly, 35*(4), 293–307.

Folger, J. P., Poole, M. S., & Stutman, R. K. (1993). *Working through conflict* (2d ed.). New York: HarperCollins.

Follett, M. P. (1940/1925). The giving of orders. In H. C. Metcalf & L. Urwick (eds.), *Dynamic administration: The collected papers of Mary Parker Follett* (pp. 50–70). New York: Harper & Brothers.

Follett, M. P. (1940/1932). Individualism in a planned society. In H. C. Metcalf & L. Urwick (eds.), *Dynamic administration: The collected papers of Mary Parker Follett* (pp. 295–314). New York: Harper & Brothers.

Fombrun, C. J. (1982). Strategies for network research in organizations. *Academy of Management Review, 7*(2), 280–91.

Foo, C. T. (1992). Culture, productivity and structure: A Singapore study. *Organization Studies, 13*(4), 589–609.

Ford, R. C., & McLaughlin, F. S. (1988). Sexual harassment at work. *Business Horizons, 31*(6), 14–19.

Frank, A. D., & Brownell, J. L. (1989). *Organizational communication and behavior: Communicating to improve performance (2 + 2 = 5).* New York: Holt, Rinehart & Winston, Inc.

Franke, R. H., & Kaul, J. D. (1978). The Hawthorne experiments: First statistical interpretation. *American Sociological Review, 43*(5), 623–43.

Freeman, J. (1978). The unit of analysis in organizational research. In M. Meyer & Associates (eds.), *Environments and organizations* (pp. 335–51). San Francisco: Jossey-Bass.

Freeman, R. E., & Liedtka, J. (1991). Corporate social responsibility: A critical approach [special issue]. *Business Horizons, 34*(4), 92–98.

French, J., & Raven, B. (1959). The bases of social power. In D. Cartwright & A. Zander (eds.), *Group dynamics* (pp. 601–23). New York: Harper & Row.

Fritzsche, D. J. (1991). A model of decision-making incorporating ethical values. *Journal of Business Ethics, 10*(11), 841–52.

Frost, P. J. (1987). Power, politics, and influence. In F. M. Jablin, L. L. Putnam, K. H. Roberts, & L. W. Porter (eds.), *Handbook of organizational communication* (pp. 503–48). Newbury Park: Sage.

Frost, P. J., Moore, L. F., Louis, M. R., Lundberg, C. C., & Martin, J. (1985). *Organizational culture*. Beverly Hills: Sage.

Fry, L. (1976). The maligned F. W. Taylor: A reply to his many critics. *Academy of Management Review, 1*(3), 124–29.

Fullerton, H., & Price, C. (1991). Culture change in the NHS. *Personnel Management, 23*(3), 50–53.

Galaskiewicz, J. (1979). *Exchange networks and community politics*. Newbury Park, CA: Sage.

Geertz, C. (1973). *The interpretation of cultures*. New York: Basic Books.

Gellerman, S. W. (1989). Why "good" managers make bad ethical choices. In K. R. Andrews (ed.), *Ethics in practice: Managing the moral corporation* (pp. 18–26). Boston: Harvard Business School Press.

George, Jr., C. S. (1968). *The history of management thought*. Englewood Cliffs, NJ: Prentice-Hall.

George, R. J. (1988). The challenge of preparing ethically responsible managers: Closing the rhetoric-reality gap. *Journal of Business Ethics, 7*, 715–20.

Gerber, J. (1990). Enforced self-regulation in the infant formula industry: A radical extension of an "impractical" proposal. *Social Justice, 17*(1), 98–112.

Gerber, J., & Short, Jr., J. F. (1986). Publicity and the control of corporate behavior: The case of infant formula. *Deviant Behavior, 7*(3), 195–216.

Gibb, J. R. (1961). Defensive communication. *Journal of Communication, 11*(3), 141–48.

Gibb, J. R. (1978). *Trust: A new view of personal and organizational development*. Los Angeles: Guild of Tutors Press.

Gilligan, C. (1982). *In a different voice*. Cambridge, MA: Harvard University Press.

Gilsdorf, J. W. (1990). Sexual harassment as a liability issue in communication. *The Bulletin, 53*(3), 68–77.

Glauser, M. J. (1984). Upward information flow in organizations: Review and conceptual analysis. *Human Relations, 37*(8), 613–43.

Goldhaber, G. M. (1990). *Organizational communication* (5th ed.). Dubuque, IA: Wm. C. Brown.

Goldin, C. (1990). *Understanding the gender gap: An economic history of American women*. New York: Oxford University Press.

Goodpaster, K. E. (1989). Note on the corporation as a moral environment. In K. R. Andrews (ed.), *Ethics in practice: Managing the moral corporation* (pp. 89–99). Boston: Harvard Business School Press.

Gordon, G. G. (1991). Industry determinants of organizational culture. *Academy of Management Review, 16*(2), 396–415.

Gouran, D. S. (1984). Communicative influences on decisions related to the Watergate coverup: The failure of collective judgment. *Central States Speech Journal, 35*(4), 260–69.

Gouran, D. S., Hirokawa, R. Y., & Martz, A. E. (1986). A critical analysis of factors related to decisional processes involved in the *Challenger* disaster. *Central States Speech Journal, 37*(3), 119–35.

Granovetter, M. (1976). Network sampling: Some first steps. *American Journal of Sociology, 81*(6), 1287–1303.

Greenhouse, S. (1989). Nestle's time to swagger. *New York Times* (Jan. 1, sec 3 F1).

Gross, E. (1975). Patterns of organizational and occupational socialization. *Vocational Guidance Quarterly, 24*(2), 140–49.

Hackman, M. Z., & Johnson, C. E. (1991). *Leadership: A communication perspective.* Prospect Heights, IL: Waveland.

Hagberg, J. O. (1984). *Real power: Stages of personal power in organizations.* Minneapolis: Winston.

Hall, L. (ed.). (1993). *Negotiation: Strategies for mutual gain. The basic seminar of the Harvard Program on Negotiation.* Newbury Park: Sage.

Hammonds, K. (1991). Corning's class act. *Business Week, May 13,* 68–76.

Harper, N. L., & Hirokawa, R. Y. (1988). A comparison of persuasive strategies used by female and male managers I: An examination of downward influence. *Communication Quarterly, 36*(2), 157–68.

Harvey, J. B. (1974). The Abilene Paradox: The management of meaning. *Organizational Dynamics, 3*(1), 63–80.

Harvey, J. B. (1988). *The Abilene paradox and other meditations on management.* San Diego: University Associates.

Haslett, B., Geis, F. L., & Carter, M. R. (1992). *The organizational woman: Power & paradox.* Norwood, NJ: Ablex.

Hatch, M. J. (1993). The dynamics of organizational culture. *Academy of Management Review, 18*(4), 657–693.

Hawes, L. C. (1974). Social collectivities as communication: Perspective on organizational behavior. *Quarterly Journal of Speech, 60*(4), 497–502.

Hecht, M. L., Collier, M. J., & Ribeau, S. A. (1993). *African American communication: Ethnic identity and cultural interpretation.* Newbury Park: Sage.

Hegarty, W. H., & Sims, Jr., H. P. (1978). Some determinants of unethical decision behavior: An experiment. *Journal of Applied Psychology, 63*(4), 451–57.

Hegarty, W. H., & Sims, Jr., H. P. (1979). Organizational philosophy, policies, and objectives related to unethical decision behavior: A laboratory experiment. *Journal of Applied Psychology, 64*(3), 331–38.

Hess, J. A. (1993). Assimilating newcomers into an organization: A cultural perspective. *Journal of Applied Communication Research, 21*(2), 189–210.

Hocker, J. L., & Wilmot, W. W. (1985). *Interpersonal conflict.* Dubuque, IA: Wm. C. Brown.

Homans, G. C. (1950). *The human group.* New York: Harcourt, Brace and Co.

Homans, G. C. (1975). What do we mean by social "structure"? In P. M. Blau (ed.), *Approaches to the study of social structure* (pp. 53–65). New York: Free Press.

Jablin, F. M. (1979). Superior-subordinate communication: The state of the art. *Psychological Bulletin, 86*(6), 1201–22.

Jablin, F. M. (1982). Organizational communication: An assimilation approach. In M. E. Roloff & C. R. Berger (eds.), *Social cognition and communication* (pp. 255–86). Beverly Hills, CA: Sage.

Jablin, F. M. (1984). Assimilating new members into organizations. In R. N. Bostrom (ed.), *Communication yearbook*, vol. 8 (pp. 594–624). Beverly Hills, CA: Sage.

Jablin, F. M. (1987a). Organizational entry, assimilation, and exit. In F. M. Jablin, L. L. Putnam, K. H. Roberts, & L. W. Porter (eds.), *Handbook of organizational communication: An interdisciplinary perspective* (pp. 679–740). Newbury Park, CA: Sage.

Jablin, F. M. (1987b). Formal organizational structure. In F. M. Jablin, L. L. Putnam, K. H. Roberts, & L. W. Porter (eds.), *Handbook of organizational communication: An interdisciplinary perspective* (pp. 389–419). Newbury Park: Sage.

Jaynes, G. D., & Williams, Jr., R. M. (eds.). (1989). *A common destiny: Blacks and American society*. Washington, D.C.: National Academy Press.

Johannesen, R. L. (1975). *Ethics in human communication*. Columbus, OH: Charles E. Merrill.

Johnson, B. M. (1981). *Communication: The process of organizing*. Boston, MA: American Press.

Jones, Jr., E. W. (1986, May–June). Black managers: The dream deferred. *Harvard Business Review, 64*(3), 84–93.

Jorgensen, D. L. (1989). *Participant observation: A methodology for human studies*. Newbury Park: Sage.

Kalbfleisch, P. J., & Davies, A. B. (1991). Minorities and mentoring: Managing the multicultural institution. *Communication Education, 40*(3), 266–71.

Kanter, R. M. (1977). *Men and women of the corporation*. New York: Basic Books.

Kanter, R. M. (1983). *The change masters: Innovation & entrepreneurship in the American corporation*. New York: Touchstone.

Katz, D., & Kahn, R. L. (1978). *The social psychology of organizations* (2d ed.). New York: John Wiley & Sons.

Katz, R., & Van Maanen, J. (1977). The loci of work satisfaction: Job, interaction, and policy. *Human Relations, 30*(5), 469–86.

Kelly, G. (1976). Seducing the elites: The politics of decision making and innovation in organizational networks. *Academy of Management Review, 1*(3), 66–74.

Kelly, G. K. (1986). Coping with America: Refugees from Vietnam, Cambodia, and Laos in the 1970s and 1980s. *Annals of the American Academy of Political and Social Science, 487*, 138–49.

Ketchum, L. D., & Trist, E. (1992). *All teams are not created equal: How employee empowerment really works*. Newbury Park: Sage.

Kets de Vries, M. F. R. (1991). Introduction: Exploding the myth that organizations and executives are rational. In M. F. R. Kets de Vries & Associates (eds.), *Organizations on the couch: Clinical perspectives on organizational behavior and change* (1–21). San Francisco: Jossey-Bass.

Kieser, A. (1989). Organizational, institutional, and societal evolution: Medieval craft guilds and the genesis of formal organizations. *Administrative Science Quarterly, 34*, 540–64.

Kilmann, R. H., & Thomas, K. W. (1978). Four perspectives on conflict management: An attributional framework for organizing descriptive and normative theory. *Academy of Management Review, 3*(1), 59–68.

Knapp, M. L., Putnam, L. L., & Davis, L. J. (1988). Measuring interpersonal conflict in organizations: Where do we go from here? *Management Communication Quarterly, 1*(3), 414–29.

Knouse, S. B. (1992). The mentoring process for Hispanics. In S. B. Knouse, P. Rosenfeld, & A. L. Culbertson (eds.). *Hispanics in the workplace* (pp. 137–50). Newbury Park: Sage.

Knouse, S. B., Rosenfeld, P., & Culbertson, A. L. (1992). *Hispanics in the workplace*. Newbury Park: Sage.

Koch, L., & Deetz, S. (1981). Metaphor analysis of social reality in organizations. *Journal of Applied Communication Research, 9*(1), 1–15.

Kolb, D. M. (1992). Women's work: Peacemaking in organizations. In D. M. Kolb & J. M. Bartunek (eds.), *Hidden conflict in organizations: Uncovering behind-the-scenes disputes* (pp. 63–91). Newbury Park: Sage.

Kolb, D. M. (1993). Her place at the table: Gender and negotiation. In L. Hall (ed.), *Negotiation: Strategies for mutual gain: The basic seminar of the Harvard Program on Negotiation* (pp. 138–50). Newbury Park: Sage.

Kolb, D. M., & Putnam, L. L. (1992). Introduction: The dialectics of disputing. In D. M. Kolb & J. M. Bartunek (eds.), *Hidden conflict in organizations: Uncovering behind-the-scenes disputes* (pp. 1–31). Newbury Park: Sage.

Kopelman, R. E., Brief, A. P., & Guzzo, R. A. (1990). The role of climate and culture in productivity. In B. Schneider (Ed.), *Organizational climate and culture* (pp. 282–318). San Francisco: Jossey-Bass.

Korte, C., & Milgram, S. (1970). Acquaintance networks between racial groups: Application of the small world method. *Journal of Personality and Social Psychology, 15*(2), 101–08.

Kotter, J. P., & Heskett, J. L. (1992). *Corporate culture and performance*. New York: Free Press.

Kreps, G. L. (1980). A field experimental test and revaluation of Weick's model of organizing. In B. Ruben (ed.), *Communication yearbook 4* (pp. 389–398). New Brunswick, NJ: Transaction Books.

Kreps, G. L. (1990). *Organizational communication: Theory and practice* (2d ed.). New York: Longman.

Kuhn, T. S. (1962). *The structure of scientific revolutions* (2d ed.). Chicago: University of Chicago Press.

Landsberger, H. A. (1958). *Hawthorne revisited: "Management and the worker," its critics, and developments in human relations in industry*. Ithaca, NY: Cornell University.

Larwood, L., & Gutek, B. A. (1987). Working toward a theory of women's career development. In B. A. Gutek & L. Larwood (eds.), *Women's career development* (pp. 170–83). Newbury Park: Sage.

Larwood, L., Szwajkowski, E., & Rose, S. (1988). When discrimination makes "sense." In B. A. Gutek, A. H. Stromberg, & L. Larwood (eds.), *Women and work: An annual review. Volume 3* (pp. 265–88).

Laumann, E. O., Marsden, P. V., & Prensky, D. (1983). The boundary specification problem in network analysis. In R. S. Burt & M. J. Minor (eds), *Applied network analysis* (pp. 18–34). Newbury Park, CA: Sage.

LaVigne, P. (1993, May). Dangerous liaisons: Training on sexual harassment and violence begins for all. *Update*, 1–3.

Legislative Commission on the Economic Status of Women. (1992, February). *Newsletter #171*.

Leinster, C. (1988, January 18). Black executives: How they're doing. *Fortune, 117*(2), 109–20.

Likert, R. (1961). *New patterns of management*. New York: McGraw-Hill.

Likert, R. (1967). *The human organization*. New York: McGraw-Hill.

Lincoln, J. R., & Miller, J. (1979). Work and friendship ties in organizations: A comparative analysis of relational networks. *Administrative Science Quarterly, 24*, 181–99.

Locke, E. A. (1982). The ideas of Frederick W. Taylor: An evaluation. *Academy of Management Review, 7*(1), 14–24.

Lott, B. (1993). Sexual harassment: Consequences and remedies. *Thought & Action: The NEA Higher Education Journal, 8*(2), 89–103.

Louis, M. R. (1977). How individuals conceptualize conflict: Identification of steps in the process and the role of personal/developmental factors. *Human Relations, 30*(5), 451–67.

Louis, M. R. (1980a). Surprise and sense making: What new-comers experience in entering unfamiliar organizational settings. *Administrative Science Quarterly, 25*, 226–51.

Louis, M. R. (1980b). Career transitions: Varieties and commonalities. *Academy of Management Review, 5*(3), 329–40.

Louis, M. R. (1985). An investigator's guide to workplace culture. In P. J. Frost, L. F. Moore, M. R. Louis, C. C. Lundberg, & J. Martin (eds.), *Organizational culture* (pp. 73–93). Beverly Hills, CA: Sage.

Louis, M. R. (1990). Acculturation in the workplace: Newcomers as lay ethnographers. In B. Schneider (ed.), *Organizational climate and culture* (pp. 85–129). San Francisco: Jossey-Bass.

Louis, M. R., Posner, B. Z., & Powell, G. N. (1983). The availability and helpfulness of socialization practices. *Personnel Psychology, 36*, 857–67.

Louis, M. R., & Sutton, R. I. (1991). Switching cognitive gears: From habits of mind to active thinking. *Human Relations, 44*(1), 55–76.

Luzzo, D. A. (1992). Ethnic group and social class differences in college students' career development. *Career Development Quarterly, 41*(2), 161–73.

Mariolis, P. (1975). Interlocking directorates and control of corporations: The theory of bank control. *Social Science Quarterly, 56*, 425–39.

Marshall, A. A., & Stohl, C. (1993). Participating as participation: A network approach. *Communication Monographs, 60*(2), 137–57.

Martin, J. (1992). The suppression of gender conflict in organizations. In D. M. Kolb & J. M. Bartunek (eds.), *Hidden conflict in organizations: Uncovering behind-the-scenes disputes* (pp. 165–86). Newbury Park: Sage.

Martin, J., Sitkin, S. B., & Boehm, M. (1985). Founders and the elusiveness of a cultural legacy. In P. J. Frost, L. F. Moore, M. R. Louis, C. C. Lundberg, & J. Martin (Eds.), *Organizational culture* (pp. 99–124). Newbury Park: Sage.

Martin, J., & Siehl, C. (1983). Organizational culture and counterculture: An uneasy symbiosis. *Organizational Dynamics, 12*, 52–64.

Martin, Jr., W. E. (1991). Career development and American Indians living on reservations: Cross-cultural factors to consider. *The Career Development Quarterly, 39*(3), 273–83.

Maslow, A. (1943). A theory of human motivation. *Psychological Review, 50*(4), 370–96.

Maslow, A. (1954). *Motivation and personality.* New York: Harper.

Maslow, A. (1968). *Toward a psychology of being* (2d ed.). New York: Van Nostrand Reinhold Company.

Mathews, M. C. (1988). *Strategic intervention in organizations: Resolving ethical dilemmas.* Newbury Park: Sage.

Mayes, B. T., & Allen, R. W. (1977). Toward a definition of organizational politics. *Academy of Management Review, 2*(4), 672–78.

Maynard, R. (1993, April). Meet the new law on family leave. *Nation's Business, 81*(4), 26.

Mayo, E. (1946/1933). *The human problems of an industrial civilization* (2d ed.). Boston: Harvard University.

McCallister, L., & Fischer, C. S. (1978). A procedure for surveying personal networks. *Sociological Methods and Research, 7*(2), 131–48.

McCarthy, K. (1991). Recovering from harassment. *Minnesota Monthly, 25*(8), 28–31; 88–91.

McDonald, P., & Gandz, J. (1992). Getting value from shared values. *Organizational Dynamics, 20*(3), 64–77.

McGregor, D. (1960). *The human side of enterprise.* New York: McGraw-Hill.

McGregor, D. (1966/1957). The human side of enterprise. In W. G. Bennis & E. Schein, (eds.), *Leadership and motivation: Essays of Douglas McGregor* (pp. 3–20). Cambridge, MA: M.I.T. Press.

McGuire, P. (1989). Product liability: Evolution and reform. *Perspectives, 17,* 1–12.

McIntosh, P. (1989). White privilege: Unpacking the invisible knapsack. *Peace and Freedom, 49*(4), 10–12.

McKee, B. (1993, April). The disabilities labyrinth. *Nation's Business, 81*(4), 18–23.

McKersie, R. B. (1993). Why the labor management scene is contentious. In L. Hall (ed.), *Negotiation: Strategies for mutual gain: The basic seminar of the Harvard Program on Negotiation* (pp. 77–85). Newbury Park: Sage.

McPhee, R. D. (1985). Formal structure and organizational communication. In R. D. McPhee & P. K. Tompkins (eds.), *Organizational communication: Traditional themes and new directions* (pp. 149–77). Beverly Hills: Sage.

McPhee, R. D. (1989). Organizational communication: A structurational exemplar. In B. Dervin, L. Grossberg, B. J. O'Keefe, & E. Wartella (eds.), *Rethinking communication: Volume 2—paradigm exemplars* (pp. 199–211). Newbury Park, CA: Sage.

Milburn, T. W., Schuler, R. S., & Watman, K. H. (1983a). Organizational crisis. Part 1: Definition and conceptualization. *Human Relations, 36*(12), 1141–60.

Milburn, T. W., Schuler, R. S., & Watman, K. H. (1983b). Organizational crisis. Part II: Strategies and responses. *Human Relations, 36*(12), 1161–80.

Miles, R. E. (1965). Human relations or human resources? *Harvard Business Review, July–August,* 148–63.

Milgram, S. (1967). The small-world problem. *Psychology Today, 1*(1), 61–67.

Mills, A. J. (1992/1988). Organization, gender, and culture. In A. J. Mills & P. Tancred (eds.), *Gendering organizational analysis* (pp. 93–111). Newbury Park: Sage. Originally published in *Organization Studies, 9,* 351–69.

Mintzberg, H. (1980). Structure in 5's: A synthesis of the research on organization design. *Management Science, 26*(3), 322–41.

Monge, P. R., & Contractor, N. S. (1988). Communication networks: Measurement techniques. In C. H. Tardy (ed.), *A handbook for the study of human communication* (pp. 107–38). Norwood, NJ: Ablex.

Monge, P. R., & Eisenberg, E. (1987). Emergent communication networks. In F. M. Jablin, L. L. Putnam, K. H. Roberts, & L. W. Porter (eds.), *Handbook of organizational communication: An interdisciplinary perspective* (pp. 304–42). Newbury Park: Sage.

Monroe, C., DiSalvo, V. S., Lewis, J. J., & Borzi, M. G. (1990). Conflict behaviors of difficult subordinates: Interactive effects of gender. *Southern Communication Journal, 56*(1), 12–23.

Morey, N. C., & Luthans, F. (1985). Refining the displacement of culture and the use of scenes and themes in organizational studies. *Academy of Management Review, 10*(2), 219–29.

Morgan, G. (1986). *Images of organization.* Beverly Hills: Sage.

Morgan, G. (1989). *Creative organization theory: A resourcebook.* Newbury Park: Sage.

Morgan, G. (1993). *Imaginization: The art of creative management.* Newbury Park: Sage.

Morgan, G., & Smircich, L. (1980). The case for qualitative research. *Academy of Management Review, 5,* 491–500.

Morley, D. D., & Schockley-Zalabak, P. (1991). Setting the rules: An examination of the influence of organizational founders' values. *Management Communication Quarterly, 4*(4), 422–449.

Morrison, A. M., & Von Glinow, M. A. (1990). Women and minorities in management. *American Psychologist, 45*(2), 200–08.

Mulac, A., Wiemann, J. M., Widenmann, S. J., & Gibson, T. W. (1988). Male/female language differences and effects in same-sex and mixed-sex dyads: The gender-linked language effect. *Communication Monographs, 55*(4), 315–35.

Mumby, D. K., & Putnam, L. L. (1992). The politics of emotion: A feminist reading of bounded rationality. *Academy of Management Review, 17*(3), 465–86.

Mundel, M. E. (1985). *Motion and time study: Improving productivity* (6th ed.). Englewood Cliffs, NJ: Prentice-Hall.

Murphy, P. (1988). Implementing business ethics. *Journal of Business Ethics, 7,* 907–15.

Nicholson, N., & Johns, G. (1985). The absence culture and the psychological contract—Who's in control of absence? *Academy of Management Review, 10*(3), 397–407.

Nicotera, A. M., & Cushman, D. P. (1992). Organizational ethics: A within-organization view. *Journal of Applied Communication Research, 20*(4), 437–62.

O'Donnell-Trujillo, N., & Pacanowsky, M. E. (1983). The interpretation of organizational cultures. In M. S. Mander (ed.), *Communications in transition: Issues and debates in current research* (pp. 225–41). New York: Praeger.

O'Reilly, III, C. A. (1978). The intentional distortion of information in organizational communication: A laboratory and field investigation. *Human Relations, 31*(2), 173–93.

O'Reilly, III, C. A. (1980). Individuals and information overload in organizations: Is more necessarily better? *Academy of Management Journal, 23*(4), 684–96.

O'Reilly, III, C., & Chatman, J. (1986). Organizational commitment and psychological attachment: The effects of compliance, identification, and internalization on prosocial behavior. *Journal of Applied Psychology, 71*(3), 492–99.

Orton, J. D., & Weick, K. E. (1990). Loosely coupled systems: A reconceptualization. *Academy of Management Review, 15*(2), 202–23.

Ouchi, W. G. (1981). *Theory Z: How American business can meet the Japanese challenge.* Reading, MA: Addison-Wesley.

Pacanowsky, M. E. (1983). A small town cop: Communication in, out, and about a crisis. In L. L. Putnam & M. E. Pacanowsky (eds.), *Communication and organizations: An interpretive approach* (pp. 261–82). Beverly Hills: Sage.

Pacanowsky, M. E. (1988). Slouching towards Chicago. *Quarterly Journal of Speech, 74*(4), 453–67.

Pacanowsky, M. E., & O'Donnell-Trujillo, N. (1982). Communication and organizational cultures. *Western Journal of Speech Communication, 46*(Spring), 115–30.

Pacanowsky, M. E., & O'Donnell-Trujillo, N. (1983). Organizational communication as cultural performance. *Communication Monographs, 50*(2), 126–47.

Pace, R. W., & Faules, D. F. (1994). *Organizational communication* (3rd ed.). Englewood Cliffs, NJ: Prentice-Hall.

Paige-Royer, M. (1987). Attention K-Mart managers. *Corporate Report Minnesota, 18*(10), 53–56.

Pamental, G. L. (1989). The course in business ethics: Can it work? *Journal of Business Ethics, 8,* 547–551.

Papa, M. J., & Pood, E. A. (1988). Coorientational accuracy and organizational conflict:

An examination of tactic selection and discussion satisfaction. *Communication Research, 15*(1), 3–28.

Pearson, J. C., Turner, L. H., & Todd-Mancillas, W. (1991). *Gender & communication* (2d ed.). Dubuque, IA: Wm. C. Brown.

Pepper, G. L. (1989). Metaphors and organizational culture research: Assumptions, concerns, and suggestions. *Speech Association of Minnesota Journal, 16,* 35–56.

Pepper, G. L. (1993). Just another day in Abilene or, "when is a 'team' not a team?" Openness, accountability, and identity in an organizational development team. In C. Bantz, *Understanding organizations: Interpreting organizational communication cultures.* Columbia, SC: University of South Carolina Press.

Perrow, C. (1972). *Complex organizations: A critical essay.* Glenview, IL: Scott, Foresman & Co.

Peters, T. J., & Waterman, Jr., R. H. (1982). *In search of excellence: Lessons from America's best-run companies.* New York: Warner Books.

Pettigrew, A. M. (1979). On studying organizational cultures. *Administrative Science Quarterly, 24*(4), 570–81.

Pettit, Jr., J. D., Vaught, B., & Pulley, K. J. (1990). The role of communication in organizations: Ethical considerations. *Journal of Business Communication, 27*(3), 233–49.

Pfeffer, J., & Salancik, G. R. (1974). Organizational decision-making as a political process: The case of a university budget. *Administrative Science Quarterly, 19*(2), 135–51.

Philipsen, G. (1989). An ethnographic approach to communication studies. In B. Dervin, L. Grossberg, B. J. O'Keefe, & E. Wartella (eds.), *Rethinking communication: Volume 2—paradigm exemplars* (pp. 258–68). Newbury Park, CA: Sage.

Poole, M. S., & DeSanctis, G. (1990). Understanding the use of group decision support systems: The theory of adaptive structuration. In J. Fulk & C. Steinfield (eds.), *Organizations and communication technology* (pp. 173–93). Newbury Park: Sage.

Poole, M. S., & McPhee, R. D. (1983). A structurational analysis of organizational climate. In L. L. Putnam & M. E. Pacanowsky (eds.), *Communication and organizations: An interpretive approach* (pp. 195–219). Beverly Hills: Sage.

Powell, G. N. (1983). Sexual harassment: Confronting the issue of definition. *Business Horizons, 26*(4), 24–28.

Powell, G. N. (1988). *Women and men in management.* Newbury Park: Sage.

Putnam, L. L. (1983). The interpretive perspective: An alternative to functionalism. In L. L. Putnam & M. E. Pacanowsky (eds.), *Communication and organizations: An interpretive approach* (pp. 31–54). Beverly Hills: Sage.

Putnam, L. L. (ed.). (1988). Communication and conflict styles in organizations [special issue]. *Management Communication Quarterly, 1*(3).

Putnam, L. L. (1989). Negotiation and organizing: Two levels of analysis within the Weickian model. *Communication Studies, 40*(4), 249–57.

Putnam, L. L., & Geist, P. (1985). Argument in bargaining: an analysis of the reasoning process. *Southern States Speech Journal, 51,* 67–78.

Putnam, L. L., & Holmer, M. (1992). Framing, reframing, and issue development. In L. L. Putnam & M. E. Roloff (eds.), *Communication and negotiation* (pp. 128–55). Newbury Park: Sage.

Putnam, L. L., & Jones, T. S. (1982a). The role of communication in bargaining. *Human Communication Research, 8*(3), 262–80.

Putnam, L. L., & Jones, T. S. (1982b). Reciprocity in negotiations: An analysis of bargaining interaction. *Communication Monographs, 49*(3), 171–91.

Putnam, L. L., & Poole, M. S. (1987). Conflict and negotiation. In F. M. Jablin, L. L. Putnam, K. H. Roberts, & L. W. Porter (eds.), *Handbook of organizational communication: An interdisciplinary perspective* (pp. 549–99). Newbury Park: Sage.

Putnam, L. L., & Roloff, M. E. (eds.). (1992a). *Communication and negotiation.* Newbury Park: Sage.

Putnam, L. L., & Roloff, M. E. (1992b). Communication perspectives on negotiation. In L. L. Putnam & M. E. Roloff (eds.) *Communication and negotiation* (pp. 1–17). Newbury Park: Sage.

Putnam, L. L., & Sorenson, R. L. (1982). Equivocal messages in organizations. *Human Communication Research, 8*(2), 114–32.

Putnam, L. L., Van Hoeven, S. A., & Bullis, C. A. (1991). The role of rituals and fantasy themes in teachers' bargaining. *Western Journal of Speech Communication, 55*(1), 85–103.

Quick, J. C. (1992). Crafting an organizational culture: Herb's hand at Southwest Airlines. *Organizational Dynamics, 21*(2), 45–56.

Rahim, M. A. (1985). A strategy for managing conflict in complex organizations. *Human Relations, 38*(1), 81–89.

Red Horse, J., Johnson, T., & Weiner, D. (1989). Commentary: Cultural perspectives on research among American Indians. *American Indian Culture and Research Journal, 13*(3&4), 267–71.

Reichers, A. E., & Schneider, B. (1990). Climate and culture: An evolution of constructs. In B. Schneider (ed.), *Organizational climate and culture* (pp. 5–39). San Francisco: Jossey-Bass.

Reilly, B. J., & DiAngelo, Jr., J. A. (1990). Communication: A cultural system of meaning and value. *Human Relations, 43*(2), 129–40.

Renz, M. A., & Greg, J. (1988). Flaws in the decision making process: Assessment of risk in the decision to launch flight 51-L. *Central States Speech Journal, 39*(1), 67–75.

Richards, Jr., W. D. (1985). Data, models, and assumptions in network analysis. In R. D. McPhee & P. K. Tompkins (eds.), *Organizational communication* (pp. 109–28). Beverly Hills: Sage.

Riley, P. (1983). A structurationist account of political culture. *Administrative Science Quarterly, 28,* 414–37.

Roberts, K. H., & O'Reilly, III, C. A. (1974). Failures in upward communication in organizations: Three possible culprits. *Academy of Management Journal, 17*(2), 205–15.

Roberts, K. H., & O'Reilly, III, C. A. (1978). Organizations as communication structures: An empirical approach. *Human Communication Research, 4,* 283–93.

Roethlisberger, F. J. (1965). *Management and morale.* Cambridge, MA: Harvard University Press.

Roethlisberger, F. J., & Dickson, W. J. (1939). *Management and the worker.* Cambridge, MA: Harvard University Press.

Rogers, E. M., & Kincaid, D. L. (1981). *Communication networks.* New York: Free Press.

Ross, R. S. (1989). *Small groups in organizational settings.* Englewood Cliffs, NJ: Prentice-Hall.

Rousseau, D. M. (1990). Assessing organizational culture: The case for multiple methods. In Benjamin Schneider (ed.), *Organizational climate and culture* (pp. 153–92). San Francisco: Jossey-Bass.

Salancik, G. R. (1986). An index of subgroup influence in dependency networks. *Administrative Science Quarterly, 31,* 194–211.

Sanyal, R. N., & Neves, J. S. (1991). The *Valdez* principles: Implications for corporate social responsibility. *Journal of Business Ethics, 10*(12), 883–90.

Sapiro, V. (1986). *Women in American society.* Palo Alto: Mayfield.

Sass, J. S., & Canary, D. J. (1991). Organizational commitment and identification: An examination of conceptual and operational convergence. *Western Journal of Speech Communication, 55*(3), 275–93.

Sathe, V. (1983). Implications of corporate culture: A manager's guide to action. *Organizational Dynamics, 12*(2), 4–23.

Sathe, V. (1985). *Culture and related corporate realities: Text, cases, and readings on organizational entry, establishment, and change.* Homewood, IL: Richard Irwin, Inc.

Schall, M. S., & Shapiro, G. L. (1984). Rhetorical rules and organization-culture: Identification, maintenance, change. Paper presented at the University of British Columbia Conference on Organizational Culture and the Meaning of Life in the Workplace.

Scheibel, D. (1992). Faking identity in Clubland: The communicative performance of "fake ID." *Text and Performance Quarterly, 12,* 160–75.

Schein, E. H. (1983). The role of the founder in creating organizational cultures. *Organizational Dynamics, 12,* 13–28.

Schein, E. H. (1984). Coming to new awareness of organizational culture. *Sloan Management Review,* 3–16.

Schein, E. H. (1985). *Organizational culture and leadership.* San Francisco: Jossey-Bass.

Schneider, K. (1993, June 2). Survey: Sexual harassment prevalent in nation's schools. *Duluth News-Tribune,* p. 4C.

Schon, D. A. (1979). Generative metaphor: A perspective on problem-setting in social policy. In A. Ortony (ed.), *Metaphor and thought* (pp. 254–83). Cambridge: Cambridge University Press.

Schoorman, F. D., Bazerman, M. H., & Atkin, R. S. (1981). Interlocking directorates: A strategy for reducing environmental uncertainty. *Academy of Management Review, 6*(2), 243–51.

Schwartz, F. N. (1989). Management women and the new facts of life. *Harvard Business Review, 89*(1), 65–76.

Schwartz, F. N. (1992). Women as a business imperative. *Harvard Business Review, 70*(2), 105–13.

Schwartz, H. S. (1991). Organizational decay and loss of reality: Life at NASA. In M. F. R. Kets de Vries & Associates (eds.), *Organizations on the couch: Clinical perspectives on organizational behavior and change* (pp. 286–303). San Francisco: Jossey-Bass.

Schwartzman, H. B. (1993). *Ethnography in organizations.* Newbury Park, CA: Sage.

Seeger, M. W. (1986). The *Challenger* tragedy and search of legitimacy. *Central States Speech Journal, 37*(3), 147–57.

Shrader, C. B., Lincoln, J. R., & Hoffman, A. N. (1989). The network structures of organizations: Effects of task contingencies and distributional form. *Human Relations, 42*(1), 43–66.

Siehl, C., & Martin, J. (1990). Organizational culture: A key to financial performance? In B. Schneider (ed.), *Organizational climate and culture* (pp. 241–81). San Francisco: Jossey-Bass.

Simon, H. A. (1976). *Administrative behavior: A study of decision-making processes in administrative organization* (3d ed.). New York: Free Press.

Smart, C., & Vertinsky, I. (1977). Designs for crisis decision units. *Administrative Science Quarterly, 22,* 640–57.

Smircich, L. (1983a). Concepts of culture and organizational analysis. *Administrative Science Quarterly, 28,* 339–58.

Smircich, L. (1983b). Implications for management theory. In L. L. Putnam & M. E.

Pacanowsky (eds.), *Communication and organizations: An interpretive approach* (pp. 221–41). Beverly Hills: Sage.

Smircich, L. (1985). Is the concept of culture a paradigm for understanding organizations and ourselves? In P. J. Frost, L. F. Moore, M. R. Louis, C. C. Lundberg, & J. Martin (eds.), *Organizational culture* (pp. 55–72). Beverly Hills: Sage.

Smircich, L. & Calas, M. B. (1987). Organizational culture: A critical assessment. In F. M. Jablin, L. L. Putnam, K. H. Roberts, & L. W. Porter (eds.), *Handbook of organizational communication: an interdisciplinary perspective* (pp. 228–63). Newbury Park: Sage.

Smith, P. B., & Peterson, M. F. (1988). *Leadership, organizations and culture*. London: Sage.

Smith, R. C., & Eisenberg, E. M. (1987). Conflict at Disneyland: A root-metaphor analysis. *Communication Monographs, 54*(4), 367–80.

Sproull, L. (1981). Beliefs in organizations. In P. Nystrom & W. Starbuck (eds.), *Handbook of organizational design*, vol. 2 (pp. 203–24). New York: Oxford University Press.

Steers, R. M. (1977). Antecedents and outcomes of organizational commitment. *Administrative Science Quarterly, 22*, 46–56.

Stewart, L. P. (1980). "Whistle blowing": Implications for organizational communication. *Journal of Communication, 30*(4), 90–101.

Strine, M. S., & Pacanowsky, M. E. (1985). How to read interpretive accounts of organizational life: Narrative bases of textual authority. *Southern Speech Communication Journal, 50*(Spring), 283–97.

Stringer, D. M., Remick, H., Salisbury, J., & Ginorio, A. B. (1990). The power and reasons behind sexual harassment: An employer's guide to solutions. *Public Personnel Management, 19*(1), 43–52.

Szwajkowski, E. (1989). Lessons for the consultant from research on employee misconduct. *Consultation, 8*(3), 181–90.

Tannen, D. (1990). *You just don't understand: Women and men in conversation*. New York: Ballantine.

Taylor, F. W. (1967/1911). *The principles of scientific management*. New York: W. W. Norton.

Terpstra, D. E., & Baker, D. D. (1989). The identification and classification of reactions to sexual harassment. *Journal of Organizational Behavior, 10*, 1–14.

Thayer, L. (1979). Communication: Sine qua non of the behavioral sciences. In R. W. Budd & B. D. Ruben (eds.), *Interdisciplinary approaches to human communication* (pp. 7–31). Rochelle Park, NJ: Hayden Book Company, Inc.

Thomas, K. (1976). Conflict and conflict management. In M. D. Dunnette (ed.), *Handbook of industrial and organizational psychology* (pp. 889–935). Chicago: Rand McNally.

Thomas, K. W. (1988). The conflict-handling modes: Toward a more precise theory. *Management Communication Quarterly, 1*(3), 430–436.

Thomas, K. W., & Schmidt, W. H. (1976). A survey of managerial interests with respect to conflict. *Academy of Management Journal, 19*(2), 315–18.

Thompson, K. R., & Luthans, F. (1990). Organizational culture: A behavioral perspective. In B. Schneider (ed.), *Organizational climate and culture* (pp. 319–44). San Francisco: Jossey-Bass.

Tichy, N., & Fombrun, C. (1979). Network analysis in organizational settings. *Human Relations, 32*(11), 923–65.

Tjosvold, D. (1985). Power and social context in superior-subordinate interaction. *Organizational Behavior and Human Decision Processes, 35*, 281–93.

Tompkins, P. K., & Cheney, G. (1983). Account analysis of organizations: Decision-making and identification. In L. L. Putnam & M. E. Pacanowsky (eds.), *Communication and organizations: An interpretive approach* (pp. 123–46). Beverly Hills: Sage.

Tompkins, P. K., & Cheney, G. (1985). Communication and unobtrusive control in contemporary organizations. In R. D. McPhee & P. K. Tompkins (eds.), *Organizational communication: Traditional themes and new directions* (pp. 179–210). Beverly Hills: Sage.

Trevino, L. K., & Youngblood, S. A. (1990). Bad apples in bad barrels: A causal analysis of ethical decision-making behavior. *Journal of Applied Psychology, 75*(4), 378–85.

Trist, E. (1981). The evolution of socio-technical systems: A conceptual framework and an action research program. Paper presented at the Conference on Organizational Design and Performance, April 1980, University of Pennsylvania.

Trotter, R. C., Day, S. G., & Love, A. E. (1989). Bhopal, India and Union Carbide: The second tragedy. *Journal of Business Ethics, 8*(6), 439–54.

Trujillo, N. (1983). "Performing" Mintzberg's roles: The nature of managerial communication. In L. L. Putnam & M. E. Pacanowsky (eds.), *Communication and organizations: An interpretive approach* (pp. 73–97). Beverly Hills: Sage.

Trujillo, N. (1985). Organizational communication as cultural performance: Some managerial considerations. *Southern Speech Communication Journal, 50*(Spring), 201–24.

Trujillo, N. (1992). Interpreting (the work and talk of) baseball: Perspectives on ballpark culture. *Western Journal of Communication, 54*(4), 350–71.

Trujillo, N., & Dionisopoulos, G. (1987). Cop talk, police stories, and the social construction of organizational drama. *Central States Speech Journal, 38*(3&4), 196–209.

Tsui, A. S., & O'Reilly, III, C. A. (1989). Beyond simple demographic effects: The importance of relational demography in superior-subordinate dyads. *Academy of Management Journal, 32*(2), 402–23.

Tuchman, G. (1978). *Making news: A study in the construction of reality.* New York: Free Press.

Ulm, D., & Hickel, J. K. (1990). What happens after restructuring? *The Journal of Business Strategy, 11*(4), 37–41.

U.S. Bureau of the Census, Current Population Reports, Series P-20, No. 462, *Educational attainment in the United States: March 1991 and 1990.* U.S. Government Printing Office, Washington, D.C., 1992.

U.S. Bureau of the Census, *Statistical abstract of the United States: 1989* (109th ed.). Washington, D.C., 1989.

Useem, M. (1982). Classwide rationality in the politics of managers and directors of large corporations in the United States and Great Britain. *Administrative Science Quarterly, 27,* 199–226.

Van Maanen, J. (1978). People processing: Strategies of organizational socialization. *Organizational Dynamics, 7*(1), 19–36.

Van Maanen, J., & Barley, S. (1985). Cultural organization: Fragments of a theory. In P. J. Frost, L. F. Moore, M. R. Louis, C. C. Lundberg, & J. Martin (eds.), *Organizational culture* (pp. 31–53). Beverly Hills, CA: Sage.

Van Maanen, J., & Katz, R. (1976). Individuals and their careers: Some temporal considerations for work satisfaction. *Personnel Psychology, 29,* 601–16.

Van Maanen, J., & Kunda, G. (1989). "Real feelings": Emotional expression and organizational culture. In L. L. Cummings & B. M. Staw (eds.), *Research in organizational behavior, Vol. 11* (pp. 43–103). Greenwich, CT: JAI Press.

Van Maanen, J., & Schein, E. H. (1979). Toward a theory of organizational socialization. In B. M. Staw (ed.), *Research in organization behavior: An annual series of analytical essays and critical reviews, Vol. 1* (pp. 209–64). Greenwich, CT: Jai Press.

von Bertalanffy, L. (1968). *General system theory: Foundations, development, applications.* New York: George Braziller.

Waters, J. A. (1978). Catch 20.5: Corporate morality as an organizational phenomenon. *Organizational Dynamics, 6*(4), 2–19.

Waters, J. A., & Bird, F. (1989). Attending to ethics in management. *Journal of Business Ethics, 8,* 493–97.

Weber, M. (1946). *From Max Weber: Essays in sociology.* (H. H. Gerth, C. Wright Mills, eds. and trans.). New York: Oxford University Press.

Weber, M. (1947). *Max Weber: The theory of social and economic organization.* (A. M. Henderson & Talcott Parsons, trans., Talcott Parsons, ed.). New York: Oxford University Press.

Weick, K. E. (1976). Educational organizations as loosely coupled systems. *Administrative Science Quarterly, 21,* 1–19.

Weick, K. E. (1979a). *The social psychology of organizing* (2d ed.). New York: Random House.

Weick, K. E. (1979b). Cognitive processes in organizations. *Research in Organizational Behavior, 1,* 41–74.

Weick, K. E. (1989). Organized improvisation: 20 years of organizing. *Communication Studies, 40*(4), 241–48.

Weick, K. E. (1991). The vulnerable system: An analysis of the Tenerife air disaster. In P. J. Frost, L. F. Moore, M. R. Louis, C. C. Lundberg, & J. Martin (eds.), *Reframing organizational culture* (pp. 117–30). Newbury Park: Sage.

Weiss, R. M. (1983). Weber on bureaucracy: Management consultant or political theorist? *Academy of Management Review, 8*(2), 242–48.

Wilkins, L. (1989). Bhopal: The politics of mediated risk. In L. M. Walters, L. Wilkins, & T. Walters (eds.), *Bad tidings: Communication and catastrophe* (pp. 21–34). Hillsdale, NJ: Lawrence Erlbaum Associates.

Williams, D. E., & Treadaway, G. (1992). Exxon and the *Valdez* accident: A failure in crisis communication. *Communication Studies, 43*(1), 56–64.

Wisenblit, J. Z. (1989). Crisis management planning among U.S. corporations: Empirical evidence and a proposed framework. *SAM Advanced Management Journal, 54*(2), 31–41.

Wong, M. G. (1986). Post-1965 Asian immigrants: Where do they come from, where are they now, and where are they going? *Annals of the American Academy of Political and Social Science, 487,* 150–68.

Wood, J. T. (Guest Ed.). (1992). Special section—"Telling our stories": Sexual harassment in the communication discipline. *Journal of Applied Communication Research, 20*(4), 349–418.

Working Mother ranks top firms (1992, Sept. 23). *Duluth News-Tribune,* p. 5C.

Yates, R. E. (1991, Dec. 22). 47 of top 100 world economies are corporations. *Duluth News-Tribune,* p. 13C.

Zahrly, J., & Tosi, H. (1989). The differential effect of organizational induction process on early work role adjustment. *Journal of Organizational Behavior, 10,* 59–74.

Zey, M. (1992). Criticisms of rational choice models. In M. Zey (ed.), *Decision making: Alternatives to rational choice models* (pp. 9–31). Newbury Park: Sage.

Zey-Ferrell, M., Weaver, K. M., & Ferrell, O. C. (1979). Predicting unethical behavior among marketing practitioners. *Human Relations, 32*(7), 557–69.

Subject Index

Name Index